CW01627313

Andrew Tunstall

SLOW BOAT TO URUGUAY

Riofrio books

Riofrio books

ISBN 978-1-9164847-0-2

"It is not the strongest of the species that survive,
or even the most intelligent;
but the one most responsive to change."

– Charles Darwin

N
RIO DE JANEIRO
BAIA DE ILHA GRANDE
BRAZIL
PARATI
ILHA GRANDE
xStorm
ILHA BELA
PARAGUAY
CANANEIA
xIrishman
IGUAZU
xToucans
PARANAGUA
xRan aground
CHILE
xTuna
Oysters!
FLORIANOPOLIS
IMBITUBA
x
Storm
LAGUNA
xDolphins
Rio Paraná
Rio Uruguay
RIO GRANDE
xGreat Storm
x
Engine explodes
CARMELO
ARGENTINA
URUGUAY
x
Aground
PARANÁ DELTA
MONTEVIDEO
xPampero
Llamas
COLONIA
PIRIAPOLIS
x
Orca attack
Police
Mt
Aconcagua
MENDOZA
PUNTE DEL ESTE
RIVER PLATE
BUENOS AIRES
LA PLATA
xStorm
SANTIAGO
PEHUAJÓ
xFlamingoes
MAR DEL PLATA
Volcanoes
Out of fuel
PATAGONIA
LAS GRUTAS
xParrots
BARILOCHE
xStupid
EL BOLSON
xSeals
PENINSULA VALDEZ
xPixies
PUERTO MADRYN
xWhales

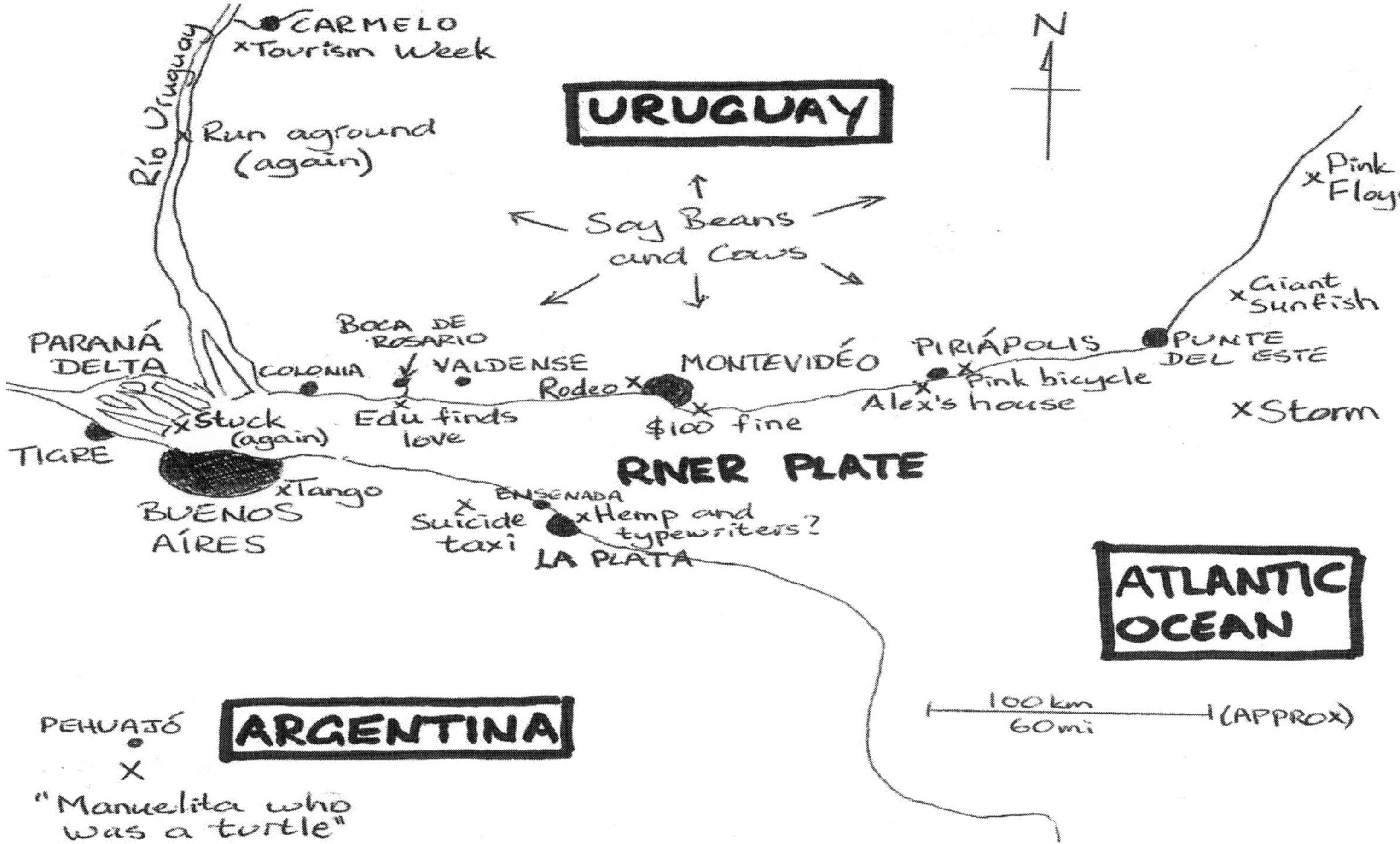

CARMELO
xTourism Week
Río Uruguay
xRun aground (again)
URUGUAY
N
Soy Beans and Cows
Pink Floyd
Giant Sunfish
PARANÁ DELTA
BOCA DE ROSARIO
VALDENSE
COLONIA
MONTEVIDÉO
PIRIÁPOLIS
PUNTE DEL ESTE
Rodeo
Pink bicycle
Alex's house
xStorm
xStuck (again)
Edu finds love
$100 fine
TIGRE
RNER PLATE
xTango
BUENOS AÍRES
ENSENADA
Suicide taxi
xHemp and typewriters?
LA PLATA
ATLANTIC OCEAN
100 km
60 mi
(APPROX)
PEHUAJÓ
"Manuelita who was a turtle"
ARGENTINA

Author's Note

Writing this book has been as much of a journey as the travelling it describes, evoking half-buried memories and re-acquainting me with all those wonderful people of South America who so selflessly embraced us and took us into their homes and hearts. They are far too many to thank personally here, but they all pop their heads up in the text and I have done my best to treat them sympathetically while celebrating their endearing quirkiness. I love you all!

I care little for convention, and have taken to naming places as we called them ourselves, with the result that I have sometimes used English place names, but more often the Spanish or Portuguese names (many places we visited probably do not have English names anyway). I tried to describe sailing in plain terms to avoid writing a technical sailing book, and the glossary of fancy sailing words at the back of the book should be sufficient to make any landlubber feel at home out at sea.

All anecdotes are stories of actual encounters, and any resemblances the characters have to real people are purely intentional. Timelines are according to how I remember them though I might admit under torture to conflating some minor interactions to ease the story flow.

I did not create this book on my own. After committing my (sometimes sketchy) memories and impressions to type, then gutting and re-constituting them so many times it seemed no book would ever see the light of day, I did not do very much at all to make it happen. I owe a debt of gratitude to patient friends and family members who waded through the first disjointed versions and were kind enough to encourage me to try again. All suggestions and ideas were carefully considered, but in the end I had to stay true to my own tastes and memory so the blame for any inaccuracies must lie squarely at my door.

Alistair Lowde has been extremely patient and his professional editing and publication input has been of inestimable value. I thank Brian Kannard for his timely and efficient assistance in realising the final publication of this book, and recommend his services as the "Bookwrangler" without reservation. Mel Rowlands did a wonderful job of producing a cover that conveys in one picture my ideas of travel, adventure and sheer fun. However, absolutely nothing would have come of this project without the unwavering faith of my wonderful, long suffering comrade-in-arms and wife Abigail. She pushed and cajoled me with just the right level of firmness whenever I slacked (i.e. often) and eventually took on the responsibility of seeing it through to publication herself. I am so proud to be married to you.

I love you Abi, this book is for you.

The author

Preface

A wall of black cloud loomed up over the southern horizon and threatened to swallow the sky. The water, even here in the sheltered little bay of Pequea, was restless and lumpy, as the rising wind funnelled the sea between island and mainland creating close, steep waves that marched unchecked through the moored boats and smashed themselves onto the narrow strip of beach below the road. I tied a third rope to the mooring buoy.

We resolved not to worry too much. The Yacht Club was full of boats; every mooring was occupied, and the locals seemed unconcerned. We knew it would be uncomfortable, and *Josephine* had an unpleasant habit of leaking in heavy rain; but we had been uncomfortable before, and the occasional bumpy night or a wet cushion was not a high price to pay for our new-found freedom.

The lush Brazilian island of Ilhabela was the perfect starting point for our new life afloat after a close friend made his mooring at Pinda Yacht Club available for preparing the yacht for living aboard with a baby. We were about to set off on a ten day sojourn to the nearby *Baia de Ilha Grande*, or "Big Bay", for our first taste of the cruising life among tropical islands before heading south to Argentina. After years in the planning, our Family Adventure was finally underway.

There was just the matter of the weather. This storm was bringing rain predicted to last three days; after that it should be balmy, and we were looking forward to getting going. I sat in the cockpit with my mum-in-law as we sipped tea and watched the approaching cloudbank. It really had gone dark. The wind was whipping up; it had risen from nothing to over twenty knots and *Josephine* was snatching at her tether like a restless horse. We convinced each other we were not concerned.

By sundown the wind had risen again to a steady thirty knots, making moving around inside the pitching boat awkward, so we went to bed early; Abi with baby Lucy in the forepeak, and Jo and our friend Dael in the two aft cabins, while I bedded down in the saloon from where I could better monitor what was going on outside.

Sleep was not easy to come by. The rising gale whistled through the rigging and the boat lurched with increasing violence. The wind increased to forty knots and the rain came thundering down. It was not long before the downpour worked its way through the seams in the deck and started to drip on us where we lay.

I tossed and turned on my bunk as the boat leaped about on her lines like a puppet. Cooking utensils clattered to the floor somewhere in the galley and Abi groaned with sea sickness. Twice I ventured out into the driving wind and rain to edge on hands and knees along the plunging deck and check the lines on the bow. They looked secure. The storm raged on and I drifted in and out of a fitful sleep.

Some time later – was it ten minutes? four hours? – I became dimly aware the boat was no longer rocking as violently, or jerking at her mooring. I lay there thinking how nice that was when it started to dawn on my muddled mind that the wind was till screaming – if anything with a higher pitch. Then there was a slight "*thunk*", followed immediately by heavier jolt that sent a sinister shudder through the boat. Almost in slow motion, *Josephine* rolled through forty five degrees, sending books and plates crashing to the floor as she quivered under an onslaught of waves pummelling her side. In a half dream I kicked my way out of my sleeping bag and scrabbled up the steps through the hatch to find myself awake in the cockpit, *Josephine* leaning over on one side, wind screeching through the rigging, my face being stung by driven rain and spray. I could hardly see. Side on in the surf that was crashing over the little beach and up onto the road, *Josephine* had broken away from her mooring and was now aground, at the mercy of a furious sea. Waves were pounding the hull, every impact weakening the boat and grinding her deeper into the sand.

Gripping the wheel I looked around in desperation. White water was sweeping over the boat and the canting deck was awash with tumbling foam. Abi and Dael had followed me up and were looking at me with big eyes. I had no idea what to do. An image of our precious little Lucy, asleep in her cabin and oblivious to the peril, flashed before me. How do you get a seven-month-old baby off a stricken yacht in a storm at night and safely to land through pounding surf? Our dream was not supposed to end like this.

"The trouble with the rat race
is even if you win it,
you are still a rat."

– Lily Tomlin

1

"So now you're a banker!" teased Mark as we loped along side by side, our breath steaming ahead of us in the winter air. It was several years earlier, seven o'clock in the evening, and dark. My friend and I had been running for about half an hour. I was starting a new job the next morning, and was looking forward to the change.

"I suppose so."

I have never really understood what that means. Is everyone working in a bank a "banker"? In truth my new job had less to do with "banking" and more to do with "schmoozing"; *Senior Relationship Manager* to be my grandiose title.

"Sounds like I'm going to spend most of my time having lunch. I'll need to keep up the running!"

We were jogging down a dark, quiet road next to a river on the fringes of Johannesburg, a clutch of houses lit up over to our right when an explosion of barking erupted from amongst the buildings.

"You hear that?" I asked.

"The dogs? Yes. Why?"

I stopped to listen. It was frantic barking, higher pitched than normal.

"Something's not right."

Then someone screamed. A woman. A deep, visceral scream that was all too abruptly cut off.

"Just a dog fight!" called Mark behind me as I sprinted up the road in the direction of the din.

Fizzing with adrenaline, I cut up between the houses, the sound of the dogs a rising crescendo. Scarcely two blocks and suddenly I was upon them: four men around a car. And a woman. The car parked in front of a locked gate, engine still running; two dogs berserk behind the gate; the boot of the car open; the men roughly trying to force the woman into it; one man with a pistol – in the woman's mouth.

There was barely time to take it in – I remember shouting at them, challenging – then they ran at me, all four of them, the armed one snapping the slide of his semi-automatic and yelling at me as one might a disobedient dog. *"Come here! Come here!"* He spat the words out with venom that left his intentions in no doubt. I thought not.

Realising if I ran straight back down the road he would be able to shoot me all too easily, I dashed for the pavement in a desperate attempt to get across and scale a wall. I did reach the wall. A row of bushes tripped me up, and before I could get to my feet they were on me, pinning me where I lay. The steel muzzle of the gun pressed cold against the back of my skull. Everything slowed to a dream. My mouth went dry and all sounds became muffled. I sensed the tension in the muscles of the gun hand as his finger tightened around the trigger and I knew I was dead. An ant struggled over the sand in front of me and I yearned to swap places. Good trade. I was not angry, I was not sorry; I was not even afraid. In that dull, long second before the end I was merely disappointed. It just seemed a *shame* I was about to die. A waste.

Then I heard them, shouting at each other; two of them tussling over something. The gun. Jammed. A third stood up to get involved, and suddenly I realised it was not yet over. Fuck that.

Lashing out and throwing them aside, I bolted. I could hear them running down the road behind me, shouting at me, at each other. Mark appeared from nowhere just ahead of me.

"What the Hell…?" he started.

"Just bloody run!!" I bellowed. He did not argue.

The sound of a motor. Looking back over my shoulder I saw our pursuers pile into a van and accelerate after us.

"Shit, here they come again! Quick, in here," and we ducked through the open gate of a church yard. "Back against the wall, and stay down!"

"They saw us! I tell you, they saw us!"

"Yes. Just wait."

The van screamed down through the gears, and as the beam of the headlights swung through the gate and lit up the driveway we flung ourselves back over the wall into the road.

"*Now* run!" I exhorted, but neither of us needed extra motivation. We flew down the road, the sounds of our erstwhile pursuers' shouts in the church grounds fading behind us.

Reaching home we called the police, then returned by car to the house where we were relieved to find the woman unharmed behind the gate with her dogs. We waited two hours for the police but they did not come. When we called again, they said we would have to wait as it was "not an emergency". Eventually we gave up and went home, leaving our contact details. Nobody called.

***

The following morning, stuck in rush hour traffic, I could not think of anywhere I would rather be. It was a great morning for traffic. I had my window down and could feel the warm spring breeze on my cheek. *'I should be dead,'* I kept telling myself. *'I should be dead.'* I resolved to grab my second chance at life with both hands and wring the most out of it, really make a go of something. I wanted to be dynamic, inspirational. That was it. Inspirational. I would be *inspirational* in my new job.

"You must be Andrew?"

"Yes, I'm the new guy, nice to meet you," I smiled at the woman behind the reception desk.

She made a call, and a woman in a smart skirt suit appeared and introduced herself as 'Lyn from Human Resources'.

"We are retrenching today, and as one of our senior managers you will be playing a part in the consulting process."

Not quite what I had expected.

"Retrenchments? Me?... On my first day?"

Incredulity.

"All senior managers are involved. You will have a private meeting room, and someone from HR to sit in."

"Hang on, this is all a bit much – what are you talking about? I don't even know the staff."

"That will make it easier for you. No emotional attachments. Let me explain how it's going to work…"

It was like something out of a bad sitcom. Every senior manager was given a list of about thirty names, next to each of which was either *'retrench'* or *'retain'*. Employees were then to be sent, one by one, for a private audience with their appointed manager, who would tell them whether or not they still had a job. To limit the emotional impact in the workplace, someone had come up with the bright idea of not letting the Retrenched return to their desks; instead their access cards would be revoked immediately, and they would be herded into the cafeteria with their fellow Untouchables for further processing before being escorted from the building, never to be seen again.

As the names to be laid off had been kept secret, *all* members of staff were made to pack their desks in anticipation of not coming back from their "interview". They were even given quaint little gifts – natty drawstring bags, emblazoned with The Bank's logo – in which to pack their family photos and personal coffee mugs. Those who were reprieved returned to their desks to unpack their little bags and replace the photographs of their children in full view of those still awaiting their fate. If they did not come back, everyone knew…

This was absurd. How could I be expected to be a part of this farce – and on my first day? *'Inspirational?'* I thought to myself. *'Hardly'*.

I sat in my little meeting room and looked at my list as my appointed HR minder busied herself making the first call.

"Can you come to room one-one-four please? Mr Tunstall is ready to see you."

I imagined the poor soul at the other end of the line, saying goodbye to her colleagues, maybe hugging them, probably in tears, wondering who on earth "Mr Tunstall" was. Next to her name I read *'retain'*. She would be going back to her desk. I looked down my list: *'retain'*, *'retain'*, *'retain'* .... to the end. All of them, *'retain'*.

"Well here's a thing," I said to my babysitter. "It seems I'm not retrenching anyone."

That was a relief at least.

"Oh, no!" she replied, flicking her manicured nails, "we are only retrenching about eight in all."

"What? But there are almost three hundred people in this division!"

"Correct. This is not a big thing you know."

I could not believe what I was hearing and made her tell me again. Stupefied, I stood up to gather my things.

"Alright, now listen to me. I don't know whose idea this was, this... this animal farm thing, but I don't think..."

"H-R" she said pointedly. "Human Resources is in charge of the retrenchment exercise."

"Well I say bollocks. If I'm a senior manager then I am going to do some managing."

I walked into the hall to meet the first name on my list. I watched her coming, nervous with round eyes.

"Helen?" I asked and she nodded. "You are not being retrenched, okay? I am sorry you walked all this way, but you still work here. Now if you don't mind, can you please take me to meet all the people on this list?"

She took me around the building dropping in at the desks of the people on my list so I could introduce myself and tell them they did not need to pack a bag.

Back home that evening my head was spinning. In the last twenty-four hours I had been sentenced to death, executed, come back to life, started a new job, and watched almost three hundred people put through one of their most emotionally stressful days at work for no logical reason. I needed to breathe. Why do we live like this?

***

That evening Abi and I huddled round a bottle of wine asking ourselves the perennial questions. What happens to us as we get older? Where does the idealism go? What becomes of our dreams? Are they discarded along the way because our lives are too full of society's expectations? Too often they are sealed in an envelope and left on life's mantelpiece, to be opened by wrinkled old hands and looked at one last time before we die. It seems to be a human condition, this striving all your life for… what? Very few people actually know why they do what they do, and precious few seem to actually *enjoy* it. We certainly did not know why we were bashing through the traffic to work every morning, but we had never really thought about it. It was just what we did. Work longer hours, earn more money, buy a better suit to prove it, go back to work to pay for it. Must keep up the payments. Ooh, look at that nice car. It's stuck in the same traffic jam…

One day on the new job, and already I was completely disillusioned with it. In a few short hours I had gone from *'Inspirational'*, to wondering what the point was. There had to be some other way of living; there had to be an alternative style of life to this mindless, soul numbing rat race. Walled off from anonymous neighbours in barred apartments behind electronic security gates, spending our days between smog choked highways and hermetically sealed offices breathing artificial air with windows welded closed to keep the corrupting breeze of the fresh outdoors at bay. This socio-political, back-stabbing, pig-fight was going to take us nowhere. We needed to get out.

"Desired Outcome."

"What?"

"Desired Outcome," I repeated. "That was what Gerald always used to say when I worked for him. Whenever there was a problem, and people were falling over each other trying to figure out what to do, he would always ask what the *Desired Outcome* was. Once we agreed on that, it was a lot easier to decide how to tackle the problem. So – in this situation, what is our *Desired Outcome*?"

"I'm not with you."

"What I'm trying to say is, let's forget about the situation we are *in*, and let's focus first on where we would like to *be*. Our *Desired Outcome* is how we would most like to be living our lives. Don't let current circumstances affect how we think about that. If we could do anything we like, what would make us happy? It doesn't have to be conventional or even "realistic" – just really, honestly, *what we would most like to do*."

It did not take long for us to come up with the idea of living on a yacht, sailing around the world. Not very original perhaps, but difficult to knock as a fantasy. And it certainly was far removed from our current lifestyle, living in a rented apartment and venturing out to drive the daily gauntlet to our respective high rise office towers. The concept made us laugh.

"Wow, can you imagine," said Abi, "spending all day barefoot?"

"And wearing shorts every day!"

"We would eat more fresh fruit. We could just pick it off the trees!" she fancied, plucking at the air.

"I like the idea of being able to sleep late, but wanting to get up early."

"Fresh sushi!" exclaimed Abi, really warming now to the theme, before she squinted at me. "Not very feasible though, is it?"

"No," I agreed, "I suppose not – but then that was the rule; it didn't have to be, remember? So, now that we have agreed we would be happy living on a yacht, going wherever we want to go, let's return to Earth and look at it objectively."

I opened a notebook, and started to list all the reasons why we were not already sailing around the world on a yacht. This was easy.

"We don't have a yacht, for starters."

"We can't afford to buy one either!" added Abi.

"No. And if we had one, we wouldn't really know what to do with it, would we?"

We both laughed. That was true. I had my first experiences of sailing on the Ijsselmeer in Holland, on holiday from my teaching job in London, and while I had subsequently learned some basics by day-racing on a friend's little boat for a couple of years, pulling ropes whenever he told me to, I had never actually helmed, much less been exposed to cruising. I had not spent a single night at sea, and did not know the first thing about managing a yacht on the ocean. Navigation, electronics, sea rescue, diesel mechanics, meteorology, radio operation, first aid, route planning, tides… I did not even know enough to list what I did not know.

"And don't forget we live at an altitude of five thousand feet, four hundred miles from the sea," Abi put in. "That doesn't help either."

"Well," I capped it off, "as you said we can't afford it. We don't have the money to just get on a yacht and take off around the world. Nice idea, but we would need to win the lottery."

We fell silent. Our first idea, while it sounded wonderful, did not seem realistic. We would need to come up with something a little more sensible, more practical. We sat at the table nudging our glasses around and looking at each other. But neither of us could think of anything else.

"Some people do it you know…"

"What?"

"Live on a yacht."

"Yes, but they're rich."

Silence again, then after a minute Abi spoke again.

"I wonder *how* rich? I mean, how much money would you need to do that?"

"I have no idea. A lot."

"I'd like to know how much. One of the reasons we wrote down just now for not living on a yacht is that we can't afford it, but we don't actually know what it costs."

She had a point. So out of interest we did a rough calculation of how much we thought we would need. The cost of a boat, plus the cost of equipping it, then what we thought our running expenses might be, as well as general living costs for, say, the first two years. We sat looking at the final figure.

"That's a fair amount of money, but I must say I'm amazed that's all it would take," I mused. "Oh well, we don't have it, so that's that!"

But Abi would not let it go.

"I wonder how much we *have*?"

"Not *that* much I can tell you!"

"I'm sure, but how much *do* we have?"

Like most people, we did not know.

"Um… lets see… two cars, we are still paying for the silver one… a little plot of land with a mortgage…"

I scribbled in the notepad, counting on my fingers and in my head, factoring our pension savings against the credit card debt, and came to a final net figure that, surprisingly, was positive. I was cheered. Before I worked it out, I imagined it to be a negative figure with all the loans and credit. At least we were solvent.

"That's what we would have if we sold everything we own, and paid off all our debt. Not nearly enough to buy a yacht and go sailing around the world."

"I guess not," nodded Abi ruefully. "How long do you think it would take to make up the difference?"

Looking again at our investments, anticipating returns on top of our monthly savings, potential salary increases and expected property appreciation, as well as the rate at which we could pay off our debts, and allowing for additional savings we could start making now, we came up with the surprising answer of five years.

"Five years?" Abi sounded incredulous. "*Five years?* All that money in just ***five years***?"

I checked my calculations.

"Yes, I think so. Maybe before. If we keep driving these old cars, and don't spend too much… yes, we could have that in five years, certainly. With the right investments of course. Maybe this idea isn't as fanciful as it sounds. We wouldn't be the first people to sail off on a yacht you know…"

Financially it suddenly looked less unrealistic. Challenging, yes – but certainly possible. We would need to have a proper strategy, and work to a strict financial plan instead of upgrading our cars whenever we were promoted… If we could not go off and live on a yacht, it would not be because we could not afford it. Realising that – given enough time – the money was not an insurmountable difficulty, we were keen to look again at the other things standing in our way.

Funny how we create barriers in our minds that stop us achieving things without even realising we have done it. We rationalised that '*yes, there are real, live people out there who already do it*', so 'unrealistic' had to be nonsense. Anything that you see someone else doing has to be realistic. It's just a matter of figuring out how *you* can do it too.

One of the "reasons" we had just written down for not living on a boat was a lack of knowledge and requisite skills. Now it made us laugh.

"That one's a bit wet. Nothing a course or two couldn't fix. We can read lots of sailing books too. Knowledge is not a barrier to anything nowadays."

So we crossed that one off.

"What else?" asked Abi, grinning.

"Um, I wrote here … this is silly… that we '*don't have the experience*' to sail a yacht across an ocean."

These were no longer sounding like reasons for not living on a yacht; they were sounding like excuses.

"Oh for goodness sake, *experience* is the reason we can't do it? Well hi-ho, lets go sailing then and get some!"

Abi was right; this was daft. All we needed to do was go to the yacht club on the local lake and ask everyone there if we could help them sail their boat. I knew from my early sailing with Gerald that skippers are always looking for crew.

"Come on," said Abi. "Remind me what the *real* barriers were?"

I looked up from the page with what must have been a simple expression.

"That's it. Those *are* the reasons we listed for not living on a yacht, sailing the world. We don't own a boat, we don't have the money, neither of us is a qualified skipper, and we don't have the experience or knowledge to be able to do it. And don't forget we live a six hour drive from the sea."

We sat there shaking our heads in wonderment as it sank in.

"My god," Abi whispered. "If we want to – *really* want to – we *can* do it."

"That's right. In five years we could have the money, and we have all that time to do the courses and gain enough sailing experience. If we use our leave to go on sailing holidays we can do this. We really can do this!"

We were stunned. It was one thing to mutter and complain about our boring routine life, and fantasise about tropical islands and parrots, but quite another altogether to be faced with making it a reality – if we dared. And that was all it would take – a little daring. We knew if we took the decision, right now – if we made the commitment that we really wanted to do this – we could do it.

***

From then on there were things to do. I investigated courses, we bought a heap of sailing books, we analysed our living expenses and started to budget, putting additional money aside to invest, and over time the process took on a life of its own.

Several months later I overheard my boss talking to our financial manager about a business unit in Cape Town that our division would be taking over. I was familiar with the business as we dealt with them regularly.

"Am I hearing that we are taking over the trustee unit?" I asked, sounding as casual as I could.

"Yes," he replied. "It makes a lot more sense for them to be part of our division."

"Who will run it?"

"I haven't thought that far. I expect we'll head-hunt someone in Cape Town."

"Why don't we send someone down from here?" I suggested. "That way we'd have someone who already knows our business and our people."

Dave laughed.

"What? Nobody wants to move from here to Cape Town. Jo'burg is where it all happens, where the money is. Cape Town is a backwater!"

"Have you asked anyone, *Dav*-id?" I called him by his full name to get his attention. It was as if he had just seen me for the first time.

"No… you wouldn't… would you? Would you move?"

"Is that an offer I am hearing?"

And that was that. I went to my desk and called Abi.

"Are you ready to move to the beach?"

Within three months we were living in Cape Town. Abi's company agreed to transfer her too, and we joined the local yacht club where I enrolled myself in a number of sailing courses. It was all just happening. Because we knew what we wanted, opportunities popped up everywhere – like the opportunity to spend five weeks cruising the coast of northern Brazil on a friend's catamaran and building the experience I needed to be able to register for my Yachtmaster exams. We saved money, stuck with our old cars, and made astute investments. Within three years I was a Royal Yachting Association certified Yachtmaster and we were ahead of schedule financially. It was time to start looking for a boat.

***

Six months passed. The second hand boat pool is not big in South Africa (we were certainly not in the market for a new one, and buying one from Europe while based in South Africa was out of the question) and it had to be the *right* boat. Patience was key. We had probably looked at ten or twelve, and come close to buying one of them, but held off as it had just not felt right. Choosing your boat is a bit like buying a house – you know when you know.

The cell phone rang. It was my friend Tony Coon from the False Bay Yacht Club, who ran a fishing equipment business as well as working as a yacht broker.

"Andrew, I've found your boat!"

Tony knew us well, and knew what we were looking for. He also knew what we had already seen.

"Is that so? Tell me about it." I tried to stay calm.

"I've just been asked to sell a *Beneteau First38.* The previous owner died several years ago, the widow is in England and doesn't sail. The boat is at the club in Gordon's Bay, but hasn't been out in years. I've been over to see her, she's a bit of a mess to look at, but she's the perfect boat for you, I know it."

"Sounds interesting, I'll certainly go and have a look."

"Here's the catch: I have other clients who I *know* will buy this boat as soon as they see her, but you're a friend and I want you to see her first. Is there any way you can go there now, before I advertise?"

"*Now*? I am on my way to work now Tony..."

"Andrew, *please* try and go today. I know you will like her, and I also know if you delay someone else will buy her. She'll go very quickly. She'll be sold by this evening."

Tony was pushing, but I liked and trusted him. In any event, he was only urging me to *look* at her.

"Okay, I'll take the day off, I'll be there in an hour."

At the end of the marina was a grubby, worn looking yacht, festooned with yards of bleached rope. Her mouldy cockpit, spattered with gull shit, was strewn with rusty shackles and tatters of old canvas. A generous green skirt of algae billowed around her waterline. There was a sharp smell of diesel below, the upholstery was old and torn, and the bilges full of evil looking black water. I called Abi on the cell phone.

"Abi, do you trust me?"

"What are you talking about? Of course I trust you."

"Then do you mind if I buy a boat?"

"What? What boat? Where *are* you? You should be at work!"

"Gordon's Bay. Tony found a boat. I'm looking at her now, she's beautiful. But I need to put in an offer before lunchtime or we'll lose her. There's no time for you to see her first, so I am asking you to trust my judgement."

"If you think she's right, then I think so too," she said, then squealed. "This is so exciting!"

And so we came to own a yacht. I suggested we rename her *Josephine* after Abi's mother, and Tony helped me sail her (the boat, not my mother-in-law) twenty odd miles across False Bay to Simonstown. The following afternoon Abi and I visited our favourite sushi restaurant run by a delightful couple from Leeds, and the kind owners put a table outside so we could sit and look across the bay with our new boat tied to the jetty in the foreground. It was surreal, sitting there sipping chardonnay and looking at the yacht that would carry us across the ocean to a new life packed with adventure. Just one more year, then things were really going to change.

Little did we realise quite *how* life was going to change.

"...men who know the price of everything
and the value of nothing."

– Oscar Wilde

2

A dandy young man with perfectly coiffed yellow hair wearing a zebra-striped waistcoat was waiting for me in my office clutching a sheaf of glossy brochures. An overdue furniture upgrade was underway, and Head Office had flown Gregoire down as a 'consultant' to 'facilitate the process'. After agreeing on one hundred and fourteen desks, stainless steel waste baskets and compartmentalised workspace dividers, we were now on to the chairs. Gregoire showed me a picture of a very sensible, practical looking office chair with the usual swivel and tilt functions. He told me the price per chair, and I signed it off.

"Now!" he beamed conspiratorially, eyes narrowing. "Those were the chairs for your staff." He flipped the page of his brochure with a flourish and held it high for me to behold. "Here is *your* chair!"

I gazed at the plush leather, the high back, the several levers and knobs that made it look more like the seat of a fighter jet.

"How much is this… *thing*?"

He told me *sotto voce.*

"*What*?! Well then, I shan't be needing *that*! Make it a hundred and fifteen of the little ones."

He was aghast. "This is a director's chair. All business heads qualify for one of these. It's a privilege you are entitled to… and it's a very good chair. Much better for your back, lots of support in all the right places," he wheedled. "You can set it up to fit you perfectly. You won't regret it."

"Yes," I replied. "They do sound much better. On second thoughts then, make that one hundred and fifteen of *these*."

Gregoire blinked at me as if I had just spoken in Mandarin. "Wha-at?"

"A hundred and fifteen of these high backed leather jobs, and you can keep the nasty little cheap ones."

"Oh no, oh no!" he exclaimed hurriedly. "We can't do that! No, that would never do, wouldn't be allowed…"

"What do you mean, *not allowed*?" I cut him short. "I'm not having my staff sit nine or ten hours a day on substandard chairs, then taking time off with bad backs."

"No, no!" Gregoire looked chastened. "These chairs are fine, just fine. They won't have problems at all with those, I assure you. They are perfectly good quality chairs, very comfortable."

"Good, then that's settled. One hundred and fifteen *little* ones. They'll do nicely, and I won't be needing the throne. Thanks for coming down."

Gregoire's departure was not, however, the end of it, and I understood enough about corporate politics to know that I would soon be hearing more. I did not wait long.

"Good morning Andrew!" boomed the voice at the other end of the line. A Senior Director From Head Office. "How are things going?"

"Oh, fine, thank you, everything is running smoothly down here," I replied casually, as if it were a normal occurrence to have a Senior Director From Head Office call me to inquire about "things". But the truth was, in all my time there, I had not taken a single call from anyone more senior than my boss's boss. This had to be something very important indeed.

"How is the renovating going?"

"Very well, thank you."

"Good, I'm pleased to hear that, very pleased." I couldn't help but wonder what he was so pleased about, as he had never seen the inside of my office in any event so had no idea what it looked like before. Another brief pause, then it came.

"I believe we have a little problem with the new furniture?"

I was going to enjoy this.

"Oh no, not at all!" I simpered. "It's all very smart, very professional. It'll create a much better impression on clients, and we are thrilled. Thank you so much."

"Now Andrew, it's not really our people I'm worried about." *Our People*. Corporate-speak, to make it sound like anybody actually gives a toss about *Our People*. "It's you. I want *you* to be happy. I heard there was a problem with your chair. You know you are very important to this organisation, and it matters to us that you are comfortable."

"Oh, I am going to be very comfortable on my new chair, it's a perfectly good chair. In fact all my staff will have the same chair, we couldn't be happier."

The line popped and clicked as the Senior Director From Head Office fiddled with the cord.

"Now Andrew, bear with me here," he said in a patronising tone. "We want you to have the director's chair. All business heads have the director's chair, it is a very good chair. Don't worry about the cost, it's one of the perks of your position."

"Yes, apparently so, but I really don't want it."

I had spent some time getting my staff to comprehend the big organogram I had drawn up showing the more junior clerks arrayed along the top of the page, and the "lines of command" going downwards, through supervisors, managers and senior managers, ending at my name on the very bottom. On this chart the clerks were the most important people in the office, and I was the least important; they did all the "real" work, and mine was the ultimate support function. The concept I had been trying to inculcate was that the managers and I worked for *them*. Now here I was being told to perch on a grand cathedra like the dictator of a small country. It just would not do.

"I don't think it sends the right message to my staff for me to be sitting on something like that," I ventured.

A heavy pause before the Senior Director From Head Office grew curt.

"Well that's not how it is seen up here. At Head Office all senior people have this chair, it confers status. The junior staff see it, and they respect it. They in turn aspire to it. So you need this chair in order for your staff to look up to you."

When I did not respond, he continued.

"If you turn this chair down, everyone will know about it, the staff will all talk about it, and how do you think it will make us look up here?"

So there it was. They wanted me to play the game and sit on this ridiculous thing so that it would not occur to anyone how ridiculous it actually was. I thought wryly that the chair cost the same as the monthly salaries of three clerks. But there was nothing more I could say.

"You will have your chair by the end of the week. You won't be sorry." *Click*, and the Senior Director From Head Office was gone.

The Chair of The Gods did indeed arrive before the end of the week, and I had it wheeled into the lunch area at midday where I had requested all the staff to be present for an announcement. I came down the stairs to find a hundred and fourteen people squeezed into the room, The Chair, all black leather and shiny chrome, wrapped in see-through plastic, raised up on the bar counter drawing curious looks.

One of the managers solemnly handed me a cardboard box. Inside the box were about a hundred folded slips of paper, each bearing the name of a clerk. I randomly drew a name, and the winning minion was presented with The Chair. From then on this ritual was performed on the last Friday evening of every month when the staff gathered for a beer or two before going home, and another corporate slave revelled in the privilege of sitting in a director's chair for a few weeks.

I never again took a call from a Senior Director From Head Office. Senior Directors From Head Office are tremendously busy, very important people, and only call about truly serious matters indeed.

***

It was barely seven o'clock in the morning but the city streets were clogged. I stood in my suit on the island between the busy lanes, briefcase in hand, watching for a gap in the traffic. Behind me the early morning sun was already bright, and the leaves of the city oaks stirred softy in the faint breeze. It promised to be a lovely day. Out *here* at any rate; in *there* it was going to be the usual treadmill. My boss had flown down from up country to do my appraisal. We would spend an hour pouring over a pre-printed 'scorecard' agreeing on my 'score' for such unmeasurables as 'transparency', 'integrity' and 'upholding the Bank's core values'. I had always found it faintly absurd. What gave this particular bank unique claim to 'honesty' as a value? And surely a score of anything less than a hundred percent should warrant dismissal? These appraisals were nothing more than a box-ticking exercise to make it look as if the upper echelons were taking an interest in the development of "*Our People*".

Adam would tell me I was good with people and commend me on my client relations, then suggest I work on my "attention to detail". I would in turn object that I was not employed to attend to detail – I had eight managers and twelve supervisors doing that, with over ninety clerks. Then we would both sign my card, and neither he nor I would ever see the report again. It was always the same. Appraisals went into a file that nobody ever looked at, but housing the files was what kept Human Resources in a job (especially now that the bank had "outsourced" the payroll function – which meant if you were not paid it was nothing to do with your employer; you'd have to fight your own fight over the phone with a disembodied voice from the call centre of a "payroll company" with which you had no relationship).

Standing there in the sun I reflected that if all went to plan this would be the last appraisal I would do. Seven more months and I should be ready to resign and go sailing. If only he knew! I looked up at Table Mountain and thought how nice it would be to go for a run up there between the rocks and the flowers instead of sitting hunched over a computer in an air conditioned office. Then it struck me: I did not need this. Not any more. Seven months was too long to wait. We could afford it now. To heck with it, I didn't need one more stupid appraisal.

I danced between the cars and sprinted up the steps to the lift. At my desk I dashed off a letter, '... *remain grateful for the opportunities afforded me blablabla....*' folded it carefully, and tucked it in the inside pocket of my suit jacket.

"Adam is waiting for you in the boardroom."

"Thank you. The fun never stops around here."

Tra-la-la.

***

I came out of the meeting with Adam a different man. I felt like Me again. I had agreed to work two months more in order to ensure a smooth handover of responsibilities, but the deed was done and the pressure was off. I would work as hard as I had before, if not harder, but it was the end and that knowledge gave me the extra energy I would need.

To pre-empt speculation in that rumour-prone corporate environment, I invited the staff for a drink that afternoon and told them of my pending departure.

"So where are you going?" asked Lwando.

"I'm going sailing!" I announced. "I am going to cross the Atlantic to Brazil and sail around South America for a year. After that, who knows?"

He was dubious. "What are you going to do for work?"

"I am not going to work. I am going to video the trip and make documentaries. I might write a book. Perhaps I will teach people to sail, or do charters. I don't know yet. That's the whole point!"

"Oh!" he said, leaning back in his chair. "My Xhosa people have a saying for this. You are '*Dreaming The Sky*' my friend! Everybody likes to Dream the Sky, but dreaming is for the night. You should live your life in the day, when you can see clearly!"

I spent the evening commute oblivious to the traffic. Looking up at the clouds with their copper bottoms I imagined snorkelling in a secluded bay off a pristine beach, then swimming back to the boat for an early dinner of conch *ceviche* and fresh limes, washed down with a *cuba libre* as the tropical sun sank blazing into the ocean. Yes, I really was *Dreaming the Sky*.

I arrived home euphoric and skipped up the driveway to find Abi already there.

"Well look at you!" she exclaimed, meeting me at the door. "Did you just sign a new client?"

"Better!" I chuckled, and bundled her into the house. Being a typical man I did not notice anything different about her.

"Sweetheart, I have some news," she ventured as I hustled her down the passage to the sitting room, but I was impatient and determined to go first.

"Ha! So do I! You're going to love this. Today I decided '*bugger it*', and I resigned. Just like that. BOOM! Done. How do you like that?"

She sat on the sofa, looking up at me, impassive.

"Well come on then," I cajoled. "Let's have a reaction. We're finally free!"

"Maybe *you* are…" she started, and I cut her short.

"No negative talk now! We *both* are. You can resign too, we need to get on with things. Come one, let's go sail the world!"

"Andrew," she said evenly. "I'm pregnant."

My immediate reaction was one of denial. Five years of saving and planning, of dreaming the dream; and now? No job, and a baby on the way? No, I thought, this was just not possible. It was never part of the plan. It had to be a mistake.

"I will need to make an appointment for a scan," said Abi.

"A what?"

"A scan. To be sure."

"What do you mean, to be sure? You're not sure?"

"Well, no… I mean, yes, but… well, we need confirmation…"

"Ah, well! You had me going there…"

And I would have no more talk of babies; there could be no sabotage. We were preparing to sail off into the Blue Yonder and I had important matters to attend to. Pregnant indeed!

***

Two friends Mark and Jevan had agreed to help me sail *Josephine* around Cape Point from the city, then up the east side of the peninsula to Simonstown, a trip of some sixty-odd miles. I had sailed *Josephine* around the point once before: overnight in miserable wet weather and I was now looking forward to making the return trip on a sunny day. It would be Jevan's first time round the point, while Mark had never sailed before at all.

We left Cape Town in the early morning under clear skies and motored past Three Anchor Bay in the lee of Table Mountain. The notorious Cape Doctor – a strong southeaster that rages for days at a time and frequently reaches over fifty knots – was forecast for the afternoon, but on this, the Atlantic side of the mountainous peninsula, we would be sheltered from it, and after rounding the point we would be sailing north with the wind over our right shoulder, propelling us up to Simonstown. But by mid-morning gusts of thirty knots were whistling down off the slopes, and we hove to and reefed the sails. It was to be the last sensible thing we would do all day.

Past Hout Bay, where the peninsula flattens out somewhat, the southeaster was blowing an offshore gale that turned into a head wind as we followed the curve of the coast towards the south east. The wind whipped the swell into a procession of steep seven-foot waves marching in close formation directly at us. As the wind was from dead ahead, and it is impossible to sail directly into a wind, the only way to make progress in the right direction without losing too much time was to run the engine and force *Josephine* head on into the oncoming sea. The pounding over the waves was relentless and after a couple of hours ceiling panels and light fittings were breaking loose in the saloon and my stomach was in open rebellion. My stomach has never taken kindly to rough seas, but I love the freedom of sailing too much to let it stop me, and now I was retching and heaving over the side as if it were my first time on a boat. It was miserable. I soon passed the stage of feeling like I was going to die, and started to *believe* I would die.

"Man, look at you!" exclaimed Mark, eyes wide with disbelief as I hung wretchedly over the rail. "And you want to sail this boat around the world?!"

He was as tough as nails, and although he had never sailed before no gale at sea was about to get him down. He showed no fear and not the slightest hint of sea sickness. I envied him his rock-solid constitution.

"Okay, how does the toilet work?" he asked as we smashed head on over another wave, shattering it like glass, the fragments glittering in the sun as they whipped back along the deck in the wind.

"You want to go *now*? In *this*? Are you crazy? You'll be beaten to death down there!"

I could not imagine anything worse than being cooped up in that tight, damp little space trying to perform bodily functions with the boat flinging me violently against the bulkheads. I threw up again at the thought. But Mark was unconcerned, and went below. Two minutes later he reappeared in the hatchway, shaking his head and mumbling to himself.

"Bloody boat!" he swore. "Threw me off the bog, straight through the door!"

"Ha ha, you idiot, you should've shut the door! Then you could have braced against it."

"I did! But when we hit that last wave I was shot right through it, took it with me. The hinges just smashed off. I landed upside down in the locker opposite with my pants round my ankles and the door on top of me!"

Jevan and I loved it. This entertaining respite from the trying conditions had us doubled up with laughter. But our delight at his misfortune was short lived.

"Hey, what's this smoke?" asked Mark, still below.

"What smoke?"

"Christ," he said, as a whitish grey cloud billowed out of the hatch and engulfed the cockpit. "It's *full* of smoke down here!"

"Get out, quick!" I shouted, and killed the engine. The smoke felt damp on my skin and there was no smell. "It's not smoke, it's steam."

We lifted the inspection hatch in the cockpit floor to discover a cooling hose had ruptured, spilling water from the system and causing the engine to overheat. The rest of the water had then been ejected as steam. It would be impossible to run the engine again this trip; we could only sail from here on. Beating down to Cape Point into an ever-rising gale was no fun. The waves were getting bigger, their tops being blown off in a welter of stinging spray by the forty knot winds, and *Josephine* was heaving and pitching over the sea, surging up the front of each wave before smashing down into the valley behind, shuddering under the impact. I was so sick I was now looking forward to my miserable death. The floor in the saloon was a mess of books, charts, life jackets, clothing and cooking pots that had not been locked securely away before we left. It was no matter; now all three of us were on deck sailing the boat, and would remain up there the rest of the way. We were bruised from being hurled against winches and each other, and soaked by the icy spray. Every few minutes I was overcome by new floods of nausea and flung myself at the lee rail to vomit over the side. My stomach was empty; all that came up was a bitter yellow froth, but that did not stop the retching. I felt so awful that my biggest fear now was *not* dying.

By three o'clock in the afternoon we were finally angling in towards the Point. We had stood quite a long way out to sea in order to build up enough room to make it past the high cliff with the lighthouse marking the southernmost tip of the cape, but the wind was up to fifty knots and we were losing ground to the relentless battering from the waves. It was going to be close. I had just made up my mind to call another tack to take us further from the rocks when there was a load bang and the headsail juddered.

"What the hell was that?" shouted Mark.

"The genoa halyard!" replied Jevan, pointing up the mast. "It's snapped!"

I peered up through the rigging to see the head of the sail had slipped about six feet down the forestay, with a short length of frayed rope fluttering from its cringle. The only reason the whole sail had not collapsed onto the deck was that it was partly furled against the storm, and the rolls of sail wrapped around the forestay were pinning it up there. It was still doing its job – though with less efficiency – but it would be almost impossible to tack again now that the sail was loose.

With no motor we had a choice: abort the trip, turn around and head off back downwind the way we had come with just the mainsail; or keep going and hope we had enough sea room to make it round the point without another tack. In spite of the roaring wind, visibility was good and we could see the rocks and cliff clearly.

"Okay boys, if we make it past this cliff we'll have a clear run downwind on the other side, and will be in Simonstown in less than two hours. If we abandon and head back, it'll take ten or twelve hours to reach Cape Town. We would get there in complete darkness in the early hours of the morning..."

I could read their minds: darkness, early hours, big port, ships, no engine, tired, cold... no, we had to try the point first.

"We should make it. It'll be close, but I think we're clear." I tried to sound confident.

The wind now gusting fifty-five knots was the strongest I had ever sailed in, and as we were blown ever closer to the cliff the waves were building to fifteen feet in the shallower water. My grip tightened on the wheel and I felt like a startled rabbit in the headlights of an onrushing car. Mark and Jevan were on the deck, clinging to the shrouds and looking expectantly at me, waiting for instructions, but there were no instructions to give. We skidded past the point, a few yards inside the outlying rocks, the incoming waves thundering in the shallow water and sending rolling walls of white water crashing against our side. The adrenalin was hot metal in the back of my throat, and then we were round into open water.

I spun the wheel as a wave lifted us up, and angled *Josephine* down the slope. Jevan released the main sheet and Mark let out the rest of the genoa as we tore off downwind, surfing the front of a monster wave, the eight ton yacht trembling under my feet like a living being, white water arching from her bows.

The headsail chose that moment to collapse onto the foredeck, half of it trailing over the side. Mark was forward in a flash – Mark, who had never sailed before – and through the flying spray and the flapping canvas and the flailing lines I caught a glimpse of him lying on his back like a stranded beetle grappling with the sail as the cliff flashed in a blur past my left shoulder. I watched the boat speed go from six to eight, nine, ten knots.... thirteen... I yelled and pumped the air. "FOURTEEN!!" A new boat record. "Yee-hah!" It was exhilarating, rampaging past the rock face at fourteen knots.

As we left the cliffs behind Jevan helped Mark wrestle the headsail into submission and lash it down. Now we were running downwind under a triple reefed main and no headsail, surging with the swells at ten or eleven knots in storm force winds. We had full control of the boat, but only just, and for the next hour surfing before the tempest we had about as much fun as three little boys could handle.

Later, the wind not having let up, I was beginning to worry about how we were going to get into Simonstown without the motor. I called my friend Darren on the cell phone. Darren was the commander of the local sea rescue station and I was going to ask him whether he and his lads fancied a bit of a drill. My idea was that they come out in the rescue boat to escort us in, and take us in tow if necessary to help us get on the marina. Unfortunately though I was still very sick, and when I throw up there is nothing subtle about it: I confess to being a bit of a screamer.

"Hello, Darren?" into the phone, then "AAAARGH!..." as I puked, bile tinged with blood dribbling down the front of my jacket to be washed away by the spray.

"Is that you Andrew? Weren't you planning to bring your boat round today?"

"Yes...AAAARGH!... yes, I'm sailing... AAAARGH!...."

"Andrew? Andrew? Are you okay?"

It was difficult to hear anything above the shrieking wind.

"Darren, yes, but I need a tow… AAAARGH!… AAAARGH!… the wind… too strong to… AAAARGH!…"

"My God Andrew, where are you? Speak to me, are you alright?"

"Everything is… AAAARGH!… everything … AAAARGH!... no motor… AAAARGH!…"

Darren had heard enough. In Simonstown, where he was on duty, the wind had been gusting sixty five knots – hurricane strength – and now all he knew was his friend was out there, screaming. He had managed to catch that we had no motor, and scrambled a full rescue.

The life boat came leaping out over the waves just as we were surfing round the sea wall of the naval harbour. I waved to Darren and pointed towards the far end of the wall where we would be sheltered from the worst of the wind. Once there we could just about hear each other shout.

"If it's okay with you, I want to try to sail in!" I yelled over the wind. "We've come this far, and I think I can sail the boat onto the marina! I'd like you to stay close to me though, in case I foul it up!" Even in this relative shelter it was blowing thirty knots.

"Are you nuts?!" Darren shouted back. "The wind is crazy, and you don't have a headsail! You have to go upwind to get in. How are you going to tack without a headsail?"

But inexperience, testosterone and adrenalin are a bad mix, and I had all three in buckets. I would show him! Jevan and Mark knew no different, so there was no dissent from my crew, and Darren had no choice but to shadow us as I tried to coax *Josephine* upwind into the marina. Of course she was having none of it, and ran off sideways towards the harbour wall. I tried to tack away and spun the wheel. Nothing happened. The gale was far too strong to be able to turn *Josephine* across the wind without the help of the missing headsail, and we skidded inexorably sideways until we ground against the concrete of the harbour wall, mangling the stainless steel tubing of the pulpit and destroying the navigation lights mounted in the bow.

So Darren finally had his way, and towed us into the marina with the rescue boat where we moored in front of a small crowd that had migrated down from the club bar. Many were the opinions about my seamanship, and none too complimentary. I was supposed to be preparing the boat for an ocean crossing, not destroying it; but I had learned some valuable lessons.

***

While I was messing about off Cape Point in my gale, in denial about where my domestic life might really be headed, Abi had made an appointment for the scan. Now I found myself standing self-consciously in a hospital waiting room where two or three obviously pregnant women were submerged in comfy sofas reading baby magazines. There was not a single magazine about landrovers, or cycling, or sailing, or even golf. Nothing at all for men; just magazines with articles on Water Birthing, Breathing Exercises and Cooking for Baby. I felt awkward and conspicuous.

We were summoned into a small, neat office to meet the gynaecologist – a very personable, down-to-earth woman who we both liked instantly. With no fuss Ursula ushered us into her consulting room and before we knew it Abi was on the bed with Ursula running the ultrasound transmitter around in circles on her tummy. The monitor showed nothing but a blizzard of black and white interference.

"Ah, look, there you go!" said Ursula.

"What? Where?" I stuttered. "Nothing, right?"

"Ha ha!" she retorted, as Abi just lay there smiling. Of course Abi knew; had known all along. "Look here, see this dot?" and

Ursula pointed to a pulsating blob. "There's your child's heartbeat. Congratulations!"

It was the most humbling thing I had ever seen. Nothing more than a pulsing spot amongst so much visual static on a black and white screen, but at the same time so much more. Feelings I did not know existed welled up out of I don't know where and I fell in love with the dot. I forgot completely that I had no job, and that our only plans for our future involved striking out blindly over the south Atlantic in a thirty eight foot fibreglass boat to who-knew-where. What I did know was that we were going to have a child, and it was the most exciting and intensely thrilling moment of my life. Abi and I walked out of Ursula's office in tears, as I resisted an urge to nick the magazines on the way out.

We sat in a coffee shop across the road from the hospital not knowing what to say. It was all just overwhelming.

"How does the saying go?" I asked. "Something about the best laid plans of men…"

"The best laid schemes of mice and men go oft awry," Abi replied. "Robert Burns."

"Yes, that's it. I thought it was John Steinbeck?"

"John Steinbeck wrote a novel called 'Of Mice and Men'. He got the idea of the title from Burns' poem."

"Oh."

I fiddled with my scone.

"So now what?"

"What do you mean, '*now what*'?" asked Abi.

"Well, you know… now what?" I repeated lamely.

I had not been thinking about this development; still less had we been talking about it. But now it really was time to take stock. I was terrified. I hated the thought of going back to work, back into the traffic. And as for the notion of leaving for the office before my child wakes up, and getting home in the evenings after it has gone to bed...

Abi, however, *had* been thinking about it.

"Well, I think it means you'd better find something to do ..."

My heart sank, and I closed my eyes. '*Here we go*' I thought.

"...until the baby is maybe six months old, and then I don't see why we can't go sailing."

I blinked like an owl. I had been so afraid of seeing our dream unravel before my eyes I had not thought it through. Instead I had been in denial, hoping – believing – that the pregnancy would turn out to be a false alarm. I hadn't felt ready for the responsibilities of parenthood, but then who does? Now that it was confirmed, and I had seen that little heartbeat with my own eyes, I was as proud and excited as any prospective father. And the more we talked about it the more we agreed that the additional member of the family made it all the more imperative that we push forward with our plans. The alternative would be a return to the exhaust fumes, the office politics, the bills and taxes and deadlines and those stupid appraisals. And I would likely only see my baby on weekends. I would be a part-time father. No thank you. This little mite was going to come and join us in *our* world; and our world was going to be islands, beaches, dolphins, sunsets, sushi and coconuts. Aah, the coconuts. There could be no other way.

"The best thing about arriving at a destination is the realisation the road does not end there."
– Robert Louis Stevenson

3

By the time Lucy Jo was born the following March, we had done a lot of work on *Josephine*, replacing all the halyards and sheets, and giving the engine a complete overhaul after my misadventures around Cape Point. We had also equipped her with a new GPS system, new sails, a wind-driven generator for recharging the batteries, new stainless steel tanks to hold four hundred litres of fresh water, and safety netting all around the deck to keep crawling babies on board. Lucy was four days old when I took her onto the boat for the first time. Not out to sea, but on board – for me rather than for her; so I could say she was on her first boat at four days.

Abi's mother Jo (after whom we had named both our boat, and the second half of our new daughter) flew to Cape Town from the UK to be with us for the birth; when her boss declined her enough leave to make the trip worthwhile, she had resigned on the spot. Bright, easy going and very practical, it did not take a lot of thought to realise she would be a perfect addition to the crew, and when I suggested it both she and Abi were thrilled at the idea.

Five months later we were ready to go. I had spent the last few months at film school, doing courses on camerawork, editing, lighting and the like, and had invested in a good quality high-definition video camera and state-of-the-art editing software. The idea was to film our adventures – whatever and wherever they would be – with a view to marketing the footage later on. In truth it was all rather vague, and aside from getting the boat across the Atlantic Ocean to Brazil we had little idea where we were going or what would happen to us when we got there. Perhaps if we had had any clue what we were letting ourselves in for we would have planned more, or saved more money – or chickened out! Naivety makes you brave, and some things really are just easier when you don't know how.

With the girls safely packed onto a flight to Brazil I made final preparations to sail *Josephine* across the ocean with three mates (we considered it unnecessarily dangerous to subject our five-month-old to a four week ocean crossing – especially considering my lack of experience). Looking at the chart of the ocean, sailing across the Atlantic did not strike me as being particularly complicated. The southern part of the ocean is dominated by a year-round cell of high pressure, driving the prevailing winds in an anti-clockwise spiral. The epicentre of this anti-cyclonic system shifts slightly northwards during the winter, but in the summer it migrates back down again bringing strong, consistent south-easterlies to the southern part of the African continent.

Perfect winds for our departure at the beginning of November. For around four days we could expect to be pushed north up the coast by these prevailing conditions, after which we would reach the latitudes of the Trade Winds – virtually permanent south easterly winds found south of the equator in all the world's oceans, caused by the rotation of the earth. These winds, named for their reliability in the days of inter-continental trade by sail, would then carry us across to South America. There was no reason to expect anything other than downwind sailing on our trip to Brazil, which is always faster and more comfortable than sailing into a headwind.

From a navigational point of view, getting from Cape Town to Rio de Janeiro should be fairly straightforward; in fact I had no doubt it would be easy without charts, or even a compass, let alone GPS. If one were to head northwest, following the afternoon sun, and sail for long enough – say a month, give or take a week – you should eventually bump into South America. And it could only be Brazil – *northern* Brazil; which means somewhere *north* of Rio. The next step would be to turn left and sail down the coast – maybe for three days, maybe for eight – until you see the iconic Sugar Loaf Mountain with the famous statue of Christ the Redeemer dominating Guanabara Bay. Simple. We did, however, have a compass, and a paper chart of the ocean onto which we could plot our co-ordinates from the GPS every day to see exactly how far we still had to go. So in theory at any rate, it should be quite difficult to sail out into the Atlantic, and *not* find Rio de Janeiro – eventually. No, getting "lost" was certainly not a concern.

There are plenty of other things that can go wrong, of course. Spend a month out on the ocean and you are guaranteed to have some bad weather and rough seas, and you will quite likely have to deal with a medical emergency at some point. Then there are the ever present possibilities of a fire on board, or a gas explosion, or being run down by a freighter in the dead of night, or colliding with a whale or a semi-submerged shipping container and sinking. But these horrors, while real, are uncommon: I was more likely to be perpetually seasick and starve to death. And at least the ocean is something like two or three miles deep, so we were not going to be washed onto rocks; at any rate not until we reached Brazil!

It would not do to dwell too much on the risks – after all, one could be killed in traffic on the way to work, but that does not keep us off the roads.

When the four of us combined our total miles of sailing experience together it did not add up to even one crossing of the Atlantic. None of us had ever been further than a day's sailing from land – in fact one of our number had never so much as set foot on a yacht in his life (he was coming as the cook: we all hoped he could find his way around a gas stove, but we had no proof of that even) and here we were committing to a trip of some five thousand nautical miles. At least most of our collective experience had been in Cape Town, notorious for its rough seas and strong winds. I have heard it said that if you can sail in Cape Town, you can sail anywhere. Well, we would find out.

Attitude was going to count for a lot. Sailing across the Atlantic was not going to be like going on a road trip in a car: there would be nowhere to pull over and park when we were tired. Getting to Rio de Janeiro would entail crossing one of the planet's loneliest stretches of ocean (there are no major shipping routes traversing the area we would be sailing through), a voyage that should take anything from four to five weeks. *Josephine* had no autopilot, which meant someone would have to be on deck at the wheel every minute of the trip, night and day, in all weather. We could expect to be at turns burnt to a cinder by the sun (there was no cover over the cockpit), swamped by rogue waves, soaked by rain and smacked by wayward flying fish, not to mention stiff and sore from standing at the wheel for hours at a time. Neither did we have a satellite phone or radio that would enable us to communicate with anyone on land; we had no internet access, so no weather reports. We would be *alone*. Four ordinary blokes – a banker, a real estate agent, a biochemist and a just-graduated-from-high-school surfer – confined to a fibreglass capsule a little over thirty feet long by ten feet across at its widest, at the mercy of the wind and ocean currents to get where we wanted to go. To a seasoned sailor this might be a side-trip, but to us ordinary folk it would be epic.

After me, the most experienced sailor on board was Dael, a thirty-year-old masters' student of biochemistry. In addition to having spent several years racing as a member of the crew on a yacht at the club in Cape Town he was an accomplished surf lifesaver, so doubled up as first mate and medic. Boisterous and highly educated, Dael knew the names of all the parts on a sailboat and what most of them did. He would be very useful on the deck and had no difficulty getting time off from his research and lecturing duties to make the trip.

It was at lunch in the Brass Bell restaurant that I first met the forty-two-year-old Rob. We were there to celebrate the birthday of a mutual friend, and the topic of my impending ocean crossing came up for discussion. A little later Rob sidled round to where I was sitting.

"Hey mate, I need to talk to you," He whispered. "I want to cross the ocean. I'm serious. Please take me."

He had never so much as been on a yacht, and here he was pleading to be taken as crew for an ocean crossing. It was admirable, but I had seen and heard it before. He was not the first person to declare with great bravado that he was "up for it" without knowing a thing about it; I had a list of at least ten people who had "committed" over the last year or two only to fall away closer to the time. The difference was that Rob did not have a beer in his hand; he was completely sober.

"I'll do anything. I'll cook!"

That clinched it. My DNA came without a cooking gene. Rob was enthusiastic in the extreme, and proved eager and inexhaustible, and an insatiable urge to learn and understand what was going on around him had him reading the full library of sailing books on board. He turned out to be a very diligent cook. He was also very funny, on the first day flinging a malfunctioning can opener overboard for being a "*can't* opener".

The third, and youngest, member of the crew was Rupert, a year out of high school and looking for adventure. We met over dinner at my neighbour's house. Practical, intelligent and witty, his bearing belied his tender age, and by the end of the evening I knew I had found the perfect person to round out the crew list. I offered him a spot, and he promptly booked himself on a sailing course, after which I was delighted to appoint him "navigator". He proved to be dependable, brave and mature beyond his years, and I might go so far as to admit he was emotionally the most stable person on a boat full of over-demonstrative extroverts.

***

I had one last debt to settle before I could leave. I owed my friend Torries a bottle of bourbon. He had won it off me in a bet. He said Abi would be pregnant before we left to go sailing around the world, and although his implication was that we would not go as a result, technically he had won the bet and I was happy to pay up. Of course there was no way I could just give him his bottle and leave – no, we had to drink it. All of it. We sat up through the night talking more and more nonsense about less and less, until in a rare moment of lucidity I confessed to being terrified at the prospect of crossing the ocean.

"I think it's brilliant what you are doing," said Torries. "We all do. Everyone is talking about you. You have to do it. Everyone I know wishes they could do what you're doing."

"That's great, but it's not so simple. I mean – what *am* I doing, really? I have no job, no house… no income… and a five month old baby, and now I am about to sail out of here and head across a bloody ocean on a small boat! It's crazy if you think about it. I don't know what I'm doing – not really. We'll have no communication with the world for a month. Anything could happen to us, nobody would ever know. And where the hell is Brazil anyway? Out there – somewhere…"

Through the whisky haze a bleary morning sun swam through the window over his shoulder. He leant unsteadily forward and fixed me with the most earnest look his blood alcohol count would allow.

"Let me tell you something," he said, waving a finger of authority under my nose. "You just listen to your old friend Torries. When you sail out of that harbour," thrusting the finger now towards the window, "it doesn't matter what happens after that. You got out. You beat the system. You've won!"

***

We left Cape Town in a stiff breeze that whipped the tops of the glittering swells to fragments that dazzled like crystal in the bright sun. A pod of Dusky Dolphins leaped and danced on our bow wave in celebration. First-timer Rob was on the foredeck leaning over the rail, almost touching the dolphins as they swam in formation under the bow. It was unlike anything he had ever experienced before and he had no words. As we drew away from Table Mountain, her table cloth tumbling from her top and down the cliffs towards the city, *Josephine* surged eagerly over the waves at nine knots. We were flying along, but with the rocking and rolling in the swell it did not take my predictably weak stomach long to rebel, and I spent the better part of that afternoon and evening throwing up violently – and very noisily – over the side. The vomiting had left me tired, hungry, wet and cold by the time we reached Dassen Island a couple of hours after sunset.

Dassen lies some forty miles up the coast but no more than about two miles offshore. We picked our way round the outlying rocks in the dark to the north side where we were sheltered from the worst of the wind and dropped anchor in flat water to steal the only real sleep we expected to get for the next month. First thing in the morning we hauled Rupert up the mast on the end of a halyard to wrap duct tape around the ends of the spreaders as they had rubbed holes in the sail the day before. Once that was done we enjoyed a breakfast of fried eggs and bacon before departing our anchorage and heading out onto the big blue open ocean.

It was another sparkling day, bright and fresh, and we were soon joined by a new pod of inquisitive dolphins that had us wondering aloud who was watching whom. Throughout the day, cruising along at a comfortable seven knots over cobalt-coloured water, we were visited by Cape Fur Seals and African (aka Jackass or Magellanic) Penguins. Around four o'clock in the afternoon we sighted our first pair of courting Southern Right Whales as they lolled about on the surface, blowing their distinctive V-shaped clouds of spray like steam from double-spouted kettles.

Right Whales owe their name to the whalers of old who coined them the "right" whales to hunt because they come close inshore to court and mate, and, unlike other whales, float when they die. A rather prosaic claim to fame of the Southern Right is the fact that the male has the biggest testicles in the animal kingdom, each one weighing five hundred kilograms – or half a ton – the combined mass of the pair constituting a full one percent of the animal's bodyweight. The crew delighted in these statistics.

"Man!" exclaimed Dael. "Imagine walking around with more than two pounds worth of testicles. Try tucking a pound of butter down each trouser leg. That's what it would be like!"

Rupert suggested the obvious buoyancy advantage of enormous butter testicles might explain why the whale's mammalian ancestors reverted to the water.

That night the wind picked up to gale force, as it is wont to do in those parts, and standing alone at the wheel at three o'clock in the morning guiding eight tons of yacht as it thundered over the waves at ten knots under a full moon was an experience that etched itself forever into my psyche. Alone and untouchable, I was flying over the crests of the waves and soaring down the valleys like an eagle, the exultant sense of liberation absolute. Silver moon, roaring wind and heaving ocean, forever. I thought of Torries and laughed out loud. No two ways about it. Yes, I had won.

***

Morning revealed a shifty and restless grey ocean. Sheets of spume were being torn from the ragged wave tops as the gale raged on, showing no sign of abating. We agreed between us that three hour shifts wrestling the wheel had been too long during the night, and adjusted the watch system to two hours on followed by four hours off. Rob was not expected to take any watches, as he was responsible for keeping us all fed – though his company in the cockpit was always welcome – but within the first few days he tried his hand at steering during my watches, and showed a natural aptitude. He steered by instinct. He could feel the boat under his feet and make the subtle adjustments necessary to keep her on course in rough weather. Before long we changed the watch system again so Rob had a full complement of three two-hour shifts of his own (all during daylight hours; we kept him off duty at night so he could sleep, and we could continue to eat well.)

Life aboard slipped comfortably into routine. Two hour watches, when we were alone (usually) on deck at the wheel, scudding over the ocean under ever changing skies and hoping it would not rain, were followed by four hours off during which we washed, ate, read, attended to general maintenance and snatched some sleep. As Rob now had his daytime shifts on the helm, the other three of us were able to alternate a day off (day mind you, not night). Rob still made dinner, but the man on his day off was responsible for lunch. Preparing lunch involved diving into that week's provision box and throwing together anything that took our fancy. Typical lunches were canned curries and instant noodles, or hotdogs. We were all responsible for our own breakfasts, which meant delving into a bucket of home made muesli, as it was not practical to serve a meal to everyone together first thing in the morning – not after a night of interrupted sleep. Between meals there was freedom to scratch around in the box and help yourself to any snack you found – nuts, dried fruit, biscuits – on condition you announced it and shared. The only rule was that if anyone was heard saying the C-word – "chocolate" – we had to break out a slab immediately.

***

Four days into the trip we marked Rupert's nineteenth birthday, and to celebrate appropriately we chose that day to bake our first ever loaf of bread. I had been given a "recipe" by a sailing friend back home which involved nothing more than mixing a can of beer with a pound of self-raising flour and a handful of salt, leaving it to rise for fifteen minutes, then shoving it in the oven for an hour. To merry it up a little in Rupert's honour we added a smashed up slab of chocolate and a generous splash of rum. The rum promptly burned off in the oven and the sweet taste of the chocolate was at odds with the salty dough, but the bread itself did not turn out too badly and was presented to Rupert in lieu of a cake, complete with musical candles. From that day on a loaf of freshly baked bread was *de rigeur* with lunch, though after Dael nauseated us with a meal of jelly-baby bread and custard it was forbidden to add anything sweet to the mixture.

The greatest excitement of Rupert's birthday came just before sunset when we caught a twenty-four pound tuna which was hauled aboard amid wild celebration just as Rob was about to open a dubious looking can of meatballs. Not knowing quite what to do with it once we had it on the boat, we slaughtered the hapless fish in a manner reminiscent of one of the more violent and bloody scenes from "Lord of the Flies", but our civilized veneer was restored as we dined with elegance on soft, pink sashimi starters followed by seared tuna steaks and fried eggs. The perfect birthday feast. Later I owned up that it was the first fish I had ever caught from a boat, though I suspect it was obvious.

As it turned out it was to be the last fish we would catch for the next two weeks. In fact it was the last living creature we saw for a long time, other than birds. There were no more whales, no dolphins, and no seals or penguins once we were more than a hundred miles from land. We were, however, accompanied by those most magnificent sea birds of all – the albatrosses. We never tired of watching them float in the air above the boat, or soar down to the water and glide effortlessly among the valleys of the ocean swells, almost flicking the tops of the crests with their wingtips as they swooped over the waves, never seeming to flap.

A study in gliding efficiency, they have evolved an incredible wingspan, the Wandering Albatross having the largest wingspan of all birds, reaching up to eleven feet. They are so efficient that their heart rate while gliding is almost the same as their resting rate, so flight is little more tiring than sitting on a rock doing nothing, a physiological phenomenon that renders distances from land meaningless. An albatross can thus spend all year at sea, occasionally sitting on the water when the wind is no good for gliding, and returning to land only to breed. Sadly, of the twenty-one species recognised by the IUCN *(International Union for the Conservation of Nature)*, nineteen are verging on extinction. The biggest single threat to their survival is long-line fishing, with thousands dying every year from drowning after swallowing baited hooks. We were quick to haul our fishing lures back on board whenever we saw an albatross.

***

A few days after Rupert's birthday we were faced with our first crisis at sea. One of the regular boat checks involved lifting up a floor board and checking the bilges for signs of any leaking. This day I lifted the board and was horrified to find the bottom of the boat awash with water. We needed to know whether we had a leak, or whether we were losing fresh water from our tanks, so in spite of the unappealing sight of it – foul with engine oil and diesel (the bilges of a boat never stay clean) – I was forced to taste it. No salt.

"Guys, we've lost drinking water. Fill all the spare containers you can find, then let's get the bilges pumped dry so we can see if we are still leaking."

As the crew set about filling bottles, cans, pots and the kettle with fresh water from the taps, the electric pump was employed to clear the bilges and I ran my eye over the parts of the plumbing system I could get to. I could find no leaking pipes or joints. Our drinking water was stored in two stainless steel tanks of two hundred litres each, linked by pipes that ran under the floor and up to the taps in the galley and heads. The tanks had been installed on either side of the saloon, under the bunks, and were difficult to get at without embarking on a serious carpentry project. Also, there was no meter, so we could not check the level. When they were filled to overflowing (there was a filler cap on deck) we knew we had four hundred litres, but after that we had to carefully estimate consumption to keep some track of how much we might have left. After this sudden loss of water we had no idea how much remained in the tanks, or whether they were still leaking. We were over a thousand miles from home, and at least four hundred from the nearest land – which was the appropriately named Skeleton Coast of the Namib Desert. Officially the driest desert on Earth, we would have as much luck finding water there as on the moon. This was a big blow and I sank my head in my hands. Now, surrounded by water, we were all going to die of thirst. How ridiculous.

"Okay, that's thirty litres in containers to add to the fifty litres of water in the emergency drums," said Dael, referring to two jerry cans we had filled back home and stashed in the forepeak where we kept the food. I did a rough calculation in my head.

"Four of us, say two litres each per day, that's eight litres, it'll last ten days. And it seems the tanks are not yet empty, the taps still run, but ten days would not see us to Brazil if the taps were to run dry now. We're three weeks away yet, at best."

"Could we turn round?" asked Rupert.

"Technically, Rupe, yes; but we'd be fighting the wind and the current, it would take at least two weeks to get back, maybe longer."

I lifted the hatch in the floor to see a dry bilge, and switched off the pump.

"Now for the test!"

We stared with bated breath, but no water came. There appeared to be no further leaking. Whatever the cause, it seemed to have been a once-off loss. But I was worried. The tanks might be close to empty and could run dry at any moment, and then we would have water for only ten days. We could harvest any rain, but could not rely on that – it might not rain. I had to make a decision. Turning back was dangerous as it would be a punishing trip against the wind, the current and the waves, with no guarantee of reaching civilization in time. Pushing on to Brazil was just as risky as there was still such a long way to go, and we might well run out of water. Turning east and heading to Namibia was another option – there may not be water in the desert, though closer to shore we might hope to find another vessel – perhaps a fishing trawler – and bum some water.

But there was a fourth option. I sat at the navigation table and studied the chart.

"We're just over a thousand miles from Saint Helena, we could get there in less than a week. It's a lot further north and would add at least six hundred miles to our trip, but I don't see that we have a choice."

And so for several days we trended northwards, falling back on the structure of routine, meeting over meals and at changes of watch, but for the most part each immersed in his own private world. I had never before spent weeks at a time confined to an area no larger than a medium sized room, yet I felt so free. It struck me this must be what it is like for astronauts in space. Out on the wide ocean you may not be able to walk away from your fibreglass pod, but you can see forever and your mental universe becomes boundless. It seemed odd to have such a notion of space at the same time as being so constrained physically, but one gains a wonderful sense of spiritual and emotional freedom out on the ocean. The water around us was a living entity – it was in constant motion, colours changing from indigo to bottle green to metal grey depending on its mood, and the sky above was limitless. It was everywhere, a Great Sky the size of which one never sees on land. Truly a Sky to Dream.

Sunrises and sunsets were special. The sun would rise behind us like an inflated grapefruit after tingeing the ruffles of cloud low on the horizon a gentle pink, and in the evenings would hang ahead of us like a suspended lantern showing the way to the west before extinguishing itself below the distant waves. Twice we were witness to the almost mythical "Green Flash" – an optical phenomenon created by the refraction of light rays of different wavelength through air of varying temperatures that causes the sun to flash a brilliant neon green the instant before it slips away round the back of the world.

But when the sun left us the Great Sky stayed. The full moon laid a bright luminous path out over the water, and when there was no moon the foaming wave crests were picked out with silver plate from the light of a thousand stars, scattered across the heavens like so many diamonds spilt across a sheet of black velvet. The stars were perfect navigational aids. We would line the boat up with the compass, identify a convenient star hanging in the rigging above us, then dowse the compass light and sail through the darkness by the star. Sometimes we would use a constellation to guide us – Orion the Hunter, or the Scorpion – the Southern Cross was a permanent comfort watching over our left shoulder and we were on first name terms with the Seven Sisters of the Pleiades, mentioned in Homer's *Odyssey* and forming part of the constellation of Taurus. A two hour shift was never so long that the positions of the stars changed materially, and the next person on watch would reset the helm to his own star. Sometimes we used the Clouds of Magellan; dwarf galaxies, containing a mere few billion stars, and the only galaxies outside our own discernable to the naked eye. Visible from the southern hemisphere, they appear as two smudges of light just off to the side of the Milky Way, the smaller of which is so faint you can almost not see it, so you need to practically look past it before it is visible in your peripheral vision. The Large Magellanic Cloud (LMC) measures only 14,000 light years across (compared to the 100,000 light year diameter of our Milky Way) and it and its smaller sister (SMC) are satellite galaxies to ours. Being no more than 160,000 light years away, their spiral shapes have been deformed over the ages by tidal interaction with our stars.

Crawling into a sleeping bag in the saloon after two hours on the wheel, I would lie awake listening to the sound of the water rushing and gurgling a few inches from my head, the creaking of the wooden bulkheads as *Josephine* rolled with the swell, the clunks and rattles of the rigging, the slap of a luffing sail or the occasional heavy thump of a wave against the side invariably followed by a choice expletive from the unfortunate helmsman as he took a soaking. They were the reassuring sounds of a healthy, happy boat at one with a benign ocean that sang me to sleep.

***

Sometime in the morning of the eleventh of December we first made out the dark grey rectangular smudge in the cloud on the western horizon that is the volcanic island of Saint Helena. We squinted at it as we sailed on, willing it closer, but it faded back into the cloud and we were left to chase its image on the GPS plotter instead. With the wind from dead behind us we were forced to gybe and sail doglegs and by nightfall the island was still some twenty frustrating miles away.

Saint Helena erupted into existence through volcanic action along the eastern edge of the Mid-Atlantic Ridge, a geological fault line with a four mile deep canyon that runs north-south along the full length of the ocean floor. The island is thus the peak of an extinct volcano that rises some nine thousand feet from the sea bed. It last erupted seven million years ago, and over the following millennia the rocky top transformed itself into a tropical island with steep cliffs plunging sheer into the sea on all sides. It was named after Saint Helena of Constantinople, mother of Constantine the First, Roman Emperor from 324 to 337 AD. (Her religious stature was assured by political foresight when she was expediently credited by the Catholic Church with finding the remnants of the "True Cross". How could Roman subjects not bow in homage to an emperor who was the son of such a woman?) The island was discovered by the Portuguese in 1502 or 1503 – depending which version of history you prefer (unless the great Chinese fleets of the fifteenth century actually landed there eighty years prior, as has been claimed more recently) but the Portuguese did not occupy the island, and in 1657 Oliver Cromwell granted a charter to the English East India Company to settle and govern Saint Helena as it was of strategic importance to British shipping between Europe, South Africa and India. Two years later the capital, Jamestown, was founded and named after James the Duke of York, later to become King James II of England. Today Saint Helena forms part of the British Overseas Territory of Saint Helena, Ascension and Tristan da Cunha, and is the second oldest remaining British colony after Bermuda. In 1840 the Royal Navy established a permanent presence on the island and used it as a base from which to fight the West African slave trade, rescuing some fifteen thousand slaves over the ensuing nine years.

The island has been visited in turn by such illustrious personages as Charles Darwin, Captain James Cook, Sir Francis Drake and Edmund Halley (of comet fame). Probably the most celebrated "visitor" was Napoleon Bonaparte, who spent the last six years of his life there as a "guest" of the Crown after his defeat at the hands of the Duke of Wellington in the battle of Waterloo. Boney died there in May of

1821, and the cottage he lived in is the second most visited tourist attraction on the island, after the 699 concrete steps of "Jacob's Ladder", by which one can climb to the top of the cliff supporting the little fort overlooking the valley that cradles Jamestown.

One of the world's most isolated places, this little five by ten mile island, surrounded by water two miles deep and over a thousand miles from the nearest landmass, has no airport and therefore few tourists to speak of. The only visitors to the island either come on the monthly mail ship from the UK that plies a route between Southampton and Cape Town, or on private yachts like ours. During our visit the locals were talking about the impending construction of an airport, but in October of 2009 those plans were scrapped by the British government. (Stop press: work finally began on the construction of the airport in January 2014.)

***

Late that evening we dropped anchor in sixty feet of water just off Jamestown, and spent an uncomfortable night rocking on the ocean swell and worrying about the anchor holding. We only had a hundred and thirty feet of chain, which was all down, but the general rule of thumb is to drop a length of chain that is four times the depth. Before turning in for the night we sat on deck looking at the line of lights that pick out the steps of Jacobs Ladder where it rises steeply out of town and up to the old fort on Ladder Hill.

"It's a British colony, they must speak English I suppose?" queried Rob as we speculated about the people we would meet the next morning.

"Perhaps they're mutants, with magic powers," suggested Rupert. "In fact, midgets. Mutant midgets!"

Dael felt the island was more likely to be populated by a colony of Swedish air hostesses, an idea that went down very well indeed. I dreamt that night of volcanoes inhabited by Swedish midgets with dragging anchors. In the morning we were surprised to discover most of the "Saints", as the locals call themselves, to be descended from South Pacific Islanders. Only the GPS convinced us we had not messed up and landed in Tonga.

In 1907 plantations of New Zealand Flax were established in the temperate highlands of the island to produce fibre for rope, and hundreds of Tongans and Fijians moved to Saint Helena to work. In 1966 synthetic fibres took over the world's rope industry and the Saint Helena flax business collapsed. Most of the people – who were by then second or third generation – opted to stay, and the economy is now sustained by the British government, over half the adult population being employed by the state. The main exports are game fish, colourful postage stamps and the world's most expensive coffee. At the time we were there, the good people of Saint Helena were hoping to make their sporting impact on the world with the island's cricket team due to make its international debut in Division Three of the World Cricket League in 2011 alongside powerhouses Papua New Guinea and Uganda.

To us the best thing about Jamestown was "Anne's Place", a restaurant with a veranda overlooking the bay that is a favourite with visiting yachties, where we tucked into a big, greasy breakfast of eggs, bacon, sausages, beans and toast. After a good feed, Rob went off on a lone quest to find Napoleon's cottage while the rest of us drank more coffee and tried to cajole some sense out of a very slow internet connection. In due course Rob returned triumphant, photos of the little general's house saved for posterity in his camera, and pronounced the Saints the "Friendliest People in the World" – quite a compliment, seeing as it was the first time Rob had ever been outside South Africa. A little later we overheard our dedicated real estate merchant trying to convince some hapless local at the bar to buy a house in Cape Town.

That evening, after a massive dinner at "Anne's", where we had stayed all day, as we rowed back to *Josephine* under a night sky that was stretched over the world like a black net through which a thousand silver pricks of light twinkled, a dolphin sighed and puffed around the dinghy setting off green flashes in the phosphorescence. I reached over the side and tried to touch it. I gazed in wonder at the green tracks of light in the water, then up at the silhouette of my *Josephine* riding so proud and serene at her anchor against the backdrop of a galaxy in full glory. I could have burst with happiness.

***

The taps in the boat had run dry the day we arrived in Saint Helena, and it took six dinghy trips with all available containers to bring back the four hundred litres needed to get the tanks full again. This time we took an additional hundred litres of water on board in drums, just in case, as the trip from here to Rio would be even longer than the 2210 miles we had covered so far, and we could ill afford another water disaster. This time there would be nowhere to go.

After I performed some impromptu dental work on Rupert (he smashed his mouth with a winch handle and Dael shot a hammed-up video of me re-shaping his shattered incisor with a metal file from my toolbox) we set our watches to Brazil time, hauled up the anchor, shook out the sails and pointed the good ship *Josephine* west across the ocean towards South America. To begin with the change in ship's time was disorientating, the sun rising at (our) 3am and setting at 3pm, but with every day westwards the time better matched the sun, and we would arrive in Brazil with our diurnal rhythm already adapted.

But for the first four days out of Cape Town, when we had surfed northwards on the swells ahead of gale-force winds, the weather for the leg to Saint Helena had been perfect, with consistent following winds and mostly sunny skies making for near perfect sailing conditions. Things were to change on the second leg. As we ventured further out onto the Atlantic and Saint Helena slipped inexorably over the horizon in our wake, a cell of intense low pressure was barrelling its way up the South American coast from the Southern Ocean. Over the ensuing days it developed into a full blown tropical cyclone, bringing with it violent winds and torrential rain that lead to some of the most destructive flooding in the history of the Brazilian state of Santa Catarina, killing over a hundred people and leaving thousands homeless.

Of course we knew nothing of this, and had been at sea five or six days when we noticed a pronounced swell coming through from the south west; a deep, wide swell that conflicted with the prevailing ocean swell driven by the south-easterly Trade Winds we were sailing on. This conflict set up a lumpy, erratic sea with frequent rogue waves coming from odd directions that reared up unannounced and slammed into the boat, shaking her like a toy and swamping the cockpit. The high cirrus cloud feathering the sky warned us we could expect some excitement, and later the following day the barometric pressure plunged. Without access to weather reports we had little idea we were headed on a collision course with a massive storm cell as it bludgeoned and battered its way up the coast of Brazil.

In due course the wind veered from easterly to north westerly, further confusing the swells running from the south, and we put a third reef in the mainsail to keep the power to a minimum for the coming tempest. Both the wind and the waves continued to build, until we were surfing down the faces of waves thirty feet high. Down in the troughs there was eerie quiet as the waves shielded us from the wind, then as we were lifted high on the next crest the wind screamed through the rigging and slammed the sails tight, *Josephine* surging in response and accelerating off the lip, carving the bottle green water into a twin bow-wave of tumbling foam. It was a wild ride. Steering demanded absolute concentration as we anticipated the movements of the water and lined the boat up to minimise the risk of being spun out or rolled over. The wind had picked up to fifty-five knots before the rain came, and when it came, it came in a deluge, as if another layer of the ocean were falling out of the sky under its own weight.

With the wind howling, the tops of the waves exploding into stinging white needles and the rain cascading down, it was difficult to read the water and we started making mistakes. Rupe and I were tied to our bunks in the saloon during one of Dael's afternoon shifts when we heard a muffled cry of alarm as the boat rolled awkwardly on her side, then our bunks pressed hard against our backs as *Josephine* climbed steeply, followed by an eerie weightlessness. Gone was the sound of running water along the hull as *Josephine* went into freefall. Our stomachs floated up under our ribs as we held our breath and braced ourselves for the impact. Time stopped. We hung motionless in the air, then a sudden, juddering crash forced us violently down into our bunks. I looked up through the top hatch at where the sky would normally be, but there was only a deep green, swirling like liquid malachite against the glass. The boat was underwater.

But *Josephine* is a resilient ship and she looked after us. She shook the water off like a duck and burst above the surface, Dael whooping like a teenager in the cockpit (I was relieved to hear he was still there!) and the rest of us falling over each other to rig our harnesses so we could get outside and join him. Then Dael was shouting again in alarm, and as I scrabbled up the steps and out through the hatch he was pointing forward and babbling incoherently.

"Shit! Shit!" he was shouting, eyes round with fright. "The boom! Shit!"

"What? What is it?" I shouted above the roar.

"I don't know! The boom! It just flew up..."

"What do you mean, '*flew up*'? Up where?"

He wore the face of a man who had just been scared out of his wits, and no wonder. He had been at the wheel when we were dropped off the crest of a huge wave and fell past a grey cliff of water to be buried in the boiling cauldron below, and now he was in shock. I squinted at the boom. It looked fine, but the mainsail was sagging, and I realised the boom was bouncing.

"The kicker has gone. Dael, there's no kicker!" I yelled into his face, and he nodded wide-eyed as if he understood. I crawled forward on my stomach over the coach roof until I reached the attachment point for the kicker to discover the steel cable had parted in the middle. The impact of our landing had had a whiplash effect on the mast, jerking the boom up and snapping the kicker. I removed both ends of the broken cable and inched my way back to the cockpit as *Josephine* twisted and bucked like a bronco on the waves, trying to throw me off. Two minutes of crawling around on my stomach on a heaving, rolling deck triggered a bout of violent vomiting.

Dael was the best foredeck crew we had and was not prone to sea sickness, so I sent him forward with some rope to rig a new kicker while I took the wheel. He was in his element clinging to the pitching deck fiddling about with shackles and tying knots, and by the time he came back, job done, was his normal cheerful self again. The new kicker worked perfectly and we had *Josephine* back under control. Then we whooped and chanted like football fans as we surfed mountain after mountain, competing with each other to set the fastest speeds.

"We are such cowboys!" remarked Rupert, wearing the broadest grin as *Josephine* plunged into the next abyss. We were running on Attitude.

For four days and four nights the storm raged around us, and for four days and four nights, two hours at a time, we clung like limpets to the wheel cajoling *Josephine* over, through and occasionally under the waves towards Brazil. Nobody knew how Rob kept a steady stream of hot meals flowing, but he did, in spite of frequently having to dash out through the hatch to puke over the side as he was afflicted by dreadful bouts of sea-sickness huddled over the gas stove in the heaving, sweaty bowels of the boat.

Nights were more difficult as we could not see, and we took regular sucker punches from rogue waves that knocked us on our side, causing the helmsman to cling desperately to the wheel under a deluge of cold saltwater, and those in their sleeping bags below to brace their feet against the side walls and ceilings of the cabins.

By the fourth night the wind had abated to a manageable thirty five knots and we were racing the swells with regular boat speeds of over twelve knots (our maximum recorded speed was fifteen, with the *cook* at the wheel!). Moon and stars were smothered by dark cloud, but at least there was no more rain, and the inky black sea around us was alive with phosphorescence, the breaking crests of the waves flashing like neon in the night. We would be lifted up from behind by the invisible mass of water, *Josephine* would hang a moment in space then accelerate down into the dark void, a brief silence shattered by a roar as the wave collapsed and tumbled beneath us, and we were riding atop a rolling cascade of bio-light that lit up the cockpit. Surfing on flashing thunder. In five days we covered over a thousand miles at the improbable average speed of well over eight knots, logging 217 miles in our best twenty-four hours.

After the fifth day of this rollercoaster ride the wind died away in the night and by morning we were becalmed. It was a wonderful opportunity to spread soaked clothes and sleeping bags on the deck to dry, and for us to plunge overboard for our first swim in three mile deep water. Dael and Rupe paddled around the boat on their surfboards – "because they could" – and Rob conjured a sumptuous lunch of canned meatballs and limp cornflakes. Most of that day was spent motoring over smooth turquoise water startling swarms of flying fish from under the bow. Knowing they are a favourite food of tuna and dorado, we dragged two rubber lures about fifty feet behind us, and in the afternoon changed course to pass deliberately under a flock of diving birds to be rewarded with two skipjack tuna of fifteen pounds apiece that Rob turned into perfect sushi rolls.

Those fishing birds were our first hint that we were drawing near the coast, and the last few days of the trip were uneventful, except for the hilarity of seeing first Rupert, then Dael, smacked on the head by rogue flying fish. There are apparently sixty four recognised species of flying fish, of the genus "Exocoetus" (from which was derived the name "Exocet" for the French-built anti-ship missile that saw extensive service in the Falklands War of 1982). Another hint of land came from a white plastic miner's helmet floating on the ocean with a little water in it and a tiny, lost black fish swimming around in frantic circles. We were closing on Brazil.

On the twenty-eighth of November, Brazil's "*Muro Verde*" or Green Wall, the forest clad escarpment running the length of the coast of Rio de Janeiro and Sao Paulo states, rose up out of the sea ahead of us topped with a thin smear of white cloud. There were boobies, gulls and frigate birds about and we could smell the trees. By sundown we reached the entrance to the bay of Ilha Grande, midway between Rio de Janeiro, fifty miles over to our right, and the island of Ilhabela to our left, which was our destination. There was still no wind, and the listless green sea, sprinkled with floating leaves, looked like thick vegetable soup. The warm, humid breath of the rainforest lent a physical weight to the air and gobs of sweat slid down our legs.

We turned left and motored along the cliffs as the sun set behind the Green Wall off our starboard bow, and as the day faded the sea ahead of us was picked out with the scattered lights of a fleet of wooden fishing boats, forcing us a couple of miles out from the shore to avoid their nets. A steady, gentle rain started to fall after dinner, and we endured a frustrating, eternal night in the unrelenting drizzle, the motor droning onwards towards the distant lighthouses on the island of Vitoria and the town of Caraguatatuba. Ilhabela, our destination, lay directly between them in the dark.

We did not see the morning sun, but a pale light diffused by a grey sky revealed a steep dark island with high peaks jutting defiantly above a ring of mist. A languid turtle paddled by as we motored into the mile-wide channel between Ilhabela and the mainland, rain gear on and hot coffee in hand. I called my Brazilian friend Ludi, who was to meet us, on my cell phone.

"*Bom dia!*" he exclaimed. It was the first outside voice we had heard on the boat for a month. "Where you are?"

"Ludi! We're in the channel off *Sao Sebastiao*. I'm heading over to the mainland to find Immigration…"

"*Whaat?!*" he cut me short, "Are you *crraizy*? Ees *Frraidai todai*! Turrn arround and come to de beetch! I weell wait you dere. I breeng yourr waif and yourr baby. We go forr passports next week!"

"But the regulations say to report within twenty-four hours…"

"No, no! What for? Don't worry! Dees ees Brraseel ma frriend!"

And so the fun started.

"What we are told of the inhabitants of Brazil,
that they never die but of old age,
is attributed to the tranquility and serenity of their climate;
I rather attribute it to the tranquility and serenity
of their souls."

– Michel de Montaigne, circa 1540

4

We had not known Ludi long. In fact I had first met him only a few months before, at the Yacht Club in Cape Town, just after he crossed the Atlantic from Brazil with Teddy, a seventy-year-old New Zealander, on a fifty-five foot sloop. I bumped into them on the jetty. Almost literally. Actually I bumped into the boat alongside them. As I was manoeuvring *Josephine* in a tight circle, the gear cable snapped and instead of going into reverse at the critical moment, she leapt ahead and ploughed into the stern of the next boat. Teddy was on his deck bellowing "Reverse! Reverse!" at me as if I were some sort of simpleton, charging ahead deliberately. I introduced myself and took Teddy and Ludi to lunch.

Now Ludi and I were together again in Brazil, and he could not have been more generous. He had put Abi, Jo and Lucy up in his beach house for some weeks before I arrived with the boat, and subsequently made it available to us all for a further two weeks so we could have a "holiday" before embarking on our travels. *Josephine* was secured to Ludi's mooring buoy at the little sailing club by the beach, and I moved into his house with the girls. It was a lovely break, reconnecting with little Lucy after two months, taking her swimming and hacking fresh coconuts from the palms outside the front door with a machete lashed to a bamboo pole. Rob flew home, Rupert went to Chile to surf and Dael agreed to stay on for a time to help with the boat.

***

The odd thing about entering Brazil with your own boat is that nobody has any idea you are there until you present yourself at the appropriate office in the nearest town, which in practice can be some days after your actual arrival. Then, suddenly, as if you have just been caught in the act of performing some nefarious deed, you are frowned at severely and sent on the most extraordinary paper-chase from one office to the next in search of the requisite permissions and stamps. The list of requirements varies depending on where you have landed, and, it would appear, who happens to be on duty that day, or who won the previous night's football. And so I had my first encounter with *Brazileiro* bureaucracy in Sao Sebastiao, the town on the mainland opposite Ilhabela.

Sao Sebastiao has an oil terminal. Tankers clog the channel between the town and the island, and the authorities in the town are used to dealing with these seven hundred foot long ships with their crew of professional sailors and engineers; but they are *not* used to dealing with thirty eight foot fibreglass sailing boats with decidedly unprofessional families on board.

First we all needed to be cleared into the country by Immigration, which in Brazil falls under the jurisdiction of the *Policia Federal*, their equivalent of the FBI. We trooped into their downtown office brandishing our passports. The amiable young policeman behind the desk with his hand in plaster was very proud to be able to tell me he had been to Cape Town and that Cape Town was very beautiful and Cape Town had very sexy girls and we are very welcome in Brazil and do we know Brazil has very sexy girls too and would we like to see a calendar of Brazilian girls in G-strings? He was so taken by us that he forgot his pistol on the counter in front of me as he went off to make photocopies of the passports.

Once that had been taken care of, the girls wandered off to poke around in the cheap clothes shops while I presented myself to the "*Capitania dos Portos*"; the Brazilian port authority that doubles as a coastguard. Ludi was kind enough to accompany me as a translator, but the problem with a translator is that it takes away your "stupid gringo" card and you can no longer just shake your head and mumble and pretend not to understand when things get difficult.

This particular day, the *Capitania* wanted to see my "*Saude*" (Health) clearance. There was nothing about that in my sailing guide. I told him I did not possess such a thing, and confessed I did not even know what it was, upon which we were despatched to the *Saude* office down the road, which turned out to be a converted shipping container, inside which one small man laboured behind an enormous desk groaning under a heap of yellow and green forms.

"*Sim, sim!*" he smiled, he could arrange everything, and could he see our forms?

"Well, we want you to give us the forms please. That is why we are here."

"No *senhor*, I merely certify them."

"Certify what? I don't have anything."

"*Es imposivel senhor.*" Surely I had a health declaration, signed by the ship's doctor?

Ah, so here was the confusion. I explained that I did not have a ship, merely a little fibreglass sailing boat; much less a doctor.

"Well you still need a health declaration."

"So where do I find one of those, if not here?" I asked.

"Who is your agent? Your agent should have them."

"My *agent*? What agent?"

I had no idea what he was talking about.

"Your shipping agent *senhor*!"

I tried in vain to convince him it was perfectly normal for me to enter the country in a private yacht without a doctor or a shipping agent, but he was used to dealing with mega-ton oil tankers and the idea of tourists coming and going willy-nilly was too novel for his provincial tastes.

"These are the clearance certificates," he said, indicating the desk piled with yellow and green forms. The green ones were for ships fifty to two hundred metres, yellow for ships over two hundred. How long did I say my ship was again?

"Thirty eight feet. Twelve metres. Actually a little less."

He blinked at me then looked at the floor a moment, frowning. It was finally dawning on him that even if I had a doctor and an agent, no form existed for a ship of a mere twelve metres.

"*Ah, senhor!*" he finally pronounced with the gravitas of one who has just solved an intractable mathematics theorem. "*Nao problem.* You do not require a form. You may go!"

But I was having none of that.

"Ludi, please tell him thank you very much, but I need something to show the *Capitania.* He believes I need a certificate, and he is not going to stamp the boat papers without something from *Saude.*"

Ludi duly translated the dilemma. The *Saude* man could offer no solution. Then I had an idea. I produced my vaccination papers (all in English) and showed him the hospital stamp. If he did not mind adding his own seal, that would be all I needed. He was delighted to do so and see the back of us, and my endorsed yellow fever certificate served admirably for the *Capitania's* purposes.

Customs was the final challenge. A Skinny Old Man and a Fat Young Man, who had never between them encountered a tourist, seemed to believe I was "importing" the boat, and were keen to charge me a deposit (refundable – how comforting) of no less than fifty thousand dollars – equal to its insured value. I was lucky to have Ludi with me, as I could explain the relevant Brazilian regulations around visiting private yachts to him in English, and Ludi in turn was able to find the legislation on the internet using the Fat Young Man's computer. Thus educated, they stamped the papers.

I came away with a sense of bewilderment at it all, but in hindsight it had all been rather easy. After all, it was settled within the same day; over the coming year I was to learn the *true* meaning of South American bureaucracy.

***

Brazil is the fifth biggest country in the world, and its population of some two hundred million souls makes it the fifth most populous too. Established as a Portuguese colony in the year 1500 and granted independence in 1822, Brazil traces its name back to Celtic mythology. Irish sailors used to talk about "*Ui-Breasil*", or the "Blessed Land", a phantom island somewhere to the west of Ireland (The Isle of Man was sometimes referred to as Brazil), permanently shrouded in thick mist except for one day every seven years. Numerous fifteenth century expeditions were despatched to search for the mythical land, including one under the august leadership of the great John Cabot (who was in fact Italian, born in Genoa under the name Giovanni Cabotto, but commissioned by the English). Cabot is generally recognised as the first European to have set foot on mainland North America (at Newfoundland) since the Vikings.

Ilhabela, or *Ilha da Sao Sebastiao* to give it its official name, has an interesting history. The island was named *Ilha da Sao Sebastiao* by Amerigo Vespucci in 1502, who had sailed as a Royal-appointed observer on the Portuguese ship that "discovered" Brazil two years previously. (The name "America" is derived from his first name.) Although it is now commonly referred to as Ilhabela (Portuguese for "Beautiful Island"), that name actually applies to an archipelago of four islands, of which *Sao Sebastiao* is by far the biggest and the only populated one. It is Brazil's largest oceanic island, measuring fifteen miles from end to end and about six across, with an extra little bit poking out of the eastern side. (Brazil's largest island of all is Marajo, but it is a "river" island; it sits in the Amazon Delta, and with its 5,500 square miles is the size of Switzerland.)

Ludi originally lived in Sao Paulo, Brazil's – indeed South America's – biggest city. He moved to Sao Sebastiao a few years back to escape the rat race and open a surf shop. Now he lives on the island itself.

"Eet was a good move frrom Sao Paulo. Life in Sao Sebastiao was more *tranquilo.*" he told me.

"So what made you leave Sao Sebastiao last year, and move again, across the channel to the island?"

Ludi clicked his tongue against the roof of his mouth and shrugged resignedly.

"In Sao Sebastiao dey announce to constrruct a trraffic light. So I must to move."

***

The next morning I decided to celebrate my legally landed status with a run. My route took me along the seafront, past the palm-roofed coconut stalls where the well-to-do ladies of Sao Paulo flit about the beaches in their flashy jewellery and oversized wrap-around sunglasses, giving them all the appearance of plump dragonflies. The beaches may be narrow and coarse, and face directly across the shallow channel towards the Petrobras oil terminal on the mainland, but the Brazilian island of Ilhabela is nonetheless "the place" for all well-to-do *Paulistas* to see and be seen.

To escape the suffocating humidity, I turned away from the beach and into the wooded hills, where the roads wind sharply up between tiers of cement houses, brightly painted butter yellow and spearmint green, stacked atop each other as they cling precariously to the steep slopes. Through the houses then the track twisted, potholed and muddy, into dank, dark forest, bringing me finally to a wooden gate in a grubby white-washed wall, where a deserted guard-hut sported a hand painted sign bidding me "*Bemvindo a Cachoeira das Tocas*". An addendum advised it would cost me three dollars to see the waterfall, but as there was nobody there I ran on through the open gate and up an overgrown path to a low brick bungalow with a corrugated tin roof. A shaggy, thin man with a full black beard appeared in the doorway. I greeted him with just about the only Portuguese I had mastered.

"*Bom dia senhor*!"

My inane tourist grin was acknowledged with a curt grunt and a twitch of the head. I tried to explain in very generic Latino, overlaid with a somewhat theatrical Portuguese accent, that I was here with my family on a sailboat and should very much like to see the waterfall if that would in order. He glowered at me through overhanging vines of unruly eyebrows and for a moment I felt uneasily like one of the city boys in that awful seventies film "Deliverance". I did not much want to have to "squeal like a pig". But then the dense scraggle of facial hair was rent by a flashing white grin: Marek, of Polish extraction, evidently found me rather novel. He proffered a shot of his home made *cachaca*, a white spirit distilled from sugar cane, rendered infinitely more potent by the fact that it was barely nine in the morning. It would have been churlish to turn down so kind an offer so I closed my eyes and swallowed hard, but with the prospect of another four mile run to look forward to back to the boat I hesitated to accept a second slug. But my new friend was having none of that. Seconds and thirds were poured, and while I sucked with mounting dread at the clear, evil spirit Marek was on his cell phone dispatching a car to the beach with instructions to round up my entire *gringo* family and hustle them into the jungle. I was clearly not about to escape.

A lurching taxi ride over the muddy, rutted track brought Abi, Lucy, Jo and Dael into the hills for their rendezvous with the hirsute Marek, who greeted them expansively at his front door, a bottle of *cachaca* in each hand.

"*Bemvindo a Cachoeira das Tocas!*" he exclaimed jubilantly, "*A Casa das Cachaca Caseira!*"

Dael grinned broadly but the girls look on dubiously. The "Home of Moonshine Cane Spirit" was not top of their list of *to-do's* on the island. At least there would appear to be a waterfall to look at. With my baby in my arms it was easier to decline a fourth shot of rocket fuel, but only after swearing a blood oath to drink with him later did Marek allow me to escape his bar and flee to the tranquility of the forest waterfall.

Unfortunately *Cachoeira das Tocas* appears to be the main breeding ground for Ilhabela's population of *borrachudos*: small, biting flies no larger than a grain of sand but more voracious than mosquitoes, their bites leave you with weeping sores for weeks, and are the reason your three dollar entry fee includes as much of Marek's home made insect repellent as you can lather onto your body. Under a liberal coating of almond and citronella, we slipped through the trees to a delightful clearing beside a stream where we spread ourselves on a large flat rock and glistened in the sun like basted turkeys.

The waterfall at Tocas (Portuguese for "caves") is a ribbon of water plunging some forty feet down a cliff over the mouth of a shallow cavern, after which the water chatters and bubbles over humps of black granite linking a series of clear pools. It is a beautiful spot tucked into the rainforest where blue butterflies the size of your two hands waft out of the jungle and over the cool dark water, and the tiniest yellow and green humming birds shimmer and dart like emerald bumblebees among hanging strings of scarlet flowers. We were the only visitors to the falls, and a wonderful morning was spent alternately lazing on the warm rock and skidding on our bums down a natural sixty foot chute of rushing water.

Around midday Marek stalked out from between the trees, barefoot and hairy, lacking only a poison-dart blow-pipe to look the part of the jungle warrior-savage. He leered at us and makes biting and slurping gestures.

"My god!" exclaimed Abi, feigning horror. "He's going to eat us!"

"Don't be silly," I said, "he's very kind. He's inviting us to lunch."

After gorging on fried fish, followed with fresh breadfruit from the forest, we adjourned with Marek to his rattan bar where I honoured my promise of sharing more of his *cachaca*. When poured over crushed lemon chunks and sugar, it became a *caipirinha*. We settled in and the potent spirit flowed. The girls eventually escaped in another taxi, but Dael and I stayed drinking with our new brother late into the evening. At some point Marek ran out of lemons for the *caipirinhas*. Undeterred, he rushed out into the forest to return in triumph with a fistful of suspicious looking leaves. They were crushed with a pestle and mortar, and used as a substitute for the missing lemon bits in the next round of drinks. I have no idea what they were – they could just as well have been an ingredient of his evil insect repellent – but by then I was some way past tasting the difference, and hopelessly past caring. I would have drunk anything. The fearsomely bearded Marek The Terrible was my new best friend in the whole world.

***

A highlight of our stay at Ilhabela was the day we spent with Ludi and his brother Adriano in the remote and rocky little bay of Bonete, tucked away around the south-east fringe of the island. It is a rough four hour hike through the forest from the nearest road, so all regular comings and goings are by boat. The island – apart from the beach resorts that make up the "tourist strip" facing the mainland – is a national park and land is therefore unavailable for purchase and development, but the fishermen who have subsisted there for generations have special dispensation to remain, and survive on fishing and gathering fruits from the forest.

Adriano and Ludi had befriended the family in the little bay of Bonete, and in exchange for medical cover and various building supplies – which they used to construct a tiny chapel – the fisherman built the brothers a delightful little cottage in the trees overlooking the bay that is theirs to use freely as a weekend getaway.

We joined Ludi and Adriano, with his wife and baby boy, on Adriano's motorboat for the trip round to Bonete early one morning, where we were met and helped ashore by the fisher folk.

"Xina" (I supposed because he looked vaguely oriental – and pronounced "Cheena") was the head of the family. Wiry and extroverted he spent the day beavering away over a fire cooking up all sorts of gastronomic delights from the forest, and belting out Brazilian folksongs on his guitar.

We sat on the balcony of the cottage under a roof of palm fronds feeding on fresh coconuts, bananas, granadillas, guavas and breadfruit plucked from the surrounding trees while Xina boiled up a pot of fish, beans and "*taioba*" – a spinach-like leaf with a milky sap that Ludi swore "*make you high, man!*"

Watching the sun sink over the sparkling sea, listening to parrots chattering in the canopy and the burbling of fresh water running down out of the mountain behind us, we sipped fresh *caipirinhas* and wondered how we would ever bear to leave this Eden.

***

The time came, however, to move on. Transferring the family out of Ludi's beach house and onto the boat was a mammoth task. The back of Ludi's van was overflowing with clothes and baby toys when he pulled up at the beach opposite *Josephine*, and we spent most of the day shuttling bags and boxes out in the dinghy. Finding somewhere for all of it to go was an immense challenge, and I was very happy to be fiddling about on the foredeck replacing missing screws in the roller furler while the girls saw to the nesting arrangements.

As a test we planned a little trip up the coast just north of Ilhabela; a coast punctuated by pretty, tranquil coves, palm covered islands and pristine beaches. We were looking forward to a week or so of snorkelling and generally lounging about before returning to Ilhabela to make any final changes to the boat or buy additional gear before heading south on our Big Adventure.

But first the storm was coming.

The channel between Ilhabela and the mainland is about fifteen miles long and a mile wide. The hills on both sides (the highest peak on Ilhabela reaches to almost four thousand feet) provide the prefect funnel for the strong winds pushed up by the summer cyclones that develop over the South Atlantic. The water is also very shallow, conducive to close, steep waves that can play havoc on Ilhabela's western beaches.

This particular storm looked to be a big one. The pressure had dropped steeply and there was an ominous stillness to the sultry air. The sky to the south east was a black wall. We went to bed early but did not sleep. And then, at half past two in the morning, pummelled by fifty-five knot winds and heavy waves, *Josephine* snapped her mooring line and was thrown against the beach.

In the cockpit there was mayhem. Tarpaulins and ropes were flogging violently and the air seethed with driven rain and spray. The screaming of the wind through the steel rigging made it impossible to communicate without bellowing directly into the ear of the person next to you. *Josephine* was leaning over drunkenly in the shallows making it difficult to get around in the dark without falling overboard.

We had to move very quickly. Any chance we had of saving the boat would be lost if we did not do something right now. Every wave that slammed against the side forced us deeper into the sand making it that much more difficult to escape before *Josephine* was destroyed and we would have to swim for the beach. I felt sick to my stomach. It was all very well "waterproofing" an eight-month-old baby in a swimming pool; but getting her off a foundering yacht in a storm at night and swimming her through the pounding breakers to shore would be a different proposition altogether.

I turned the ignition key after a backward glance at the water for any stray ropes that might tangle themselves in the prop, and my heart leapt with relief as the twenty-three-year-old diesel Perkins roared into life. Dael and Abi were wrestling the thrashing bimini cover down so I could see the bow as I gunned the throttle with the wheel hard over to try and twist *Josephine* round and up onto her keel.

We had only been in the sand a minute so were not buried too deep, and inch by inch, in spite of the waves smashing her back again, *Josephine* heaved her bow across and pointed into the storm. Now she was taking the waves head-on, shattering them into pellets of spray that leaped high in the air to be swept the length of the deck like volleys from a shotgun.

Under full power, *Josephine* dragged herself out of the sand and came upright. Ahead of us was chaos. The other boats in the bay were a mass of dark shapes leaping about wildly on their lines. We would have to push as hard as we could into the waves between all these moving obstacles to escape this hell. I could barely see through the spray that stung my face with its flying needles and burned my eyes with salt, but with Abi and Dael on either side signalling the positions of other boats we somehow made it to open water without hitting any of them.

As soon as we escaped the demolition derby in the little bay we turned north and ran helter-skelter with the wind and waves up the channel in the dark, using the GPS to see where we were going. At the top of the channel we rounded the point of the island and out of the fierce wind. Even here it was blowing twenty-five knots, coming down off the hills, but compared to the sixty knots in the channel it was like being becalmed. We felt our way carefully in the dark as close to the little beach of Jabaquara as we dared and put down two anchors.

By 5am the sea had calmed somewhat and the wind was gusting a benign fifteen knots as the adrenaline subsided and we nestled into our sleeping bags to sink into a collective coma. Sometime mid morning, the storm having passed, we motored back round to the club and reattached *Josephine* to her mooring with two new lines. High up the beach near the road lay the remains of a twenty-five foot sailboat with no mast, no rudder and no keel. Like us, she had obviously broken free in the storm, and been rolled over by the waves before being dumped above the high tide line. Her deck was split open, she was half filled with sand and there was a gaping hole under her bow. A motorboat had suffered a similar fate, and lay sprawled across the rocks, her back broken. It was a sobering reminder that our new lifestyle, while affording us immense freedom, came with its risks.

"I would rather wake up in
the Middle of Nowhere
than in any city on Earth."

– Steve McQueen

5

Midway between Ilhabela and Rio de Janeiro is *Baia de Ilha Grande*, or Big Island Bay, named somewhat unimaginatively after the big island that sits in its centre, which has been named in turn – you guessed it – "Big Island". The island is a two hundred kilometre square forested reserve that rises out of the bay and climbs to its highest point some three thousand feet. The forest-clad slopes are home to such threatened species as the Maned Sloth and Brown Howler Monkey. The south side of the island is also host to the Broad-snouted Caiman (a fact that perhaps unsurprisingly is not trumpeted in any of the tourist literature, that side of the island being something of a surfing mecca). Over a hundred smaller islands scattered throughout the sixty mile wide bay provide refuge to large colonies of frigate birds and boobies, and offer an almost inexhaustible choice of good snorkelling spots and secluded beaches tucked away under coconut palms. A ten or twelve hour sail eastwards from Ilhabela along the coast towards Rio de Janeiro, *Baia de Ilha Grande* presented the ideal environment for an introduction to the cruising lifestyle, and for us to come to grips with the video gear we would be using to film our adventures.

***

There is a reason Brazil is so green. We left Ilhabela under pregnant skies and it soon started to rain. It took thirteen hours of mostly motoring (with a little sailing at four knots when the faintest of breezes wafted off the mainland) to reach the high headland of *Punta de Juatinga* that marks the western edge of the vast bay of *Ilha Grande*. Here the rain let up for the first time and our spirits lifted when we were greeted by a pod of maybe fifteen dolphins creating the only disturbance on mirrored water reflecting a grey steel sky. Just after dark we found the elongated bay of *Saco de Mamangua* off to our left, where we anchored between two other yachts opposite what looked like a hotel cum restaurant. It started to rain again so we did not go ashore to investigate.

The morning mist lifted just after nine o'clock to reveal an inlet so long and narrow, with sides so high and steep, we could have been anchored in a Norwegian fjord but for the steaming rainforest sweeping down thick and lush to the water's edge. Leaving our overnight haven, we ran before a kindly breeze that carried us out between the cliffs and lifted us round the corner to Paraty Mirim, a tiny settlement with a very old but freshly painted white chapel dominating the shoreline.

About two hundred yards out from the beach the depth dropped sharply from fifteen to three feet and we thudded – not for the last time – into a sandbank before pulling back and dropping anchor. Dael and I launched the dinghy and motored into the mangrove forest up the knee-deep little river that bisects the beach, fouling the prop continuously in the sand, at times lifting the motor clear and dragging the boat on foot through the shallows. We came upon some tin shacks in the trees but not the "town" we were expecting. The closest sign of life among the corrugated iron was a discarded plastic doll with one eye.

Back at the beach, having collected the girls from the boat, the only evidence of civilization other than the gleaming white church with its yellow window frames was a bar at the south end under the canopy of a vast "*guarda-sol*" or "sun umbrella" tree (*Terminalia catappa* – actually a species of almond tree, native to Asia and possibly brought to Brazil by Chinese sailors in the fifteenth century). Nero, the owner of the bar, forty and balding with a cropped grey goatee, wearing a black vest with a gold eagle motif and sporting a plaster cast on his hand (like the policeman who stamped our passports), grinned at us through silver teeth and served up a delicious local fish dish, baked with sauce that tasted of apricots, and some revolting bony deep fried chicken balls. We sat under the tree in our shorts quaffing cold beer in the warm rain.

Puttering back to *Josephine* in the dinghy we noticed strange dark shapes on the sand eight feet below and I swam down to find the bottom littered with hand-sized purple pansy shells. A little further on I spotted a giant starfish in the water which I retrieved to show Lucy. As big as a large serving dish, bright orange with red horns adorning its top side, it was an impressive creature, but Lucy found it somewhat unnerving, all arms and pointy bits.

That night it rained heavily, and after going ashore for a few more drinks at Nero's bar, Dael and I walked a mile down a muddy track through the forest barefoot, sucking on our beers and clutching a chess set, hoping to find another watering hole that might still be open. Eventually we heard singing and music, then saw a light piercing the jungle, only to discover an evangelical church service in full swing. We beat a hasty retreat into the dripping trees guiltily clutching our by now empty bottles.

***

About a mile off the beach at Paraty Mirim sits the immaculate little island of *Ilha Cotia*, on the far side of which is an exquisite, well protected anchorage in twelve feet of champagne water, which we visited the next morning. A two minute stroll along a sandy track lined with bromeliads – one of which flaunted a spectacular head-high purple flower – through forest trembling with birdsong, took us over a low isthmus to a tiny beach on the southern side. In the shallows were big, smooth, round rocks to climb over and dive off, one of which was rent by a large crack that provided refuge to a sooty huddle of quivering velvet bats.

We did not have the beach to ourselves; we shared it with two hairy old men in tight speedos carrying lurid purple and pink pool noodles. They had come from the mainland in an ostentatious plastic-looking motorboat, and flounced about in the warm shallows holding hands and intruding on the scene as I attempted to shoot some video of Lucy paddling in the rock pools.

Back on *Josephine* for an afternoon siesta we were roused by the sound of a loud motor, followed by a persistent tapping against the hull. I poked my head out of the hatch and came face to face with a very brown, nutty looking man in a bright yellow shirt.

"Eu sou o rei das ostras senhor!" he proclaimed rather too loudly into my face.

Indeed. The King of Oysters, no less. Bearing out this claim, the same credentials had been hand-painted along the side of his dented aluminium boat.

"Um... *cuanto?*" I enquired, trying my best not to look or sound like the naïve gringo tourist I was.

The Oyster King grinned, flashing a set of dazzling teeth. "*Dez Reais para vinte senhor!*"

What was that? Ten Real for twenty? Could that be right? Two dollars?

With a Copperfield-esque flourish he whipped the grubby sheet off a battered polystyrene cooler box full of fat oysters nestling in ice that he had wedged under his seat, at least half out of the sun.

"Do you think they're alright?" asked Abi, appearing beside me.

"No, I don't. I think they're in big trouble. They're all about to be eaten!"

We spent tea time slurping succulent oysters with fresh lime juice and cracked pepper, chased down with a bottle of chardonnay. All very proper.

***

After two peaceful nights at anchor off the island, we left the environs of Paraty Mirim early in the morning of Christmas Eve and headed for *Praia dos Mangues* on Ilha Grande, my mother-in-law at the wheel sporting a Father Christmas hat with white pigtails. It rained all the way and her ensemble was a little limp and soggy but it did not dampen her yuletide spirit.

With all the motoring, as a consequence of the lack of wind since Ilhabela, our diesel was running low and after thirty miles we were forced to divert to the mainland in search of fuel. We had been out of Paraty Mirim five and a half hours when we passed *Punta de Gambelo*, no more than a name on the chart and non-existent in the Pilot Book, but behind which we found the newly created resort village of Portogalo with its little strip of sand, smart marina with fuel jetty, swanky holiday homes and a cable car to ferry the rich and lazy between the beach and their hilltop houses. We anchored off the beach for the night with all our signal flags gladding up the rigging and celebrated Christmas night in yet more rain.

From Portogalo it was only ten miles across the bay to Ilha Grande and the beach of *Praia de Mangues*. After filling the tanks with diesel first thing in the morning we motored over in persistent rain then stayed in the boat until lunchtime, reading and trying to keep Lucy amused, hoping for a break in the weather. By the afternoon it was still raining, but we were starting to suffer from cabin fever, so dashed a couple of hundred yards in the sodden dinghy to a floating restaurant – named, reasonably enough, "*Restaurante Flutuante*" (which I mis-translated as "Flatulent" much to my own juvenile amusement). There we had lunch and drinks on the tarpaulin-covered raft with its plastic furniture and bar, anchored forty yards from the beach, with a rope attached to a wooden dinghy that could be winched between the restaurant and the shore to ferry clients across. It did not stop raining all day, and when the wind blew the rain came in sideways under the tarpaulin drenching everyone. Nobody seemed to mind, and at least it was a *warm* soaking and the beer was good.

When evening came we motored *Josephine* round a headland to Abraao, the only town on the island, where we tramped through the muddy lanes of the hip little tourist trap with its bars and nightclubs and shared an overpriced pizza washed down with a couple of *caipirinhas*.

The weather so far had hardly been out of the top drawer for an introduction to the fantasy life of yacht cruising – rain, rain and more rain, followed by some rain; but it finally let up during the night and we left Abraao at nine o'clock the next morning in bright sun, the forest steaming. Once again there was no wind so we motored all day, leaving *Baia de Ilha Grande* behind us as we started our return towards Ilhabela, reaching *Ilha Couves* at sundown. It had turned into an uncomfortable sixty mile trip wallowing in a miserable swell that left Abi thoroughly seasick. We worked *Josephine* into a tiny bay in the crook of the L-shaped island, protected from the ocean by a thickly forested hill, high above which a cloud of frigate birds circled, black against the sky. Soon after we settled a fleet of wooden fishing boats – maybe seven – arrived trailing their nets from mechanical arms which were then folded away like the wings of giant insects as they anchored around us for the night.

***

The next day dawned balmy. Of course we should have known the sun would shine; we were on our way back, our little cruise all but over. I sipped my morning coffee on deck watching the mist rise like smoke from the distant mountains on the western horizon as the little wooden trawlers hauled their anchors, unfolded their wings and set off for another day's fishing. After breakfast we went ashore to explore and shoot some video. A short walk through a thick bamboo forest – some of which was fifty feet tall and a foot in diameter, another legacy of the Chinese voyages of exploration in the early fourteen hundreds – took us to a second beach where we found the modest house of an extended fishing family, their wild spinach patch alive with hopping rabbits. The fishermen said they had no fish to sell us. We snorkelled the morning away among the rocks off their beach and after a late lunch left for *Ilha Anchieta*. The fifteen mile trip took two hours. There was still no wind.

The three square mile, crescent shaped island of *Ilha Anchieta* (sometimes known by its other name of *Ilha dos Porcos*) is a National

Park, with some seventy two species of bird recorded in its dense forest. In 1983, the Sao Paulo Zoo released breeding colonies of capybaras, capuchin and tamarind monkeys, agoutis, armadillos, opossums and coatis – in fact almost every South American small mammal not endemic to the island – into the trees. Of course they have flourished in this protected habitat, and being used to man and unafraid, attract hordes of tourists to the island.

From the little strip of beach off which we anchored, complete with a clear stream gurgling out of the forest and running across the sand, it was a short fifteen minute walk along a muddy trail through the cool shade of the jungle canopy to the main beach with its concrete jetty where the schooners from the mainland disgorge their camera-toting day-trippers. Semi-domesticated capybaras, the world's heaviest rodents, graze among the ruins of a defunct prison. (Male capybaras often grow to 65kgs, the weight of a small man, the biggest on record having been over 100kgs. They are prolific grazers, the name "capybara" coming from a Guarani word meaning "Master of the Grasses".) We divided a banana between some extroverted Tamarin monkeys in the trees and glimpsed a pair of agoutis, then walked back through the forest under the anticlimactic impression of having just visited a tropical theme park.

In the morning we found a thirty foot wide natural tidal pool with soft sandy bottom to take Lucy for a swim attended by a cloud of inquisitive little yellow and blue striped fish. The clear water, colourful fish, smooth round boulders under a tropical sun, *Josephine* swinging on her anchor in the background while a family of capybaras cavorted in the stream that spilled out of the forest behind us… *this* was why I had given up working in a bank.

***

Our drinking water was getting low (we had not yet mastered the art of harvesting sufficient rain to keep up with our water use, in spite of the incessant downpours), so we motored eight miles over to the mainland where the chart showed a yacht club at *Baia de Ribeira*. On arrival we discovered the club only catered for powerboats, and the marina was not deep enough for us with our keel. We could not get in.

We were driving in circles debating what to do when a toothless old man in grey shorts and a grubby green T-shirt puttered out of the marina towards us in a bright red wooden dinghy with a clanking outboard motor belching blue smoke. I asked him where we could get water.

"Ah, *agua*? Follow me *senhor*!" he grinned, and made off, beckoning over his shoulder. Threading our way between moored boats, closer and closer to shore, the depth down to six feet, I was about to abort when he pulled up at a little yellow buoy. It was shallow, and uncomfortably close to the rocks – I really did not want to moor here, and told him so.

"*Nao, nao, senhor*!" he assured me as he reached down below the buoy and pulled on a rope. "*Agua doce!*"

Attached to the end of the rope was a plastic hosepipe, gushing water. It was a permanent flow coming clean and fresh off the mountain under gravity, clear as vodka. We filled the tanks then tossed the free running hose back overboard.

The bay of *Baia de Ribeira* was full of mooring buoys and fishing boats. We tried to anchor there for the night but the boats were all too close together, swinging and knocking against each other, and by ten o'clock we realised we would get no sleep constantly worrying about it, so hauled anchor and returned to *Ilha Anchieta* in the dark.

The water behind us was a brilliant glow of luminous phosphorescence stirred up by the prop, and after anchoring Dael dived over the side. It was a dark night; there was no moon, and we watched spellbound as his every movement set off a magical green light show in the black water.

***

With a forty mile trip ahead of us to Ilhabela, and being New Year's Eve, I was keen to get an early start the next day to ensure we arrived in good time for the evening's festivities. Greeted with a warm sunny morning and no wind, I was pleased to think the last part of our trip shaped to be a comfortable bimble over a flat sea. Not seeing any point in waking the others at seven o'clock for so simple a procedure as hauling up forty feet of anchor chain and then beetling off under motor, I resolved to do it alone, with no fuss, and surprise them with the progress we had made towards Ilhabela when they eventually surfaced. Not to mention how impressed they would be with what a thoughtful skipper I was to have left them sleeping; and so clever too, to raise the anchor all by myself. So, with the best intentions, I tried to get us underway without waking anyone.

I stood on the foredeck looking down into the clear water watching the links of chain rise from the depths and bend clanking over the bow roller on their way to the windlass from where they were fed safely into the anchor locker. It was barely a minute before the anchor itself loomed into view, trailing a cloud of billowing grey mud. I wasn't having *that* on my nice white deck, so I locked the chain off with the anchor hanging just below the surface, returned to the cockpit and engaged reverse. After dragging the mucky anchor backwards through the water for a minute in an attempt to rinse the worst of the mud off, I left the wheel and dashed forward to check it was properly clean before heaving it up on deck.

Now I should know better than to take my hands off the wheel while going backwards. Forwards, yes; but not backwards. Going forwards, the rudder trails along behind and when left to its own devices is held straight by the flow of the water. But going backwards is another matter altogether, as the rudder, being now the leading edge of the entire boat, bites into the water and…

Too late I realised what was about to happen. I was half way along the deck when it suddenly occurred to me, and I made a desperate dive back towards the cockpit but was too late and could only watch in horror as the wheel spun madly and slammed to a halt.

The rudder, under pressure from the water, was forced round and wedged sideways under the hull. No amount of heaving on the wheel could free it, and for fear of damaging the steering cables, I gave up trying. The rudder was jammed over on full lock. Next I tried the emergency tiller, a four foot long hunk of wood with a metal bracket that slots directly into the top of the rudder shaft, thereby bypassing the complicated (and delicate) system of chains and cables connecting it to the wheel. Some good hard heaves on the tiller, followed by several full-blooded kicks, with Dael in the water kicking the rudder itself for good measure (everyone of course by now fully awake and more than a little annoyed), yielded nothing. The rudder was stuck, and the boat would only go in a very tight left hand circle. That was not going to be a lot of use.

What was obviously needed was to harness the same power that had forced it round in the first place; it would take the pressure of the water to push it straight, and the only way to do that would be by getting the boat moving and dragging the jammed rudder through the water. Under her own power, *Josephine* just went in circles; we needed a tow.

After a four hour wait, during which I put up with merciless and cruel abuse (*it was an accident – I didn't want to wake you – yes, I understand I woke you up anyway – I said I was sorry – yes, I do know I am very stupid*) we finally spotted the first boat of the day coming out of Ribeira (but not before Dael had rigged an elaborate breathing system with the hosepipe so he could spend prolonged periods underwater trying to dislodge the rudder with a screwdriver – a fruitless project that at least had the twin benefits of keeping us amused and him quiet.)

The day's first power boat finally arrived, packed to the gunwales with sun worshippers, and moored at the jetty on the main beach. I paddled over in the dinghy after first looking up "rudder", "stuck", "left" and "tow" in the English to Portuguese dictionary, and in the most horrendous Portuguese *patois* managed to convince the driver to take a rope and tow us around in clockwise circles. Sure enough, after about a minute, there was a dull thud beneath our feet and the steering was back, to loud cheers on both boats. Abi just could not resist pointing out that if I had only woken someone up in the first place, not only would we have avoided the morning's drama, but we would almost be in Ilhabela by now. Yes dear.

We motored most of the forty miles in the absence of wind, but the breeze came through towards the end and for the last two hours we had a glorious sail over a glittering sea in sparkling sun. It was an uplifting finish to what had not always been an idyllic trip.

***

Back at Ludi's little sailing club in Ilhabela there were a lot more boats than before. Temporary moorings had been dropped between the existing ones to accommodate visiting boats from the mainland who had come over to celebrate the New Year, with the result that the boats were closely packed, forcing us to deploy all our fenders. With so little room between boats I dread to think what the outcome would have been had another nasty storm come up from the south. It was tricky just getting to our buoy; so much so that we were forced to go too near the beach and ran aground again (this was becoming a bad habit) and had to rely on propwalk* to twist the keel off the sand.

That evening Thibaut (Marek's Belgian nephew from the *Tocas* waterfall) came on board with two Dutch friends bearing gifts of beer, and from the boat we had a grandstand view of the town's impressive New Year fireworks display. I am ashamed to admit I entered into the Brazilian spirit of things by firing off an out of date parachute flare (my weak defence being that we had seen several locals do the same). It was actually the first time I had ever fired one. In spite of having it explained fully on my yachtmaster course, I had never let one off – or even seen one go for that matter – so was keen to get some practice. And, yes, I messed it up.

Instead of pointing it straight upwards, above the boats, it struck me as a far safer idea to point it at a forty five degree angle in the direction of open water. There was some logic to that, except that they are manufactured to keep burning while they fall from a thousand feet, and unless you fire it straight up, it will not *reach* a thousand feet in the first place. The chute deployed with the flare only five hundred feet up – if that – above the last row of boats. Directly below was a wooden tourist schooner riding oblivious on its mooring. Watching the blazing incendiary wobbling under its chute, descending directly

* Propwalk can be an annoying phenomenon, and some boats suffer from it worse than others. *Josephine*, with her fin keel, is one. As soon as you engage reverse gear, the rotation of the prop pulls the stern of the boat over to one side and instead of going backwards, you pivot on the spot. The boat will not go backwards until there has been enough time to generate sufficient momentum; but by then, of course, she has often swung so far sideways you are going in the wrong direction. Occasionally though, as in this case, the ability to spin the boat on the spot can be useful.

over someone else's boat, was agony. I don't think I breathed for the full minute of its descent; there was nothing at all I could do but watch. Thankfully, somehow, it drifted ever so slightly off course at the last second, and landed fizzing in the water alongside the schooner. I needed another of Thibaut's beers.

***

It was time to move on. It had been over a month since we arrived in Ilhabela, and our "test" cruise around Ilha Grande, in spite of the wretched weather, had been proclaimed a success. Last little problems with the boat were ironed out: the foot of the headsail, damaged in the ocean crossing, was repaired, and a portable two-ring gas burner procured and balanced on top of the now malfunctioning stove as a temporary measure until we could find somewhere to buy a new one.

Our last couple of days were spent tied to the jetty of the upmarket *Yate Clube Ilhabela* where we took full advantage of their generous four day courtesy arrangement, enjoying the plush facilities and spending as much time as possible in the swimming pool with Lucy. We worked on her "waterproofing" with a game that involved pushing her to each other under the water, to which she reacted with big smiles and wide open eyes, automatically holding her breath. Babies really are natural in water if you get them in young enough.

Our original plan – if you could call it that – had been to sail south all the way to the southern tip of the continent and investigate Tierra del Fuego in December and January, when the channels are relatively free of ice, then take our time exploring the coast of Argentina on our way back up again between February and May. Now it was already January, and we were still in Brazil. And although the plan remained much the same, we now expected to reach Tierra del Fuego only towards the end of February as a result of having spent a month longer than anticipated around Ilhabela. The first part of our journey south would involve a sail of about three hundred miles to Florianopolis, the city on the island of Santa Catarina, where we looked forward to visiting Abi's cousin Alastair, his lovely Brazilian wife Marianna and their daughter Thalissa.

However, in what was later to become a pattern, circumstances threw a spanner in the works the day before our departure. The wind picked up to gale strength from the south west, blowing the stern of *Josephine* hard against the concrete of the floating pier. We were sitting out the squall in the comfort of the coffee shop in the clubhouse and by the time I saw what was happening to the boat, and could sprint back through the rain to tighten the anchor lines and pull her away from the dock, the transom has already been damaged. Chunks of gel coat had been smashed off revealing naked fibreglass, and I was worried that if not attended to smartly, water would get into the fabric of the hull between the glass fibres leading to de-lamination and weakening the structure. So the next day, instead of setting sail for Florianopolis, I was faced with a messy repair job. And I have a chequered history with fibreglass.

"There is nothing, absolutely nothing,
so much worth doing as
simply messing about in boats."

– Kenneth Grahame

6

If fibreglass had been invented in medieval times it would have been condemned outright as a dark art. Working with it sounds simple enough on paper, but if it really was so straightforward I do not suppose there would be quite so many people doing it professionally. I for one did not pick it up naturally.

At some point I had taken to canoeing (or, strictly speaking, kayaking) as a competitive sport. In South Africa that means you race marathons, down long, remote stretches of the wildest rivers, in a very narrow, fragile and decidedly unstable fibreglass kayak. You typically race twenty-five miles at a time, and in the longer races you do that over several days in a row. The boat needs to be very light, as it is often necessary to run along the bank, or over a hill, lugging it on your shoulder. Unfortunately – or fortunately, because it makes it more fun – you are bound to encounter rapids and weirs along the way, and a certain amount of damage to the boat is inevitable. It is not uncommon to see a contestant cross the finish line with his kayak splinted together with the branches of a thorn tree strapped in place with gaffer tape, or sitting in the half submerged centre of what used to be a rigid kayak but is now folded around him like a deflating lilo.

Many canoeists are therefore accomplished fibreglassers, but I was always too lazy to do my own repairs and after races would drop the boat off at a workshop on my way to the office and pick it up a day or two later looking like new.

***

One year, in a pact fuelled by beer, my mate Pete agreed to partner me on the *Dusi*. The *Dusi* is a seventy-five mile race down a particularly remote river spread over three days. There are a number of sections virtually impossible to paddle – and certainly too dangerous for the sponsors' stomachs – that have been designated compulsory *portage*; which is to say you get out of the water and run. With your boat. The *Dusi* has somewhere between twelve and twenty miles of running, depending on the water level; precious little of which is run on anything at all resembling a road. The race is hard on body and soul.

Pete had never so much as seen the inside of a kayak, so we took ourselves off on holiday to train for a couple of weeks prior to our big race. We had a couple of runs along the highway humping our K2 (two-man kayak) until all the skin had been rubbed off our shoulders, and spent a good few hours thrashing about on the water of a nearby lagoon.

The problem for all beginners is that these craft are very unstable, and it takes a long time to train your core muscles to balance comfortably. I had not given Pete much time to master it at all, but after two weeks we could more or less paddle together in a straight line on calm water without toppling out too often. But I was dreading the rapids we would encounter in the race.

***

The day before the race we had to drive six hundred miles across country to Durban, our eighteen foot kayak lashed to the roof of the car. The trip took us through the wild and remote countryside of Transkei with its rugged mountains, steep valleys and tumbling rivers.

In the afternoon we spotted such a river from the car, snaking through a gorge way below. It was irresistible. I handed the keys to my nephew in the back seat, turned him around and sent him some five miles back down the road to wait on a bridge we had crossed a little earlier. I told him to expect us in about an hour.

Now as exciting and near disastrous as it was, the tale of the river is not the story here. Suffice to say it took us a whole hour to even *reach* the water, never mind get downstream to the bridge. We battled down the slope through thick thorn bush until our legs and arms were slashed to a bloody mess, and on reaching the river discovered it was a raging torrent. We got in anyway, and it was not pretty. To this day I have no idea how we did not lose the boat, but several hours later we arrived at the bridge; bleeding, bruised, badly shaken – and on foot. The kayak would no longer float. We had managed to destroy it, and nearly ourselves too. The tattered remains were tied to the roof of the car and we set off in the dark for the last six hours of the drive to Durban where our friend Mark was waiting up for us at his mother's house.

It was almost midnight by the time we had the ruined kayak upside down on Mark's lawn, and everything was wet with dew. He whistled through his teeth when he saw what we had done to our boat. In addition to several cracks, there were five ragged gashes that needed to be repaired, and a nasty fist sized hole had been punched amidships, between the two cockpits.

I eyed the little brown bottles of magic potion which constitute a fibreglass repair kit.

"Okay Pete," I said brightly. "Let's get to work."

Pete looked from me to the chemicals and back to me.

"You mix the resin then."

"Um… I'd prefer it if you did it. I haven't worked much with fibreglass lately, so if it's all the same…"

Pete chewed his lip, and it occurred to me that I was not the only one here who had actually never done this before at all. We had just driven six hours with a shattered boat, debating how long it would take to repair, and neither of us had thought to admit he did not know how to do it.

Pete, however, had at least *seen* it done, so that made him the expert. He poured about half a pint of resin into a tin, and I made ready with the catalyst. Mark swigged his brandy and sniggered.

"Go easy Pete, it's important not to put too much in," I said knowledgeably.

The catalyst was in a little plastic dropper bottle, and Pete dribbled about five drops of the magic fluid into the resin while I stirred.

"That's probably enough now."

In truth we had absolutely no idea how much was enough, or too much; so that would just have to do. Anyway, we knew that "too much" would harden the resin too quickly, leaving it brittle; whereas "too little" and it would take longer, but finish more flexible. Better to err towards "too little" then. In any event, we still had ten hours to the race start, so it could take all night to set for all it mattered. Once we had positioned the patches in place and brushed them with wet resin, we rewarded ourselves with a beer which we quaffed standing proudly around our handiwork, congratulating each other on a tremendous job. It did look a fine piece of work, all sticky and glistening under the garden lights.

We went to bed happy in the knowledge that while we slept, the catalyst would be activating the resin, and those gluey patches would be toughening and hardening. Our abused boat would be healing itself and tomorrow we would rampage down the river in our once again indestructible craft.

In the early morning we were a lot less pleased with ourselves. The patches, which had been in place for five hours, were every bit as wet and sticky as when we had slapped them on. This could not be right?

We scratched our heads, then I noticed how utterly wet everything else was out there on the grass. The dew had been very heavy, and we had been too tired, or a little drunk, or both, to think to pull the boat under cover. I reasoned the dew must have kept the resin from setting.

"Well, not to worry," I said, trying to sound convinced. "Let's lash the boat on the car and be off. The wind will help speed up the drying, and once the sun comes up the patches should harden in no time."

Soon we were driving along the highway at seventy miles an hour trying to hurry the drying process on the sorry kayak strapped across the roof, watching blobs of resin drip off and blow in the wind all over the windscreen. Then I made my second big misjudgement. I put the wipers on to clear the view.

Tacky resin is nothing like rain water. When wiped lightly across glass with a rubber wiper, it does not go away; it does a terrible thing. Instantly the windscreen was transformed to a translucent sheet glowing alternately white and red in the lights of the traffic ahead. I was forced to slow the car to a crawl and drive with my head out of the window in the cold dark air for the next hour. By the time we arrived at the start of the race, my neck was stiff, my hair matted with gobs of sticky resin, and my face frozen.

I found some acetone and cleaned the resin out of my hair as best I could, then we heaved the canoe down into the car park. The largest patch slid off in my hand like a soggy slice of bread and honey. The resin had not even *begun* to set, and here we were at race registration, the start gun due in less than thirty minutes. Things were looking dire. There was no time now to patch the boat again.

"Only one thing for it. Duct tape!"

The next quarter of an hour was spent scrounging as much spare tape as we could convince people to let us have (duct tape, which as everyone knows binds the universe together, is the first absolute essential in any survival kit). Five minutes prior to the start, as the other competitors were warming up on the water, there we were, hunched over our boat, frantically trussing it in yards of silver tape. The boat should at least float, but we would have to be really careful in the rapids not to tear the tape off sliding over the rocks.

"What the hell are you two doing?!" bawled a voice behind me.

It was Mike Foreshore, or "Backwash" as we called him. Backwash was exactly the guy you did not want knowing your business when you had messed something up. He was the self-appointed party wag and now we knew we would be in for a rough time in the pub.

"Shit, fixing your boat already? The race hasn't even started! Bwaahahaha!!"

And as he trotted off towards the water we could hear him shouting, "Hey, check out Tunstall's boat, it looks like Tutankhamun!"

As if the ribbing was not bad enough when we eventually got on the river with half a minute to spare, the boat immediately began to take on water; so quickly in fact that only our heads were above the surface when the starting gun fired. The field thrashed off downstream in a welter of spray and flashing paddles, while we sank beneath the waves with as much dignity as we could muster. We hauled ourselves up the bank, emptied the boat of water, hoisted it on our bruised shoulders, and started to run. It was the beginning of a long, long day.

Ten years later, in Ilhabela, I repaired the damage to *Josephine's* transom with globs of epoxy glue applied with an ice cream stick. My excuse was that I should save the fibreglass for emergencies.

"There is a fine line between fishing and just standing on the shore like an idiot."

– Steven Wright

7

The city of Florianopolis straddles the narrow strait between the hilly island of *Ihla de Santa Catarina* and the mainland of Brazil at about twenty seven degrees south, some three hundred nautical miles from Ilhabela. The modern city centre is on the island; on the mainland is the sprawling industrial area. A fifty-five foot high iron bridge supports a six lane highway connecting the two, and the rest of the forty mile long wedge-shaped island is residential. With some of Brazil's most popular surfing beaches along the east side, facing the ocean, and a broad shallow lagoon in its centre – a popular spot for kite surfing – it is little wonder that the island is one of Brazil's premier holiday destinations.

On reaching the north of the island after an uneventful two day sail from Ilhabela, we anchored off the wide sandy beach at Jurere. Jurere was, according to my pilot book, the only suitable place for *Josephine* on the whole island. The charts indicated a yacht club in downtown Florianopolis, under the big road bridge, but there did not appear to be so much as a quay in the way of facilities. In any event the bay between the island and the mainland is very shallow and without a more detailed chart I was not keen to venture in there. The other problem was the bridge itself. To get to the club we would either have to sail fifteen miles only to discover we might not fit under the bridge and have to turn back; or sail eighty miles around the island and back up the other end of the bay, which would be a terrible waste of time – especially if, as was apparent on the chart, there were no real facilities at the club anyway.

Abi's cousin Alistair, however, who lived on the island, was adamant there were other options. As I had already discovered in Ilha Grande, the pilot book was either out of date or just inadequate, so I was only too happy to accept his word for it when he told me I could anchor off the beach at Armacao, a mere twenty minute walk from his house. A small fishing fleet operated out of Armacao, which suggested to me it might not be too bad an anchorage; but it was mention of the house that decided it for the girls and plans were made to move the boat.

We met up again with Rupert who was back from surfing in Chile with his friend Dan, and camping nearby. The two of them joined us for the trip around to Armacao, as did cousin Alistair, his wife Marianna and their six-year-old daughter Thalissa. It turned out to be a rather lumpy forty mile sail on a choppy sea, and both Marianna and Thalissa were violently seasick. Rupert and Dan were in fine spirits though, and we towed the dinghy behind the boat while they took turns standing up in it "surfing" the swells. Hooking a twenty-five pound skipjack added to the day's fun and we all looked forward eagerly to that evening's tuna steak feast.

The trip was far from over once we reached Armacao, as anchoring turned out to have its challenges. The bay is all but fully exposed to the northerlies, and there was a moderate northerly blowing when we arrived. A medium swell was running, with four foot waves breaking onto the beach. The fishing boats were small, open, wooden affairs, attached to buoys, and crammed in the east corner where a rickety old wooden jetty provided a hint of protection. It was too shallow for us behind the jetty, and there was no room to anchor among the fishing boats anyhow. It was obvious we would have to make do in the swell and deploy two anchors.

Setting them was a tricky job in the rough conditions, and Rupert was flung head over heels over the side when the boat was tossed on a swell as he leant over to secure a trip line. He had the presence of mind, while airborne, to grab hold of the guardrail, so finished dangling outside the boat but holding on, a look of shocked surprise on his face. There was quite a crowd of onlookers gathered on the busy beach by the time we had our boat securely anchored.

After tidying up it was time to go ashore in the dinghy. I took Alistair and his family first and somehow managed to run the dinghy through the waves and up onto the beach without mishap. Lulled by this fluke into believing it was easy (I had never before beached a dinghy through waves), I went back for the lads. This time I got it all horribly wrong, and was caught out between waves on the way in. Gunning the game little 4hp outboard motor full ahead was barely enough to keep us in one place against the backwash running from the beach, and when the next wave hit us we had no chance. The stern of the dinghy lifted, the engine howled in protest as the prop came out of the water, and in slow motion the boat tipped up on its side in the leaping white water. In a desperate attempt to prevent it capsizing, engine and all, I leapt into the surf giving the boat a violent shove as I went. My weight gone, it fell back level and skidded sideways in the tumbling foam to the beach, still upright. It was a close call and not my most dignified landing, and we looked like rank idiots to the watching fishermen. But up at the house in dry clothes Alistair did a sterling job searing the tuna and we spent a very pleasant evening swapping tall fishing stories over several bottles of red wine.

***

In truth I am not a particularly accomplished fisherman. The tuna we were devouring that evening was in fact only the fifth fish I had ever caught from my boat (the first four having been caught on the ocean crossing a few months before) and the only form of fishing that really appeals to me is fly fishing. I had enjoyed my first experience of that spiritual pastime a few years previously.

"Is that Andrew?" came the brogue over the line.

"Hello, yes it is. Norman?"

"Aye," replied the Scot. "Ah was just thinkin', d'ya like fly fishin'?"

"Oh, very much, I do indeed!"

"Well then, that's grand! Nigel and I are goin' t' Dulstroom t'morro, d'ya fancy comin' alon'?"

Part of my job was consulting to companies with large pension funds, helping them structure their investments and benefits. One of my bigger clients had a corporate hideaway up in the mountains near a little town well known for its trout streams. Norman, a heavy set Scot of around sixty with a keen mind and a very sharp, dry sense of humour, was the Financial Director. Nigel was the Human Resources director, in his mid-fifties, very easy going with a perpetual smile and a mischievous glint of eye. He was everyone's favourite grandfather.

"Norman, I would love that, thank you very much!"

This would be very good for corporate relations. We were in the middle of trying to convince them to restructure their pension fund in a way that should make them – and us – a lot more money. And I liked them both, so it would be fun.

"Be sure," he went on, "t' bring all your gear t' ma hoose this evenin' then, so I can pack the car, then I'll pick ya up at your hoose in tha mornin'."

My mind raced.

"Fine, fine. I'll see you later then. I know where your hoose is. *House*! Your house…" But he had already rung off.

For several seconds I sat staring at the phone, then jumped with a start when it rang again.

"And one more thing," Norman went on, as if he had never left, "don't forget ta bring tha lovely Abigail!"

"No, of course not, fine. I'll do that…" and he was gone again.

***

Now I had never been one for fishing, in spite of having spent most of my childhood on the banks of a quiet river in the rural village of Henley-on-Klip, named after the better known village on the Thames. It must have been something to do with the tranquil, winding course of the Klip through the overhanging willow trees and the little weir at the end of the village near the hotel that inspired the name.

As children we spent all our time, when not at school, swimming in the river and messing about with boats. Most of my friends in the early days, before the village expanded beyond the banks of the river, had boats of one kind or another. We would congregate on the water of an afternoon in all manner of craft, from open canoes, kayaks, and windsurfers with their masts missing to a few modern fibreglass dinghies and one old, somewhat rotten, wooden lifeboat. Richard Carpenter's father worked at the city airport, and Richard had the inner tube of the wheel of a Boeing 747 which was the envy of all. There was no sailing, the river being too narrow and winding for that. Anyway, no mast would have stood a chance, what with all the overhanging willows and leaning birch trees, so most of us therefore paddled or rowed, and on the odd occasion that someone had access to an outboard motor we would rope up and be towed down the river like a line of rowdy washing.

And then we fished.

At any rate, that was what we called it. We would toss our gear in a dinghy and row off downstream to a tree-covered little island where we would pitch a tent, make a fire and deploy our fishing rods. Hooks carefully baited with flour and corn – unless we found a hapless cricket in the grass – we would cast into midstream, prop the rods on cleft sticks, and wait.

I for one became very good at this. Waiting, that is. The other boys were forever landing fat juicy carp, feisty yellowfish and be-whiskered catfish, but I was unlucky. Unlucky, or clueless. I only remember landing one small "silver" (as my knowledgeable friends called it) and it was foul hooked and very little. I used the same bait as everyone else, the same sized hooks, cast in the same places, at the same times of day, but no luck. I would watch the little red float bobbing in the water, and when it was tugged under I would strike and … nothing. Maybe I struck too hard, or too late. I never knew. In truth it didn't really bother me much though. Watching my friends hunched over in the wet clay gutting their slimy fish – blood, entrails and mud oozing between their bare toes – was quite enough to convince me that the fun was in the hunt, not the kill. After a time I would sneakily not bait my hooks at all.

Back then, on that little island, there was not much science to the activity we called "fishing", and certainly no art. We simply squeezed pulp onto a hook, then squatted in the mud like Dickensian urchins and stared at the impassive black water waiting for something to happen. Which in my case, did not.

By contrast fly fishing, involving, as it does, hiking down pristine mountain streams and finding quiet secret pools with delicious sunny banks for taking afternoon naps, is noble and therapeutic. And it truly is an art. To whip that cane and get that little fly singing through the air, to drop it on that exact spot under that little overhanging bush beneath which that fat hungry trout is waiting just for you ... to present that little fly to that fish, with the right little twitches on the line, so that he recognises his favourite dinner flicking about on the surface ... *that* is art.

***

But of course it did not start out that way for me. I stared at the phone, ready to snatch it up should Norman call a third time to continue the conversation. It was a few moments before I accepted he really had gone this time, then I called my friend Patrick.

"Pat? Tunners here. Listen mate, I think I might have a slight problem..."

"What's up?"

"Well, I've just let myself in for a weekend of fly fishing with the directors of the Boart pension fund."

"Ho, very nice!"

"Um, yes... the problem is I don't have any gear. No rod, nothing."

"No worries!" chuckled Pat. "You can borrow mine."

"That's what I was rather hoping. Thanks." I hesitated. "There's one more thing ..."

"What's that?"

"Uh, well… the thing is… I've never actually fly fished before. At all that is. I've read about it, it's really interesting, the theory, so I can sustain a conversation, and I think that must be why I was invited…" I paused. "I think I might be in trouble here."

Patrick giggled like a girl. I did not find it funny at all.

"Okay," he sighed. "Come past my house after work and pick up my gear, I'll give you a dry run on the lawn. It's really not that difficult."

He was still tittering as I put the phone down.

I breathed out slowly and told myself that Patrick had good gear, that he was an accomplished fisherman, that he would make everything okay, and that I would do just fine, and Norman would never know, and I would bag a load of trout, and we would finish the weekend with Norman signing the multi-million dollar contract we had been pushing for.

***

That afternoon, after work, dusk found me on Patrick's lawn, fly rod in hand, yanking it up and down above my head as if I were signalling to a parking aeroplane, the nasty little feathered hook whipping around my head in the fading light until it embedded itself alternately in a tree, Patrick's shoe, and my ear. But it was already dark, so that would have to do, and I dropped it all off at Norman's *hoose* where he made me even more nervous commenting with approval on my rod.

"Och, would ya look at that then! Beautiful! That belongs to a man who knows his way around a trout!"

I felt sick and smiled wanly.

The next day I drove the four hours to Dulstroom with Norman, to "get everything ready" before the arrival of Nigel and the lovely Abigail, who could not get away from work for the earlier drive.

Norman became more and more animated the closer we got to Dulstroom, until by the time we arrived he was bursting like a little schoolboy on an unsupervised outing. He was straight out of the car and laying his fishing gear out on the grass. It was late afternoon.

"Och come on now, we can unpack the car later. Tha poor little buggers; we've kept 'em waitin' for us all day!"

He was clearly determined to have trout with every meal, starting tonight. Filled with trepidation I followed him down the slope behind the grey stone cottage to the water's edge. I peered over the pool, to the weir at the far end hewn out of the local rock, over which water was pouring in from the pool above. There were low bushes and reeds whispering on either side of the pool, and here where we stood, facing the weir, was the only clear bank for easy access to the water. It seemed the obvious place to start.

"A'right now laddie, you take this 'un, an' I'll head off up t'other one up there," said Norman, and clomped off round the pond in his boots to scale the weir. I watched him swinging his cane atop the stones, the yellow line with its minute fly on the end whipping back and forth before describing a final graceful arc away and out of side beyond the wall. It was a relief that he would be fishing some distance from me, and that he was facing the other direction.

I looked dubiously at my rod and tried to remember what Patrick had told me. Forearm back and forth between ten o'clock and two o'clock… ten o'clock and two o'clock… it felt stiff and mechanical.

First I had the fly hook itself in the end of the rod, and as I tried to flick it loose the line wrapped into a terrible knot. I picked away at it gloomily and noticed Norman looking down from his wall. I smiled and shrugged as if this was just one of those things that happens to even the best of us from time to time, and he nodded sympathetically.

Then I set to unravelling the mess and avoided looking in his direction again.

Once I had everything disentangled I tried anew. I waved the rod with vigour, sometimes thrashing the surface of the water with the tip, but it seemed the harder I tried, the less inclined the fly was to… well, fly. It caught in the bushes, it flopped onto the mud, it tangled itself back into the reel, it even caught in my boot, but never did it venture near the water.

I was in an idyllic environment – a peaceful pool, the muted burbling of gently trickling water, the reeds suffused in a yellow glow as the sun eased herself gently towards the horizon – yet I was sweating and getting frantic. Once or twice I even thought the bubbling water sounded suspiciously like the distant chuckling of Norman up on his wall… surely not? Don't look up…

Eventually, in desperation, after checking surreptitiously that Norman was not facing my way, I unravelled the line in coils on the mud, picked up the fly, and flung it over the water as hard as I could with my left hand. It dropped obligingly onto the surface; not much more than a few feet in front of me to be true, but at least in the water. I resolved immediately that it should stay right there the rest of the evening, and whenever Norman looked in my direction I smiled back nonchalantly and allowed myself a few stylish little twitches at the line. He was not to know the fly was not out in the middle somewhere. I breathed a self satisfied sigh and congratulated myself on my expert subterfuge. There would be no dishonour in not catching a fish; this could just be a dud pool.

My tranquillity was short lived. I understand now that the trout in those pools, reared in farms and accustomed to being fed with pellets, were inclined to approach people on the bank, mouths agape, expecting a meal. So it was no surprise at all to this particular trout when I tossed what looked like a perfectly edible mayfly in its path. This was to be expected of me. The real sportsmen, like Norman, cast their flies way out over the water and tried to catch their fish through stealth and ruse; whereas actually all the fish wanted was to be hand fed from the bank.

There were several seconds of thrashing and splashing before it got through to me what had happened. This stupid fish had gulped down my offer, and was now well hooked at the end of my line. I had no idea what to do. Patrick had filled my head with romantic descriptions of playing trout in exotic mountain streams but I could remember nothing and terror swept me.

"Norman!" I bellowed, my composure crumbling completely. "NOR-M – A-AN! I've got one! A FIII-IISH!!"

In seconds he was next to me. "Get it in then laddie!" and I hauled at my line hand over hand – having long since dropped the rod – dragging the surprised trout flopping over the mud and onto the grass. There was not much finesse to it, and certainly no *art*.

The fish and I gaped at each other.

"Well done then! That makes three now," exclaimed Norman, clapping me on the back and pointing at his bag. "That should do it. Let's go up t' hoose and clean up."

Up at *t' hoose* my next challenge awaited me. The fish needed to be gutted and cleaned. I wished I had paid more attention to my childhood friends rendering their fish for the fire on that little island all those year ago.

I peered anxiously over Norman's shoulder as he expertly whipped the innards out of his two trout and tried to memorise his technique before I set about hacking at mine. It was not pretty. The knife would not go in; then it slipped and I gashed the side of the fish; then it went in, but too deep, and I pierced the spine. I severed the ribs and struggled to get the intestines out. When I cut my finger the first time, Norman politely went indoors to "open a bottle of wine" and left me to it. He was either being very kind and sparing me further humiliation, or was just disgusted with what he was seeing.

***

Later that evening, after Nigel and Abi arrived and we served them up a triumphant dinner of trout stuffed with flaked almonds, we set about the wine. It was a particularly friendly Merlot and a merry log fire was crackling in the hearth. The conversation became easier with each bottle, until some time well beyond midnight when even the frogs had long since packed up their choir.

The warm spirit of Bacchus had risen high in me.

"Norman," I announced. "I have something to confess!" I spoke with deliberation, pronouncing each syllable separately in a vain attempt not to slur. "…co*n-fesssh!*"

Norman's eyes twinkled at me over his glass.

"Och aye laddie, ah think y'do," he agreed, nodding sagely.

"Well, then," I continued, closing an eye so I could focus on one of him. "That trout I caught this afternoon: I have to tell you, that was the first one I have ever caught… *in my life*!"

I flung myself back in the chair with a flourish, opened my other eye and looked again at both of him.

His faces merged into a blur of smiles.

"Really now?" he exclaimed, with a theatrical feigning of incredulity, cocked his head over, and chortled into his wine. His ruddy cheeks glowed in the firelight as he looked up at me again.

"Well ah never! Ya know, ah could have sworn, the way ya pulled that bugger in, it was tha first bloody trout ya ever *saw*! I'm surprised ya *recognised* it!"

The truth, they say, will always out – but we had feasted regally that night. We shared many bottles of good wine, and thus was I inducted into the brotherhood of fly fishermen.

***

For several years after that I would accompany Norman and Nigel to the remote village of Rhodes high in the mountains of the Eastern Cape for the annual Bells Whisky Fly Fishing Festival, where local farmers would throw open their homes to accommodate visiting fishermen from upcountry, and at the final dinner at the end of the week the mayor would dole out generous portions of his special sheep penis stew to all the big city financial men, who had no idea what they were eating.

"A loaf of bread" the Walrus said
"Is what we chiefly need:
Pepper and vinegar besides
Are very good indeed –
Now if you're ready Oysters dear
We can begin to feed."

– Lewis Carroll

8

One morning shortly after our arrival in Florianopolis, Alistair bundled us into his car for a drive around the island. He needed first to call on a woman he had been speaking to about getting involved in his plans for an international school, so we drove round the west side of the lagoon to her house "for breakfast".

Marina met us outside her gate. To describe her as effusive would not do her justice; she was uncontainable. An extrovert among extroverts, and great fun.

"Welcome to my home!" she proclaimed expansively, sweeping all six of us up the stairs like a hen would her brood of chicks. Her seven-year-old son, Tommy, was already carrying Lucy in his arms. "Breakfast is almost ready!"

And what a breakfast it was. Her sister Sandra, on a visit from Italy, had been slaving in the kitchen. Fried eggs, toast, mince, bacon, sausages, kidneys, beans, tomatoes, not to mention the wonderful Brazilian coffee and a selection of teas. We fell upon the table and ate royally.

Happy and replete, I walked through a sliding door with my coffee onto a high balcony overlooking the lagoon. Marina was still at full volume inside. "Try the bacon! Who needs more coffee?! Why aren't you eating that?! TOMMY, PUT THE BABY DOWN! …"

One of the wonderful things about travelling without much of a plan is that you have little idea from one day to the next who you are going to meet or what you are going to be doing. Here we were, in the lovely house of someone we did not know, scoffing the most extravagant breakfast we had seen in months. I was just marvelling at it all when Marina breezed outside and caught me in my reverie.

"Have you ever sailed a canoe?" she challenged me.

"Um, er, no… I don't think … a *canoe* did you say?"

"Yes yes, a canoe!" as if I were being particularly slow-witted. "A fishing canoe. Have you ever sailed one?"

"Well, uh…n-o..."

"Then you absolutely must!" she announced with a flourish, and surged back indoors to dish out more eggs.

***

Eventually, after managing to convince Marina we had no further need of breakfast, she hustled us back down the steps to the gate and we spilled over the road to the edge of the lagoon. There, tethered to a tree, was a blue and red painted wooden canoe about the dimensions of three bath tubs end to end. In no time she had it rigged with a mast and a single square sail, and my family ensconced under a willow tree with a box of muffins and a case of beer. Marina was taking no prisoners. I was thrust into the canoe, alone, and shoved away from the bank before I knew what was happening.

"Sail!" she bellowed, as Abi and Jo giggled at me from the safety of their tree. "You sailed across the ocean; surely you can manage a canoe?!"

I had little idea what was expected of me, but it was a lovely warm day with a gentle breeze ruffling the water, and it did not take long to grasp the basics. Sailing is sailing, after all, and with a cord attached to each of the bottom corners of the sail I was able to twist it around on the mast and slip along perpendicular to the wind. I lay back with the tiller wedged under my armpit, bare feet over the side in the sun, and fancied myself an intrepid explorer, sailing one of the great rivers of Brazil. I idled and daydreamed my way across the lagoon and back for an hour. It was bliss.

Gliding my way back to the muffins and beers I realised I had lost some ground downwind and would need to head back up slightly to make the landing. It was not to be. The absence of a keel made it impossible to make any headway upwind, and the best I could do was run the canoe into some trees about fifty yards down the bank, jump out, and wade it back through the mud.

"What the hell are you doing? I thought you were a sailor!" howled Marina with glee. I didn't mind at all, it had been a most agreeable diversion.

Back up at the house, full English breakfasts overlaid with muffins and beer still weighing heavily in our stomachs, we were confronted with a table groaning once more under a load of sticky risotto, tender steaks and delicious truffles. Sandra had been busy while we were out.

"Lunchtime!" pronounced out generous host, pulling out the chairs. "You sit here. Where is Tommy? Tommeee!! Take more rice – that's better. Red or white wine for you? Tom-MEEE, LEAVE THE BABY NOW! You like my canoe then? SOMEONE GET THAT PARROT! No, that is not enough, take another piece of steak…" as her twelve-year-old daughter chased down the errant parrot and popped it squawking back in its cage.

The steaks were luscious and succulent, the risotto delicious. Eating again was not to be resisted, and after the day's second feast we could hardly move. I vaguely remember lying inert on a sofa next to my distended stomach, groaning quietly to myself, when my self-pity was disrupted by Marina yelling at me again.

"Does Lucy like Toucans?!" she demanded.

"What? Toucans? I suppose… everybody likes toucans… what are you talking about?"

"We have toucans!" She was triumphant. "Lucy must see the toucans!"

With that we gathered up our stomachs and were once again bundled down the stairs and out into the garden, blinking in the sunlight like overfed moles.

"We keep the toucans back here!" announced Marina, disappearing through the bushes behind the house. "They are very tame, Lucy will love them!"

We burrowed after her until we came upon a small aviary. Two beautiful green toucans with yellow and purple bills perched side by side on a branch, and Marina lifted them up, one in each hand. The larger bird stretched over to nibble delicately at her ear which made her giggle. It was a surprisingly girlish little giggle from someone so ebullient.

"Here you are," she proffered a bird. "Give this one to Lucy!"

Poor Lucy was all of eight months old and not even walking; now she was expected to do something with a live toucan. She looked dubiously at it and hid her face in her mother's shoulder. Then she peeped out again and chuckled at the colourful bird with its incongruous large bill. The toucan cackled at her, and Lucy dissolved with laughter. The toucan seemed to be laughing too, and Marina had tears in her eyes.

"Children love them!" she gushed. "They are like therapy. You have a happy baby!"

***

Marina did not think much of us keeping the boat moored at Armacao.

"What the hell is it doing there?" she asked, incredulous; as if I, of all people, should know better. "Why is it not at Paulet's oyster farm?"

I had absolutely no idea what she was talking about.

"Oyster farm?"

"Yes, of course! I will call him, and we can move the boat tomorrow."

She was not inviting dissent, and I was not inclined to offer any. Anything to do with oysters sounded like progress.

In the morning we made quite a crowd on the little beach at Armacao. There was the full complement of *Josephine's* normal crew plus Alistair, Marina, her two children and her sister Sandra. That made no less than ten people waiting to be ferried out through the breakers in our little inflatable dinghy.

Somehow the feat was accomplished without mishap and after we had everyone safely aboard Dael and I set about disentangling the twin anchor chains. For several days *Josephine* had ridden on two anchors, being blown first this way and then that, with the result that the two chains were wrapped so tightly round each other Dael had to don a mask and dive to untangle them.

Half an hour later we were sailing out of Armacao in bright sunshine with a fifty mile cruise ahead of us to find the mystery Paulet and his oyster farm. Marina produced a bottle of whisky from her bag and passed it around the cockpit "to take the nip off".

Round the outside of the island, the wind was blowing stiffly from the south forcing us to beat all the way down, alternately heading out to sea, then back towards shore. It was an uncomfortable trip, pitching over the swell, and both Marina's children were violently ill. To make things more miserable, we endured a rain squall in the late afternoon, so when we finally rounded *Punta do Frade* ("Friar Point") on the southern tip of *Ihla Catarina* and sailed by the huddle of wooden restaurants on the beach at *Pantano do Sul*, there was great relief all round.

The bay between the mainland and the island is very sheltered – not even a south wind seems to be able to push the swell through the gap between the light on *Punta dos Naufragados* ("Shipwreck Point") and *Ilha do Papagaio Grande* ("Big Parrot Island") so while we had a good breeze to sail by, the water was flat calm. The sun came back and spirits rose.

"Okay Marina, where is the oyster farm?"

She waved vaguely northwards. "That way."

"How far?"

"Not far."

"Could you show me on the chart?"

"No, I know his house. Just keep going, I'll tell you when I see it."

This did not sound encouraging. The shore was an almost uninterrupted jungle, but several miles to the north we could see the masts of two other yachts.

"Up there by the boats. He said there are other boats anchored nearby."

Another half an hour passed, and the depth dropped to barely seven feet. We were running out of water, our keel clearing the muddy bottom by mere inches. Marina was shouting into the cell phone at Paulet who was making a valiant attempt to be heard. No description of the house helped; there just was not a low white house with an orange roof anywhere in sight. (It turned out later than you can only see it from the road.)

As we edged up the bay, the depth down to five feet and the keel carving a groove through the soft mud, we saw the telltale blue buoys in the water.

"The oysters!" exclaimed Marina. "Paulet's oysters!"

Yes, she was sure; even though we could see no building matching the description of Paulet's house.

We deployed the dinghy and Alistair, Marina and I went ashore to investigate. We had indeed arrived at Paulet's oyster farm, and Paulet himself, a soft spoken, retiring man with a gentle smile, greeted us on the concrete slipway.

Once everyone was ashore, Paulet walked us up to his lawn and presented us with the biggest bag of the fattest oysters I think I have ever seen. No less than six dozen, each bigger than my fist; I could barely lift the bag. Lemons and cracked black pepper were conjured from Marina's ample handbag and Paulet produced a sharp knife. It started to rain again as we levered open the first oysters, but it was a steamy tropical rain and nobody minded. There we sat, leaning against a wall looking over the bay at *Josephine* serene on her anchor, and feasted on the fat, succulent shellfish as the water ran warm down our backs. Just another one of those moments that money could never buy.

***

Our original plan had been to leave Florianopolis and sail all the way to Argentina; a trip of a week, maybe a little more, to Buenos Aires. But illogical and petty bureaucracy reared its head, and the *Capitania dos Portos* in Florianopolis refused to allow us to leave "his" port for a foreign destination. Instead he insisted we go to the port of *Rio Grande do Sul,* some three hundred and fifty miles south of Florianopolis, to clear out of Brazil. His logic was that as Rio Grande is the most southerly town, we should exit the country from there. I knew very well it was not a regulation; in fact it could endanger my family as in the rough waters of the south it is a lot safer out at sea than close inshore. I asked – through Alistair, who was translating – what he would have done had I said I was leaving for, say, Africa, which is east of here? He replied he would indeed then have cleared me out, but I would not be permitted to change my story now. I was stuck. I knew very well that it was not in his jurisdiction to tell me where to go, or to decide whether or not I could leave the country – unless he impounded the boat, which he had no cause to do – but Alistair would not countenance arguing with him. With great reluctance I acquiesced. I was sorry I had not gone to the *Policia* to clear immigration first; I doubt even *this* Port Captain thought he had the authority to over-ride a passport exit stamp.

Having to call in at Rio Grande meant we could not head as far offshore as we had planned, so would now need to take better account of the coastal weather conditions. There was a bit of a southerly blow looming over the next few days, and then the northerlies were forecast to return. A northerly was what we wanted, but we would need it to set in for four days to be sure of reaching Rio Grande before it changed again. We had been told by a sailor in Ilhabela that Imbituba, some thirty miles south of Florianopolis, has a good harbour, and although thirty miles might not be much of the three hundred and fifty we needed to cross off to get to Rio Grande, every bit would help. We decided to head there to wait for the weather window.

***

After a lazy, late breakfast we waved goodbye to Paulet and his oysters and pointed *Josephine* south. Six uneventful hours later we found ourselves inside the breakwater at Imbituba. A sea wall extends north from *Punta de Imbituba*, behind which container ships dock to unload cargo destined for Florianopolis, there being no possibility of constructing a deep water harbour in the city. There is not much else in the port of Imbituba, and certainly no facility for yachts. We anchored just off the beach in ten feet of water, protected from the ocean swell by the sea wall some three hundred metres behind us.

The flat, hard beach, inside the protection of the wall, is lined with a row of tin-roofed wooden huts. These are the weekend houses of families who live in the surrounding hills, and from Friday to Monday the beach is a thoroughfare: pedestrians, bicycles, horses and carts, motorbikes and even cars ply up and down the beach until all hours of the night as people swim, fish, cook, drink and dance on the sand. All very festive, and very Brazilian. We went ashore for a swim and Lucy squealed with delight at her first experience of body surfing as I ran through the shallows dragging her naked in the tumbling wash. Behind the beach we found a small, clean bakery and an internet café, but not much else. We were surprised, having understood Imbituba to be somewhat more consequential.

The following day we discovered the town of Imbituba was in fact over the hill on the south side of the point, after asking an old man in the street if there was any pizza to be had locally. He was thin and bent under the weight of his oversized maroon beret and bristly white moustache.

"No, no pizza here," he whistled past his last remaining tooth. "Only in Imbituba!"

"Uh… but… *this* is Imbituba, is it not?"

"*Ah, nao senhor*! This is a fishing settlement. Imbituba is that way," pointing to the south.

After a half hour tramp in pelting rain we found the missing town. The first shop we saw was "Imbi Wave", a little surf shop. I could not resist, and when I came out I had bought my first board. It was grapefruit pink with a flaking yellow band around the edges and a tasteless green cut-out of a palm tree had been used to patch a hole in the top. Nine feet long, it cost me all of thirty dollars. I walked it two miles back to the beach in the downpour where I set about teaching myself to surf as the rain lashed down and thunder rumbled around me. I confess to having very limited success, alternately digging the nose into the sand and almost castrating myself on the skegs, and toppling off backwards to see my new board shoot up into the sky like an orange trident missile launched from a submarine. But I did manage to stand up twice – albeit briefly – and that evening, with sand in my ears and a persistent salt-sniffle, I shared a celebratory beer with Dael. I was a surfer dude. Well, sort of.

***

That night the anticipated south wind came through at thirty five knots, and had *Josephine* dancing from side to side on her anchor chain. The beach, being low, did not offer much protection from the wind. We were sheltered from waves of course, but the gale blew unchecked over the shore.

Now one of the surest ways to alarm me is to wake me up on a boat at 2am and say something like 'I don't mean to alarm you, but you'd better come and… .' Dael's voice pierced the skin of sleep and tore it wide open. I sat bolt upright, alarmed.

Stupidly, before going to bed, I had left a tarpaulin rigged to catch rainwater for drinking, and in this wind it acted like a sail. We were blowing backwards, away from the beach into deeper and deeper water, dragging the anchor through the sand. The anchor drag alarm was not set either, and by the time Dael woke me the water depth had gone from ten feet to more than thirty and we were far enough from the beach that the wind coming off the shore was blowing up choppy waves that were smacking against the bow, pushing us still further out. We had only a few feet of chain lying on the bottom; not nearly enough to hope for the anchor to re-hook itself.

Less than a hundred yards from where the waves were pounding the sea wall behind us, I gunned the engine into life and we started hauling the anchor chain with the windlass. After less than a minute the chain jammed. We let a little out, then tried again. Same result.

Dael was in the bow monitoring the chain and I was at the wheel. Communication was difficult in the wind and rain. He was gesticulating wildly that something was wrong. I joined him on the foredeck.

"The anchor won't come up. It's caught on something."

I peered over the bow while we operated the windlass again, and as the chain tightened a dark mass rose to the surface of the water. It was like a giant ball of black spaghetti wound onto a fork. A bloody fishing net.

Dael hacked at the tangled nylon with his knife while I used the engine to keep the boat in position and quickly the net was cut away, freeing the anchor. That net had quite probably saved us from being blown clear across the harbour onto the wall and seriously damaging the boat. We had just had another lucky break.

***

Two days later, after the rain, we left Imbituba while the last of the southerly was blowing itself out. Beating to windward over a choppy sea was unpleasant, and the entire family was seasick, but after twelve hours the wind switched and from then on we had something of a roller-coaster downwind ride at up to eleven knots; it was still rough, but with the wind now from behind we were going a lot faster. It was exciting but tense as the boat wallowed and rolled on the diagonal swells and very little sleep was possible. Dael and I spent all of our waking time on deck, but the girls definitely had it worse below, Jo doing all the cooking and Abi having her hands full with Lucy. Abi was horribly seasick but could not come out on deck or lie down to sleep except when Lucy was taking a nap. I did not envy either of them, and in hindsight it was just as well the Port Captain at Florianopolis had sabotaged our plan of sailing non-stop to Buenos Aires. It would have taken too long and been too unpleasant for the girls.

As it was, the trip to Rio Grande lasted two and a half days. For the last sixty miles the depth was less than thirty feet, and the strong winds over the shallow water made for close, steep waves which had us even more on our toes. At least we were sailing downwind. A year later, in these same treacherous waters, I was to learn what it is like to sail *upwind* in these waters.

***

The south coast of Brazil is flat, for hundreds of miles, with no features whatsoever on which to take compass bearings to orientate yourself. At night you can sail along the coast with the aid of a series of lighthouses, each with its own flashing code, but in the day there is nothing to be seen unless you can spot an actual lighthouse tower (and figure out which one you are looking at). Thankfully we have that modern wonder, the Global Positioning System (GPS), the satellite signals for which the American military have been kind enough to make available to all and sundry.

The first hint of the existence of the city of *Rio Grande do Sul* is the marked increase in freighter traffic as ships converge from Buenos Aires to the south and Santos to the north. Rio Grande boasts Brazil's second biggest port, so a sharp lookout is required on the approach. We crept ever closer to the coast the further south we went, not wanting to overshoot the entrance channel and have to double back up into the wind and current, and eventually away to the south-west we spotted the high derricks of the port silhouetted against the pale sky. Now we just needed to find the buoys marking the entrance channel through the shallow water.

"Music is the mediator between the spiritual and the sensual life."

– Ludwig van Beethoven

9

We sighted the first buoys marking the Rio Grande channel some three and a half miles out to sea. The wind strengthened the closer we came to land, and as we sailed into ever shallower water, the waves became more savage. By the time we reached the entrance to the long double breakwater that juts some two miles out to sea, the wind was gusting close to fifty knots and it was all we could do to control the boat under three reefs. *Josephine* was continually overpowered, rolling over and yawing to windward. The entry itself was tricky, sailing in on tumbling waves at eleven knots, but once between the breakwaters we dropped the sails as quickly as we could on the flat, brown, river water and motored towards the distant docks with a welcoming pod of dolphins blowing and puffing around us.

Past the container terminal, monstrous freighters and tugs lining the docks, we picked our way through the channels of the estuary for three hours with the aid of the GPS and the depth sounder – the marker buoys are somewhat sparse – then by the old town, miles of deserted quays with dilapidated grey warehouses, all smashed windows and rust. It may be Brazil's second biggest port, but it appears its glory days as a trading hub are past. After some ten miles fighting the out-flowing current in steady rain we had all but reached the yacht club when we heard a voice booming, loud and clear, above the din of the motor and the wind.

"YOU WILL PARK HERE!"

It seemed to be coming from the sky.

"OVER HERE!"

Was it God?

Then we saw him. Majestic in a flowing white gown with grey hair and beard. God? No, Gandalf. "He's put on weight," said Abi. Standing tall in the rain and wind on a wooden jetty with a loudhailer to his face surrounded by an entourage of at least ten smaller folk – hobbits perhaps – scurrying about with ropes. He defied argument, so dog tired, wet and cold, we came about and made fast to his jetty in the shadow of a four storey motor yacht that looked like a gigantic plastic kitchen appliance.

Gandalf strode towards me like a Portuguese galleon in full sail, his white robes billowing in the wind.

"I AM LAURO!" he thundered, his voice echoing off the rain-clouds like some distant cannon. "I AM THE DIRECTOR OF THIS MUSEUM! YOU HAVE WATER AND ELECTRICITY HERE, AND YOU CAN STAY AS LONG AS YOU LIKE. IT IS FREE.

THAT MEANS NO CHARGE! AYRTON WILL SHOW YOU THE SHOWERS!" and he turned on his heels and sailed away into the trees. I had not even spoken.

Ayrton was his security guard; a short, portly individual with a tight uniform and a big gun, hovering in Lauro's considerable shadow. Gimli, almost, without the beard. He beamed when I alluded to his racing driver namesake, and slapped me rather too hard on the back all the way to the showers while exhorting me in rapid Portuguese to some or other dubious end. Within minutes he had confided in me that he used a shipping container in the museum garden for illicit sex. He was also the best "*churrasceiro*" (braai master) in Brazil, and we would indeed discover this truth for ourselves as he was going to lay on the mother of all "*churrascos*" just for us. (He never did.)

In time we discovered we had arrived at the *Museo Oceanografico*, a semi-governmental museum-cum-aquarium loosely affiliated to the local university for research purposes. During the day it was open to the paying public, and boasted a very neat and tidy hall of exhibits, including a tank of living axolotls and an array of whale and dolphin skeletons. There was a pond full of de-oiled penguins, and another, deeper one housing an enormous sea-lion. He had been rescued as a pup, and now lived here permanently as, according to Lauro, the poor creature "*have forgotten the nature*".

It turned out the yacht club was actually right next door, but we seemed to be a lot better off at the museum. Not only was it free at the museum, but there was a depth problem at the club: when the south winds blew – as they often did, for days at a time – the water in the two hundred mile long *Lagoa dos Patos* ("Duck Lake" – Brazil's largest lagoon) that fed into Rio Grande from the north, was blown upcountry and all the boats with draught in excess of about four feet were stuck in the mud at their moorings.

That first evening Lauro invited us into his "kitchen", an olive green painted wooden cabin mounted on stilts over the water with a fridge and gas stove, and a long table down the middle surrounded by about twenty plastic chairs. The walls were adorned with signed flags from visiting boats, photographs of boats, carvings of boats, little model boats and other assorted nautical bric-a-brac like fishing floats, sailors' hats and miniature anchors. A team of research biologists, as well as a documentary film crew, were in attendance that evening and we dined sumptuously into the night on sausages, cheese and cake, sharing stories of the sea. Lucy had pride of place all evening on Lauro's lap. It was an unexpectedly festive end to our three day sail, and for good measure just happened to be Abi's birthday. Candles were magicked from somewhere and planted in a cake in her honour.

Lauro turned out to be quite a character. In addition to being the Director of the Oceanographic Museum, he owned a Boat Museum in the town, and was the founder and patron of the local "Sea School". This privately run school, dependent solely on donations from benefactors, takes as students around two hundred under-privileged children, and every subject on the curriculum has some or other bearing on the sea. The students are taught to be cooks, carpenters, electricians and the like, and for the older ones a number of trades are combined and they are taught to build boats from scratch. I asked Lauro what I thought to be a logical enough question.

"I assume fishing is on the syllabus?"

Lauro stopped in his tracks. He turned slowly to face me, his finger raised high in admonishment, then, in a melodramatic stage whisper, hissed "Fisshhh-errr-mans! I *h-a-te* fishermans! *H-A-ATE* them! Murderers! MURR-DERR-ERRS!!" shaking the finger and going almost purple.

We were asked to donate anything spare on the boat to the school, and were only too happy to part with several lengths of rope and a life ring. I thought better of offering any of our excess fish-murdering gear.

***

Originally visiting Rio Grande under duress merely to complete exit formalities and clear out of Brazil, we ended up staying, for a number of reasons, three weeks.

I had ordered – and paid for – another South American pilot guide to supplement the book I already possessed, but it had been delayed in the post and only reached Florianopolis after we left. Alistair wasted no time in forwarding it to Rio Grande, c/o Lauro at the museum. He was assured by the Brazilian postal service it would get to us in twenty-four hours. Of course it did not.

Another reason for our prolonged stay in Rio Grande was our fresh water pump. It had been installed, new, no more than six months prior, but in Rio Grande it packed up and no amount of re-wiring, cleaning or general cajoling could get it to work. In the end we bought a replacement pump, which took several days to be delivered.

After all was said and done though these were really not much more than excuses to linger, because we liked it there. Lauro was very good to us, throwing open all the facilities of the museum, including the (normally private) research laboratory with its permanent internet access. We wanted for nothing and it was fun getting to know another town.

One afternoon we saw another yacht working its way up the channel from the direction of the old docks. She flew a German flag, and looked to be slightly bigger than *Josephine*. The obviously added-on doghouse over the centre cockpit, as well as the washing hanging out to dry in the rigging, told us she was a cruising boat. The large grey

Capitania dos Portos launch shadowing them told us they were in some kind of trouble.

The new boat, *Afun Davu,* duly arrived alongside and I helped make her fast. Two short humanoids, neither of them standing as high as five feet, were on board. The one with the bushy moustache we took to be the male.

"My name iss Werner. I am Bavarian. I like beer!" he announced himself. He may have been short but he was very powerfully built, muscles bulging out of his red vest in all directions.

"Ach, ja, he alvays say ziss!" chimed his even shorter wife with her purple rinse and smoker's cackle. "I am Emmy!"

And with that they where whisked away by the Port Authorities to explain some previous indiscretion and we did not see them again the rest of the day.

In the morning they were back.

"Ja!" pronounced Werner. "Zey are very stupid here. Zey vont to fine us because ve do not stamp out of Florianopolis. But zey know ve leaf because ve tell zem before and now zey say zey vait for us here because ze *Capitania* in Florianopolis report us. But how zey report us here if zey don't know vere ve go? Obviously zey know vere we go, so how zey can say ve don't tell zem? Ziss iss impossible I tell zem, but zey don't listen!"

Impeccable logic, except that Brazilians – in fact South Americans generally – are big on paperwork. Bureaucracy rules, and they love the Rubber Stamp. It is all very well reporting your movements, but if you don't afford them the opportunity of embossing your papers with an assortment of Stamps, you can get yourself in all sorts of trouble.

In the end Emmy paid a two hundred dollar fine to "make zem go avay". (Emmy note, not Werner; Emmy forbade Werner from getting involved in the debate as "*he get under ze skin of ze people and zen zey go crazy*".)

And so we came to know Werner and Emmy from Bavaria. Werner was a physiotherapist, and ex-bodybuilder. He was immensely strong – I once saw him tottering along the jetty clutching four six gallon diesel drums in his two hands – all full. Trapezoids knotted, moustache quivering, he looked like a caricature straight from the pencil of Albert Uderzo. And he was fifty five years old.

It was odd that our Bavarians should be so indignant at being fined by the authorities. By their own admission, they had arrived in Bahia, in the north of Brazil, after crossing the Atlantic from Europe, spent six months there, then sailed south to Ilha Grande and anchored in the little town of Paraty for a further fourteen months. At no time did they so much as get their passports stamped, let alone report the entry of their boat into Brazil. In Paraty they had been anchored right opposite the town quay, in full view of everyone, illegally – for over a year! So much for the three month tourist visa.

As Emmy told me enthusiastically: "Zey see us every day. Zey know us! Ve are ze short people wiss ze folding bicycles!"

"Ach ja," added Werner. "Zey don't care. Normally you haff no problems wiss ze aussorities in Brazil. Only you haff problems ven you go to zem!"

He had a point.

Werner was very proud indeed to be Bavarian. Much more so than German in fact.

"Ze Bavarians are ze true Germans. Ze pure Germans. Ze usser Germans are more mixed, ja. I am from Regensburg. Regensburg is one off ze older towns in Germany and indeed it could be ze oldest, ja!"

He held forth to anyone who would listen that the only reason the Germans lost The War was that the Italians surrendered; if not for that we would all be speaking German, and quite frankly we'd all be better off.

Although he was generous to us, and certainly very funny, he sometimes made it difficult to be empathetic. He would unashamedly relate stories from his time in the exotic north of Brazil.

"Ve come into ziss place, and ve see a man sitting on a rock in a dive soot, but it is very hot, *very* hot, and ve sink '*vot iss ziss? He is crazy!*' And zen, ve come closer, and indeed ve discover ziss iss no dive soot; he iss black! But he iss *very* dark, ja!"

He had a similar story about a man standing on a yacht with a wetsuit hanging next to him, until Werner noticed the wetsuit moving, and "off course also zen ve see ziss is not a dive soot, indeed zis iss hiss girlfriend!"

I supposed Regensburg to be very Aryan.

Regensburg, to listen to Werner, is the centre of the civilized universe. He had been to Peru, where he was charged nine dollars to "*visit ze Inca Steps*". He found this ridiculous.

"Vot iss ziss? Ziss is just steps. Off course ze Incas must haff steps to go up, ziss iss normal. And zey tell you ziss steps is six hundred years old, and zen you must pay to look at it. Zen I tell zem, '*In Regensburg, ve haf indeed many buildings older zan ziss, and you can see zem every day and you never pay to look at zem.*' But zey understand nussing."

***

As a physiotherapist, Werner was in demand at the museum. He delighted in sharing his undoubted knowledge of human physiology with all and sundry, and was regularly called upon to massage stiff backs and aching legs. Some of his best patients came from *Josephine*.

Of course it is impossible to find the space for a proper massage in a thirty eight foot sloop populated by four adults, a nine month old baby, several dozen teddy bears and a ton and a half of LEGO, so a venue was needed. Then Werner discovered the Antarctica Exhibition – a converted shipping container with maps and photographs of the adventures of the likes of Scott, Shackleton and Amundsen, and bits of whale baleen and a stuffed albatross suspended from the roof. There he found the perfect massage bench – which of course explains why the security guard, Ayrton, had a spare key and would use it for secret liaisons of his own in the dead of night.

As luck would have it, on this particular night Ayrton had made plans. There the poor fellow was, leading his *amore* stealthily through the darkened garden headed for the Antarctica container, when he noticed the light had been left on. Imagine his surprise on opening the door to see my mother-in-law lying on her tummy under a towel, Werner sweating and grunting on his knees behind her. Ayrton and his girlfriend bolted into the night.

Every day after that Ayrton would leer at Werner and make obscene gestures with his fingers, and as his English – like Werner's Portuguese – was non-existent, there was no way of clarifying what had actually been going on. In any event I doubt whether any attempt at explaining would have changed Ayrton's mind about what he believed he had witnessed.

Quite a community developed at the little wooden jetty during our three weeks in Rio Grande. At one time there were as many as five boats, and, as the jetty is a small one, we rafted up two and three abreast. Climbing over and through other boats is a great way to meet people, and there were some real characters in residence.

Henry the Uruguayan, seventy-two years old, tall and slim with a neatly cropped silver beard, had spent twenty-five years of his life in Africa. Now back in Uruguay, he was making a living from sailing, working as a delivery skipper with the occasional bit of racing thrown in. He had been forced to stop over in Rio Grande for repairs while on his way north delivering a fifty foot yacht from Montevideo to Angra dos Reis (near Rio) when the headsail tore in a storm and a wave broke over the cockpit crushing the stainless steel bimini frame. (Months later, in Uruguay, we met several people who knew him, and the standard question on hearing we had met him was "What had he broken?")

Henry liked to talk about his time abroad, and one of his favourite topics was red meat: specifically, the cooking of it over a flame. As in most countries with any sunshine, the Uruguayan rituals around the fire have taken on a nationalistic flavour, to the point you would think Uruguayans are the only people on the planet who know the first thing about how it should be done. Henry would expound at length on the relative virtues of the English barbecue and the Uruguayan *asado*. He pointed out that while the *asado* (like the Brazilian *churrasco*) is a slow, drawn out affair involving multiple burnings of flesh to provide a series of small courses, the traditional English-speaking regime is different.

"The English only adopt barbecue after they colonise Australia with its good weather. In places like Australia and South Africa, people wait and wait for the fire to be ready; and then, when is ready, after a long time, everything suddenly is cook and you must eat all in one time or it come cold on your plate. Then is finish and everyone go home!"

He went on to promote his favourite theory on this difference between this and the "*gaucho*" way:

"In Africa," he explained, "when the Afrikaners stopped in the bush to *braai*, they had to be quick or the cattle would be stolen by natives or eaten by lions." He contrasted that with Uruguay, where there was nothing more threatening than the odd capybara or armadillo running about, so the *gauchos* could afford to be more *tranquilo*.

And in England?

"In England they must cook all very quick before it rain."

Pepe Blau, a fisherman from the Balearics, was there too. Big, jovial Pepe. Between fishing seasons in Majorca, he would fly to wherever he had left his yacht the previous year and sail it to another part of the world. Now he was on his way north from Uruguay, heading for Rio; and he was doing it his way.

"You should see my charts!" he announced one night when the subject was navigation. He rummaged around under his navigation table and emerged with a single spiral-bound booklet.

"Look at this, here!" he said, stabbing at the page with a meaty finger. "A port, a railway line, a bus station.... and further up, a swimming beach... then hotels, here an island too." He let the book sink to his lap. "And guess what else?" he asked, followed by a dramatic pause. "Look here, when I get to the end of the chart? I just turn the page, and there you are! It continues! Fantastic!" he proclaimed, brandishing his South American road atlas. He was sailing up the continent following the shore using a route map as a guide.

Another boat in our floating community was the Argentine flagged *Azul*. Oscar, retired and balding with a comfortable waistline, built the steel *Azul* himself some twenty years previously, and had sailed here from his home port of Bahia Blanca with his friend Omar, "*just for the funny of it*". The inside of *Azul* was adorned with pictures drawn by Oscar's children as toddlers, though they were now in their late teens. One of his daughters was named Lucy. Oscar gave our Lucy a teddy bear that used to belong to his little girl and had been a mascot in his boat for fifteen years. It was a kind and touching gift.

Oscar's companion, the heavily smoking Omar, made up for his lack of English by just grinning at everyone all the time. He had very yellow teeth, like old ivory, and smoked continuously. I would regularly see him looking a little furtive in the museum garden at night, hovering under a tree waiting for his latest "date" to arrive at the gate. I wondered whether Ayrton had tipped him off to the Antarctica container.

One morning Marcos appeared out of the air. He was just there, hovering about. Impossibly tight black jeans, a cropped black beard, black pony tail and multiple silver Gothic earrings. Out of the ether he materialised on the jetty, wanting to practice his English. A part time teacher of English in the town, the thirty-five-year-old Marcos was also the lead guitarist in a local heavy metal band. Always happy to meet locals, we had him aboard for a cup of coffee and he stayed two days.

He turned out to be good fun. By day he walked us around the old town and give us history lessons, then dropped us off at his mother's for lunch while he popped out to deliver a quick English class. By night he took us pub crawling. On the third day he had an inspired idea.

"I have band practice this afternoon. You wanna come?"

I certainly did, if he meant it?.

"Yeah, that'd be great. Come and meet the guys!" he enthused. "In fact, why don't you bring your video camera and shoot us?"

I was introduced to the band in a rented lock-up garage that had been converted into an impromptu studio. Posters of John Lennon and Whitesnake were pinned to the egg boxes that lined the walls as soundproofing. A drum kit took up half the space, and the lead singer, Miro, was squeezed between his microphone stand and a hatch in the wall that opened behind him into a little kitchen that obviously doubled as a bar.

It was immediately evident that Marcos had done a sales job and the rest of the band was very excited about being filmed. They probably thought I was their ticket to MTV.

"Is okay we do our own songs first?" asked Marcos.

That was fine with me; in fact I would prefer that.

Cheyenne duly launched into their first track and played five on the trot while I filmed away. It was a heavy, raucous sound, no doubt the real thing; with Nick's energetic drumming and some intricate guitar riffs from Marcos, they almost got away with it, but for Miro, the vocalist. He certainly looked the part with his wild eyes and crazy long hair, but he missed more than just the occasional note. It occurred to me, as the session went on, that while he had the signature gravelly voice that lends the necessary "street cred" to any hard rock band – and this was *Hard* – he might do better to scream less and sing more.

As the final crescendo of frantic drumming, screeching guitars and Miro's labour pains reverberated around the egg-boxes and ebbed away, they lowered their weapons and looked at me.

"What do you think?" asked Marcos.

The silence had a stunned quality. All eyes were on me. Clearly the video camera made me an authority.

"Uh, very good," I ventured. They stared. "Hard – HAAAARD, yeah! Right on!" I thought they might appreciate some "cool" English. They did. I then went on to point out that while I am hardly a music critic, I enjoyed their sound; they had good chemistry, were obviously having fun, and it came through in their music. All safely non-committal.

"Cool man, right on!" replied Marcos, nodding. "But what about our songs man, how about our songs? What do you think of our songs?" They wanted more.

"Um, yeah… your songs… good melodies, good guitar riffs, catchy – I like the sound – obviously I don't understand the words – but good sound guys!" I finished with a cheesy double thumbs up.

There was a hush. We looked at each other for an awkward moment, then a wave of laughter swept round the room. What had I said?

Marcos stumbled towards me wiping the tears from his eyes. "My maaaan…" he exclaimed, pointing at Miro, "… is singing in English!"

Thankfully Miro had a sense of humour and appeared to appreciate the joke as much as everyone else. I tried to soften it by explaining how it is often difficult to make out the words of English-language rock songs sung with different accents, and that it is not always that important so long as the sound is good.

No harm was done, and Miro presented me with the printed words to his latest English-language composition. I record it here, lest it be lost to the world of art:

"SNORING ENGINE, TYRES EATING THE ROAD"

Snoring engines are buzzing… within me realise my machine.
Here it is always nice and hot
Before and after who is in charge here I am

The one hundred miles per hour…
Just stop to give you ride come into my car, trust me
I will take you to where I want.

I with you hand in you with your hand on me
Come on, work right!
Let the bliss together.

I go from here to the enjoyment final.
Groans, heat, sweat, wind…
Snoring engine, tyres eating the road…
Impact! Twisted metal,
Meat with meat is involved.

After the rehearsal we walked together down the road, beers in hand, carrying guitars and playing impromptu football with a discarded melon. It was all so Brazilian.

Marcos stopped off at a corner shop and presented me with a potted palm for the boat. Back on the jetty he insisted on being winched up the mast to see the view, and we just got him down again before a storm broke.

***

A few days later Marcos had another treat lined up for us. This time he invited us to join him at an "underground punk concert". Who could resist?

Dael and I duly presented ourselves outside a rundown little hall at midnight with Werner the Bavarian in tow. Marcos and his brother Anderson met us at the door and whisked us inside past the bouncer. We were obviously VIPs. The five of us swelled the crowd close to twenty and the show kicked off.

It was awful. The band consisted of four individuals in silver studded black leather with spiked up blue and red hair, screaming through their lip rings into microphones that reproduced the sound as a loud, grinding, popping static. The heavy THUMP THUMP THUMP of the drums was clear enough, and seemed to be all that mattered. The crowd – with the exception of us – was made up of members of the bands scheduled to follow on, their little brothers, and the bouncer. There was a twelve-year-old boy in football kit selling beers out of a backroom, but within the hour he had passed out drunk and the beers were "free".

Werner – the only person not wearing black, in a dayglo orange lycra muscleshirt – parked himself directly in front of the stage where he proceeded to film as much of the act as he could with his cell phone. He had never seen anything like it – not even in Regensburg. Unfortunately the punks chose that moment to turn the floor into a mosh pit, and as they jumped around cannoning off each other Werner was knocked over. The nuggety Bavarian was up and flattened two of them before Dael and I could wrestle him outside. One of his victims was the bouncer, who looked very sorry with his crimson cockscomb bent over to one side.

The music was rubbish, but we had swallowed enough beer to make it all worthwhile, and we laughed all the way home.

***

Lauro had a boat of his own. Tethered to one of the stilts supporting his kitchen was a canoe. And what a canoe. Carved out of a single tree trunk eighty-five years earlier and apparently weighing a ton, it stepped two masts with gaff rigs and had thwarts to seat ten people. Lauro spread himself in the stern, one arm flopped over the tiller, a beer in the other hand, while the rest of us hoisted the sails. There were several of us on this little booze cruise – Sergio, the owner of a recently arrived seventy-seven foot racing sloop; some of the Brazilian crew from *Lady Genyr*, the hundred foot, four storey luxury motor yacht that took up two thirds of the jetty and had air conditioning and eleven toilets; the lecherous, grinning Omar from *Azul*, who was forbidden to smoke; and Dael and me from *Josephine*.

Sailing a canoe that is close to a hundred years old was thrilling, and as we plied the shallow waters of the lagoon, the red sails taught and sheets humming, I wondered what adventures the boat had witnessed over the years. It had originally been a fishing canoe, part of a fleet that used to harvest the waters off the beach in the days before boats had engines. It had then been abandoned in the harbour, until Lauro rescued it for his Boat Museum. Once restored by the students at his school, he thought it a waste to let it stand as a static display in a hall, and had it moved to his private jetty. Not being a sailor at heart, he had committed the sacrilege of installing a stinking single-cylinder diesel engine which admittedly made it a lot more practical to use, but on this day there were enough sailors on board to convince him not to fire the diesel and it was not until late in the evening that we found ourselves back at the museum, all sensibly drunk and brothers for life.

***

The day finally dawned that our new water pump had arrived and been installed (and was actually working) and the weather forecast was favourable for going south. As we had already overstayed the exit stamps in our passports by almost two weeks, we thought it would be prudent to ship out of the country without delay.

Both *Azul* and *Afun Davu* were planning their departures too; *Azul* to Uruguay, and *Afun Davu*, like us, to Buenos Aires. We thought it would be fun to sail south together and prepared to leave on the same morning. The Bavarians on *Afun Davu* left at seven o'clock, the Argentines on *Azul* an hour later; but knowing we had a faster boat in *Josephine* we frittered most of the morning away and only got going around eleven. As we were casting off Lauro presented us with a silk Brazilian flag the size of a large table cloth. We hoisted it up the mast and cruised down the channel past the commercial harbour and the port hooting our farewell as fishermen, stevedores and shoppers on the promenade waved us on our way.

Between the breakwaters the dolphins were waiting for us, and rushed around the boat in excitement as we hauled the mainsail up and pointed *Josephine* south.

"Buenos Aires, here we come!" I shouted, and we all cheered. It was a lovely sunny day with the perfect breeze at our backs, and we were thrilled to be sailing to Argentina.

We were not to know that fate had a little surprise in store for us that would see us making landfall in another country altogether.

Anchored at St Helena, Mid Atlantic, with the Royal Mail Ship behind.

Rob graduates from cooking to helming across the Atlantic

Dael working on deck during the ocean crossing

Rupert in charge

The crew celebrates a sucessful ocean crossing in IlhaBela.

Left to Right Rob, Dael, Rupert, the author.

The author in Parati Mirim, Ilha Grande

Jo does her shift on a rainy Christmas Day, 2009

The author and Lucy in Florianopolis, Brazil

Ilha Ancieta, Baia de Ilha Grande, Brazil

Mist rises from the jungle in Baia de Ilha Grande

Capybaras

"If you'll be my bodyguard
I will be your long lost pal,
I can call you Betty,
and Betty when you call me
you can call me Al..."

– Paul Simon

10

The breeze ruffling the shimmering sea slacked off to a mere ten knots, so we ran the motor to give *Josephine* a little extra push and charge the batteries. But we did not run the motor for long.

No more than two miles out of Rio Grande, the engine developed a dry rattle, coughed, then stalled. I restarted it, it ran – again the rattle – less than a minute, then it stopped again. And try as I might, I could not restart it a second time.

"What happened?" asked Abi.

"It rattled and died."

"Yes, I saw that. What's wrong with it?"

I had absolutely no idea. I am not a mechanic. I can replace a fan belt, or even change an oil filter; but the inner workings of an engine block remain a mystery to me.

We were faced with a dilemma. We did not fancy the prospect of another layover in Rio Grande, we were bored with it; and anyway it did not look like the best city for trying to get a yacht engine repaired. Added to that, the prospect of retracing our steps through the breakwaters and up the channels to the museum, against the out-flowing current, with only sails, was an unattractive one to say the least. There there was the spectre of getting all our passports and customs papers re-stamped. No, we were finally out, and not about to go back in.

The alternative was to sail on to Buenos Aires as intended, then at the last minute try to use the motor, however sick, to get onto a dock. There are some fifty-five yacht clubs in the greater Buenos Aires, so getting the motor repaired should pose no problem. We opted to keep going.

We sailed well that first day, catching *Azul* the same afternoon, in spite of her head start.

"*Josephine, esta muy rapido!*" hailed Oscar.

"Maybe not quite so *rapido* my friend!" I shouted back. "We have lost our engine!"

Oscar insisted on coming alongside and throwing me his aerosol can of "*Kwikstart*". I did not want to mess with the engine, fearing I might do yet more damage trying to start it again. If it had one start left in it, I wanted to save that for our arrival in Buenos Aires. Apart from that, those aerosols are not recommended for diesel engines. His English was not quite up to having this explained, so I went through the motions of pretending to try his spray, so as not to give offence.

Three more hours of good sailing brought us abeam of *Afun Davu* as the light was starting to fade over a purpling sea. We were making six knots in a fifteen knot breeze, but the Bavarian boat had only her headsail out as we came up on her.

"Ach ja, ve go slowly on. Ve are careful, ja!" Werner shouted across to us.

'*I'll say,*' I thought to myself. I was not sure how "careful" it actually was to hold the boat back in such good sailing conditions. It can be a treacherous bit of coast, with funny currents and shallows, and a tendency for very sudden, strong winds with steep, breaking seas. I think going faster is more careful, so you can get out of there before the elements conspire a change for the worse.

That night we were forced to gybe out to sea as the wind veered, and early next morning as we came back towards the coast at the end of our dogleg passed *Azul* for a second time. She had motored all night, and been able to take a more direct route.

After looking again at the chart I began to think it would be unwise to try getting into Buenos Aires without an engine, what with all the container ships we could expect to encounter on the River Plate. After debating the pros and cons, we settled on Piriapolis, in Uruguay. Pepe (with the road atlas) had told us there was a very good harbour in Piriapolis – although my pilot book, of course, said nothing, (the new one had never arrived in the post from Florianopolis). Also, Oscar was headed there with *Azul*, so we would have Spanish speaking friends on hand to help with communication.

The three-hundred-odd mile sail to Piriapolis was comfortable and uneventful. The sun was bright and warm, the consistent following winds of between ten and twenty knots ensuring we maintained good boat speed without straining anything. We shared the ocean with albatrosses and petrels, Right Whales and dolphins, but caught no fish, and arrived off Piriapolis in the late afternoon after two nights at sea.

There was a light breeze blowing offshore as we tacked up close to the thronging beach and dropped anchor, half a mile from the harbour over to our right. We were unsure how to raise anyone on the radio, as all the Spanish between us amounted to little more than "*gringo*", "*tequila*" and "*Real Madrid*" (the first two might be Mexican) and were happy to see out the afternoon and bed down where we were for the night. In the morning I would go ashore and look for Alejandro Martin, a resident sailor who had been recommended by a mutual friend as a good man to know if we ever found ourselves in Uruguay.

No sooner was the kettle boiling for afternoon tea, than an inflatable boat, driven by a young *Uruguayo* in naval uniform, came out of the port and pulled alongside. After a cheerful exchange of greetings, during which he welcomed us to Uruguay and introduced himself as Oaxington (pronounced "Washington") he managed to convey to us with a combination of slow Spanish words, some broken Portuguese, and a good deal of gesticulating, that we were illegally anchored and would have to move a hundred yards further back from the beach. This we were fortunate enough to be able to do with little fuss even though we had no motor, by hauling up enough chain to allow the anchor to drag slowly over the sand in the offshore breeze for a few minutes.

The encouraging upshot of this encounter with Oaxington, once we were able to explain to him we had no motor, was a promise to come out again before sunset and tow us into the harbour. At any rate that was how I interpreted our conversation; but evidently Oaxington had misunderstood my Portuguese, or I had misunderstood his Spanish, for we spent the rest of the evening waiting for the mystery tow, which never arrived. It was a still, warm night though, anchored off the busy beach gazing at the twinkling town lights and listening to the jolly sounds of a carousel, and we were quite happy to be left alone until the morning.

After breakfast the following day I made my way into the harbour, tied the dinghy up on the mussel-encrusted slipway next to a somnolent sea lion, and set off up the road in search of Alejandro with the aid of a rough map scribbled in the back cover of a paperback. It was a beautiful morning, dew sparkling like diamonds in the branches of the tamarisk trees lining the promenade, hungry egrets stalking the shallows between smooth round pebbles.

Within thirty minutes, I had found Alejandro – or Alex – at his house, and he and I were now back in the harbour borrowing a dinghy with a bigger motor than mine to go out and tow *Josephine.* Less than an hour after I had left the boat, I was back on board at the wheel with our "tug", manned by the competent Alex, lashed alongside. It was all over by ten o'clock – *Josephine* was securely moored to the quay inside the harbour and we found ourselves ensconced in Alex' house enjoying coffee and cake with his family.

Alex was a bull of a man. Forty-two years old, standing six foot five in his socks and weighing a hundred and twenty kilograms before breakfast, he had played rugby for Uruguay and been the national heavyweight boxing champion in his day. He left home at the age of seventeen, speaking not a word of English, and made his way to the Caribbean where he picked up a labouring job in a boatyard. He went on to work on boats and in yards all round the world, eventually becoming a successful skipper and delivering countless yachts across the world's oceans. Alex now has some 360,000 sailing miles in his logbook.

That morning he regaled us with amusing stories of his exploits, one of which involved a visit to Moorea, an island near Tahiti, where he was the skipper of a ninety-eight foot catamaran. He and his crew were anchored off a quiet beach when in the distance they saw an approaching motor boat that seemed to be trailing something large and awkward through the water. They watched as the motorboat drew nearer, until they saw what they thought looked like a cow dragging behind. And indeed a cow it was. A frozen cow. Apparently the cow had come all the way from New Zealand (presumably in the hold of a ship) for a "party" that coming weekend. The locals had nowhere to keep it frozen, so submerging it in sea water being the next best thing, would Alex mind terribly if they tethered it to his boat for a couple of days while it slowly thawed?

Alex agreed to tie the frozen bovine to his catamaran in exchange for an invitation to the party, and they had a deal.

"It take two days for this cow to come soft!" he told us.

The party, when it came, went on for three days, during which time nobody was allowed to leave. Alex was not even permitted to return to his boat to collect swimming trunks, and was forced to go swimming in his "interior pant". When too tired to drink or dance, he sneaked surreptitious naps hidden under a palm tree. After the party Alex and his hard drinking crew were known to the whole island, and for as long as they remained in Moorea were feted wherever they went.

***

Later that afternoon our new friend accompanied me back to the harbour to have a look at *Josephine*'s rattling engine, and it was soon obvious it would need to come out. Alex wasted no time arranging an overhaul in the meticulously clean workshop of a friend, and within a few days we had lifted the engine out with the aid of the boom and loaded it onto the back of Alex's truck.

"How long do you think this will take, Alex?"

"Ah," he replied. "I think one week to dissembly, one week to work, and one week to insembly. Then you go. Is like this."

We had not planned to spend three weeks in Piriapolis – but then we had not planned to destroy the engine, either. Three weeks did not sound unreasonable under the circumstance. Not that we had much choice. The matter was now out of our hands, but I was confident that in Alex we had found an ally.

In the event a further week was added for a holiday (it was carnival week); then another for "reparation" of the starter motor and alternator; yet another for the "enginating" of the injectors; then there was another holiday... and so it went. We resigned ourselves to an extended layover in Piriapolis and decided we may just as well make the most of it.

***

The town of Piriapolis was founded in 1893 by Don Francisco Piria as a holiday playground. Pan de Azucar, the third highest peak in Uruguay at 423m, stands five miles back from the beach, topped off with a hollow concrete cross inside which a spiral staircase winds up to little portholes in the arms that offer a spectacular view over the town and across the bay. The Don turned the hill into a quarry, reducing one side to stone from which the signature Hotel Argentino, as well as the mile-long sea wall that supports the *ramblas*, were built. Since his death the town of Piriapolis has been gradually supplanted by the glamorous, glitzy Punte del Este as Uruguay's premier holiday town, but with its wide, flat beach remains popular as the slightly cheaper, more family-orientated alternative.

Not long after we arrived in Piriapolis, I noticed a yacht anchored about two miles away from the harbour, across town at the far end of the beach. It was *Afun Davu*, carrying Werner and Emmy, who had also decided against going directly to Buenos Aires. They too had engine problems and needed help getting into the harbour. I went out to them in my dinghy, accompanied by Dael and the eternally grinning Omar from *Azul* (Oscar's chainsmoking sidekick). We helped Werner lash his inflatable to the side of *Afun Davu*, as Alex had done alongside *Josephine* a few days before, then Omar clambered aboard the yacht to steer (Emmy wanting nothing to do with it) while Werner stayed in his dinghy to operate its powerful motor.

Thus we set off across the bay towards the harbour; Werner alongside providing the push, Omar making a go of what appeared to be dodgy steering on *Afun Davu*, while I dashed around them in circles in my own dinghy shouting instructions and generally trying to look like I was co-ordinating the operation.

Omar was making heavy weather of the steering; the boat was all over the place, and it appeared there must be some sort of problem with the hydraulics. Yet Omar seemed to be rather enjoying the whole affair; in fact he was almost beside himself, roaring with laughter at everything and nothing, and waving his hands around above his head instead of maintaining a firm grip on the wheel.

"Ach, vot you are doink?!" Werner was shouting from his dinghy, "You don't must turn ze veel so much!"

"*Jaja! Soy una pirata! Yeeeeeee!*" responded the excited Omar.

"What's the hell's he doing?" Dael quizzed me.

"No idea. He's saying he's a pirate."

"No, vot iss ziss nonsense?" bellowed Werner, now getting angry. "Go careful on, ja!"

"*Holaaa! Andres!*" Omar called over to me in delight. "*Mirame*!" as he spun the wheel again.

"No Omar, I'm not watching you! And you just look where you're going please!"

"Andrew, ziss iss no goot!" Werner was verging on apoplexy. "Make him stop ziss or I shall strike him, ja!"

Only then did the realisation dawn on me that Omar was in fact drunk. It was barely ten o'clock in the morning, but come to think of it I had noticed he smelled faintly of red wine. Poor Werner, down alongside in his dinghy, doing his Bavarian best to be efficient, with an inebriated *Argentino* in command of his stricken yacht spinning the wheel with abandon and almost running him over. A quick change in personnel was needed.

I pulled alongside the yacht and Dael shimmied up the side to relieve the sodden Omar, who by then had already left the wheel, draping himself over the guardrail from where he could smoke a cigarette and leer down uncomprehendingly at Werner, who fumed ineffectually back at him.

With Dael at the wheel came a marked improvement in our progress, and in due course we goaded *Afun Davu* through the harbour entrance and round towards the quay. But just when I thought we had everything under control – *Afun Davu* coasting ever closer to her berth, *marineros* standing by to catch ropes – the impetuous Werner cast himself and his dinghy free of his yacht and sped back out into the basin from where he could get "*a goot view off ze operation.*" Now his yacht was without power, and under the gentlest of breezes blowing over the quay, the twenty ton *Afun Davu* slowly, inexorably drifted off in the opposite direction, eventually coming to rest against *Azul* on the opposite wall.

Thankfully *Azul* was a steel boat, and Oscar was a friend. With long ropes and many hands we were able to work the Bavarian yacht away from *Azul* and over to the quay where we finally made her secure under the concentrated scrutiny of a staring Omar the Pirate, now swaying on the dock clutching another cigarette and a bottle of red wine.

***

With both *Azul* and *Afun Davu* as neighbours, we were well on our way to recreating the little jetty community we had enjoyed in Rio

Grande some weeks before, and would often have dinner on each other's boats. One evening Emmy cooked up a feast of *eisbein* and *sauerkraut* for all and sundry in the harbour, and we used lumber from the boatyard to build an impromptu table to seat twenty. It was a fun evening, quaffing beer and wine under the stars between the boats that loomed silent and dark above us on their stands.

But life in Piriapolis just would not have been the same without Big Alex. Nothing was too much trouble for him. Over the three months spent waiting for our engine (yes, three months) Alex would regularly pile us all into his van amongst his wife and two little boys, and drive us across the countryside to the trendy beaches of Punte del Este, the shopping malls of Maldonado, the fascinating little ocean museum put together in someone's private shed (where Alex's younger son, Diego, was made to wait in the car because "*last time he dissembly the museum*") and the cable ferry across the lagoon at Jose Ignacio.

One of Alex's personal favourite places was "*Booger King*" in Punte del Este with its "*berry essellent boogers*". We were taken there several times. One day on the way to *Booger King* he caught sight of someone he knew by the roadside.

"We must to go around the block and come again in the street where is this old man just for to say hello."

We pulled up opposite a grey concrete bench, whereupon sat an grey old man with a long grey beard in faded grey clothes. Greetings were exchanged, a few salutary words shared, and we were on our way again without so much as getting out of the car.

"Do you see his hand?" asked Alex.

"No, I can't say I noticed his hand. Why?"

"It is destroy. He make a bad thing. He take a young girl in his house – young, young girl…"

"How young?"

"Oh, berry young.... less than thirty!"

"Oh, *that* young."

"Yes, of course! And they are drinking, and they sleep, and the fire come and eat his hand and he jump in the swimming pool to put away the fire. Now his hand is destroy."

"That's terrible!"

"Ah, but he berry rich," went on Alex. "Have many big land!"

"What is he doing just sitting there like that? He looks like a hobo."

"He say me he wait for someone to help him cross the street. But he don't ask me, and we go. If he want I help him, he must just to ask. But he not ask me."

I wondered whether that was a South American macho-complex: one too proud to ask for help, the other too proud to offer.

Alex really did have a big heart, though sometimes his kindness was almost too much. To be "*Alejandro-ed*" was akin to a sort of semi-voluntary kidnapping; not altogether unpleasant, but very time consuming. It could be frustrating when you had something more important to do – like read a book, or take an afternoon nap, or lie around doing nothing. Driving back one day from the hardware store with Alex, the local vet went by in the opposite direction and waved.

"Do you know him? He the doctor for the animals. He a berry essellent man."

"No, I don't know him."

"Do you know his house?"

"His house?..... um....no, I can't say...."

"No problem, we look now!" and spinning the car around we were off back the way we had come. I resigned myself to being Alejandro-ed once again and was duly shown the vet's rather unremarkable house. But Alex was not done.

"He have a partner too – I show you his house!"

Then of course I had to see where they worked – even though it, like both houses, was shut.

"No problem, we just pass to look".

It was not just we who were ferried around the country in Alex's van. One day he came by the port to pick me up to "go for a drive". There were two other men already in the car, who Alex was taking for medical appointments. "Now you go to see the hospital!" he announced with pride. One was an old man in a homburg hat who had been at Alex's house repairing his CD player, and managed to shoot himself in the eye with the laser. Alex explained that the old man shared a little house with his very fat, out of work computer technician son, aged forty, who refused to get out of bed before midday. The son's wife, who worked some afternoons as a cashier at a local supermarket, lived with them, and by all accounts spent most of her day in bed too. The old man worked all day then came home and cooked the meals and cleaned the house. He grinned toothlessly over the seat at me and told me he had a wonderful son.

***

The other passenger in the van was "Lejo"; middle-aged, overweight and balding, dressed in the broad black and yellow stripes of Penarol football club that made him look like a bumblebee. He had taken up beach soccer on a sudden impulse to get in shape. Someone had kicked the ball hard against his calf whereupon the muscle turned dark purple and a web of swollen blue veins erupted all over the leg like angry roots. He was now struggling to walk.

Lejo ran a light shop in town. For many years he had worked there behind the counter, and when the owner one day announced he was closing the business, along came Alex and bought the entire stock for ten thousand dollars and kept Lejo on. Within four months the stock was sold, Alex's ten thousand was recouped, and with the change Lejo was able to keep the store running by himself. Alex took no further interest in it.

"No, I was just to help him. I cost nothing. Now he have the shop, and when I need something, I pay. This is not my business."

I found it difficult to reconcile this Alex with the Alex who would not help an old man across a busy street unless he asked.

There were of course other colourful characters in Piriapolis, and not all of them Uruguayan. Being a pleasant, easy place to live, lots of foreigners seem to stop in Uruguay and never leave.

First there was Lennart, a sixty-year-old Swede in a little boat called *Cabo dos Hornos*, who had left everything behind in Sweden and set off in pursuit of his lifelong dream to sail around Cape Horn. He duly achieved that then ran out of ideas and stopped in Piriapolis "*to sink aboud id*". That was four years ago, and he was still sinking aboud id. Now he spent his time between the internet inside his boat in the harbour, and "Rotanda" – the local pub, on the side of a roundabout. Lennart was not afraid of a drink and once he started would not stop until he was unconscious. Then he would hide in his boat for several days to rebuild his courage for the next assault on his poor liver. He rationalised this for me one day, explaining it was all about balance.

"You canned haff fun effry day!" he pronounced in that melodic Swedish warble that Jamie Lee Curtis so successfully pulled off in the first Beverly Hills Cop movie. Then he admitted, "Yes, you can probably haff fun withoud drinking; bud why risk id?"

Lennart had a Canadian friend who went by the name Drake; a wiry, fit and very extrovert fifty-year-old Canadian who is the only person I have ever seen complete a twenty-five mile mountain bike race with a hangover, on an old single-speed shopping bicycle complete with basket on the handlebars. Perhaps he was still drunk.

There was also a very loud American couple about. Jean announced herself to us in the harbour one day as "the local representative of the Seven Seas Association" – a network of people (mainly American) with "an interest in cruising" according to their website. Her chief role seemed to be welcoming sailors to Piriapolis and trying to get them to swap their perfectly good books for the crappy torn paperbacks she had in the boot of her car. Her massively overweight husband Ralph, his arms wreathed in colourful tattoos, staggered about the place on hideously swollen legs with a constant wheeze. At every turn he ran Uruguay down and told me how useless everything was, "unlike the States". He and Jean would organise regular monthly lunches for the resident ex-pat community.

"Anyone is welcome, the only condition is they must be English speaking!"

We found this anomalous with choosing to live in a foreign country and managed to avoid these exclusive events. I never did understand why they had chosen to live there. Perhaps they were running away from something.

And then there was Laurence. Laurence, Irish, thirty-three, had been cruising the world with his wife when they stopped for a layover in Piriapolis to do some work on their yacht. A naval architect by profession, after sketching some rough designs for a pilot boat Laurence had been commissioned by the Uruguayan government to supervise the building of a boat in Montevideo. When we met him he was nearing the end of his second year in Uruguay. We never did see his yacht though – by the time we arrived, his wife was at sea, sailing it back to the UK, alone, in preparation for a solo ocean race.

In Laurence we found a kindred spirit. In addition to sailing he was a keen mountain biker and runner, so Abi and I had a running partner in Piriapolis. In time we became very close. He helped us arrange some work on *Josephine* (there was a leak in one of our water tanks) and even lent us his car when he went to the UK for a few weeks. Laurence would pop by the boat most mornings for coffee and pastries on his way to work, and doted on Lucy. She in turn adored her "Leelaw".

One such morning Laurence appeared at the boat bearing a gift. A bicycle. Actually it was not much more than a heap of rust, with no pedals, but the frame was sound enough, and with a little tender loving care and some new pedals it polished up quite well – and bright pink. It was just the thing for those early morning runs to the bakery.

Then a few days later an orange boat arrived flying a French flag.

"Ah, *Karthik*!" exclaimed Laurence. "That was their bicycle you know. They gave it to me when they were here last year."

That afternoon, while I was off somewhere, Abi heard someone fiddling around outside the boat, and poked her head out just in time to see a man making off with her pink bicycle.

"Excuse me, where are you going with that?"

"This is my bicycle," came the gruff reply.

"No, its *my* bicycle!" she retorted.

"Where did you get it?" challenged the Frenchman.

"From Laurence."

To that the Frenchman snorted and stalked off – with the bicycle. Abi was alone at the time and did not know how to stop him.

When I returned to the boat and she told me the story I was furious, but thought it best to double check with Laurence before making a scene and embarrassing myself. By the time I had been able to clear with Laurence that yes, it really had been *given* to him, the orange boat had left – pink bicycle and all.

Alex became animated that evening when I related the story to him.

"Ah, yes, I remember him to last year! That Frenchman! He is a fucking!"

"What, you know him?" I asked.

"Of course! Last year he steal me. He take my blocks from my boat. But I catch him, and then he go away berry fast! He is a stealer man!"

It seemed the Stealerman had just done it again. But as things turned out, it was not to be the last we saw of him.

***

During our enforced hiatus in Piriapolis, we bade farewell to Dael as he left the boat for an independent backpacking sojourn around South America, after which he flew back to his university responsibilities. Rupert was still surfing his way around the continent after our ocean crossing, and several weeks later made his way to Uruguay to come and see us. He slotted into the family straight away, and it was an easy decision for both him and us that he join the boat for the rest of the year.

The harbour in Piriapolis had cats. They lived amongst the rocks piled against the breakwater, and while we were there one had kittens. Most afternoons we would walk Lucy along the wall to feed them, and it was on one such expedition that I noticed a whelk the size of my fist stuck to a rock about two feet below the surface. I pulled it out, and saw it was the same as one Paulet had shown me at his oyster farm in Florianopolis. I remembered too that he, as well as his staff, had been effusive in their praise of its gastronomic value. Back on the boat, I boiled it until it frothed, yanked it out of its shell with a screwdriver and bit into it. Not bad at all. Quite rich. So without further ado, I co-opted Rupert and together we dived off the seawall with gloves and a net bag, and harvested some five dozen more – but not before being severely stung about the face and neck swimming through a cloud of jellyfish. They trailed long wispy threads of poisonous stingers like an invisible curtain across the rocks, and diving and twisting between them to get at the snails I amused myself by imagining I was a pilot dodging barrage balloons above London during the Blitz. Until, that is, it occurred to me I would have to be German.

For good measure we also collected a large pot of mussels. After scrubbing the shells, I boiled and cut up the whelks while Rupert cooked the mussels with rice and vegetables, and that evening we sat down to a large bowl of paella. It was delicious – and free – and the burning welts around our necks just made us feel even more like intrepid hunter-gatherers.

***

As tranquil a place as Piriapolis was, there were exciting moments too. One night we were woken by a loud commotion in the harbour. It sounded like someone was being beaten up. Rupert and I shot out of the boat and sprinted across the yard in the direction of the bathrooms, from where the noise was coming. It was the noise of pure rage. There was a man's voice and he was screaming in English.

As we dodged barefoot between the boats in the yard, we almost ran headlong into Jo, who was striding purposefully in the other direction, signalling us to stay quiet.

"Go back!" she hissed. "For goodness sake!"

"But what the hell is going on?" I gasped, short of breath.

"It's only *Werner*! He lost it with the security guard. Now the *Prefectura* is here, and they are threatening to arrest him. Stay out of it, you'll only make it worse!"

"*Lost* it? Lost *what*? It's eleven o'clock at night for heaven's sake!"

But Jo was waving us away. We followed, and she grinned enigmatically all the way back to the boat. The sound of Werner's wrath was still ringing across the yard. It was all very odd.

"So are you going to tell us?" I asked as we clambered aboard, and Jo dissolved in a fit of giggles.

"It was nothing! We were using the ladies loo for my therapy session and the guard saw the light. When he came in and found Werner massaging me on the bench – well, he didn't think it was right."

"Oh, not again – shades of the Antarctica shed in Rio Grande! This *is* funny!"

"When he asked what we thought we were doing," she went on, "Werner replied in German and made massaging motions with his hands. Obviously the guard got the wrong idea altogether."

"Yes, no wonder! Ha ha!"

Rupert was loving this too. He had heard all about the incident with Ayrton at the museum in Brazil.

"At that point it would have been fine," continued Jo, "only Werner refused to leave. He couldn't see why the guard wouldn't let us finish up and it turned into a flaming row."

This was getting better and better. I did not suppose Werner would have confronted Ayrton in Rio Grande with quite as much bravado; Ayrton was armed.

"So the guard called the navy and now Werner wants to fight them all."

I could see why she didn't want us in there. We retreated into the saloon and put the kettle on as we waited for the din to subside. Eventually Werner appeared alongside our boat, alone and breathing heavily. I wondered whether he had killed them all.

"Zey are so stupid!" he ranted. "I am a professional! Zere is nobody using ze toilets in zis time off night!"

It was an outrage and he had worked himself into a Teutonic lather. He assumed the stance of an old-fashioned prize fighter, fists high and turned backwards. “When somebody show me ze provocation I take it up, ja!” he shouted, dancing about like Jack Broughton.

It seemed once they had managed to get him out of the women’s bathrooms, both port security and the navy had lost the stomach for a confrontation and released Werner on his own recognisance. Just as well for them probably.

Alex just loved the story when I related it to him the next day; by now he had met Werner and formed a firm opinion of him.

“Unbelievy!” he exclaimed. “If you put him furious, he is untalkable!”

Lucy’s first birthday was one of the social highpoints of our time in Piriapolis. I hoisted the number one signal flag to the top of the mast and we bought cake for everyone in the port. Alex and his wife Rita went one better; they organised an *asado* at their house, which was attended by all our friends from the other boats in the harbour as well as the locals we had come to know. Lucy had been walking for two months and was strutting her stuff with Alex’s boys while the adults tackled a challenging pile of meat which was washed down with an endless supply of beer and single malt. All very civilized.

Sitting dram in hand on his balcony overlooking the bay as the sun sank orange and bloated over the River Plate while yet more hamburgers sizzled in the fireplace, we were grandly entertained with another of Alex’s stories. When he and Rita first met, Alex had a cat. Not an ordinary cat mind you; a *gato montana*, or “mountain cat”. Something close to a small puma by the sounds of it, which would attack anyone and everyone at the drop of a hat. Once it got out of the house and ambushed a pedestrian, and Alex had to rush out onto the street to rescue the unwitting victim.

“I must to put the separation to the cat and the man,” he explained. “The cat bite me a lot! My arms are destroy.”

Rita could not go to the bathroom alone at night, and Alex's forearms were permanently lacerated from wrestling the cat under control. But Alex loved his cat, and it would go everywhere with him in his car, much like a dog; except that Alex could never actually *put* it in the car. If he tried, it would savage his arms; so they developed a ritual.

"We have understanding. I open the door, and I stand, but I no look, and very slowly, he come, and he looking to the car, and if I watch, he don't come; but if I watch another way, he go in the car. Always is like this."

One day Alex arrived home and realised the cat was no longer in the car. "*Where the cat can to be?*" he asked himself. The last time he had seen the cat was when he stopped for fuel. "*Ah yes, the gassy station!*"

"So I return there, but nobody see the cat. Then one old lady across the road she say to me "*Yes, I see the cat; he take one dog, and he go! Boom! Like this!*" (clapping his hands) "*Now the cat is inside the engine of the car of the man, and the man and the dog is inside the house, and they wait for you and the dog is berry bad.*"

So Alex ventured down the road, found the house of the man of the very bad dog, and heard his cat growling under the bonnet of the car of the man. He then returned to the gassy station for coffee and a sandwich, and waited.

"One hour and half, then when I see the light of the house go down I know they are sleeping, and I return to take my cat, and I go".

He did have to coax it out with a sausage though.

***

By now it was early May and we had been in Piriapolis about ten weeks when shouts of "Andrew! Andrew!" pierced my afternoon nap and dragged me woolly-headed into semi-consciousness. What the hell...? Everyone on the boat was asleep; then I recognised the voice.

"Oh God, it's Alex," I muttered to Rupert, who was now also awake. "I really don't want to be Alejandro-ed."

But Alex was so kind, it would not do to be rude and lie low.

"Just coming!" I yelled as I struggled up, tripping on the steps. "Yes Alex!" I tried to appear alert and awake. It was an effort.

"We go now for your engine!" he announced from the quay.

"What?...um... yeah.... okay.... " then a pause as it sank in. "What, now?"

"Yes, of course!" he exclaimed. Everything with him was 'of course' as if there could never be any doubt.

"Ah," I replied. "Of course...."

'*Right, **now**?*' I thought to myself. The boat was a mess; it certainly was not ready to receive the engine. And I had fallen asleep after getting back from a run, was filthy, and pretty sure I smelled terrible. I could have done with a shower. And I wanted to film the return of the engine too, so needed to get the camera gear ready...

Alex picked up the business end of our hose where it lay on the dock.

"You have soap?"

'*Ah good,*' I thought, '*he's going to let me have a quick spray-down*'.

"But of course!" I shouted back. "Just a minute...."

Wading through the scattered cushions and baby toys to reach the heads, I grabbed a clean pair of shorts from the laundry bucket. Finding the soap took several minutes. I smeared it all over my chest and arms, generous under the armpits. After matting my hair down with a thick coating, it was back up through the cockpit and onto the quay.

Alex has just finished washing his hands. From a water bottle. With his own soap, from his car. He had not been thinking of my need of a shower at all. And my hose was nowhere in sight. It had been borrowed by someone from another boat.

"Okay, we go now!" announced Alex, holding the car door open for me.

There I stood; filthy, almost naked and covered in a layer of soap, hair spiked up like a punk, and no hose.

"Yes Alex, but of course."

***

Autumn was slipping towards winter and a steady drizzle was leaking out of a grey sky when a low, very old wooden sloop with *Yamandu* painted on her prow crept into the harbour. In the little boat were two wet men: one enormous, the size of Alex; the other shorter, but next to his shipmate seeming a lot smaller than he really was. We immediately dubbed them Asterix and Obelix. The little *Yamandu* came gently alongside the wall behind us and tied up. I noticed they had no motor – they had done a better job of getting in than we had.

With the rain teeming down, we watched the two Gauls wrestle a white tarpaulin over their boom like a tent. The wind was lifting it up like Marilyn Monroe's skirt and blowing the rain in sideways. It did not look like they were in for a comfortable night. I donned my jacket and ventured outside.

"*Hola!*" I shouted above the wind. "Hello!"

Asterix gave a cheery wave. "*Hola*!"

"Do you speak English?!"

"*Ahmmm… mas o menos*!"

That seems to be the stock answer for everyone in Uruguay. More or less. What it actually *means* is "*Yes, if I absolutely have to, but I'd rather not as it is a little embarrassing.*"

"Good. I don't speak Spanish, sorry!"

"Okay, no problem, we speak English for you!" Asterix had an easy, open laugh for someone so wet and cold. I would have been thoroughly grumpy in his state.

"Please get out of this rain, you're making me cold to look at you. Come aboard our boat and get dry. Dinner will be ready in half an hour, and we've made too much!"

They were delighted, and provided excellent company.

Their real names were Eduardo (the medium sized one) and Alejandro (the enormous one). Both were Uruguayan. They had set out from Montevideo in their beautiful seventy-five-year-old boat intending to sail the eighty miles to Punte del Este, but after fifty miles in atrocious weather were only too happy to put in at Piriapolis. In the end they stayed three days, and we had them over for dinner and drinks each evening, getting to know them well. Little did Edu and I know it was to be the start of a long and enduring friendship that would take us thousands of miles together by sea, sharing all manner of adventure across three countries. It was a chance meeting that would change the course of his life.

"Ach, but ziss iss a choke!"

– Werner the Bavarian

11

With the engine finally back in the boat we were preparing to leave Piriapolis after having been there almost three months, when Laurence announced he was entering a triathlon, and would Abi like to enter too so they could compete in the "mixed team" category? They had, after all, run together a few times.

I found this a ridiculous notion, and said so. We were finally supposed to be sailing again.

"Why would you want to waste another two weeks hanging about here after we've already been here three months?" I asked Abi petulantly. "And it's not as if you've been training for this triathlon – you wouldn't exactly miss it!"

"Well I just think it would be fun, and after everything Laurence has done for us here it would be nice to do it with him."

"This is stupid," I snorted. I really was grumpy, I wanted to get on.

"Why don't you do it too?" Abi ventured.

"What? Now you are being ridiculous," and I sulked.

Later that day Alex came by to visit. He had heard about the triathlon.

"Ah Andrew, but of course, you must to race with my bike!"

He had a lovely new mountain bike that he had paid a lot of money for. It was his pride and joy.

"No Alex, thank you. I am not interested."

"Ah but you are fit! You should to race!"

"No, I'm not fit. I've been running a little, but not much, and have not been on a bicycle for six years. Anyway, I can't. We're leaving Piriapolis this week."

The next day I accompanied Abi and Laurence to enter their silly triathlon.

"Alex tells me you are racing on his bike?" asked Laurence.

"He says what? *I'm* not racing. I told him that. You're lucky we're still here at all mate."

"Come on!" teased Laurence. "You're staying now for Abi, you may as well enter the race and do it yourself."

"It's eight days away for God's sake. There's no way I'm entering any triathlon, and that's final!"

***

Immediately after paying for my entry I ran 15km and got back to the boat shattered. The triathlon would consist of a 12km trail run, followed by a 24km mountain bike ride and 3km paddle in the sea in a plastic canoe (the type that is rented out to holidaymakers on the beach). My problem was that I had not run anything longer than 10km in a year; I had not paddled a canoe at all in that time; and I had not so much as *sat* on a bicycle in six years. Literally. And now I had eight days to prepare.

Legs stiff and sore from my inspired 15km run, the next morning I borrowed Alex's bike and climbed the two hills that were to be part of the following week's race course. They were hell. After the two climbs I cycled along the beach road for a way, and by the time I was done I had tendonitis in my left knee and a stiff back to add to my already sore calves.

I awoke the next day – Sunday – with knots in my back, sore legs, a painful knee and bruised bum from Alex's saddle. There was no option but to get back on the bike though, if I was going to do this ridiculous race. The hills felt worse the second day and I was reduced to walking up both of them. Towards the end of the ride, coasting downhill under braking, the handlebars came loose and spun away beneath me, and I was pitched head first over the front wheel onto the tar, bashing my knee and shoulder. Fortunately there was no damage to Alex's new bike – which landed on top of me – but I was utterly spent.

Monday dawned. I sat in the boat feeling sorry for myself nursing a painful shoulder, a grazed and swollen knee, stiff back and neck, tight calves, sore bum and a bruised ego. '*Maybe I really am forty five after all*' I thought gloomily. This was not looking good. I lay back down on my bunk and admitted to myself that the best thing today would be to get some rest.

Tuesday I felt a little better, although my knee still hurt, and I joined Laurence for a "technical" ride. That is to say we went slowly and carefully over the rougher parts of the bike route, to check it out. It had been raining all night and the course had been reduced to a bog. Not being any good at riding uphill on tyres caked with mud I was forced to walk the bike. Alex's shoes (I had no cycling shoes of my own on the boat) were clogged with mud, bits of gravel cemented into the cleats. I took the bike back to the harbour for a good wash before Alex saw it, then after taking it home to him I returned to run over the course. The wet clay made it almost impossible to run and I slipped and fell three times. Race day would be impossible if it was this wet.

My sore throat started on Wednesday morning. Lucy had been fighting a cold for five days, so it was only a matter of time before one of us went down. I gargled an antiseptic and looked out at the rain. There was no sign of it letting up. It occurred to me that this might be a good thing. If it was muddy enough, *nobody* would be able to ride over those rocks, and we would all be in the same position pushing our bikes. As I am a better runner than cyclist, this might suit me. I started to fantasise about being competitive – *maybe if I could have a good run and be up near the front, then not lose too much on the bike if we all walked… maybe targeting a top ten finish would not be unreasonable? Nobody knows me here. I could use the element of surprise!*

Reality Check: What was I thinking? Over-ambitious, over-confident, over-aged, overweight… *idiot.* It was my first time on a bike in six years; I'd do well to finish the thing and still be able to walk afterwards.

Thursday was designated another "rest" day on account of the weather – it blew a gale all day and the rain did not let up. I gargled antiseptic again and nursed my aching knee. All this rest had to be doing me good – like an Olympian, peaking for the big event. Hah!

The weather on Friday morning was much improved, scattered cumulus dazzling white against the pale autumn sky. I drenched my sore throat with antiseptic and ventured out for a short jog. My new shoes gave me a blister for my trouble.

Saturday – the evening before the race – we were all invited to Alex's house for a "*pancho* party" (a *pancho* is a hotdog.) Alex and Rita grilled a mountain of little pink sausages, wrapped around with bacon, in the hearth. Werner and Emmy were there too.

"Tomorrow is big race!" Alex boomed at me. "You go fast!"

"I wouldn't know about that…"

"Ha, I see you in the street, running. You go strong!"

"Alex has been bigging you up all over town," observed Laurence with a grin.

"What are you talking about?" I asked warily.

"He's been telling everyone you're some or other champion and you're using his bike. I think you should expect quite a crowd."

This I did not need. It was ridiculous.

"Ach so," came in Werner, very serious. As a physiotherapist who had also been a competitive weightlifter, he was particularly interested in my training regimen. "Tell me about your trainink. I know about ziss sinks. Tell me vot haff you done?"

When I told him I had just done my first bike ride in six years, his expression changed completely.

"Ach, but ziss iss a choke!" he dismissed me with a wave and stalked off shaking his head.

No doubt. How had I got into this in the first place? We really should have sailed away a week ago. This was going to be silly.

***

Race day dawned beneath overcast skies, a strong wind from the south making it nippy. We collected paddles and lifejackets at the check-in point, put our bikes on the racks and laid out our kit. The start was scheduled for ten o'clock.

The race got underway in cold weather with a useful tailwind, and I slotted in comfortably enough behind the leader at the start of the run. We dropped the rest of the field almost immediately, and although I knew this would be too fast for me for to maintain, I was content to run at this tempo for the two miles of waterfront and build a gap before the hills started. I focused on the black running tights in front of me and tried not to think about how fast we were going.

Our lead had stretched to some two hundred yards over the chasing pack when I took a last look before turning left away from the sea and up the first hill. And what a hill! About three hundred yards long, but *so steep* – it was all I could do to not walk. Legs burning, short chopped stride, lungs bursting… and this no more than eleven minutes in! The race would take over two hours; what kind of trouble could I get myself into being this out of breath so early on?

At the top of the hill Black Tights just took off. I barely managed to keep him in view for the rest of the run, losing sight of him periodically on the more technical parts of the trail, but at the end of the seven miles came into transition still in second place, only about a minute down. I had been able to limit the damage so far.

Alex and Werner were beside themselves.

"*Venga* Andrew, you go strong!" from the enthusiastic Uruguayan, and "*Ach nein*, ziss iss too fast!" from the more cynical, knowing Bavarian.

A minute in a run is about three hundred yards, and looks like a lead that can be controlled; but once you get on a bike it opens to twice the distance, and suddenly closing it down looks a lot less feasible. A gap like that on a course with a lot of turns means you don't see the competitor ahead, and your psychology changes. You go from chasing someone you can see, to worrying more about the person behind you, who you can't see.

The first hill on the bike was hell, but short; and anyway, as I still could not see anyone behind me, I was content to pace myself and just try to maintain a rhythm and get the hill over and done with. Just over the top I turned onto the rough stuff, and was abruptly forced off the bike by my lack of technical skill and left walking. I dragged the bike up a narrow track over sharp rocks and remounted at the top of a rise, then rode the brakes for the full three hundred yards down a steep, stony, tight path with trees on my left and a wire fence on my right, the rocks and roots in the path all trying their utmost to throw my front wheel out and snag my handlebars on a fence post. Finally I made it to the bottom, dismounting again to lift the bike over a ditch and onto the gravel road. Looking back I was relieved to see no pursuers.

Ten minutes later came another really steep climb (this time on tarmac, thankfully) and it was all I could do to not walk; then left off the road into a wet and muddy forest where I somehow managed to keep the wheels turning through the cloying mud, over the roots and between the rocks to the brow of a hill.

Down the other side I was braking again, dodging more rocks and dismounting to negotiate a swamp, carrying the bike through a gate back onto the road where I was able to get underway once more. From there I knew it was just two miles of tarmac road back to the transition – and then I would have to ride it all over again. The second lap was going to be purgatory.

By the time I started lap two, I was cramping badly in both calves. My lack of fitness meant the extreme exertion of standing to work up the steeper parts of the route had eaten into my legs, and I was pleased to have a flat couple of miles along the beachfront in which to spin in a lighter gear and try and recover.

I suffered up the first hill once more, again managing somehow to keep the bike moving, until I reached the turnoff to the bush track. Almost immediately I went off line and hit a large rock which stopped me dead. There was no chance of a remount as the slope was too steep, so I set off up the path on foot, as fast as I could (which probably was not very fast). After some minutes I became aware of someone puffing behind me, and turned to see the third placed athlete breathing down my neck. It occurred to me that once he caught me he would probably go past, and then I would be giving up places the rest of the ride.

This notion gave me a surge of adrenalin, and from the summit I took off down the narrow trail next to the fence as if I were being pursued by some incarnation of hell itself. I was petrified; thorny branches whipping past my face, the fence a blur at my right hand, the bike bucking and leaping over the rocks with a life of its own. The only reason I didn't fall off was I was too frightened, and when I made it to the road at the bottom I even jumped the ditch without slowing before I looked back up the hill and saw … nobody! I had ridden away from him. That felt good, and infused with a new confidence I powered off down the road.

A couple of miles on gravel, with nothing more than a few erosion ruts and one or two sharp turns to contend with, and I was climbing the last steep hill of the day. Determined not to be caught, I alternated sitting and standing to vary the muscle groups and made it up to the turn into the forest.

Unfortunately the adrenalin, and the extra effort it had induced, now brought on another bout of cramp, and as my left calf screwed itself into a tight ball it was all I could do to get my foot out of the cleat and down to the ground before falling over. I was reduced to walking again. I tried to run, but the violent contractions in my leg made that impossible, so I hobbled up the muddy track until the slope levelled off and I was able to get back on the infernal bike.

The plunge down the other side was one of the most terrifying things I have ever done on a bicycle. It was a very narrow, slippery track with steep drop-offs into black pools of unreadable depth lined with ragged tree stumps and sharp boulders. The trail itself was littered with rocks; some rooted firmly in the clay, others just piled loosely on top of each other. I knew it was no more than half a mile, then it would be back on the road the rest of the way; I just needed to negotiate this obstacle course without losing more time. Half standing to keep my weight on the pedals, allowing the bike to pivot under me like I had seen on television, I positioned my body well back over the saddle, loosened my grip on the handlebars as much as I dared and allowed the front wheel to find its own path. I bounded down the hill holding my breath.

I had no idea a bicycle could do that. It was like riding a horse. Cavorting and leaping over the rocks with my heart in my mouth, I tore down frozen with terror but somehow defied the laws of physics and stayed upright. It was like an extreme video game, where the path keeps coming at you and you have to react without thinking and try not to hit anything.

I dropped steep down into the last left turn, keeping it tight to avoid the swamp I knew was coming up, and that was when I saw him. A back-marker, still on his first lap. He had stopped and climbed off, and was picking his way through the mud on foot.

For me it was too late; I was simply going too fast to have any hope of stopping. I jerked the bike over to the right missing him by inches, but was carrying too much speed to be able to correct. I shot by the far side of the swamp and ploughed into a nest of jagged boulders. The front wheel slammed over sideways and the bike catapulted through the air. Momentum threw me clear over the rocks, and I came down on a gatepost. Fortunately, although it was the thickness of a telegraph pole, it was rotten and disintegrated under the impact, uprooting two more posts in the process. I marvelled as I lay there in a heap of broken stakes and rusty barbed wire with nothing worse than a bleeding shin and a scraped forearm.

Pulling myself together, I retrieved Alex's beautiful new bike from the sucking mud and sped off down the road for the final stretch to the beach. I had no idea what was going on behind me, or how much time I had lost on the leader, but I knew I was still second. I was determined nobody would catch me in these last two miles of the ride.

Almost before I knew it I was back in transition, jumping off the bike, snatching up my paddle and lifejacket, and running down the sand dragging a canoe. In my socks. I ran into the surf, kept running until it was thigh deep, then clambered on and paddled furiously over the breaking waves and away from the beach.

The offshore breeze had turned the remains of a southerly swell into a short chop that was difficult to negotiate in the very wide, heavy plastic canoe, but it would be the same for everyone. Then I saw Black Tights again. He was closer than I expected, which gave me another rush of adrenalin and I set off in pursuit.

It was a two mile (3km) paddle from the beach to the harbour and back, and I was about three minutes off the lead. After several minutes I looked back to find Black Tights and I were still the only two on the water, so was able to relax a little and concentrate on closing down the gap ahead. At the half way point I thought he looked a little closer, though I couldn't be sure; but as I turned I was alarmed to see the third and fourth placed athletes on the water, working together, powering up on me. That was all I needed – second all day, then lose two places in the last ten minutes!

That is not going to happen. I dug in again, really hard. *Another half mile.* I managed to surf a few runs, even in that ridiculous plastic tub, and pick up a little speed, and with half a kay to go realised I had actually made up quite a bit on my friend ahead. The chasers behind were making no gains, and I went at it even harder as I realised Black Tights had not read the water correctly. He had allowed himself to be forced downwind and was now battling the waves from side-on trying to reach across to the beach, whereas I was riding them in.

But in the end it was not enough, and as I surfed in on the shore-break I watched my quarry running up the steps to the road, and over the finish line. I dragged my canoe up the sand and jogged in a very tired, but happy, second.

"*Prima puesto! La primera master*!" blared the public address system. "First place!"

It was a little while before it sank in that he meant me. "Master" was anyone over forty; so I *had* won – if you look at it that way. All things considered I had nothing to be unhappy about, with a gold medal and a thousand pesos to take back to the boat.

Abi and Laurence finished happy and tired after a storming paddle which saw them move from seventh to fourth in the mixed doubles race, just missing out on the podium, and we all adjourned to Alex's house to grill hamburgers in the fireplace of his sitting room.

"I say you go fast!" beamed Alex. "Is my bike!"

He was thrilled. Not even the nasty, deep scratches to the paintwork of his smart new aluminium frame bothered him. "Ha, look at this! Now I tell everyone is a champion do this to my bike!"

"Ach ja," chipped in Werner. "I tell you ziss voss no choke!"

"No two languages are ever sufficiently similar to be considered as representing the same social reality."

– Edward Sapir

12

It was mid May when we finally sailed out of Piriapolis, our engine whole again. Three months had gone by, but it had not been wasted time; we had a lot of fun and made some good friends, and by the time we left the sleepy little beach town was almost home. Not that we were sorry to be on our way; the promise of new adventures was pulling again.

Forty miles to the west, within sight of the capital Montevideo, lies the rocky little island of *Isla Flores*. There was no information in any of our guide books, and very little detail on the charts; but our new friend Eduardo (Asterix from the little wooden *Yamandu*) assured us it was possible to stop over on the island.

"So long you know the authorities, because normal ees not allow thees," he explained.

And he, apparently, *did* know the authorities. That is to say, he knew the lighthouse keeper. Some time back he had arrived there unannounced and without a permit, but because he happened to number the then 'Miss Uruguay' among his passengers that day, an open invitation to come back again anytime was easily elicited. Now Edu had secured the necessary permission for us to visit, and was adamant the old stone harbour was safe.

"Yes, no problem, you can get een," he assured us. "Eet ees deep."

***

We had planned to meet up with Edu at the island around five o'clock in the afternoon, when he should be there with a couple of his friends for an *asado*, but we were a little late sailing out of Piriapolis, and when we finally arrived at *Isla Flores* after a day of pleasant sunshine (but with a chilly breeze) it had been dark almost an hour. There was no moon. Wary of the rocks south of the island, we stuck to the twenty foot depth contour round the point, then turned back up the other side towards where the old harbour was meant to be. We could see nothing. The light from the lighthouse made it worse as it swept around in its arc and blinded us every twelve seconds. We ventured as close as we dared in a twenty knot onshore breeze under a blanket of darkness, then from twenty yards away could just make out the shape of the stone breakwater. The entrance looked tight, and in the dark, with this wind, it was a definite no-go.

We tried calling Edu, but his phone was off. There was no sign at all of any activity on the island. No boat was in the harbour, and there certainly did not appear to be an *asado* on the go. Reluctantly we agreed on discretion as the better part of valour, and turned for Montevideo.

But just as we faced south and bore away, faint red and green lights pricked the gloom ahead of us, and a white sailed ghosted out of the darkness. It was *Yamandu*.

"*Hola!*" cheered Edu, waving with his free arm while holding his *mate*[*] thermos and clinging to the tiller with the other. "Nobody come, I am alone! But don' worry, for me ees the same. We make an *asado* now!" He was irrepressible.

It was agreed we should anchor outside the harbour for the night. Edu attached *Yamandu* to our stern with a long rope so she could float off downwind, and we dropped our anchor in twenty feet of water. The barbecue on deck was fired up in spite of the now bitter cold, and we feasted on medium rare "*cuadril*" (a similar cut to rump steak) and sausages washed down with a very agreeable Argentine wine.

It turned out that Edu's friends had pulled out at the eleventh hour. He himself had originally set sail around four o'clock, only to realise – horror of horrors – he had forgotten his *mate* and was compelled to turn back. In the end he did not leave Montevideo until it was already dark.

"No problem for me!" he exclaimed, flashing those white teeth. "But I can't call you because my phone ees at home. I forget. Ha ha!"

After dinner we settled down for the night, Edu sleeping in *Josephine's* saloon, but later the wind picked up to over thirty knots and we were being blown towards the island. The anchor was hauled up and we motored out another half mile before putting it down again with a hundred and twenty feet of chain. The depth was still less than

* Mate – pronounced "mutt-ay", the stress on the first syllable – is a hot drink infused from the caffeinated herb "yerba mate", and drunk out of a wood or leather gourd – itself called a 'mate', to keep things simple – by sipping it through a silver straw, or bombilla. It is more than just a hot drink in Uruguay; it is a fixation. Uruguayans go everywhere with a thermos of boiling water wedged under one arm, and most have scars on the backs of their hands from spilling their mate while driving. Edu is no exception to this national obsession.

twenty feet, but within half an hour, in spite of all that chain, we were dragging again. We watched the GPS as we were blown back twenty metres, then stopped. We kept a close eye for half an hour, then without warning we dragged again, another twenty yards closer to the island. This pattern repeated itself, with periodic drags whenever the action of the waves whipped up by the thirty knot wind worked the anchor loose. The bottom was rock, and the anchor was alternately snagging and coming off again, and the additional weight of *Yamandu* hanging off our transom and bucking like a bronco was not helping. We sat at the chart table, eyes glued to the GPS screen as, bit by bit, we were blown closer and closer to the island. This was not going to stop until we were on the rocks. Obviously that would not do, so once again we weighed anchor; only this time we motored round the southern tip of the island, looking to get out of the worst of the wind, but where we would be among a lot of hazardous rocks. We tucked in close behind the lighthouse, between the cliff and a wreck, in fifteen feet of water, then dropped anchor with as much chain as we thought prudent given that we did not want to swing in too wide an arc. But *Yamandu* was leaping and snatching at her tow-line, and within minutes we were dragging again. At least this time we were being blown away from the island, not towards it.

But after a couple of boat lengths the anchor held again, and we spent the next hour staring at the GPS and making small talk. By one thirty, with the anchor seemingly set, we agreed to take turns at ninety minute anchor watches until daylight. I took the first watch, and by three o'clock, when I woke Edu, the wind had dropped to around twenty knots. We had not moved at all during my watch. By sunrise the wind was down around fifteen knots, and though exhausted we were all in good spirits. Not even the discovery that *Yamandu*'s towline had somehow wrapped itself around our rudder could dampen the mood.

Rupert was zipped into a wetsuit and sent down into the frigid brown water to sort it out while the rest of us hugged steaming hot coffees and imparted uninvited wisdom from the comfort of the cockpit.

After breakfast we chugged around to the old harbour, seagulls mewing and wheeling high and white against an ivory sky. Edu worked the little *Yamandu* carefully into the tight space between the dun stone walls as we watched from the deck of *Josephine*. The moustachioed lighthouse keeper, ubiquitous thermos nestled in the crook of his elbow, was on hand to take a rope. With *Yamandu's* three foot draught Edu was being very careful; with our six foot keel I was taking no chances at all, and tied up to the outside of the quay.

Isla Flores was first developed in 1527 as a quarantine camp for arriving immigrants from Spain, and for those individuals not fortunate enough to survive the quarantine period a cemetery sprang up at the northernmost end of the island. The camp was destined later to become a prison for political prisoners.

The lighthouse in its one hundred foot white tower was built by the Portuguese in 1828, during one of their ascendant moments on the river, and at the time was billed as the worlds "most expensive". The Uruguayan navy still keeps a two-man team on the island to maintain it, and it remains the most important physical navigation aid for ships approaching Montevideo.

We found the ruined buildings on the island crumbling and dangerous. Collapsed roof beams poked up into the sky where walls had toppled in heaps of worn, red bricks. We nosed around the rubble for an hour, disturbing hibernating toads and mindful of the last remaining sagging roofs, then collected some driftwood and lit a fire under an old brick oven. The leftover meat from the previous night was cooked for lunch, and in the late afternoon we piled into our boats for the eight mile sail to the Uruguay Yacht Club in Montevideo's little port of Buceo. There was the lightest wind, and we were content to glide slowly away from the island into an expansive sunset of pinks and purples with Edu's little *Yamandu* alongside flying her cherry red spinnaker. The winking lights of Montevideo beckoned us as we sipped the remains of a bottle of wine and Lucy practiced her new walking skills by tottering up and down the deck in her harness.

***

The city of Montevideo provides the "highest quality of life in South America"; or at least that was so in 2007, according to a Mercer Human Resources Consulting survey. It is not difficult to believe. There really does seem to be little or no violent crime. Alex had told me about a recent bank robbery in Montevideo.

"Is berry danger Montevideo, you should to be careful!" he warned me as we were preparing to leave Piriapolis.

"Really? You think so?"

"Of course! It was okay before, but now is danger. They steal a bank last year!"

"Who?"

"Two mans from Argentina. They cross the river and they steal one bank."

"How do you know they were from Argentina?"

"Because they catch!"

"Oh, they catch do they? Well, that doesn't make Montevideo sound too berry danger to me…"

"Ha ha, I tell you, take care! This a big problem. There was never before this problem. This the first in ten years!"

I was delighted to hear one bank robbery in ten years was considered a crisis. But when I related that conversation to Edu – who actually *lives* in Montevideo – he was cautious.

"Ah no my friend, ees not true. We have crime. Ten years? Heh heh heh! Thees ees too much. No, we have problems in that time also. I think maybe ees seven years. No more."

***

Montevideo was founded by the Spanish in 1726 to guard the northern shores of the Rio de la Plata against occupation by the adventurous Portuguese, and by 1776 the city provided the main naval base for the Spanish fleet in the South Atlantic. Site of the first ever football world cup in 1930 (which Uruguay won by beating Argentina 4-2 in the final) Montevideo seems to have taken international relations to a new level by twinning with nineteen* other cities around the globe (including no less than four in Spain).

The other thing about Montevideo – as Piriapolis – is that everyone speaks Spanish. Most times, that means they speak *only* Spanish. This is something that can almost be overcome with infinite patience, wild gesticulating and a sense of humour; but I defy anyone to try it over a radio.

In Edu's yacht club in Buceo we attached *Josephine* to one of the club buoys in the middle of the little bay. The standard procedure is to call the "*lanchero*" (the *marinero* who drives the club launch, or *lancha*) and ask him to pick you up from your boat. It is a complimentary "taxi" service provided for guests of the club. All very civilized. So, on our first morning, I set the VHF radio to channel 71, the "working" channel of the port. (Of course, being the working channel, everyone with a radio gets to listen to your entire conversation.) In hindsight it would have been a good idea to think about what I was going to say; to prepare my sentences. But I did not.

* as at 2010

"Lancha lancha lancha, velero Josephine," I began. So far so good. Normal radio procedure.

El lanchero responded, then waited for my message.

"Josephine here, uh... um.... puedo... puedo... puedo..... aah.... puedo... ", floundering, then with sudden inspiration "... *voy a tierra!"*

To his credit the *lanchero* acknowledged and motored over, straight faced, to pick us up. My loyal crew, however, were anything but straight faced. Quite the contrary in fact.

Abi and Jo were almost in tears, and Rupert was brandishing the video camera with glee after getting my ramblings on film. What had come out was "*I want... I want... I want... aah... I want... I go to Earth."*

This was not the first time I made an idiot of myself trying to get to grips with a new language. Several years ago, backpacking around Europe, I had found myself in Olomounc in the Czech Republic trying to book into a hotel where nobody spoke English. I have no idea what inspired me, but before I could do anything about it I heard myself asking, as fluently as you like, "*Sprechen zie Deutsch*?"

"*Ach ja!*" came the reply from the perky receptionist, and she launched into an incomprehensible German monologue.

Unfortunately I did not catch any of it, as the only two sentences I knew in German were "Do you speak German?" (which I had just used up) and "*Ich sprechen nicht Deutsch.*" I followed up my opening gambit with the latter. She held me in a vacant stare. Why had I asked her whether she speaks German, only to then tell her that I do not?

Some years later I had occasion to present myself to the TAM airline desk in the airport of Recife, Brazil, as my backpack had not arrived with me on a flight from Sao Paulo. No English was spoken there either. I remembered there had been a time in my life (many years earlier) that I almost spoke Italian, and with Portuguese being a Latin language, I was sure I should be able to make myself understood.

"*Parla Italiano?*" I asked the clerk hopefully. She flashed me a dazzling, but mute, smile. So that would be a 'no'.

As luck would have it, just at that moment, a real Italian walked past and overheard me, and came to see if he could assist.

"*Io sono Italiano,*" he said, "*e parlo anche Portugese.*"

Perfect. An Italian who also spoke Portuguese.

"*Quale e il probleme?*" he asked helpfully.

I went completely blank. Twelve years is longer that I thought, and under pressure I could not remember a single word of Italian.

After trying unsuccessfully for several minutes to establish the nature of my problem, bits of Italian started to seep back into my addled brain, and I was able to stutter that I had "lost my luggage".

The Real Italian looked bemused, so I said it again. He hesitated, but when I told him a third time "I have lost my luggage", he shrugged and passed the message on.

The clerk nodded gravely, then turned to me and smiled.

"*Bravo senhor!*"

I thought sarcasm was a little out of place. I wished I knew how to rephrase my sentence to point out that *they*, not *I*, had actually lost my luggage. We stood around looking at each other for a time.

"I'm not sure you understand," I tried again, slowly, in my best Italian, "but my luggage is missing. It is L-O-S-T."

"*Si, si,*" confirmed my translator; that is what he told her, and she is very happy for me.

I was nonplussed. The Real Italian then bade farewell, and I was left standing alone again in front of the help desk while the pretty clerk continued to smile sweetly at me like a model in a toothpaste commercial.

It was at this point that the obvious solution occurred to me, and I called my friend Danilo in Mozambique with my cell phone. (Of course it was around three o'clock on the morning in Maputo.)

Once I had Danilo and the airline clerk talking to each other in Portuguese, things changed quickly, and there seemed to be a lot more concern. It became apparent I had been urging the Italian to impress upon her that I had *found* my luggage, rather than *lost* it. She thought I had merely stopped by to share my good news.

Now in Uruguay we needed to come to terms with Spanish. Fortunately a lot of Spanish words are the same as, or at least similar to, English; so that if you pronounce the English word with a Spanish accent, you almost get away with it. Words like "*confusion*", "*stupido*" and "*simple*" are common currency. One cannot always guess though. I assumed "tuna" would be one of those words – it does, after all, sound somewhat *latino* – but I discovered that when you tell someone you caught a "tuna", they are not sure whether you mean you hooked a prickly pear or a student rock band. (The correct word for tuna – the fish – is in fact "*atun*".)

Armed with a veritable library of dictionaries and phrasebooks, we were primed to take up the challenge of, if not learning the language, at least learning our way around it. (Though I have always been a little wary of phrasebooks, ever since my sister gave me my first one as I was leaving London on a bicycle trip to Milan. I opened it randomly and the first thing it taught me to say in Italian was "*non sono i miei gemelli*" – "these are not my cufflinks".)

Getting to grips with a new language is always instructive when it comes to your own: I find I understand English a lot better since I started to learn other languages. There is not a simple "word for word" swap – the grammar of course changes, but the range of meanings of words is different too. Sometimes Spanish has three words where we have only one, and vice versa. Take the English word "have"; it means to "own" or "hold", but we also use it to illustrate the past participle, as in "I *have* seen it". And of course it means something like "must" in "I *have to* go". So there is no straight translation into Spanish for "have". If you just learn that "to have" (as in to hold, or own) is "*tener*", and you then use this verb to replace "have" in every instance, you might find yourself saying things like "I *hold* seen it", or "I *hold* to go", neither of which makes any sense at all.

We had fun sitting in the boat with our small mountain of books discovering "Middle Aged Spread" translates as "The Curve of Happiness". A sleeping pill is a "*somnifero*" and a smile is a "*sonriso*" (which I rather like; it sounds a bit like "sunrise"). Then there is "*estar en bolas*" – literally "to be in balls" (or "naked") and as a mushroom is a "*hongo*", what else could a bowler hat be but a "*sombrero de hongo*"?

Food always makes for important learning matter. We diligently tried to memorise that *cordero* is lamb; *albondias* are meatballs; *solomillo* is sirloin; *calolos* is tripe; *crestas* are crests – whatever they may be – and *pipirrana* is fish, peppers, tomatoes, hardboiled eggs and onions. "*Ciervo*" is venison, usually deer in South America; one evening in a restaurant we overheard a woman describing it to a small child as "*carne de Bambi*". A mountain climber is an *alpinista* in Spain, but not in South America; here the correct term is *andenista.* But of course. And we delighted in memorising phrases like "*mi importa un rabano*" – "a radish is important to me" (when you don't care about something) and "*estoy aburrido como una ostra*" – "I am as bored as an oyster".

After making a fool of myself that first morning at the Montevideo yacht club, it was agreed that calling the *lancha* presented a great opportunity to practice Spanish so long as we planned what we were going to say beforehand. We would take it in turns to call, and it was against the rules to use a sentence that had been used before. So sensible phrases like "*Tengo que andar en el club*" (I have to go to the club) or "*Quieriamos salir el barco*" (we would like to leave the boat), while being technically better than my first effort about going to Earth, were quickly exhausted. Then it was more imaginative phrases like "*Tenemos quatro passageros para te*" (we have four passengers for you) or "*Estamos listo para llegar en el restaurante*" (we are ready to go to the restaurant) that came in useful.

But it became more and more difficult to come up with new phrases, and Rupert finally killed the whole thing off one morning by proclaiming into the radio "*Debo comer una jirafa!*" To his eternal credit the patient *lanchero* presented himself at the boat and took us ashore without a word. We never knew whether he was just being polite, or whether Rupert's Spanish was so bad the *lanchero* had not picked up that what he actually said over the radio was "I must eat a giraffe".

***

Uruguay being very much a country of "the land", *gaucho* (cowboy) culture is strong, and just about the biggest event on the sporting calendar is the annual rodeo in Montevideo. There are in fact two, in the same week: the upmarket one, in the city, for the tourists; and the "local" one, near the airport, in a somewhat dilapidated brick stadium surrounded by tall Eucalyptus trees. Of course we made for this one.

The taxi dropped us amongst the gum trees in a merry confusion of wandering livestock, smoky buses and mobile *chivito* kitchens. The forest was dotted with little encampments each with its own smouldering fire, a few tatty canvasses strung up for shelter, and circa-1950s pick-up trucks. Most camps also had at least one pony and cart, and housed an extended family for the week; grubby toddlers romping in the dust, mums and daughters managing the home front, dads checking sons' riding gear and imparting final advice before the show, and toothless grandparents lounging against the trucks sipping *mate* out of gourds made from cows' hooves.

Closer to the whitewashed stadium we ran a gauntlet of stalls selling everything from roasted peanuts, leather clothes and hot water (for *mate*) to replica samurai swords, colour prints of Victoria Falls, and posters of Homer Simpson alternately done up as Che Guevara, Bob Marley or Elvis Presley. There were little Eiffel Towers made from coloured glass, carved wooden elephants with big painted eyes, and fat Buddhas cast in resin. T-shirts were on sale proclaiming such pop wisdom as "CANADA DRINK", "NOBODY CARE IN THE CORNER BABY" and "E-BY THE BLACKER CULTURE MOVE ON", but nothing could eclipse the ultimate postcard; a picture of Mickey Mouse, done up as a pirate, standing sword in hand over an open treasure chest on a tropical beach, under the title "MICKEY IN LESOTHO".

The rodeo itself was a whirlwind of thundering hooves and swirling dust, overlaid with the loudest public address system under which it has ever been my misfortune to stand. But it was nothing if not exciting. Eager young men – a lot of them teenagers – taking turns to see how long they could remain in the saddle on horses that showed absolutely no inclination whatsoever to be sat upon. Like the American rodeo, there was an eight second cut-off, and anyone who could remain seated on his mount beyond the eight seconds would then be awarded points for style. Of course a good many did not make the eight seconds, and there was plenty of excitement for the frenzied crowd as rider after rider was ignominiously hurled to the ground, and often trampled for good measure. The ambulance was kept busy, the crowd happy.

By the end of a breathless afternoon the people's favourite, and reigning Uruguay champion, had carried the day. To rapturous applause he charged around on his lap of honour at full gallop with a box of the sponsor's *mate yerba* held aloft in one hand, the Uruguayan flag in the other. All the way home in the taxi we were treated to pony noises by Lucy, and the next day we procured a bright green inflatable donkey for the boat.

***

There are not a lot of foreign yachts in Montevideo; certainly not from further afield than Buenos Aires at any rate. So when a boat with a foreign flag shows up, everyone notices. And so it was when we awoke one morning to see a bright orange, French flagged boat attached to one of the club's buoys. And there, on the deck – a pink bicycle. *The* pink bicycle.

I co-opted the *lancha* to take me over. Alex's "stealerman" was on deck.

"Good morning!" I shouted, trying to be civil. We had never met.

He glanced up briefly, then continued with what he was doing. There was no return greeting.

"Hello there!" I tried again. By now we were alongside, and I was holding onto his boat. He grunted. Not very communicative today then.

"I have come to talk to you about my bicycle."

That made him look up.

"What bicycle?"

"The one you stole from my wife in Piriapolis."

He remained unmoved.

"This is my bicycle," he muttered, looking away again.

In truth it was not a great bicycle, and I did not really want it at all; but there was a principle at stake, and his curtness was not making me sympathetic. I could see we were heading for a stalemate though, and as the bike was on his boat, not mine, he held a territorial advantage.

"Okay, that's fine, we'll let the authorities sort it out. I have reported the theft to the *Prefectura*, and they are looking for you. When they find you here, they are not going to allow you to leave. Then we'll get to the bottom of it."

Now I had his attention. He gawped at me, eyes wide. Before he could speak, I tapped the *lanchero* on the shoulder and we sped off.

Back aboard *Josephine* Abi asked me what had happened.

"Nothing much. I don't want the rubbish old thing anyway. But I told him I've reported the theft and the *Prefectura* are hunting him down."

"But you haven't... have you?"

"Of course not, but he doesn't know that. Let him stew."

Unsurprisingly, within the hour *Karthik* was a receding orange dot on the horizon. A moral victory had at least been won.

***

After several days heaving and bouncing on our buoy in the harbour, Abi was fed up. When the wind blows from the south – which it does often – the little port of Buceo gets the worst of it, the waves marching straight in through the harbour mouth, making for a very uncomfortable mooring. Putting up with rocking and rolling is one thing when you are out at sea making a passage, but it is quite another when you are moored at a yacht club. With Lucy now walking, it was rather dangerous inside the boat, especially when we were cooking.

Jetty (or "walk on") moorings certainly exist in Buceo, but they are in short supply, so probably half the boats in the club are on buoys. I also knew – or had read in any event – that there is a depth issue here. My pilot book stressed that it was inadvisable for any boat with a draught of more than five feet to venture too far into the harbour, and certainly not to attempt docking at a walk-on mooring. Edu, however – whose home club it was – laughed that off.

"No man, thees ees not true. Look at that boat!" he said, pointing to a forty footer. "And there another…. and thees one, eet has a keel weeth two metres. They are all on the jetty, ees no problem!"

He had a point. I could see the boats for myself, and they were reasonably big.

"Alright," I replied. "See if you can arrange something for us."

The next day he was back, triumphant.

"Okay my friend, I organise you thees mooring on the jetty. Ees of a man not here now, ees no problem for you use!"

Jolly good then. We fired the engine, cast off the cursed buoy, and tootled off in the direction of the jetty.

About half way – which was less than a hundred yards – it occurred to me we were going rather slowly. I gunned the motor a little, but it made no difference; we were making one knot. Usually six is easy. I looked back to see a cloud of brown mud billowing up from the propeller. The depth sounder was not reading anything; the swirling mud was too thick.

"Edu!" I shouted across to the jetty where he was waiting. "We are in mud, it's too shallow here!"

"No no, ees a channel!" he insisted.

"This is not a channel; I tell you I am stuck. Look, the boat is not moving at all now!"

"Are you sure?"

"Yes I am sure!"

"No, ees eemposseeble!"

"Well I'm telling you, it's too shallow."

"*Bueno*, go around," he said, waving his arm.

After managing to get back to "deep" water, we tried approaching the jetty from another direction, but with the same result. This was just not going to happen. Reluctantly we returned to our buoy.

"Sorry, but thees ees not normal," lamented our friend. "The water ees low today."

The next afternoon, on returning to the club from visiting the local market, we discovered *Josephine* neatly tied up to the jetty, Edu in attendance.

"You see!" he announced with pride. "I tell you ees deep enough! The East weend blow, and the water ees up, so we move your boat. Yesterday ees not normal. *Thees* ees normal my friend!"

It certainly was a pleasure to be out of the swell, have our hose connected to a tap, be plugged into the electricity supply, and able to get on and off the boat without embarrassing ourselves over the radio.

The east wind continued to blow, then veered south east and blew some more. Waves rolled in through the harbour entrance and pummelled the far beach. The wind raged. The water rose, and rose, until the next day our jetty was completely submerged under the opaque brown water of the River Plate. We were now tied fast to something we could not see, and once again dependent on the taxi to get us to the clubhouse. The electricity panels were submerged and the power cut. For two days we floated around above the jetty. There was certainly more than enough depth now. But we could not leave. We were tied to the jetty with six lines, all attached somewhere under the thick brown water. Somewhere down there we also had a hose connected to a tap, and a plugged in power cable.

"Thees ees not normal!" Edu assured us.

On the third day the wind abated and the water ran back out of the harbour again. All of it. We woke in the morning to see bare mud under the jetty we were tied to. The depth sounder would not register;

it was too shallow. The keel was stuck fast, and we had to rig a rope ladder to climb *up* to the jetty that the day before had been submerged somewhere below us.

"Don' worry," said Edu. "Thees ees not normal *at all!*"

We still could not leave. Yes, there were boats as big as ours on the jetty, that was true – but I wondered how many of them ever managed to go sailing.

***

By now we were getting into winter and it was far too late in the year to consider venturing any further south. Tierra del Fuego was certainly out of the question, and the girls had no stomach for another three hundred mile sail in rough seas even to Bahia Blanca. We held a family council, and decided to winter in Buenos Aires. There are a lot of sailing clubs in Buenos Aires, and it is a lot cheaper to keep a boat in Argentina than anywhere in Uruguay. We also liked the idea of getting off the boat and exploring some of Argentina, so plans were made to visit our next country.

"We dance the music, not the steps.
We are painters.
We paint the music with our feet."

– Carlos Gavito

13

There is a popular myth that tango grew out of the brothels of Buenos Aires, but as pointed out by Christine Dennison in her book *Histroy of Tango*, it is more likely to have been popularised there, given that Tango was the music of the working classes and the brothels were the only places where working and middle class men mixed comfortably. Live music was laid on to keep them entertained as they drank and waited for the women – who were in scarce supply in that immigrant city of the early twentieth century – and the men passed the steps on by dancing with each other.

For a time tango remained the primary entertainment of the poorer classes, but when more and more young Argentine men from wealthy families were sent to France to round off their education (Argentina was after all one of the wealthiest countries in the world at that time) they took the tango with them to Paris, where it did not carry the same social stigma as it had back home. Thus was born the tango craze of Paris around 1912. Once it was all the rage in the world's most fashionable of cities, it was an easy step back across the Atlantic to high society Buenos Aires, where tango was then danced by the middle and upper classes "as it is danced in Paris".

Tango in Argentina was forced underground after the ousting of President Juan Peron in 1955, when the military government imposed after-dark curfews in the streets and forbade gatherings of more than three people. Those measures effectively rendered tango evenings illegal until its resurgence after the downfall of the military regime in 1983, following the debacle of the Falklands War.

Known variously as "The King of Tango", "*El Zorzal*" (The Songbird) or more simply "*Carlito*", Carlos Gardel remains history's most recognisable face of Tango. He was in the vanguard of the growth of tango singing in the early twentieth century, his rich baritone and movie star looks lending him massive popular appeal. After his untimely death in a plane crash in Colombia in 1935, his body was carried in procession through the streets of Montevideo, Paris and Rio de Janeiro. Though there are no definitive records, he claimed to have been born in Uruguay, and lay in state for several days in Montevideo. His voice is still heard in the streets of twenty-first century Buenos Aires, and buskers to this day dress themselves in his trademark pinstripe suit and ubiquitous fedora – a hat similar to the trilby with its pinched front, but with a wider brim, bent down over the eyes. (Curiously, the fedora came into being as a women's fashion item in the late nineteenth century, and was subsequently adopted by men as a middle-class accessory around 1920.) Ironically, the last song Gardel performed before his death was "*Adios Muchachos*", which has since been regarded with such superstition it is never played at a *milonga* (a venue for dancing tango, usually serving drinks and snacks).

No stranger to controversy during his lifetime, Gardel was apparently shot in the leg in a bar-room scuffle by no less than the father of Ernesto "Che" Guevara.

***

No visit to Buenos Aires would be complete without experiencing tango, but first we needed to get there. Not a very long way across the River Plate to be sure, but a long way bureaucratically speaking. We were about to enter our third South American country, and if the first two were anything to go by a lot was going to depend on which offices we visited, and who was on duty that day.

In Montevideo we met a Frenchman who had been to Argentina and said to try avoiding the paperwork in Buenos Aires if we could; that the city of La Plata, about forty miles south east of the capital, was a lot easier. All the offices we would need to visit were within easy walking distance of each other and there were no queues. That settled it for me, and as I was the one dealing with the authorities, that view carried the day and it was off to La Plata.

A relatively young city, La Plata was only founded in 1882 as a new capital for the State of Buenos Aires after Buenos Aires city was effectively removed from state control when it became the Federal Capital. La Plata was briefly, between 1952 and 1955, renamed "Eva Peron City" after the death from cancer of that working class icon at the age of thirty-three, but this politically expedient move was reversed when the military came to power.

The thirty mile sail across the river from Montevideo was bitterly cold. Winter seemed to have arrived the previous night, and the daytime temperature for our trip was about eight degrees Celsius. At least the sun was shining. Edu jumped at the chance to join us; he had never before crossed to Argentina by boat. For my part, I was happy to have him along, imagining as a native Spanish speaker it would make things easier on arrival at the yacht club on the other side (quite apart from the fact that we had by now grown so fond of him and enjoyed his company).

The River Plate between Montevideo and Argentina is littered with dangers to shipping, boasting as it does the highest concentration of hazardous wrecks of any waterway on the planet. Fortunately they are all marked with buoys, and shortly after our departure we sailed past the buoys that denote the grave of the *Graf Spey*, the Nazi battleship that was so badly damaged in an engagement with the Royal Navy off Punte del Este in 1939 that her captain scuttled her off Montevideo, to commit suicide three days later.

Our destination in Argentina was the little sailing club "*Club Regatas*", tucked away up a quiet creek in Ensenada, a satellite town that hosts La Plata's port (the city of La Plata itself being about five miles inland). The harbour of Buenos Aires is becoming more of a passenger terminal with a steady increase in the number of cruise liners and ferries docking in the city, and as the freighters and tankers give way to a tourism makeover, Ensenada is growing rapidly as an alternative commercial port. It is already Argentina's main hub for beef and grain exports.

We arrived at the entrance to Ensenada just before dark. In the northerly wind, both breakwaters were buried below the brown waters of the river, so for a good mile or more we needed to be very careful to stay in mid-channel and steer well clear of the red and green poles poking out of the water that were mounted on the submerged concrete walls. Once beyond the beach and in the river proper, we motored in the gloom past a hut raised on stilts off to starboard with "*Prefectura*" painted on the front and sporting a large Argentine flag. I exchanged friendly waves with the duty officer as we went by. A little further down we come to a crossroads in the waterway. Staying within the markers – which was not easy, as it was now dark, and they were not lit – we turned right, then crept another mile up a dark, tree-lined creek past half submerged, rusting hulks of abandoned trawlers until we spotted a clutch of yachts amongst the willows off to our left: Club Regatas, according to the sketch we had been given by our French friend.

As recommended in the pilot book, we called the club on VHF channel 71, introduced ourselves and requested assistance at the marina. In the middle of the discussions, a third party came over the air asking who we were and where we had come from. It was the *Prefectura*, who advised us in no uncertain terms that we should have announced ourselves to them on entering the channel. We had in fact sailed right by the *Prefectura*'s hut overlooking the water, and the duty officer had returned my wave; I had therefore appeared obvious that they knew about us, and seeing as we are foreigners and could (one imagines) be excused for not knowing all the local procedures, why had they not called *us* as we went by, instead of just waving? Another example of the frustrating illogic of South American officialdom.

Not looking forward to another round of bureaucracy, but taking heart from the fact that we were in Ensenada under advice from fellow travellers who had assured us it would be easy, we found ourselves at the club gate in the morning, waiting for our taxi. ("Us" being the whole family; for while it is the responsibility of the skipper to attend to paperwork, the presence of Lucy invariably cleared a path through the worst of it.)

Our taxi, when it arrived, was a beat up old Nissan driven by "Leo". In another life Leo was Tom Jones. His black shirt and black slacks were too tight and his white socks were too white. Flashy silver chains hung around his neck and across his open chest, glinting almost as much as the oil in his afro. Suspended from the rear view mirror was a rotating disco mirror ball, and a yellow nitro cylinder in the boot meant Lucy's pram could not go in.

It turned out that Leo did not know Ensenada as well as might be hoped, but what he lacked in geographical knowledge he made up for with enthusiasm. We tore through the town like a tornado leaving pedestrians, bicycles, horses and carts scattered in our wake. Scything through the central district, racing round the *plaza*, flying over speed bumps, mirror-ball bashing the roof, the only thing going faster than Leo was his meter as it racked up the miles. Despite mounting evidence to the contrary, Leo insisted he knew exactly where the *Prefectura* office was, and I was really wishing I had not let Edu leave early that morning for Uruguay (he, as a Uruguayan, not needing to register with Immigration); it was going to take someone with rather better Spanish than mine to control this lunatic.

Then, just as we were charging headlong out of town again, Leo having decided the *Prefectura* must have moved after he had been unable to track it down in the centre, who should I glimpse sitting at a bus stop but our French friend Yves – the same Yves who had sent us here in the first place. Perfect!

Leo screeched to a halt in a cloud of blue rubber smoke and hurled the car back up the road in reverse, gearbox screaming in protest. We slammed to a stop a foot away from the bus shelter. Yves was up on the bench cowering in terror clutching a bag of groceries. It took him several seconds to register who I was, but once he recovered from the shock of almost being run over inside a bus stop he was able to tell us the way to the *Prefectura*.

The *Prefectura* seemed to have no record of the previous evening's radio admonition, which was just as well, and I presented our five passports and the boat papers. All were stamped. Happily Ensenada did not have a *Migraciones* office, so the *Prefectura* took care of immigration as well as boat clearance, which saved some time.

Crazy Leo then proceeded to drive all around town in search of Customs. I had a more or less vague idea where it might be, as the *Prefectura* had given me directions, but I again made the mistake of deferring to the local knowledge of our taxi driver. Unsurprisingly, it turned out he had no idea where it was, so eventually all I could do was force him to return to the *Prefectura*, park the car, and wait there for me while I walked.

I found what I was looking for in a pre-fabricated office abutting a container yard behind the port, and there the real problems started. First the customs man wanted photocopies of my boat papers and *Prefectura* clearance. He could not – or would not – make them in his own office, so once more I tore up the town driven by the inspired Leo Schumacher, this time searching for a photocopier. We made it back to Customs alive just before closing time, with said copies, only to be presented with forms to complete. These forms were very comprehensive, and quite obviously intended for large ships, as they required a full inventory of the entire contents, from engine parts and tools, through all foodstuffs and galley provisions, to the personal effects of the crew. They were also hopelessly outdated. I was expected to declare, among other things, just how many caged birds, typewriters, bars of soap and coils of hemp rope were on the boat, but there was no provision for such modern valuables as computers or video cameras. In addition to the declaration of contents, there was a list of crucial questions to be answered, among which was "*Have the rats and mice on board exhibited any strange behaviour or deaths?*" (Tricky one; there were only "yes" or "no" boxes to tick.)

I pointed out there was no time for me to return to the boat to check all the contents; he said it would be okay to bring the completed papers tomorrow; I said I was driving to Buenos Aires the next day, "for a meeting"; he agreed my wife could bring them in, so long as she had a copy of my passport. It was closing time and he just wanted me out of his office.

In fact I really *was* planning to go to Buenos Aires the next day – to visit the yacht club at Puerto Madero and arrange a mooring. Leo undertook to collect Rupert and me at nine thirty, and I did not sleep well anticipating the drive. Hardly surprisingly come to think of it, when morning came Leo showed up at the boat with a friend in tow to inform us that his car was at the panel beaters (we never did find out why) and that Walther here would be taking us to Buenos Aires instead. Walther was short and fat, with narrow sloping shoulders, no neck that I could see and his head was capped off with greasy lank hair that swung like a curtain around his ears, lending him the air of a greased turnip. His personality enhanced that image. Walther tried all the way to Buenos Aires to convince us he could arrange cheap girls in the city – which he no doubt could – but when we arrived at the yacht club and paid him for the drive he was so disappointed he tore off in a cloud of dust without so much as saying goodbye. He had obviously been hoping to get in on some girlie action paid for with the dollars of his new *gringo* friends.

That evening, back at the boat (Rupert and I having returned from the city by bus) Abi met me with the unwelcome news that the story at *Aduanas* had changed overnight, and they had refused to accept the forms she went to drop off. It would appear now only the

Commandante of the boat had the authority to physically hand them over the counter.

So in the morning – now day three – I went to *Aduanas* to deliver the customs forms. They asked me where the boat was. I said Club Regatas, then foolishly told them we were leaving the next day (never tell them anything unless they ask!) to go to Buenos Aires. I really should have known better.

"Ah, not so fast!" said *senor Aduanas.* "Your port clearance is for entering La Plata; before we can sign your customs papers, you need clearance from the *Prefectura* to go on to Buenos Aires".

This was utter nonsense; invented-on-the-spot South American bureaucracy at its best. Where does one ever require clearance to *leave*, before you can be fully checked *in*? But I was never going to win this argument, so I stalked back down the road to the *Prefectura* where I was kept waiting for over an hour before a man in a brown uniform could see me. When I explained that I was going to Buenos Aires the next day and needed clearance to leave, I was told I must present myself just prior to leaving, so to come in tomorrow. I objected on the grounds that until he stamped me *out*, customs would not stamp me *in*. The brown uniform shrugged. I told him I would be leaving at four thirty in the morning, and his office would not yet be open. He said that would not be allowed, as it was a requirement that I report to the office before departure. My Spanish was not good enough to get into the logic of the whole thing; to point out that the rationale for all this reporting was safety, but that by limiting my movements with his office hours he was potentially *compromising* the safety of my crew; we may run into bad weather or arrive at our destination in the dark as a result of having our departure delayed. It was easier simply to lie, so I told him I had just changed my mind and was now planning to leave that very evening. Straight away the papers were stamped without further fuss.

Back at *Aduanas* everything now appeared to be in order, except that I would have to come back tomorrow to collect the signed forms as the "chief" needed to approve them, and he worked in another building. This was getting too much. I objected, but was met with casual indifference. Then I pointed out that I would be leaving that very evening whether they liked it or not, and as the *Prefectura* had already stamped my exit, I had no choice but to leave; and that if my customs forms were not stamped in time, he would have to explain himself to the Navy. This did the trick, and a minor official was despatched to search for the chief, who was easily found, and everything was signed off.

So the paperwork, for which I had been sent to La Plata because it would be "quick and easy", had taken three days, with the threat of a fourth. I was feeling more and more inclined towards the Bavarian method of dealing with officialdom. *Ignore zem altogezzer.*

***

It was a very cold day indeed. The thirty-odd mile sail up the river to Buenos Aires was, thankfully, in full sun, but we shivered whenever the sail cast its shadow over the cockpit. Earlier the brown water had been stirred up by the west wind we were beating into, but later in the day the wind dropped, the water settled, and we motored into the most beautiful sunset. *Josephine* was gliding over quicksilver streaked with mauve and lavender that turned a soft shell pink as the sun hung ablaze over a line of grey cloud pencilled just above the horizon. Then a deep orange glow infused the water, and as the shining orb slipped behind the edge of the world it seemed to explode in giant slow-motion, sending tongues of rose and violet flame across the heavens.

The southeast skyline was a stepped silhouette of black skyscrapers inset with myriad little jewels of shimmering silver. Buenos Aires.

Formally founded in 1580 by Juan de Garay under orders from the Spanish Governor of the River Plate, Buenos Aires was labelled the "Gateway to the Land" for ships arriving from Europe. For many years, ships from Spain had been travelling in large convoys (to avoid pirates and privateers – mostly British) across the ocean to Panama where they were unloaded, their cargo heaped onto donkeys and carried over the isthmus to the Pacific coast. There the cargo was re-loaded onto ships that sailed south to ports in what is now Peru. Politics and conflicting financial interests precluded Spanish merchant shipping from using Buenos Aires as the "gateway" it was touted to be, and so for the first thirty years the port was little more than a landing stage for private ships and smugglers, the town supporting a population of a mere five hundred *Portenos* (as the people of Buenos Aires were – and still are – known).

We arrived after dark to discover the harbour entrance lights shown on the charts did not in fact exist – or if they did, they were not working. Fortunately there was enough ambient light from the city to be able to pick out the channel buoys floating in the river, which we followed into the port. Once inside we found the lights for the Puerto Madero dock did not exist either, but after motoring cautiously around the harbour we discovered, in the far south east corner near the ferry terminal, a stone canal that lead under a road into the dock that is host to the club and its marina.

On our earlier visit to Buenos Aires by taxi, Rupert and I had met with "William", the *Capitania* of the port. William (who was actually Guillermo, but preferred the Anglicised version having spent some time in England) served as both Harbour Master and manager of the yacht club. He spoke excellent English but was at a loss to explain his thick Dutch accent. I called him over the radio and he placed the necessary request with the authorities to halt the busy road traffic and open the swing bridge to let us in.

"*Yacht Club Puerto Madero*" is really a yacht club in name only; the club thing is a legal technicality to get around tax issues, but it is effectively a commercial marina. And it does have excellent facilities. Comfortable walk-on moorings are available with water and electricity, and it is completely sheltered from both swell and wind by virtue of being inside an old dock in the heart of what is now the very upmarket financial district. A more glamorous setting for your boat you could not wish for – if you wish for glamorous, that is. The club is surrounded by glass and steel high rise office towers and hotels with trendy steak and sushi restaurants, coffee shops and ice cream parlours on their ground floors. The very helpful marina staff will arrange to have your laundry collected, diesel delivered and gas bottles filled. They will also order you a taxi if you need one – which you generally don't, as there is a twenty-four hour club launch to take you across the dock to the "town" side whenever you like, and an intercom on the far side so you can call when you come back and want to be collected. All the shops you might need are within comfortable walking distance, as you really are in the city; and all tourist attractions are easily accessed by public transport – you are a few minutes walk from rail, bus and metro stations. The clubhouse itself has wonderful underfloor-heated bathrooms with plush shower facilities, and free 24-hour WiFi. Unfortunately there is not much else – no restaurant, no bar, no lounge to relax in – as the "clubhouse" is really just a venue to be hired out for corporate events. So it is sterile and boring, unlike a real club.

All this convenience costs a bit of course, but less than one might expect. For a 38ft boat, we paid 900 pesos (or $240) per week – which, considering it was less than $10 per person per night for accommodation in what is arguably South America's most happening city, seemed pretty fair.

Looking at the other boats on the marina, it was obvious we were in the centre of a big hustling metropolis – flashy yachts and power launches with telling names like "*SuperEgo*", "*Stress*" and "*Impaciente*". "*Anestesia*" must have belonged to someone in medicine, but we could not guess who would have called their yacht "*Another Muppet*".

Immediately on making *Josephine* fast to the floating pontoon inside the basin, a local sailor appeared alongside and introduced himself as Fabian. Having been to Cape Town the previous year on his friend's boat, and visited our home club, he was delighted to be able to welcome us to his city and we went on to become close friends.

Under his advice, I booked a table for the tango show at "*Confiteria Ideal*". One of the older, more traditional *milongas* in the city, it was used as a set in the 1996 film "*Evita*", starring Antonio Banderas and Louise Ciccone (otherwise known simply as "Madonna"). Ms Ciccone is now famous for setting the Guinness World Record for "Most Costume Changes in a Film" (in "*Evita*" she changed costume eighty-five times, handily beating Elizabeth Taylor's effort of sixty-five in "*Cleopatra*").

Just off *Avenida 9de Julio*, near the Obelisk, we found *Confiteria Ideal* in an old stucco building with a vast, hangar-like interior. The walls were panelled with dark wood to a height of about twelve feet. Off-white paint peeled the rest of the way up to a twenty foot high pressed ceiling held up by a forest of orange marble pillars as thick as elephants' legs. Light came from twenty-one elaborate electric chandeliers with half their bulbs missing. A fifteen by fifteen foot square space between the elephant legs served as a dance floor, surrounded by cheap wooden tables covered with plain linen tablecloths. We sat on plastic chairs. The hall had all the acoustics of an empty barn, and the food – when it eventually came – was dismal.

But we had come to the right place for tango. Tango had been danced here for a hundred years, and in spite of the popularity of so-called "tourist" tango – extravagant spectacles staged in lavish venues with five star meals (and matching ticket prices) – *Confiteria Ideal* still offered real dancing, up close. The amateur feel of the whole evening – indeed the dancers really were no more than accomplished amateurs – added to its authentic flavour. "Painting the music with their feet" as the great Gavito had put it, they carried us through the full spectrum of emotions that colour the history of the restless, artistic, spirited, tragic, hopeful, vivid city that is Buenos Aires.

***

The plan being to spend the winter in Argentina, the "club" at Puerto Madero was not a long term option, being the most expensive place to keep a boat in all of Argentina; but the greater Buenos Aires boasts something in excess of fifty yacht clubs, all of which are modestly priced, and most of which offer a courtesy period of a couple of weeks to foreign yachts. Our new friend Fabian arranged through his contacts for us to take *Josephine* to the Tigre Sailing Club, up the *Rio Lujan* in the Parana Delta.

The delta is a 17,500 square kilometre alluvial basin formed by the *Rio Parana* that sweeps south out of Brazil and Paraguay through the northern part of Argentina and into the River Plate. The *Rio Uruguay* constitutes the north-eastern limit of this wetland, which, at almost the size of Wales, is the world's biggest delta not flowing directly into the sea. The southern limit of the delta is defined by the much smaller *Rio Lujan*, on the mainland (south) bank of which one finds Buenos Aires' highbrowed suburbs of San Isidro, San Fernando and Tigre.

These outlying towns are the water sports Meccas for the city's middle classes, and it is here one finds most of the yacht clubs.

Tigre actually sits on an island bounded by canals with its north side facing the *Rio Lujan*. It was founded in 1820 after heavy floods destroyed the existing settlements in the area, and owes its name to jaguars (not tigers) hunted there in earlier years. Now Tigre is a popular tourist town, providing convenient ferry services into the delta, as well as across the River Plate to Colonia and Carmelo in Uruguay.

Faced with the short hop up the river from the city centre into the *Rio Lujan* and the Tigre Sailing Club, we had two options:

The direct route, straight along the coast, is less than twenty miles but the water is very shallow in places, and the channel markers are unreliable due to the shifting nature of the mud banks. It is a good idea to obtain recent waypoints from someone at a local sailing club, but even with good waypoints, in a boat like *Josephine* with a draught of seven feet, it is only practical when the water is high. Local sailors talk of the "tide", but really it is not the tide that counts; as with almost anywhere on the River Plate, what matters here is the wind. Most of the hundred and fifty mile long "river" – which ranges in width from twenty miles at its narrowest, to a hundred and twenty at its widest, and is thus celebrated as the widest river on earth by those who consider it to be a "river" in the strict sense – is no more that fifteen feet deep; not much volume for gravitational pull of the moon to have a result, and the river is too long for the six-hourly tidal cycle of the deeper coastal water to flow in and out to any effect. (Even in Piriapolis, which is close to the sea, fluctuations in the water level are dictated by the wind; there is no noticeable tidal rhythm at all.) The wind plays havoc with the depths in the coastal channel just off Buenos Aires, and in a south-westerly, even at nominal "high tide" there can be less than three feet of water – and that in a dredged navigation channel. If we chose to go this route we would need to wait for a northerly wind.

Our second option was to head north out of Puerto Madero and intersect the main shipping channel *Canal Emilio Mitre* about four miles offshore, dredged to about forty feet to accommodate freighters, then turn west and follow it upstream into the *Rio Parana.* Once on the *Parana* – which carries shipping hundreds of miles inland to Paraguay – a route south through the Delta through tree-lined channels would bring us into the *Rio Lujan.* Although twice the distance it is still only a one day trip, with the advantage that it is deep enough and can be undertaken at any time, irrespective of the wind.

Always keen to explore new places, we went for the second option and a day out on the waterways.

It was another cold day on the river. A fifteen knot westerly breeze was nice to sail on for the first half hour, but after we reached the shipping channel and turned upstream it was coming head on and of no further use to us. The sails were put away and we motored the rest of the day. Against the current of the mighty *Parana*, which was running at between two and three knots, we made frustratingly slow progress, but once we entered the delta and turned south into the wooded *Canal Honda* the current was with us, and we flew. Shortly after being treated to yet another spectacular River Plate sunset, the molten ball of the sun suspended in a net of winter branches black against the deep lavender sky, we drew near the *Rio Lujan.*

The approach to the *Lujan* was marked by an increase in traffic; small ships laden with timber, Canadian canoes carrying small families to their homes among the trees, motor launches heading back to the countless yacht clubs, and rowing boats. Particularly rowing boats. There are no fewer than fifteen rowing clubs in the delta, mostly in the suburbs of San Fernando and Tigre. (The Buenos Aires Rowing

Club, based in Tigre, was the first to be established, back in 1873.) This evening the canals were dotted with the red flashes from LEDs mounted on the prows as oarsmen bent to their task and we were kept on our toes dodging through a flotilla of single sculls.

A right turn at the end of the *Canal Viluncacion* fed us into the *Rio Lujan*. The river shone under the lights of Tigre town, easily recognisable by the giant Ferris wheel that dominates the skyline at the popular *Puerto dos Frutos.* On the right side of the river heading upstream, just beyond the Ferris wheel, we found Tigre Sailing Club. It was announced by a little wooden sign standing crooked on the grass in front of a weathered timber building with a narrow canal leading past it to a row of mooring poles tucked under overhanging trees.

Fabian had called ahead as promised, and on the lawn to welcome us was the club *marinero.* Pavlo was excited to meet us and very keen to try out his English from the bank, waving his arms and shouting "Come aaahhnn!" and "Fuuuck!" in greeting.

To the left of the narrow entrance, along the side of the clubhouse, was a wooden jetty. The water was so low the jetty resembled a first floor sundeck. Pavlo stood there looking down on us as we fouled the keel in the mud and lurched to an ignominious standstill directly across the entrance.

"Come aaahhnn!" he exhorted, but it was no use; we were firmly aground. Reversing back out into the river was impossible; with the keel stuck, the prop walk merely swung the stern against the wooden piles holding up the jetty. We were going nowhere.

We threw lines up to the jetty and made fast, and I managed – just – to clear the gap with a flying leap and introduce myself to Pavlo.

Apparently there was no problem. This was not the normal depth, and it would be a good metre deeper in *una hora,* at which time we would be able to motor in with ease. In my mind I could hear "*Thees ees not normal*".

The appointed hour came and Pavlo was confident we would now be able to get in, but I could see the water had not risen an inch. My Spanish still being poor, it was easier to let him see us try than to argue, but it proved, of course, to be pointless. Pavlo then made a phone call, and a few minutes later his sidekick Manolo arrived. The two of them then proceeded to try to tow us out of the sucking mud with a rowing boat. It was pitiful. They heaved gamely on their oars and fell over each other like a pair of Stooges, but they would not have been a match for the eight ton *Josephine* even if she were *not* rooted in the river bed.

Another ninety minutes ticked away, by which time it was getting on for midnight and we were cold, tired and hungry. The water had risen slightly – maybe six inches – so we tried again. Although the bottom of the keel was still embedded, the boat was riding high enough that with full throttle we could just make way. We ploughed our way up the sludgy canal to a mooring, Pavlo alongside in his dinghy spurring us on with exuberant "Come aahhns!" and "Fuuuucks!" at the top of his voice. It was all so novel and exciting for him. Getting between the poles and into position to tie up took some doing, as it was shallower there again, but a combination of engine power and elbow power (heaving on ropes around the mooring poles) got us in.

The next morning Pavlo came over to us in the launch and showed me the water taps and electrical points hidden in the bushes opposite our boat, and to explain that either he or Manolo would be on call every day to collect us from the boat and ferry us across the river into Tigre and back. That would be very convenient indeed as there was no bridge over the river to town.

***

Now that we had found a secure, cheap place for *Josephine* to spend the winter, discussion turned to what we should be doing with ourselves. The original plan – way back – had it that by now we would be sailing north again, to Brazil, having spent the end of summer exploring Tierra del Fuego. The enforced layover in Uruguay had well and truly put paid to that idea, but the thought of sitting around in the icy mud of Tigre for four months waiting for the return of summer was somewhat unappealing.

A week earlier we had joined our friend Marcelo in Buenos Aires to celebrate his fortieth birthday party, and he and his delightful wife Lili had planted in our minds the idea of an Andean skiing holiday. None of us had tried skiing before. It was winter after all, and we were in Argentina with no plans; and it would be a chance to see Patagonia. Unanimously in favour of a break from boat life and a change of scenery for Lucy, we were soon scouring the internet for suitable accommodation in San Carlos de Bariloche, nestled in the Patagonian Andes and home to one of Argentina's prime ski resorts.

We were off on a road trip.

"It is the Peace of Thousands of Years."

– Fridtjof Nansen

14

The drive back to Tigre in the rental car was horrific. I had somehow contrived to leave Buenos Aires during rush hour and the traffic was crazy: there were too many lanes, too many one way streets, and not enough signs. And, predictably, I had no map. As I had told Abi that morning: "*I don't need a street map; I'll just make my way north-west. Tigre can't be hard to find.*" Of course with all the high buildings and lights there was no sky by which to navigate so "north-west" quickly became a somewhat abstract concept. In any event if I had had a map it would have been impossible, in that traffic, to take my eyes off the road to look at it. I got myself hopelessly lost and what had taken fifty minutes by train, took me almost four hours by car. I arrived in Tigre well into the night, and long after Pavlo had packed his *lancha* away and taken himself off to bed.

'*Right then*', I thought, '*only one thing for it: nick a canoe from the town slipway.*' Luckily there is very little crime, so nobody locks their boats in Tigre. I paddled the borrowed canoe across the river to the club, planning to sneak it back early enough in the morning that nobody would notice it missing.

We awoke the next day to find *Josephine*'s bow resting on bare mud. The water was so low the inlet valve for the head was sucking air, making it impossible to flush. The boat was canted over at an uncomfortable angle and stuck fast, the kitchen sink outlet buried in the sediment so the washing up water would not drain away. The shore power plug had been torn from its socket as *Josephine* settled so low the cable no longer reached all the way down from the bank. With no power, no sink and no loo, we were very happy to be leaving on a six week road trip to Patagonia.

After hauling the dinghy on board and lashing it to the foredeck, we summoned Pavlo on the radio, only to be told the water was too shallow for the *lancha* to reach us. I used the illicit canoe to ferry the family and a ridiculous amount of sodden luggage (yes, the canoe had a leak) to the clubhouse in six trips. Many of the other boats were far worse off than we were. High and dry, the boats with full keels had toppled drunkenly over on their sides, while the fin keelers – like *Josephine* – squatted in the coppery mud, their keels driven into the riverbed like piles. This was a good time to be going somewhere by car.

Pavlo loaded us into his *lancha* "*Okay, yeah, come aaahhhn!!*" and we made our way across the river to the car, dropping the leaky canoe off at the slipway *en route*. It was so shallow out on the river that the launch's prop fouled the bottom twice. As we disembarked with our bags Pavlo gave me an earnest lecture about the dangers of driving, warning me to look out for trucks and buses, to obey traffic lights, to respect the police, to wear a seatbelt… he must have thought I had never driven a car before.

Disentangling ourselves from the suburbs around Tigre was a challenge. Signage was sporadic and mostly irrelevant, the roads bearing only a passing resemblance to the map. Some roads on the map just did not exist, while others existed for a way, then just ended. And there were roads – *real* roads – that did not appear anywhere on the map at all. We spent the best part of two hours negotiating the crumbling industrial outskirts of the greater Buenos Aires, winding sixty kilometres through a labyrinth of traffic-choked, smoke-clogged streets, diverted by countless roadworks, burst water mains and construction sites, until finally escaping the suburban decay onto *Ruta7*, the national road that would take us a thousand kilometres westwards across the country to Mendoza. *Ruta7* was busy, a seemingly endless procession of heavy trucks coming in towards Buenos Aires. Most of the road being single lane, progress was slow as it was all but impossible to overtake.

Some time in the late afternoon we came to a roadblock, and as we were waved down I realised my lights were not on. In Argentina it is law to drive with your headlights on at all times of the day.

"*Buenos tardes senor,*" intoned the solemn policeman. "*Donde estan sus luces*?"

Only one way to handle this. I was certainly not going to speak a word of Spanish.

"Oh, um… hello officer! Is something the matter?"

"*Sus Luces – donde estan*?"

"I'm sorry, what's that..?"

"*Luz, luz*!" he persisted, flashing imaginary lights with his fingers.

"Ah, *loose* you say?"

I stepped out of the car, and crouched to look underneath.

"What is loose?" Then with my best stupid gringo smile, "Do you speak English?"

He was stumped. Beckoning me to follow him into the privacy of a little office at the side of the road, he showed me a chair, sat down at a desk and pulled out a notepad. He scribbled something on it, and pushed it over to me. It said simply "$100".

I understood immediately, but stared uncomprehendingly at the page.

"*Cien dollar,*" he said, peering at me from under the peak of his cap.

"Pardon?"

He tapped the page with his pencil. "*Cien dollar.*"

"Ah, I see!"

I started to scribble. He leant over the desk to see what I was doing, and I shielded the paper as I busied myself. After a long minute I sat up and pushed the paper back to him. He stared at it nonplussed. I had drawn a map of the Atlantic Ocean, bordered by the outlines of Africa and South America. There was a wavy line from Cape Town to Rio, then down to Buenos Aires, and a picture of a yacht. On the yacht was a family with a baby.

"See?" I exclaimed. "This is us!" pointing first to myself, then to the car outside. "*Nosotros*! In our *barco*! We come to Argentina. We love Argentina!"

I reached over the table and pumped his hand. "*Viva Argentina! Football! Lionel Messi!*"

He was at last beginning to thaw. I did not let up, telling him how wonderful everyone in Argentina was, how Argentina would surely win the next world cup, and what did he think of my *espanol*?

He had nowhere to turn. He could see he was not going to get me to understand I had been stopped for my lights. Far less was he going home with a hundred dollar payoff in his pocket.

"*Muy bien,*" he sighed, pushing himself back from the table, resigned to his bad luck. "*Bienvenidos en Argentina!*"

He clapped me on the back and walked me back to the car, friends. We drove off hooting and waving, lights on.

A combination of the delays in getting off the boat and the dreadful roads out of Tigre conspired to limit us to two hundred and fifty kilometres for the day, and we arrived tired and road-worn in the unheralded town of Junin well after dark. I pulled over to ask a policewoman whether there was a hotel nearby, and she directed us to the recently built *Piedramore*, a swanky but surprisingly priced hotel-cum-convention centre on the main road. Tall pillars, lots of pink marble, very grand. We were the only guests, and the only diners in the restaurant. It smelt of floor polish.

The following day we drove eight hundred kilometres, with a stop for lunch at an unlikely-looking roadside *parillada.* The establishment existed for the benefit of long distance truckers, and the wholesome fare was cheap, the meat excellent. Drinks came by the litre, and Abi's sparkling water was served in an antique silver and glass soda syphon. Later, coming into Mendoza after sunset, I managed to get us lost by following signs for "Maipu", believing it to be a suburb of some standing but which turned out to be a rural neighbourhood outside the city with not a hotel anywhere in sight. After driving through a run down suburb of closed factories and dilapidated warehouses we eventually found our way to the centre of the city and checked into the very smart *Hotel Argentino* on the main square. We booked in for two nights so we could have the whole of the next day to explore.

The city of Mendoza was founded by the Spanish in 1561. It sits on the most active tectonic fault line in Argentina, and in 1861 was almost completely destroyed by an earthquake measuring over seven on the Richter Scale. A full third of the town's population of twenty thousand was killed. The most recent big earthquake struck in 2006, injuring a few people but fortunately killing nobody. For the last hundred years it has been developed as a wine region, and at the turn of the twentieth century thousands of immigrants came from Europe to grow grapes. One billion litres of wine is now produced in Mendoza every year.

For our day off from our road trip, we decided on.... well, a road trip. The idea was to motor through the foothills to the northwest of the city, into the Andes and up towards the border with Chile from where we hoped to get a glimpse of the mighty Aconcagua – at 22,831 feet, the highest mountain in the world outside Central Asia.

Our map was up to the usual Argentine standard, with roads either missing, or ending nowhere. It took an hour of driving around in circles before we were able to extricate ourselves from Mendoza's lowerbrow suburbs and progress vaguely north-west. Though not initially sure, it turned out we had chanced upon the right road, and for the next two hours we drove over a vast, wind-torn plain of brown stones. Andean foothills gathered themselves in folds to our left before we turned west and twisted between them on winding gravel, zigzagging our way ever higher, negotiating tight switchbacks, our attention drawn to the hazards of the road by signs warning of "*pronounced curves*". Watched by herds of enigmatic llamas, we looped up and up into the thinning mountain air.

The intersection with the Upsallata road, which connects Mendoza to the Chilean border at Punta del Inca, gave us our first breathtaking view of snow-capped Andean peaks arrayed across the horizon, a row of jagged white teeth on brown gums biting into the sky.

Punta del Inca itself was a disappointment. Aconcagua, which is otherwise visible from the main road, was shrouded in cloud. We took a photograph of where it should have been, then waited a long time for bad food in a frigid, snow-covered wooden restaurant with an unlit fireplace, before driving an hour and a half back down to

Mendoza along the main road. On the way into town we measured a four kilometre long row of stationary trucks lined up on the opposite side of the road waiting to climb the pass the next day. If this was a daily routine, I was glad we had climbed into the mountains by the scenic route that morning.

***

After two nights in Mendoza we joined the famous *Ruta40* and headed south towards Patagonia. Construction of this national road was begun in 1935, and continues still. Our first section, from Mendoza to San Juan, was a double-lane highway, but much of the southern section of the road is still gravel. The road spans over five thousand kilometres from the border with Bolivia in the north, down the length of the Argentine Andes to Rio Gallejos in Tierra del Fuego. Ranging in altitude from sea level to more than 16,000 feet, *Ruta40* crosses twenty seven Andean mountain passes and traverses twenty National Parks. It is an epic trans-continental road, in the same mould as the famous *Route66* in the United States. It struck me as a great idea to ride it some day on a bicycle.

Patagonia is not a country. It is not even a state within a country. A region that straddles the southern parts of Chile and Argentina south of the Rio Negro, Patagonia is more a state of mind. It is the condor floating high between the frozen peaks; the endless open plain dotted with sheep; it is guanacos, volcanoes, glaciers and biting wind; Darwin, Chatwin, Slocum, Magellan and Drake. But most of all Patagonia is big sky. A high dome of eggshell blue arches over infinity.

All day we had wide open plains on our left dotted with extinct volcanoes, and on our right the ramparts of the mighty Andes reached high into the sky. For several hours we negotiated a tarred road in such disrepair that driving on the gravel verge was both quicker and safer.

Sheep silhouetted in clouds of orange dust were harassed over the road by *gauchos* on sturdy horses, backlit by the late sun. A wildcat, and later a rhea, darted across ahead of us. The mountains in the glow of afternoon were layered yellow, ochre, gold, rust, steel grey and black. An old man with a walking stick flagged us down in the middle of nowhere hoping to sell us a fossilised mussel.

Around six that evening we reached the sparse settlement of Barrancas and tried the newly built *El Porton* hotel, only to be told it was full. At the end of a dusty track lined with the shacks and corrugated iron sheds of Argentina's rural poor, the hotel looked deserted but for the bored receptionist, and it was clear that nobody wanted the inconvenience of guests. Secretly I was glad to be told the hotel was "full" as I preferred to keep going. Two hours more in the dark saw us the remaining 120km to Chos Malal where the wind was bitter and dust swirled in the tungsten glow of the streetlights.

Nestled at the foot of the Andes surrounded by conifer forests, Chos Malal was established in 1887 as a waypoint for cattle drives. Now the focus is tourism, excellent access to the Andes making it a popular climbing destination. After a few false turns in the dark we found the town centre set a few miles back from the road with no signposting, and checked into the clean and simple *Posada Anlu*. As three of the four of us were down with flu (Granny being the exception) we took the next day off. It was a day of howling Antarctic winds rasping against the corrugated tin roof, but indoors we slept heavily.

***

The final six hour drive to Bariloche took us into a world of cobalt blue lakes, sheer black cliffs, soaring white peaks and roiling mist. If gods exist they surely must live here. On the southern side of Lake

Nahuel Huapi, squeezed between the shore and the little mountain *Cerro Otto*, we found the quaint, eclectic town of Bariloche.

The name "Bariloche" is derived from Mapudungan (the language of the local indigenous people, the Mapuche) and means "People from Behind the Mountain". The town of San Carlos de Bariloche, to give it its full name, was formally constituted in 1902 on the site of a trading store erected by one Carlos Wiederhold, a German who had crossed the Andes from Chile in the late nineteenth century. Now it is a tourist town. In the winter it offers good skiing, and in the summer climbing, hiking, mountain biking and sailing are popular. The surrounding network of crystal glacial lakes provides excellent fishing and is a photographer's dream.

Lake Nahuel Huapi ("Jaguar Island" in Mapundungan), with its more than three hundred and fifty kilometres of shoreline, is home to one of the world's mythical monsters, *Nahuelito,* first reported in 1922 and described as a "giant serpent". Numerous zoological expeditions have been mounted to detect evidence of this elusive creature, none with any success; but, as with Loch Ness, myths die hard. As recently as 2006 photographs of the beast were anonymously delivered to the offices of *El Cordillero Edicion*, a local newspaper, and were duly printed causing a sensation. The tourist spin-off is self-evident.

Che Guevara, referring to the nearby village of San Martin de los Andes and considering settling there, wrote in the diary of his celebrated motorcycle trip with boyhood friend Alberto Granado, "*only the Amazon jungle had the same strong pull on us that this did*". In a letter to his mother he described it as "*a wonderful spot amid a virgin forest with a beautiful lake.*" One wonders how the contemporary history of South and Central America might have been different had he succumbed to temptation and stayed.

We found our hotel and met Jorge. Jorge, who peered with electric blue eyes over a bushy grey moustache which gave him the appearance of a well-fed walrus, was the owner of *Ruca Piren*. I had hit on his rustic little *posada* in a search of the internet ("...*private Jacuzzi for two but only in large herds*" – I pictured a hot tub of cavorting wildebeest). Jorge loved that we were cruising on a yacht, proclaiming himself "*fanatico*" about water sports. He had a small sailing boat of his own moored on the lake, which he used for tourist day-cruises in the summer.

From our rooms we looked out over the lake and the little island of Huemul, where after World War Two an obscure Austrian scientist by the name of Ronald Richter set up a secretive laboratory, under Argentine government funding (thanks to Juan Peron), from where he undertook to produce the world's first Nuclear Fusion energy, to be delivered in handy wine-bottle sized containers. Richter snubbed the Argentine scientific community, not even allowing student visits to his laboratory, and when he reported to Peron in 1951 that he had been successful in performing "*thermonuclear reactions... on a technical scale*" his claims were met with considerable cynicism. Peron appointed a committee of eminent scientists to analyze Richter's results, and after they found the Austrian's work hopelessly inadequate the facility was shut down – but not before some seven million US dollars of Argentine tax payers' money had been thrown at it (equivalent to over three hundred million dollars in today's money).

On our first morning it was raining and very cold, and little Lucy was ill. We took her to the local hospital where we found a charming and helpful paediatrician within five minutes. The diagnosis was a low level tummy bug, there was no need to worry; and no, there was no charge. We liked Bariloche already. I dropped by the local pharmacy and outdid myself yet again asking in Spanish for "*something because you are a small baby and you have an upset stomach*". To her credit the pharmacist kept a straight face and the medication was handed over.

With the sun shining bright the next day, it was time to orientate ourselves, and we piled into the car for a day drive around the lake and its environs. Nahuel Huapi and its sister lakes are glacial; valleys scoured out by moving ice five million years ago during the Miocene, now filled with meltwater run-off from the surrounding mountains. The scenery is dramatic. Dazzling icecaps crown sheer faces of rock that plunge thousands of feet into frigid, misty lakes, fed by rivers that writhe through narrow gorges, by turns shallow and tumbling white, or deep and placid reflecting the green of the forest pines.

On the scenic road through the forest of Park Llao-Llao, we stopped where a gap in the woods affords a spectacular view over the waters of *Brazo de la Tristeza* to the lofty *Cerro Capilla.* The branches of the trees dripped lichen and moss, clouds skated across a mirror of teal blue water. The *brazo* is a ten mile long fjord that branches south-west off the lake, and here at the viewpoint was a trailer with the word "LOMITOS" hand-painted on a board. Manfredo, in his sixties, with unkempt beard, shabby leather waistcoat and yellow teeth, sold not only the advertised beef sandwiches, but hot chocolate, *hongos de pino* ("pine mushrooms" – or truffles) and scented candles.

Manfredo showed us pictures of his Saint Bernard with its eight puppies, and of his motorbikes. In his youth he had spent four years traversing the globe on a 1000cc Honda Goldwing, and was delighted to meet fellow travellers. His daughter laboured away in the trailer over our steak rolls while Manfredo regaled us with stories of Asia's Karakoram Highway and the Silk Road. I was desperately sorry my Spanish was not more adequate.

A little further up the road was the most fantastic panoramic view over Bariloche. The waters of the lake shone in the sun like lapis lazuli, and merged into rivers that spread away between the mountains towards Chile as far as we could see. The distant Andean horizon was a white saw blade. Far below us the rolling green fields were mottled with flecks of white where week-old snow lay frozen in the hollows. We stared at the lake until our eyes watered but there was no sign of the great serpent.

"Snowboarding is an activity that is very popular with people who do not feel that skiing is lethal enough."

– Dave Barry

15

Abi and Jo were looking forward to their first experiences of learning to ski, while Rupert and I were determined to snowboard. Although neither of us had tried before, Rupert was a surfer so could be expected, at the very least, to have some "board sense"; and I had spent many a happy hour flopped in front of the television, beer in hand, watching the X-Games and reckoned I had a pretty good grasp of it.

We had of course picked up a few tips from friends. Useful pointers like it being "all in the hip movements" conflicted to a degree with other sage advice like "don't move your hips"; and we had been alternately advised to "keep your weight on the back foot" and "spread your weight evenly"; to "keep the board flat" and to "ride the edges"; to "steer with the back foot", and to "use the edges to steer". It was difficult to see how we could go wrong.

Determined not to waste any money on classes, we downloaded some free "lessons" from the internet. This turned out to be of limited use, but we did pick up such gems as "*If you ride Belligerent bindings or use the Belligerent Sinch Strap retrofit kit, insert your foot, then bend over to lock the lever down into the buckle.*"

OK.

We were further exhorted to "*Eat Healthy for strong bones and muscles*", and reminded that "*most of the time accidents are due to other people thinking that they are the shiz nitz and when they are not.*"

Got it.

The girls, however, being girls, and infinitely more sensible, determined that lessons would be the way to go, so Rupert and I dutifully escorted them to their first meeting with Justo, a stout and jolly middle-aged fellow with the easy charm of a family doctor who was to arrange their instruction. I hung about looking generally knowledgeable while he explained what they could expect to get for their several hundred dollars, and I quietly congratulated myself on having had the foresight to get all my tuition free off the net. Then Justo turned to me.

"And you," he asked, waving a gloved hand to include Rupert. "Will you be requiring lessons too?"

"Us? Oh no," I replied airily. "We will be snowboarding."

Abi rolled her eyes.

"Ah, you are snowboarders!" affirmed Justo. "Good, okay then." He nodded and turned back to the girls.

"Where are you from?"

"South Africa and England."

"A-*ha*, so you are not Brazilian then. That is good, very good."

How so?

"Ah, Brazilians!" he sighed, holding his hands up in the air in mock surrender. "They are very difficult. They sign up for lessons, and after half an hour they don't want to listen anymore, and they take the lift to the top of the mountain and roll all the way down. We are forever rescuing them. They are very dangerous, we cannot tell them anything. They think this is the beach!"

I smiled and avoided Rupert's eyes. This was, of course, exactly our plan. Except for the half hour of lessons.

Newly kitted out in the requisite gear, trudging between the restaurants and coffee shops, a snowboard slung with studied nonchalance over my shoulder, I felt distinctly cool. All those years spent watching the Winter X-Games, and here I was, a snowboarder at last! I could have walked around like that all day. In hindsight perhaps I should have.

The problem with this image was that after studying the map over hot chocolate, Rupert and I were forced to admit that slopes with names like "*El Condor*", "*La Garganta*" (The Throat) and "*Diente del Diablo*" (Teeth of the Devil) would be better off left well alone – at least until tomorrow. We settled on familiarising ourselves with our boards on the more benignly named "*Bambi*".

Bambi was not much of a slope in the classical sense; more an ever so slightly elevated corner of an old car park. When we found it, it was crowded with toddlers zipping about on mini skis with their mothers floundering behind, hand bags flapping in the wind, and fathers standing in all the most inconvenient spots taking pictures. It did, however, afford us our first opportunity to step into our bindings, and the subsequent discovery that yes, snow can be hard.

After pitching over our boards several times as kamikaze children swooped around us, their mothers still in game pursuit, we gave it up and retreated to the pub to soothe our physical and emotional bruises with a well deserved whisky. Watching through the window the goings on of *Bambi*, we resolved never to go there again, but to adopt the Brazilian method and go straight up the mountain, as had been our original plan, and find a real slope.

For Abi and Jo things were progressing rather better. Justo had arranged as their instructor a phlegmatic Ukrainian by the name of Valery, who in his day had been a member of the Ukrainian Olympic cross-country skiing team. For some reason he just could not get his head around Jo's name.

"*Zhou*?" he tried. It sounded Chinese.

"Jo," she repeated.

"Ah, *Show*?"

"No, *Jo*." She spelled it for him. "J-O."

"Ah, yes. Jay-*Oh*!"

Rupert and I could hear him bellowing from the pub as my mum-in-law wobbled off down the slope.

"Yes, Jay-*Oh*! Okay! That's good, Jay-*Oh*!"

***

It was a few days before Rupert and I made our way back to *Cerro Catedral* (the Tour de France was showing live on television), by which time Abi and Jo's daily lessons were bearing fruit. The four of us took a cable car (after being subjected to compulsory blood pressure tests in the queue) for the twenty minute ride up to one of the higher points on the mountain where a busy restaurant offered a superb view of Nahuel Huapi to the north, and the high Chilean Andes to the west.

Up here was a bigger "learning ground" – a shallow bowl in the mountain, about the size of three football fields, with a lift running up one side of it. Compared with *Bambi*, it was nice and spacious and might have proved a useful nursery – if only we had the patience.

Unfortunately though, we had noticed a well-wooded, interesting-looking run from the cable car, and as we rose higher we had tracked it back up here. I managed to convince Abi and Rupert to join me in exploring this exciting looking option back down the mountain. My logic was that we had all day, so we could go carefully and take it easy; and surely by the time we reached the bottom of the mountain we would know what we were doing? It seemed intuitively simple – like teaching yourself to swim by throwing yourself out of a boat.

If we had only bothered to study the ski map, we might have been warned by the fact that the major part of that particular run went by the ominous name of "*Avalancha*".

From the restaurant, we looked down over a relatively easy looking path running away across the mountain towards our left for about half a mile before it opened onto a large, sweeping slope. There we could see skiers and snowboarders diving down at great speed, but a few were cruising sideways, quite slowly. I convinced Abi and Rupert it would be easy, and we set off. Jay-Oh had more sense and stayed with Lucy in the restaurant.

The first path – the "easy looking" one – turned out to be a narrow, rocky, lopsided track with a very awkward sideways camber that kept shovelling our boards over the side. We found it impossible to even stand still without sliding diagonally, slowly but inexorably, over the edge. Eventually we had to admit defeat and walk.

We trudged along for twenty minutes to the end of the track, where it petered out and we found ourselves standing at the top of the big, open slope we had seen from the restaurant. This was "*Avalancha*". It was very exposed, and a lot steeper than it had looked from back there.

As we stood contemplating our folly, three people on snowboards came up behind us.

"*Todo bien?*" one of them asked.

"Uh… yes, I guess… we're just a little nervous about this…"

"Oh, don't worry," he assured us in English. "It's not so bad. We are not very good at all!" and they plunged down The Avalanche as if they were shooting a Red Bull commercial. Great.

There was nothing really for it but to have a go. I made a few brave comments for the video camera, then stood up on my board and instantly started to slip sideways down the mountain. The only way I could stop was to sit. I tried standing again with the same result. After persevering some minutes, I discovered the best way to arrest the "death slide" was to go with it and generate a little momentum, then angle the board across the slope and slightly downwards. Suddenly I was gliding smoothly along on my upper edge, traversing the slope with no slippage at all. I was exultant. It was the one bright moment of the day, and well worth all the trouble, skimming across the face of the mountain as if on air.

Rupert followed with similar results, but Abi let us get ahead before starting down – she being a far more competent skier than we were snowboarders. Perhaps it was the lessons.

The thrill of that first ride did not last long. In spite of the relative success we were having, we were losing too much altitude too quickly. We needed to traverse the slope to a lodge a few miles away, about thirty degrees to our left, but were not competent enough to make the angle. Every time we fell we slithered down the icy slope and lost more height. In the end we had no option but to walk back up and across. (Abi on the other hand had stayed too high, and we have a hilarious video clip of her tobogganing down the frozen slope on her behind, skis shouldered and heels pedalling the ice as if she were descending on a bicycle.)

It was getting late. The mountain was in shadow and freezing up. Little balls of ice were tumbling down around us. The steep slope, with its slick surface, was no place for beginners and we spent the next hour slogging on foot over the crusty ridges with their stark scrubby bushes showing up black against the white.

The sky was darkening when we came weary upon the lodge, only to discover the last lift for the day had gone. We were on our own, and still half way up the mountain.

"This is just great!" exclaimed Abi. "Now what?"

"Now we have to ski down, that's what. It should be a lot easier from here. There's a run – the one through the trees – remember we saw it from the cable car?"

But the path was narrow and winding. Other people, experts who were making full use of the last minutes of twilight, were swooping down off the Avalanche and charging in a blur amongst the trees. We would have to be very careful not to be hit in the gloom.

We were falling again. The path was too steep, we were generating too much speed every time we stood up. It was not wide enough for us to manage turns to slow ourselves. Our only option was to keep sitting down. Once I smashed so hard into Rupert I really thought I had broken his arm with my board. Luckily nineteen-year-old limbs are made of rubber.

We slid, we fell, we rolled, we scraped our way down the hard sheets of ice with their protruding tree roots and balls of frozen mud for another two hours. Our mitts were frozen solid and beneath our jackets we were drenched in icy sweat. Everything hurt from falling – bum, knees, shoulders, wrists, hips.

More than anything, we were exhausted from getting up. There is a technique to standing up strapped to a board on a slippery surface, and I had not mastered it. After ending up on my bum, I would first lift my legs high to get the board in the air, then roll over and line the board up with the slope. Then I would hook the fingers of my right hand under the edge of the board, and heave against it to pull my body off the snow and stand up. I was forever trapping my mitt under the board as I came up and catapulting straight across, head over heels, ending in a worse tangle then before and scrabbling madly on the ice to get out of the way before being run over. I would invariably then be facing the wrong direction, and have to repeat the entire process. When I did manage to stand, I would grind ten yards along the ice, hit a tree root, and flip over on my face shovelling another scoop of slush down the neck of my jacket.

On the flat or slightly uphill sections, because we carried no speed, we would slide to a halt. Then we would have to remove our frozen mittens, unclip, stomp up the slope, sit down, clear the ice from the board and bindings, clip back in, re-mitten, heave up, fall back, heave again – only to start sliding slowly sideways, or backwards, and have to sit down and do it all again. It was some hours before we eventually ran out of ice altogether and were able to shoulder arms and walk the rest of the way down in the dark on lumpy, frozen mud.

Back in the pub, while Lucy chased a boisterous St Bernard puppy between the tables, the rest of us nursed our scrapes and bruises – and egos – and recovered our collective sense of humour with spicy mulled wine. I picked up the familiar sound of English at the table behind us, and we introduced ourselves to two Geordies. They had just arrived, and were keen to learn to snowboard.

"Can you recommend anyone for lessons?" they asked.

"Hey!" chirped Rupert. "We taught ourselves today. It's easy. Rent a couple of boards, go to the top of the mountain, and just practice all the way down. At the bottom, if you are not dead, you will be snowboarders!"

I for one felt more dead.

"I pictured a low timber house with a shingled roof,
caulked against storms, with blazing log fire inside,
the walls lined with all the best books,
somewhere to live when the rest of the world blew up."

– Bruce Chatwin, "In Patagonia"

16

Our skiing adventure over, we hit the road again and made our way south from Bariloche deeper into Patagonia through mountains heavy with snow, in the direction of El Bolson. A "*bolson*" is a raised desert valley with a central shallow lake, the word derived from the Latin for a "large purse". According to our guidebook, the town of El Bolson, a hundred and thirty kilometres from Bariloche along *Ruta40*, is famous for its Pixies.

We pulled over for lunch outside a little diner called "*El Zuchini*" with a striped pumpkin painted onto a board by the door. The interior décor was pine, pine and more pine; pine ceilings, pine bar, pine shelves, pine tables and pine chairs with shamrock motifs burnt into their backs. The pine-clad walls were hung with pine-framed beer labels. Two friendly sisters, who could almost have passed as pixies, ran the place. One had Lucy in her arms before we could order and whisked her into the kitchen to see pictures of her own daughter who was the same age.

Of the four specials on offer, they were out of both *Cordero Patagonico* (lamb) and *Trucha Patagonica* (trout); but there was *Pollo Patagonico* (Chicken), which was tough, and a *guiso verduro* (vegetable stew) which had been infiltrated by gristly fragments of sausage.

***

We found the town of Esquel a further hundred and fifty kilometres down the road. Even smaller than El Bolson and lacking pixies, it marks the "economic border" of Patagonia in that from here on south the Argentine Government implements significant tax breaks to encourage businesses in this under-developed region of the country. Fuel from the government-owned YPF filling station in town was half price. We slept the night on hard wooden beds in an A-frame pine construction with a creaky loft that smelled of stale cigarette smoke and thrummed with starving mosquitoes.

In the morning we left *Ruta40* and turned east. The sweeping plains of central Patagonia unfolded before us under a pale yellow sun that lifted like a balloon above the eastern skyline. Under a high ceiling of washed out turquoise we left Esquel behind us and headed out across the stony winter landscape, old snow lying like foam in the hollow shadows. The jagged white peaks of the Andes receded in the rear view mirror as we motored past frozen puddles of mud gleaming in the watery morning light. I looked up at the delicate porcelain sky and could imagine it shattering at any moment into a web of hairline cracks. The tarred road sagged like uncooked biscuit between edges that had crumbled from repeated freezing.

After some four hundred kilometres the road joined the *Rio Chubbut* and followed its meandering course as it snaked around remote farmsteads pinned with naked poplar trees. The Chubbut owes its name to the Tehuelche word "*chapot*", meaning "shining" or "flashing". The river glinted silver from its stony floodplain a hundred metres below us.

By late afternoon we had crossed a continent and came upon the Atlantic at Puerto Madryn. "Porth Madryn" was established by Welsh immigrants on Patagonia's east coast in 1865, who named it after the estate in Wales belonging to their leader and sponsor, Sir Love Jones-Parry. To this day the town flag is the sky-blue and white Argentine stripes with the red dragon of Wales at its centre. The clipper *Mimosa*, that brought those first Welsh settlers, remains prominent on the town coat of arms, and Puerto Madryn is twinned with Nefyn, a small town in North Wales. On the nearby peninsula the settlers came across bustling colonies of flightless, swimming birds they are said to have named *pen gwyn* after the souls of drowned sailors. (This etymology has been disputed, as *pen gwyn* actually means "white head" in Welsh, and penguins generally have black heads – although the Magellanic Penguin, which is ubiquitous on Peninsula Valdez, does have a white head with a black face.)

The modern Puerto Madryn is sustained by fishing, tourism and Argentina's largest aluminium smelter. The town itself was not particularly imposing when we drove in, but the recent construction of a "shopping centre", as highlighted in all the tourist propaganda, seems to have given it new credibility.

Driving along the seafront we stopped to watch a pair of courting Right Whales as they lolled and wallowed in the shallows just off the beach. To our left gulls wheeled and mewed above red fishing boats at the end of the mile-long *Storni* Pier, constructed to support the export of aluminium. Closer in the rusting hulks of long-abandoned trawlers lay decaying on the sands of low tide.

From a tourism point of view it is not Puerto Madryn *per se* that is the attraction; it is the nearby Peninsula Valdez. The 3625 square kilometre peninsula has been a UNESCO World Heritage Site since 1999. It was declared a nature reserve as far back as 1778, and owes its name to the Spanish minister who motivated it. The peninsula is a refuge for guanacos, maras and rheas, as well as colonies of Magellanic Penguins, Elephant Seals and Fur Seals. Between May and December Right Whales come to the protected bays on either side of the peninsula to court and calve, and Orcas patrol the eastern beaches where they have refined the technique of deliberately beaching themselves through the surf to take seal pups off the sand.

We drove the long, straight gravel roads of the peninsula past family groups of guanacos haloed by the winter sun with their large round eyes and long lashes. Rheas sprinted ahead of us like startled old ladies with their skirts hiked up.

Although the original *estancias* – sheep farms established by the Welsh settlers – still operate, the only town on the peninsula is the small Puerto Pyramidis, named after the angular headland north of the beach. The town exists solely for the servicing of the tourist industry, which revolves around whale watching. It boasts one fuel station, one automatic bank teller – on wheels – and a scattering of rustic hotels, restaurants and drinking holes. Licences have been issued to a select few operators who launch enormous rigid inflatables from the beach, jammed with life-jacketed tourists, out into the bay for a close up experience with the romancing whales.

Las Restingas Hotel, dominating the beach with its heavy blue paint job, afforded a dramatic view over the sea with the sun reflecting brilliant white off the explosions of spray from the breaching whales. A battery-powered singing and dancing penguin that lived on the bar had Lucy bopping along in the lobby to a blues rendition of Merry Christmas, and the only way to separate her from it was to get her to tuck it up under a blanket for a sleep.

A short drive from our hotel found us atop *Punta Pyramidis*, looking down twenty metres from the mud cliffs inset with fossilized bivalves, onto a five metre wide shelf of rock jutting out over the water. This is one of the main breeding grounds for the fur seals that congregate in their tens of thousands every year, but we were a few weeks early, and on this day there were no more than six or seven seals taking the sun on a rock. We could but imagine the chaos of noise and smell a month later.

Dinner that night was in *La Estacion*; a cosy, rustic restaurant with a wooden interior dressed in rock memorabilia. We ate surrounded by posters of Bob Marley and The Beatles, old vinyl discs and record sleeves suspended from the ceiling. We could buy wind charms of penguin feathers and whale bone, and wooden carvings of armadillos.

***

The northernmost point of Peninsula Valdez goes by the somewhat unimaginative name of *Punta Norte*. It sports a long gravel beach overlaying a rocky shelf that extends, submerged, some hundred metres out to sea, from where it then drops off into deeper water. The shelf is scored with narrow channels the seals use to get to the beach during their spring breeding season. Punta Norte is one of the world's largest Elephant Seal breeding grounds, and the one made famous by David Attenborough as the place where Orcas are to be seen propelling themselves through the rocky channels onto the beach to prey upon young seals. The Orca – or Killer Whale – is an apex predator. Not even man is a natural enemy. Fittingly perhaps, the genus name *orcinus* means "Kingdom of the Dead", and the name Orca is derived from the Latin "*Orcus*", a Roman god of the underworld.

The "Punta Norte Orca Research" group monitors orca activity year-round, and Juan, the park ranger on duty in the lookout hut when we visited, showed us his calendar onto which all Orca sightings are noted. He tore off a picture of an Orca and gave it to Lucy.

Down on the beach was one solitary female elephant seal, and as we watched she hauled herself into the water to lie wallowing in one of the channels. By the end of the month (August) there would be thousands of elephant seals fighting for space on the stony beach with the dreaded orcas patrolling the drop off.

Above and behind the beach, where a railing has been constructed to keep tourists from getting too close and disturbing the breeding seals, was a sign. On the sign was a picture of a nurse, drawn in the Pop-Art style of Andy Warhol, with her finger to her lips. It looked more like a Guinness advertisement you would expect to find printed on a tin tray in a pub in Hammersmith. Above her were written the words:

"THIS PLACE IS NO HOSPITAL…
BUT THE IMPORTANCE OF SILENCE
IS THE SAME ONE.
…THANKS!"

We elected to cross the centre of the peninsula on our way back to the hotel in Puerto Pyramidis rather than follow the coast, in the hope that we might be lucky enough to see some of the land animals that thrive there. We were not disappointed. Driving slowly we saw, in the scrub, a pair of maras, those long-eared little desert creatures that look so like hares their English name is "Patagonian Hare", but which are not actually hares at all: they are rodents, closely related to the capybara and guinea pig.

***

Back on the mainland two days later, after a two hundred kilometre drive north from Puerto Madryn, we came to San Antonio Oeste and pulled up at the "*El Colonial*", a roadside motel next door to an overnight truck-stop with a *parillada* and a shocking pink *whiskeria.* (It was only the following year that I learnt a "*whiskeria*" is really a brothel, and they are always painted pink.)

The hotel reception desk appeared abandoned, but we hung about for some minutes until a swarthy, indigenous looking man materialised from somewhere behind the building. He showed us the rooms, took our money, advised us the restaurant "*no funciona*", and, as mysteriously as he had appeared, vanished. The inside of the room was bare brick with a domed ceiling, reminiscent of old photographs of World War Two air-raid shelters. I felt like I was in a kiln. There was a strong smell of pine scented air freshener and carpet shampoo.

Seeing as the restaurant "*no funciona*", and the abutting truck stop looked a little on the seedy side, we piled into the car with our rumbling tummies and followed the signs for eight kilometres to forage in Las Grutas.

Las Grutas is by all accounts a booming tourist town, boasting, despite being in Patagonia, the beach with the warmest water in Argentina. The water in the shallow San Matias Gulf is trapped inshore by the ocean currents and bakes in the sun with very little turnover, with the happy result that temperatures near the beach average 25degC. Even in winter the temperature seldom drops below 22degC. A high concentration of iodine has invested the waters with miracle healing powers that are reputed to be of particular therapeutic benefit to the old and the very young.

There was not much "booming" evident when we arrived. The reported quarter of a million summer visitors were long gone, and most of the three thousand permanent inhabitants seemed to be in hiding. But the empty beach was beautiful – miles of hard packed sand running along the base of fifty foot high sedimentary cliffs, pocked with hundreds of fist-sized holes, each home to a pair of green Burrowing Parrots. The parrots were out for their evening constitutional, perched in couples atop the street lights, or barrelling up and down the beach flashing their fiery red tummies and squealing up a merry din. As the sun sank behind the empty hotels the still sea was rendered in muted pinks and lavender. A small pod of bottlenose dolphins slipped languidly through the smooth water in tight formation while four flamingos dabbled in the shallows. A few minutes' walk north and the cliff became a series of caves hollowed out of the limestone by the sea over millions of years. They inspired the town's name – "The Grottos".

Dinner was served in "Aladdin", the only restaurant we could find that was open, with the blue genie from the Disney film prominent on the sign. I ordered chicken from a middle-aged waitress with glasses like prisms, but after being scolded for not choosing seafood changed my order to "*Cazuela de Mariscos*". I was not sorry; it was an excellent seafood pot-stew. The only other people eating were a family at the next table, who turned out to be the owners. The matriarch was a heavy woman with heaped up hair and strong African features. She had Lucy on her knee within minutes, sharing her *mate*, and marvelled at how we had sailed our boat across the ocean to visit her restaurant.

In the morning, with the restaurant at our bunker still "*no funcionando*", we left early and made good progress, stopping twice to photograph guanacos. The road was long and straight over the chessboard-flat landscape, taking us past a number of dull grey salt pans picked out with rosy flamingos. The monotony of the road was broken only by the occasional bored rhea and a dead armadillo.

By mid-afternoon I was driving the car on reserve. Stupidly I had opted not to stop in Rio Colorado with the tank half full, and now in the middle of nowhere the needle was in the red. The map showed names of places like *El Principio* and *Cotita* that did not appear to exist on the ground, much less manifest filling stations. We followed a hand-painted sign for *Hucal* off the highway along a dusty track. After ten minutes with no evidence at all that we were approaching a town, I thought it prudent to return to the main road. It would not do to run out of fuel here; it was quite possible there would not be another car this way for days. We managed another twenty kilometres, driving slowly, to the nondescript settlement of *Peru* (which actually means "turkey").

There was no evidence of fuel here either. Fronting the road was a whitewashed police station, but it was locked up, and when I knocked I succeeded only in raising the interest of several large dogs on chains. Round the back was a lamb on a rope, and two calves tied to a cart of hay. A new looking Volkswagen car gave us hope, and I banged noisily around some adjacent sheds, shouting greetings.

"*Hola, hola! Buenos Dias!*" (bang – crash – thump).

Eventually a skinny, peroxide-blonde woman of around thirty appeared. She looked Russian. I was invited indoors. The gloom was opaque after the bright sun, and it was a full minute before I could see I was in a fly-blown tuckshop that sold potato crisps and fizzy drinks. I explained that we needed fuel. She suggested we try the "*gommeria*"; if it was closed, we could find *Senor Juarez* at his house, "*third on the left*".

I felt sorry for her and bought a dusty packet of biscuits – they turned out to be stale – and walked over to the corrugated iron shed with the yellow "*gommeria*" sign. Nobody was selling tyres today; the shed was padlocked. More precious fuel was then used up driving between the gum trees on a bumpy track to the second in a row of five identical cinder block houses. A woman in an impossibly tight pair of shiny track pants was hanging up washing. She told me through the white plastic pegs clamped between her stained teeth that *Senor Juarez* was out; and no, she had no idea when he would be back. I wondered where he could possibly have gone.

Back at the store, the fading Russian doll gave me a dirty five-litre plastic can with a cracked lid which I took with me for when I would finally run out of fuel and need to hitch a lift.

I coaxed another ten kilometres out of the car before the fuel finally did run out and we trundled to a halt under a gum tree. The first car to come along stopped and I met yet another "Alejandro". This one was thin and greying and forty in a beige safari suit, and worked on a gold mine in San Juan. He drove his little white Japanese car with its heavily cracked windscreen very fast. Touching two hundred kilometres an hour, we reached a filling station in less than fifteen minutes, and moments later I was back on the side of the road hitching in the opposite direction, a full can of fuel at my feet.

This time I was picked up by a truck driver. "Maxi" was in his twenties, driving the family business. He worked a six day, five thousand kilometre round trip from Buenos Aires to Catamarca in the north, down to Puerto Madryn and back to Buenos Aires. He said in Argentina, any long distance truck driver would stop for someone waving a plastic can.

"*y Argentina, como es? La gusta?*"

Yes, I told him, I liked Argentina very much. He asked why. I mentioned the wide open spaces, the friendly people, the culture, the mountains, sea, climate…

He looked faintly disappointed. I asked him what the matter was.

"*No ti gustan los asados*?" he asked, looking almost hurt.

"*Ah, claro*!" I replied. "*Mi gustan mucho los asados. El carne de Argentina es el mejor del mondo*!"

Reassured that Argentina's meat was the best in the world after all, he beamed and puffed up like a pigeon. He was still smiling when he dropped me back at the car with my can with the cracked lid.

Much later that afternoon we came into *Pehuajo* past a family of six on a horse and cart in choking dust, driven by an old man in a floppy hat who nursed a litre of beer as children fought for room with four large hounds. Another family sat beside the road with a tent and a bonfire. The central avenue was lined with people, their cars parked between low scrubby trees as they sipped *mate* and flew kites. Tattered remnants of several kites hung strangled from the power lines.

The streets of the city formed a grid of low concrete buildings, gusting wind, choking dust, swirling plastic bags, ribby dogs and tumbleweed. Only the central *plaza* sported some fine colonial buildings with smart new paint jobs. All appeared to be government offices – police station, magistrates court and some or other agricultural organ of state. Near the plaza we found Hotel *Las Nogales* – "The Walnuts". It was clean and reasonably priced.

Breakfast at The Walnuts was served in a cavernous colonial-era ballroom with high ceilings, glass chandeliers, dark panelled walls and a long bar. It was scattered with the memorabilia of past grandeur. Silver serving trays adorned the walls between framed newspaper cuttings from the fifties, the head of a deer with one horn, and an old polo stick from Pakistan. In one corner was an ancient piano with yellow ivory keys, and in another a desk with a collection of silver and brass letter knives and an inkpot. Nobody could tell me anything about the polo stick.

Ours was the only table in use. I wondered what Pehaujo had ever offered to warrant the construction of this hotel, and decided it must be the lake. We would look at the lake. After breakfast we drove out of town to the end of the street, over a rutted track and onto a raised bank overlooking a sombre grey pan supporting a sewerage works and a few demoralised ducks.

The most interesting trivia I could glean from a cursory search of the internet was that the *"… city is well known in Argentina because of Maria Walsh's song 'Manuelita', who is a turtle"*.

At four o'clock that afternoon we arrived back in Tigre and summoned Pavlo. He crossed the river from the club in the *lancha* to pick us up. He was delighted to see us.

"Yeah, cam *aaaahhhnnn*! Fuuuck!" as if he had never expected to see us alive again.

It was good to be back. For the trip across the river to the club, Lucy sat on Pavlo's lap "driving" the launch. Pavlo leant out of the window flashing his dazzling smile, honking the horn and waving at girls in the other boats. Back at *Josephine* I presented him with a little black and white television set we had earned in Piriapolis by returning empty beer bottles.

"The waterways are charged with magic,
but nothing about them is more magical than
the difference made by the few feet of water which
separate the boat from the land."

– Robert Aickman

17

Back at Tigre Yacht Club not much had changed since we left for Patagonia. The water was as low as ever, and *Josephine* still stuck fast in the mud. We tried to move her a little way back from the shore into slightly deeper water in preparation for our departure but she would not budge; not even with the engine full astern, and two winches with ropes attached to the aft mooring poles. It was too shallow even for a depth reading. We realised that to move back out of our hole we would have to pay close attention to the fluctuating water levels, and steal inches whenever the chance presented itself.

There was a buzz of excitement on board. The road trip had been great fun, but it was time to go sailing again. Winter was almost over, and we were looking forward to heading back north, where the turquoise water, sandy beaches and laden coconut palms of Brazil beckoned. We were planning a six month cruise up the coast, after which we would sail to the Caribbean, calling in at the little-visited country of Suriname on the way. We already had something like thirty hours of video, and felt all it lacked before we could make something of it for television was more "tropical island" stuff.

Early the next morning we managed to winch the boat a few more inches out from the bank with the help of a little extra water. The bottom of *Josephine* 's keel was still sunk in the sediment, but any progress was welcome. If we could just get her back another two metres, over the mud bar behind the mooring, we would be in deeper water and possibly able to force our way through the sludge of the canal to the clubhouse, if not out onto the river. It would be a start.

I checked the weather forecast for the next few days and the wind looked perfect for the two hundred mile sail east to Piriapolis the following week. If we could just get out of the club on Sunday or Monday, we could motor the forty miles to Colonia then wait a night or two for the predicted north westerly…

Mud aside, before sailing we were faced once more with the fearful Argentine bureaucratic system. It was time to jump through the hoops of *Migraciones, Aduanas* and the *Prefectura*. Being in Tigre, the closest place we could get immigration done – according to all the guidebooks – was Buenos Aires. I was dreading having to travel over an hour each way by train, then legging it backwards and forwards across one of South America's biggest cities between remote government offices with their erratic working hours. This was the whole reason we had entered the country in La Plata in the first place (not that it had turned out to be all that convenient there either). Unless…

I remembered that in La Plata it was the *Prefectura* who had affixed the immigration stamps to our passports – now if only the local *Prefectura* in Tigre could be convinced to do the same… who knew? It was worth a shot. I hailed Pavlo and he dropped us on the far side of the river near the *Prefectura* office. I was not at all optimistic I would be able to prevail upon them to stamp our passports, and as much as I was going to try, was mentally preparing myself for an additional fifty mile trip with the boat to La Plata in the next few days – water and mud permitting, of course. A return to the joys of Kamikaze Leo and his taxi, and the nineteenth-century customs office, would still be preferable to throwing myself at the mercy of Big Bureaucracy in the capital city.

But first I was going to try in Tigre. The *Prefectura* were to be taken by storm; the element of surprise would be key. Behind the counter were four uniformed men and one woman. Perfect, a crowd.

"*Buenos dias todos,*" I greeted them all at the top of my voice. "*Como andan?*"

Flashing my best Friendly Gringo grin I thrust Lucy at the woman so I could dig around in my bag for the papers. Our blonde and giggling sixteen month old had never been refused before, and it was not going to happen today. The woman was only too delighted to take her, and the men remained mute as they watched Lucy being lifted over the counter. Like a boarding party, we were in.

I launched into a staccato Spanish explanation of the fact that we wanted to leave for Uruguay, that the *Prefectura* at La Plata had kindly stamped us into the country, and could these good fellows please be equally kind and stamp us out? On the counter I constructed a mound of five passports, the boat papers, my skipper's licence, payment receipts from Tigre Sailing Club, yacht insurance policy, the crew list, my open water scuba diving card, international drivers licence and some laundry slips from Uruguay, all the while confessing that my Spanish was not too good and asking their forbearance on that matter. As the uniform in charge eyed the growing pile of papers with bewilderment, Lucy liberated herself from the woman and fled under the counter. Confusion reigned.

They were not used to foreigners in this office. The only boats they processed belonged to locals. That is to say, Argentines and Uruguayans, neither of which need a passport to cross between the two countries.

"*Pare senor.* Stop. *Por favor,*" implored *el capitan*, holding up his hands. "*Primera, ustedes nessesitan ir en migraciones.*"

I told him yes, I understood perfectly that immigration was the first step, so would he please be so kind as to stamp our passports, as his fine colleagues in La Plata had so efficiently done on our arrival.

"*No senor, no es posible.* We don't do that."

He was not going to be harassed into complying.

"*Nessesitan ir en el capital. Migraciones son dentro el terminal de Buquebus en Puerto Madero.*"

Of course I knew this very well, but feigned amazement. To the capital? But that would take a whole day! Was he sure there was no other way?

Knowing as well as I there was not, but at the same time not wanting to be the one to disappoint us, he neatly passed the buck by directing me down the road to the local river bus terminal, where Argentines and Uruguayans regularly pass through flashing their identity cards. He suggested I check there for confirmation.

This redirection was an excellent development. I was now in the happy position of being able to present myself at the ferry terminal with great authority.

"The *Prefectura* says you are to stamp our passports, as they have cleared us to leave!" I announced grandly to the girl behind the counter, who could not have been a day older than nineteen. She was more than a little intimidated at the mention of the mighty *Prefectura* and was most obliging, stamping our passports and boat papers without a murmur. We stepped back out into the winter sunshine feeling liberated.

Not a quarter of an hour later we were back at the *Prefectura* brandishing our five stamped passports. The *capitan* who had dealt with us just minutes earlier had gone off to lunch, and it was left to a young cadet to emboss the boat papers with the stamp of the *Prefectura*. *Migraciones* was *Migraciones* – if they had stamped our passports then who was he to question it? It could not have gone more smoothly. Somewhat irregular, indeed, in that I had not bothered to visit Customs; but I really did not have the energy to go through the farce of declaring in full the number and nature of any typewriters, caged birds, or hemp rope we were removing from the Argentine economy, or explaining any "strange behaviour and unusual deaths" among our rats. We were out! Or so we thought.

Getting the paperwork done meant we *may* leave; but it would be up to the mud sucking around our keel to decide whether we actually *could* leave. Next morning the water was even lower. There was no detectable movement in the boat; not even when powerboats went past and sent their wakes washing against us. It was as if we had grown more roots in the night. It was so shallow that parts of the channel bottom were visible along the banks. We would be going nowhere today.

It was very disappointing, as the weather from the next day onwards would be perfect for the two hundred mile sail to Piriapolis – wind northerly, offshore, fifteen to twenty knots, in 20degC daytime temperatures. We would hug the Uruguay coast in smooth seas and cruise along at seven knots in warm sunshine for maybe thirty hours.

Instead we now faced the prospect of sitting around in this foetid swamp for another day or two until the northerly blew itself out, and the water flooded back into the delta to disentomb us.

***

This mud-enforced hiatus in Argentina was a good time to get things done on the boat that had been waiting for my attention, not the least of which was the stove. For eight months now we had not been able to use it at all; not since the oven and one of the two rings had packed up back in Brazil. All our meals were being cooked on the portable double-ring gas cooker we had bought in Ilhabela and balanced on top of the stove, where it was prone to sliding around with every movement of the boat. Abi and Jo had coped admirably (you will remember that I do not cook) but were by now fed up.

Sailing being a popular pastime in Buenos Aires, the city and its environs abounds with good chandlers. From one close to Tigre I bought deck caulking, some new rope, plugs for an extension to the shore-power cable and a shiny new stainless steel gas stove. In the shop its dimensions were perfect for the boat, and it seemed to me it should be a simple matter to remove the old one and drop the new one into place.

After lunching on a lot of red meat and a not inconsiderable quantity of beer (it is sold by the litre – what do you do?) in the local pub beside the river, our brand new stainless steel stove on the floor next to our table, Rupert and I humped it back across the river in Pavlo's *lancha*. Somehow, between buying it and getting it to the boat, the stove had grown and would not fit in the galley. Of course I only discovered this after I had removed the old one, damaging it beyond redemption in the process, so now the commitment to the new one was absolute. We spent several hours hacking away alternately at the steel of the stove and the woodwork of the boat with a range of saws and files to create a big enough space. It was miserable work in too cramped a space after too many beers and with too many women overseeing our progress.

Abi started it.

"I thought you measured the boat this morning."

"Yes".

"So what happened? Did you not measure the stove in the shop?"

"Of course I bloody did," I huffed past the screwdriver clenched between my teeth.

"Then I don't understand why it won't fit. Did you measure it before or after all the beer?"

I was on my back with my head in the little gap under the fridge, my hands round the sides of the new stove, fiddling with a screw I could not see. I would ignore that question.

"So why don't you take it back?" she suggested after a pause.

"Because," I replied testily into the bottom of the fridge, "we have already left the country if you remember, so I don't suppose we have any rights. And because I completely destroyed the old one getting it out. And because I have now *dissemblied* the ruddy boat. That's why."

Finally, after hacking away a few more pounds of wood, we were able to lower the new stove into position. It was not pretty, but it was in. More or less. The gimbals were not properly centred, so the whole thing leant forward drunkenly, but a few lead weights from a dive belt strategically placed in the bottom of the oven fixed that. I hoped we would not all die from lead poisoning.

As we were congratulating ourselves Abi peered over my shoulder.

"And just how are we supposed to work that?"

"What do you mean?"

"You can't see the knobs!"

She was right. We had mounted the stove in the precise position that the retaining bar across the front obscured the knobs. A spider monkey would not have been able to get its hand in there to operate them.

"And look, the oven door won't open!"

So a further hour was spent ruining the remaining woodwork with saws and chisels to reveal the knobs, and another layer of wood planed off the bulkhead to allow the oven door to open.

"Have another beer!" Abi suggested unhelpfully.

"You know, I believe I will. I obviously didn't drink enough; I am still so thirsty, and I have a headache."

***

At the end of another night imprisoned in the icy mud, we awoke to the same bitter cold but noticed the water was lapping slightly higher. The wind had not swung, so we were not expecting the level to rise – perhaps this was the extra few inches of high tide? There was nothing to lose and we decided to have a bash.

After going ashore to disconnect the water and power, and heaving the dinghy up over the side and lashing it down, we gunned the motor in reverse. *Josephine* moved about a foot back, then stuck fast. Alternating the motor between forward and reverse repeatedly, each time edging the stern a little further into the canal, we bulldozed our way through the mud.

About half way out of our mooring we stuck fast again, and no amount of revving the engine made any difference, so we waited. After thirty minutes the water was another inch higher, and with more of the same bashing and shoving we broke our way out. Ploughing through the sludge of the canal, we made the hundred yard trip to the clubhouse (but not before getting stuck twice more on the way) lifting our feet up as we crossed the club's underwater power cable. We were reassured by an old man who shouted a familiar refrain across from another the bank "*no es normal*!"

It was an immense relief to be free and coasting through the delta through the brown reeds with their black ducks and white egrets on our way to the open waters of the River Plate. We slipped out of the delta with the sun setting behind us, the sky an orange firestorm and the river ahead a soft undulating carpet of tangerine. With the northerly breeze pressing firmly in the sails, *Josephine* made a steady seven knots as a long skein of cormorants strung out above us, coiling like a wisp of smoke against the dimming sky.

Josephine pushed on through the night with a purpose, and sunrise found us off Montevideo, where the water had changed overnight from the turbid brown of the river to an olive sea. It was still cold, but we thrilled to the albatrosses and petrels that circled the boat again. By late afternoon, as the high clouds turned to streaks of gold leaf laid over a pale ice blue, we reached Piriapolis. We had all had enough of the cold winter and were keen to get back to Brazil. The only reason for stopping in Piriapolis was to drop the girls off with Alex who had kindly offered to drive them to the border, from where they planned to catch a bus to Rio Grande. Rupert and I would continue on with the boat and reunite with them at Lauro's museum.

It was good to see our friend Alex again and we were invited to his house for "*humboogers and wheeski*". On hearing how much we liked Argentina, and Bariloche in particular, he was appalled.

"But Buenos Aires is berry danger!" he warned.

I pointed out Buenos Aires is a big city, and big cities anywhere have their dangers; and that we were not planning to live in Buenos Aires; and anyway, he had told me Montevideo was danger too.

"No, I tell you this, *Argentina* is berry danger!"

I reminded him we had just spent a couple of months in Bariloche, and that we had not seen so much as an electric gate or a burglar bar. I could not say I remembered seeing a policeman either.

But Alex was adamant.

"No, you can't to live in Bariloche," he persisted.

"Why ever not?"

"You be divorce in five years."

"What?"

"Yes!"

"What are you talking about? Abi loves Bariloche. She wants to live there too."

"Ah no, not for this; the problem is the young girls!" he explained, wagging a finger.

"*Young girls?* Wow... Alex, um… I don't think…."

"They are very persistent!" he dismissed me with a wave. "If you don't go with them, they put furious, and they tell your wife they sleep with you, and then who she believe, you or the young girls?" he asked, raising his eyebrows. "I tell you this, your wife put you out in four month. Watch!"

"It was morning, and the new sun sparkled gold across the ripples of a gentle sea."

– Richard Bach, Jonathan Livingstone Seagull

18

Edu jumped at the chance to help sail *Josephine* the three hundred miles up the coast to Rio Grande do Sul in Brazil. It would be his first ever "ocean" sail – that is to say, his first experience of sailing outside the *Rio de la Plata*. Not that sailing the River Plate is anything like sailing on a river in the normal sense; at its narrowest it is as wide as the English Channel, and with depth ranging from thirty five feet at its deepest, to less than three in places, when the weather gets up the water does too; it can be very rough. It also has the world's highest concentration of wrecks, and in the shallow water most of them present a serious hazard to navigation. So Edu, in spite of being so excited at the prospect of his "first ocean sail", was in fact already a pretty accomplished sailor.

Getting out of Uruguay involved the normal bureaucratic nonsense. At least this time I had not bothered with customs when we came in, so that was one less bit of paperwork to worry about on the way out. Werner had been on the money about only having problems with the authorities when you go to them.

The closest immigration office to Piriapolis was at the airport, so Alex took us there in his car. Unfortunately for us there was a particularly sulky fellow on duty who would not answer the intercom phone, even though he could see us clearly from where he was, no more than ten yards away on the other side of a glass door. He was looking straight at us, impassive. A security guard shrugged and said he was like that, we would just have to wait. When eventually the glass doors opened for a planeload of tourists, the sullen immigration officer made us wait until he had finished with all the passengers before looking at our passports. He then cross questioned us for fifteen minutes before finally declining to stamp them – no reason given – and sent us to Punte del Este. He never so much as smiled. Very un-Uruguayan.

The Immigration office in Punte del Este was closed. Alex roused a guard, from whom he extracted a phone number for the "*migraciones*" officer. We called. It was his home number. He had gone home because "nothing was happening" at work. He told us to come back in the afternoon. We objected, he said he would come back to work in twenty minutes. An hour later he arrived. It seemed his car had not started. Then he had been unable to start his wife's motorbike. In the end he borrowed his neighbour's car to get to us. He smiled a lot in spite of these travails. Very Uruguayan.

The forecast was good. We could expect this southerly to veer gradually over the next twenty-four hours and settle to a westerly, which would allow us to sail a broad reach up the coast on water blown flat by the offshore breeze.

As always I ran through a safety briefing before we left. Rupert was of course familiar with the boat, having lived on it for almost a year, (not that it ever does any harm to refresh safety procedures) but Edu – the newcomer to ocean passage making – was somewhat bemused by it all.

"Ha, ha! Yeah! Don' worry man!" was his reaction when I started to discuss watches.

"I'm serious Edu – we'll do shifts on the helm during the day of three hours at a time, followed by six hours off. If the weather is unpleasant, we can shorten it. Night watches, between 6pm and 6am, will be two hours at a stretch."

Edu chuckled. "Yes, okay. We see!"

I put his cavalier reaction down to his excitement at getting out to sea for the first time, and allocated Rupert the first watch, to be followed by me, by which time I had no doubt Edu would have settled down and I could hand over to him.

It was an idyllic start to the trip as we set sail from Piriapolis on a balmy mid-morning with the wind blowing gently from the south. The air was rent with the farewell mewing of gulls as we rounded Punte del Este that first evening. We were circled by inquisitive sea lions and almost sailed straight over a basking sunfish. The sunfish is the biggest bony fish in the world (sharks and rays are cartilaginous) and a big one can weigh over two tons. Curiously, they also have the fewest vertebrae of any backboned animal (a mere sixteen). It was the first one Edu had ever seen as it lay there on its side; a buoyant pudding, one fin up in the air like a wafer. As the sun sank behind the luxury apartments above the beach we sat together in the cockpit sharing a steaming pot of chicken curry. After Punte del Este we reached in a light breeze never more than about a half mile from the flat, wild beach that stretches two hundred and fifty miles northwards from Uruguay's holiday mecca to the border of Brazil, and on another hundred miles to the city of Rio Grande do Sul.

That night Edu overslept before each of his two watches. The first time I actually heard his alarm go off, and when it finally stopped I assumed he must be awake and getting ready to relieve me. Then ten minutes later it went off again, and kept bleeping for some time. Eventually it stopped, but it was Rupert's head that appeared in the hatch to ask me what time it was. He too had heard the alarm and was wondering whether he had overslept.

"No, it's Edu's shift, he must still be asleep."

Rupert dug the sleeping Uruguayan out of his bag, and I was eventually relieved on the wheel. Edu did not mention it as he took over, so neither did I. I guessed he was well aware of his *faux pax*, and embarrassed enough without me rubbing it in.

Six hours later, however, it happened again. In the minutes leading up to the change of watch, there was no sign of stirring in the saloon where he was sleeping, and exactly on the hour I found myself hollering down the hatch like the town crier to wake him up. Then I suffered the indignity of a further fifteen minute wait up in the frigid night air as he boiled water for his *mate*. I was annoyed, but held my tongue. Conditions were very good for sailing and it was going to be a short trip; there was no need to fall out with a friend.

Our first sunrise found us becalmed. Gentle zephyrs merely wrinkled the ocean's skin, so we were subjected to the rhythmic drone of the Perkins engine. At least using the motor meant we could run the fridge and recharge the batteries. Attended by ever-watchful albatrosses, and kept a sharp lookout for amorous whales lolling about in pairs inshore. To our left was an endless beach, a strip of mustard-coloured sand underpinning a layer of shrubs so tightly packed they resembled a cultivated hedge. Painted in sweeping brush strokes above the line of bush, layers of dunes in ochre shades rolled away and merged with the distant horizon. For mile upon mile we motored along this flat but starkly beautiful coastline, a giant strip map unrolled and pinned in place by the occasional lighthouse. At times we were so close inshore we would wave to a fisherman.

The several hundred mile trip up the coast can be navigated – at night – solely by the lighthouses. They have been spaced at regular intervals of around forty miles, so you can always sight the next light before the previous one vanishes over the horizon behind you. Each light, of course, has its own "signature", which is recorded on the charts; so when you see, say, a double flash every ten seconds, it is impossible to confuse with a *triple* flash every *twenty* seconds. Foolproof, surely. Or so I thought.

We were slipping along around midnight no more than a quarter of a mile from the beach, which we could make out in the dark by the ghostly pale line of the sand in the starlight. There was no moon. Somewhere astern was a lighthouse beaming out its single bright flash every fifteen seconds, and we knew that in about another hour we should see the next one show itself over the horizon ahead of us. A triple flash every twenty five seconds. We knew this, because as the competent skipper I am, I had familiarised myself with the chart and the characteristics of all the lighthouses up this stretch of coast. The intrepid ocean captain, I could tell you anything.

All was peace and calm, until Edu, at the helm, broke the spell.

"What ees thees?"

I heard him from below where I was watching the kettle boil, and popped my head up through the hatch.

"What is what?"

"Ees a strange light. What ees?"

I hauled myself into the cockpit and peered over the spray dodger to see a very definite triple flash in the darkness up ahead.

"O-ho!" I declared with great authority. "That would be the next lighthouse. Three flashes!"

Edu rubbed his chin. "So soon?" He sounded dubious.

"Yes. Well, I admit we seem to have made really good time, but there's no mistaking it. Three flashes alright! Aim straight for it."

"Straight for eet?" with big eyes.

"Oh yes," I confirmed, quite sure of myself. "It's at least twenty miles away, maybe a little more, and right on the coast. As we are so close to the beach, we can aim straight at it for at least the next two hours. After that it will seem a lot higher, as it stands twelve metres tall, and we will be able to see the tower against the sky."

How pleased he must be to have me as a skipper, able to rattle all this information off the top of my knowledgeable head.

After a minute, as I was pouring the coffee, Edu started up again. "Seems a strange heading thees."

I came back on deck and handed him a coffee. "How do you mean, strange?"

"Well, I had to change the course with thirty degrees to the port and aim thees light as you tell me."

That had to be nonsense.

"Impossible. That lighthouse is on the coast, just like all the others. We should be able to just press on straight. You've made a mistake."

He looked baffled. "No, for me ees funny. The compass reading has definitely change, and we are sail now more on the wind also."

The wind angle was definitely tighter, but that did not mean we had changed course; we could just have had a wind shift. But the compass? I checked it, and he was right – we were aiming for the light, but heading thirty degrees further west than before. It made no sense: after all, lighthouses don't *move*?

"Let's have another look at the GPS," I muttered, and went below. "Hmm..... no, we should be aiming for that light, definitely. Perhaps there is a local magnetic anomaly here affecting the compass. That happens. Don't worry about it, just keep aiming for that flash."

I snuggled down into my sleeping bag, coffee in one hand and book in the other. Aah, the life of a competent sea captain with everything under control!

"Andrew, please come back. Something ees not right here. Thees light ees coming very bright."

Was there to be no rest?

"Alright, I'll check the GPS again," I mumbled with resignation. I read our co-ordinates from the screen and plotted them onto the paper chart. Yep, spot on, right where we should be, twenty-five miles south west of the triple-flashing lighthouse.

Hang on... twenty-five miles? The full code of the light on the chart read Fl(3)25s12m22M. That was a triple flash every twenty-five seconds, from a twelve metre high tower, visible from twenty-two miles away... but we were still twenty-*five* miles away, so we should not be able to see it at all. Yet not only could we see it clearly, Edu was remarking on its increasing brightness.

I felt that first knot in my stomach when you realise something is just not right, and hardly noticed smacking my head on the hatch cover in my haste to scramble back on deck. The light, triple-flashing, that we were now aiming straight for under my confident instruction, really was getting bright. And the flashes were very quick. And there was no beam. This was no distant lighthouse whirling around in its glass dome: no, this was a stationary light, winking on and off three times, very rapidly. And it was an awful lot closer than before.

With a rush of adrenalin, the reality burst upon me. This was the flashing code of an east cardinal mark. There would be a big steel buoy bobbing in the sea marking some or other hazard in the water immediately ahead – rocks probably – and warning us to stay to the east of it. And we were sailing flat out straight at it.

"Turn to Starboard, immediately! Bear off, bear off!!" I barked, letting out the main sheet just as a large steel yellow and black buoy loomed out of the dark and surged past our port side. We missed it by about six feet and were lucky to avoid whatever obstacle it marked lurking just beneath the surface.

Edu and I sat there looking dumbly at each other for several seconds. My god, what had we almost done? In hindsight it should have been obvious. The three flashes were very quick, and set a lot closer together than any three flashes from any lighthouse. It was just that I was *looking* for a triple flash, and not *expecting* to see anything other than the lighthouse. A salutary lesson had been learned, and I felt suitably chastened. Competent skipper indeed.

By the second night Edu was really getting into the spirit of things. Very excited about being "*een the ocean man!*" he stayed up for Rupert's first evening watch, then sat through an hour and a half of mine too.

"How much time?" he eventually asked.

How nice it had been to have company for three quarters of my watch, but how I would not envy him half an hour from now, taking over for his two hour stint after being on deck all this time.

"Thirty more minutes," I replied. "Then she's all yours my friend."

"Okay, I go to boil water, see you," and he disappeared below. I guessed he was going to get pretty tired, he would be needing that *mate.* I remember doing the same thing on my first overnight sail, staying up with other people on their watches, then feeling like death when it came time for my own. He would learn his lesson, like I had.

Conditions were very pleasant so I was not worried, and without an auto-helm he would have to cling to the wheel so there would be no danger of him falling asleep on the job.

Half an hour later, however, there was no sign of Edu. It was such a pleasant evening, sailing at a steady seven knots in the warm offshore breeze, that I let it be. I was rather enjoying myself. Obviously all his socialising on other peoples' shifts had exhausted him.

Another hour passed before Rupert's shaggy head appeared. He looked confused.

"Is it still your shift? What's the time?"

"One o'clock. And no, I'm halfway through Edu's shift. Did you see any sign of him on your way up?"

Rupert glanced back inside. "He's asleep, shall I wake him?"

"No, not to worry, I'm quite happy here for now. Thanks."

It was another twenty minutes before Edu appeared and announced cheerfully, "Okay, now I take my turn!"

I could only think he really believed the shift scheduling was a joke, and we were in fact all just being rather grown up and taking turns when it suited us. I told Rupe to set his alarm forward so Edu would be left alone at the wheel until sunrise. The next day Edu was pretty shattered, and that evening it was easy to get him to agree it would be a good idea to have regular two hour watches the rest of the trip.

Our third and final night, on our approach to Brazil, found us gliding on a gentle warm breeze, the boat whispering over a velvet black sea. Phosphorescence illuminated our wake like the underwater lights of a swimming pool, and ribbons of shining green and silver flashed from the bow, dissolving into the hissing foam. We scoffed the dregs of the giant pot of chicken curry.

The lights of Rio Grande were approaching at six knots, rising and dipping beyond the gentlest of swells. There were still no waves. There was no moon either and a spray of bright stars were twinkling up at us from the water. The great wheel in the sky that is the Milky Way arched overhead and completed itself in the reflection below. The word galaxy comes from the Greek "*galaxias*", for milky, the name given to our arc of starlight by the ancient philosophers. The English name "Milky Way" was first used by Chaucer in his poem "The House of Fame" in 1380.

We were well fed, toasty and snug in our woollies. It was surreal. We watched a DVD concert in the cockpit, and felt we had been transported to this magical place by the music. Edu broke into a stupid grin, I started to giggle, and Rupert burst out laughing. Not a word needed to be spoken. We looked at each other and laughed until we cried. It was just one of those rare moments when life is perfect. A sublime end to a special trip in sparkling weather with the ideal breeze and close friendship, soaring albatrosses, courting whales, magnificent sunsets and *A Delicate Sound of Thunder* under a bowl of brilliant stars. I decided I like my life.

Fishing boats in Piriapolis, Uruguay

With Alex and his son Diego in Piriapolis

Lucy learns to walk in Piriapolis

Lucy's first birthday party at Alex's house

The author with the pink bicycle in Piriapolis,

before the incident with Alex' s Stealer Man

A precious family moment

Edu and Alexssandro (Asterix aand Obelix) on Yamandu

Gauchos in Uruguay

Lucy has her first ever pony ride

Jo, Abi and the author in Bariloche, Argentina, 2009

Abi gets to grips with the basics in Bariloche

Lake Nahuel Huapi at sunset

"The best way to deal with bureaucrats is with stealth and sudden violence."

– Butros Butros-Ghali

19

Not being as brave as our Bavarian friends who had spent almost two years in Brazil incognito, I did not want to risk short-cutting the paperwork in case something blew up later. We would be in a right fix if we got into trouble at sea and needed to be rescued by the *Capitania dos Portos*, or if we fell victim to crime and needed to report to the *Policia Federal.* No, it would be prudent to bite the bullet and sacrifice yet another day of my life to the bureaucratic machine.

Now if you want to confuse the authorities in Brazil, arrive in the country with Edu and Rupert on board, meet Abi and Jo and Lucy off the bus, add them to your crew, then send Edu home. Your boat papers, if you do everything correctly, will say three of you entered the country, then you were six, and now you are five. I knew only too well this is not the kind of juggling that impresses the ever-suspicious authorities in that *narco*-cursed part of the world. Especially if you have a South American of your very own on board, doing all your translating (Edu speaks fluent Portuguese). And so I suspected when I walked to town from the boat in the morning with Edu by my side it was likely to get messy.

Before anyone else can process your arrival you need to be stamped into the country by the *Policia Federal*, and on the whole I have found them to be the best of the lot. Perhaps you need a certain level of education to be admitted as a recruit into the *PF*; they invariably speak good English, and are always engaging and polite.

The girls had already been through immigration when they entered Brazil by bus, so there was no need for them to come with us to the police. Rupert and I went along with our passports, and Edu with his ID card (Uruguay being part of the so-called *Mercosur*, a common-market arrangement between Brazil, Argentina, Uruguay and Paraguay, Edu did not need to travel with a passport). I handed the friendly policeman our documents. He asked for the crew roll, and I handed him the one from Uruguay stating there were three people on the boat. He counted us. Three. So far so good.

After stamping our passports, the policeman handed me a document printed in bright red ink listing details of the boat, specifying three crew, with the instruction that I was to bring it back before departing Rio Grande. This was potentially problematic, because I knew very well that when we left Rio Grande there would be five of us on board, and Edu would not be one of them. But I had enough nous to realise this would be something better dealt with when the time came, and not to open a can of worms by raising it now. Someone having left unexpectedly for personal reasons would be easier to explain after the event than someone *intending* to leave all along. It is always easier to beg forgiveness than to ask permission.

Rupert returned to the boat, his passport stamped, and Edu and I made our way to Customs. They had moved to a new building since our previous visit. Well hardly new; in fact it dates back some 170 years. It was the original customs and excise building constructed on the orders of Dom Pedro II (full name Pedro de Alcantara Joao Carlos Leopoldo Salvador Bibiano Fransisco Xavier de Paula Leocadio Miguel Gabriel Rafael Gonzaga) the second emperor of Brazil, and was in the final stages of renovation when we visited. It is a beautiful old stone building painted white and orange with heavy wooden floors and thick teak roof beams.

Behind a desk just inside the door was a stooped old man with dark rings under his eyes and the yellowing moustache of a nicotine addict. He looked forlornly at my papers, said everything looked okay, and that I did not need anything else. Apparently I could go.

But I knew better than that. I could well imagine the trouble at the next place if I had nothing to show, and asked for that in writing, with a stamp. Such impertinence seemed to arouse him, and he proceeded to cross-question me about the crew list of five (I had managed to get two lists from Uruguay, and was now showing him the one that had my family on it – the one I intended to use when the time came to leave Brazil again). He demanded to know who Edu was, where the family was, and how come the *Policia* document showed a crew of only three entering the country. This was all highly irregular, allowing half the crew to take a bus from Uruguay and we were instructed to come back in half an hour. Thirty minutes later Edu and I were back, but there was now a different problem: could we come back in another three hours, as there is a "change of supervisor" today?

At three thirty, when we returned, our morose old man Tall Skinny had been joined by a short, swarthy colleague with his customs officer badge, star and all, hanging ostentatiously round his neck like so much bling. Fat Shorty had new requirements for us. First of all, we should have an official letter from the *commandante* of the boat (er… that would be me) stating who the crew are, and specifically that Edu is *not* part of the crew; and secondly, a certificate of health for the boat – this because we had been in Argentina, and everyone knew that the entire population of Argentina was very sick and dying from that year's fashionably dreaded Mexican Swine 'flu.

So off we went on a ten block walk to find the *Saude* (Health) building, then up three flights of stairs to a door with a frosted window at the end of an empty hall. A Jean Reno look-alike invited us in. We briefed him on our situation, and he went off to "get papers" after kindly giving me the go-ahead to use his computer to draft a crew declaration. I typed and printed the letter, signed it, and for good measure franked it with a very important-looking rubber stamp I found lying in a drawer.

The health questionnaire covered things like "*has anyone on board had a headache?*" (what, *ever?*) and "*do you make water on board?*" (which I took not to mean "*do you pee?*"). In due course our *Saude* certificate was issued, and we sprinted the ten blocks back to Customs making the evening cut-off at the door with about sixty seconds to spare.

It appeared this paperwork was now all in order at last. Then it was time for more questions. "What do you do for a living?" I was asked.

Before I could speak, the ever helpful Eduardo chimed in: "He's a banker!"

Now this, of course, was no longer true. But it would look awfully suspicious if I contradicted him with something like "No no, actually I used to be, but now I'm a movie director"; and still more suspicious if I told the truth and said "Actually, I don't work at all". It would have been way beyond the comprehension of Tall Skinny and Fat Shorty that, at my age and in my modest traveller's dress, I could be sailing around the world in my own yacht without a job. I would absolutely have to be up to something nefarious. So I decided to go along with the banker thing, and after admitting that, yes, I am on vacation, I noticed out of the corner of my eye the Tall Skinny leafing through my passport and pointing out to a colleague that I seemed to have been on vacation for rather a long time.

I could see this was not going well, so pretending not to have noticed, I asked their boss – into who's august presence we had been ushered – "How do you say 'sabbatical' in Portuguese? You know, extended leave on half pay, for a year?" He did not understand the question.

I was worried they might next ask for details of my employer, and was aware that if they did I would have to brass it out and use the details of my last banking job. There was then of course the risk they might actually check. Seeing as I had resigned almost two years previously, this could go tits up.

Eventually everyone appeared satisfied enough, but after we were hustled out of the office, instead of being free to go, we were escorted even deeper into the building, to an underground car park. Nobody was telling us anything, and Tall Skinny was still clinging to my wad of documents. Then we saw two vans, three or four heavily armed policemen and a couple of dogs waiting for us, and realised they were getting set to accompany us to the museum to see for themselves this mystery family on this phantom boat with its irregular crew list.

It was all quite annoying, after spending the day to-ing and froing between government departments. Still, it was not as if we had concealed guns or drugs on board, so it was merely going to be an inconvenience. I just do not like being messed about though, so by the time we reached the museum my sense of indignation at the injustice of it all was almost getting the better of me.

The head honcho of our little boarding party was a thickset, shiny-bald man in civilian clothes sucking on a lollipop, reminiscent of that eighties television cop in the brown suit. Like Fat Shorty back at HQ, Kojak wore his badge of office dangling round his neck. He gave Ayrton, the museum security guard, an imperious wave as our convoy charged through the gate in a cloud of dust. I suggested that, out of respect, we should present ourselves at Lauro's office first. It might be a good idea to have the Director of the Museum in attendance, as his presence would be every bit as imposing as Kojak's, and he was a friend. But it was not to be. There was not a moment to be lost. Why, Abi and Jo may be unloading the contraband as we speak!

We descended on the boat like a marauding Mongol Horde and Abi and Jo were summoned out onto the jetty, eyes wide at the sight of the dogs, the guns, and the bullet proof jackets. Kojak was in his element, but he had not banked on a sleeping one-year-old and a protective mother. He was not going to have it easy.

"Just where do you think you're going?" asked Abi in a strident voice as the first soldier made to step over the guardrail onto the deck.

He teetered for a moment, half on and half off the boat, then withdrew his boot and replaced it on the jetty. He did not understand English, but knew he had not just been offered a nice cup of tea.

"My baby is asleep. If you wake her up there will be trouble!" she scolded Kojak. "And as for those boots! What do you think this is? There will be no boots on my boat!"

This was the first time it had been *her* boat. I don't know if someone was quietly translating, or whether the tone of Abi's voice just made the meaning plain, but the soldier obediently removed his boots while

Kojak said nothing, his badge hanging suddenly rather limp around his neck.

As "*Commandante*", it was ruled that I should accompany the search team. Now *Josephine* is not a large boat, which meant the search team would have to consist of only one man and his dog. The other men looked a little let down. After helping the sock-footed soldier manhandle his wriggling Labrador down the hatch, I sat in the saloon as he exhorted her to search.

"*Busca, Busca*!"

She made a beeline for the plastic bag hanging by the chart table, and before I could stop him the soldier had his hand in and pulled out a shitty nappy. I wished I had a hidden camera.

Next the dog took an inordinate interest in the floor, so I was instructed to lift the boards. Unfortunately for all of us, that very morning I had had to unblock a toilet pipe, and in spite of my flushing several buckets of water through the system after the job, the revolting residue of brown sludge that lined the bilges had left a very exciting smell – to a Labrador. I had to pull up all the floorboards before I could convince the soldier there was nothing more in there than the smell of the unspeakable, and then he made to go into the forepeak cabin.

"*Bebe, Bebe*!" I warned him. He took a cautious peak at little Lucy fast asleep among her teddies, and his face dissolved into the hugest smile I had seen all day. He backed out of the cabin on his toes with his finger to his lips in case either of us should accidentally speak.

"I too have a baby," he whispered in Portuguese, as if it were a conspiracy. "She turns one today!" I gave him a congratulatory handshake.

Back on the jetty he assured Kojak there was nothing at all untoward in the boat, and the *narco* squad trooped off to their vans thoroughly dejected. Except for the soldier, who was still grinning as they sped away.

***

Three days later, getting out of Rio Grande was shaping to be as inconvenient as getting in. To complicate matters, our plan had changed, and although I had the girls on the crew list, they were now going to continue their trip to Florianopolis by bus, and Edu had agreed to stay on a little longer to help Rupert and me with this next leg. I was well aware that crew changes do not sit comfortably with the authorities, who usually deal with Korean trawlers and Panamanian-registered freighters. Such clients are not in the habit of dropping crew off arbitrarily all over Brazil.

First we called again on our old friends the *Policia Federal* where we were attended to by a kindly old man who could not find the stamp. After rifling through several drawers with no success, he brightened and announced the stamp had been taken to a ship in the harbour, and we should come back in the afternoon. I pointed out we needed to leave soon on account of the weather, so he decided we did not need a stamp after all, and that we in fact only needed to clear out with the police from our "*ultimo porto*" in Brazil. This was more like it. (I also knew it to be true.) One of his colleagues, however, disagreed vehemently; we *did* need to be cleared by the police to leave Rio Grande, and the *Capitania dos Portos* would not allow our boat to leave town until he had seen our police clearance.

We took our leave and undertook to return that afternoon when the stamp was back. In hope we then went to see the *Capitania*. Captain Porto (that really was his name) was very excited to meet me and proudly told me he had a cousin in Cape Town. When I told him I had lived there, we were immediately brothers, and I think he would have stamped anything. He confirmed he did not need to see any police clearance, as we were not leaving the country, and *Josephine* was cleared to leave Rio Grande. So that was that.

I rather hope the police are not now looking for us for not going back and signing out with them – though I doubt it. As Werner had pointed out, "Zey don't really care."

"The Storm is Master
Man, as a ball, is tossed twixt winds and billows."

– Johann von Schiller

20

Edu, Rupert and I departed Rio Grande around three o'clock in the afternoon on a warm breeze that filled the sails for the eleven mile trip through the channels past the old docks to the open ocean, whereupon it promptly died. We were reduced to motoring most of the next twenty-four hours, nonetheless making good progress over a sea as flat as a plate. The last of the winter's Falkland Current gave us an extra knot northwards, and again we spent most of our time within half a mile of the dunes. The engine allowed the use of the little electronic autopilot and fridge. It was all very relaxed and civilized.

By the evening of the second day a little westerly came through again, and we sailed well through the night at around six knots in the calm water just offshore. We made good eighty-seven miles in the twelve hours of darkness without so much as a single tack. It was idyllic and we wondered aloud why so few people cruise these waters. We were soon to be reminded.

Sometime on the second morning we sailed through a picturesque fleet of little wooden fishing boats, gleaming smart and white in the sun with their royal blue gunwales. Working in pairs, they were dragging nets between them, each below its own entourage of albatrosses and gulls. We were hailed by a fisherman holding up a fish the length of his arm, but with the headsail poled out and sailing a steady seven knots were not inclined to turn around. A group of some twenty birds broke free from the fleet to circle us, and we recovered our fishing lures in a hurry to avoid snagging a greedy albatross.

For some minutes we were escorted by Kerguelen's Petrels – looking like giant black pigeons with their stubby beaks – the ubiquitous Black-browed Albatross, and the immaculate Yellow-nosed Albatross with its striking black wing markings and bright yellow tip at the end of its black and red bill.

It never ceases to amaze me how benevolent conditions at sea lull one into a sense that all is well, and will ever be so: but how quickly things can change. The wind started to build in the afternoon, swung north, then north east, forcing us to take down the pole, harden up, and eventually tack away from the coast. By dusk, the wind was above thirty knots, the sea building. Being ten miles offshore we were now pushing against the Brazil Current coming down from the warm waters of the tropics. We went into the evening with three reefs in the main, the headsail furled to a number three.

Night became positively awful. The waves grew to a parade of slab-sided double story buildings, their tops turned to stinging spray by winds in excess of fifty knots. We beat ineffectually in and out of the coast until half past one in the morning, making no northward progress against wind and current whatsoever. Inside the boat everything was wet from salt spray, the floor slick from a mix of spilt diesel and vomit. Eventually we hove to and tried to get some sleep, alternating one hour shifts in the cockpit, huddled under the spray dodger, looking out for ships as we drifted south across the Tramandai shipping lane. Rogue waves hit us at a rate of three or four every hour, and when they broke into the cockpit the canvas spray-dodger was no protection at all. We finished each of our watches soaked and shivering with cold.

By sunrise, having been pushed back seventeen miles while hove to, we set the sails and resumed beating into a slightly reduced gale of thirty-five knots. The sea was confused and lumpy, the swell from the south clashing with the waves worked up by the wind from the north. We took six big waves in the cockpit that first hour. Gradually the wind dropped to a more manageable twenty-five knots, and at three that afternoon we had clawed back the seventeen miles lost to the previous night's drift. By early evening we were ten miles better off than we had been the same time the previous day, but the wind was back up to thirty five knots and climbing. The sea was rising again too; it did not look promising.

We had a number of options:

One: Heave to for another night, losing miles to drift again, and hope for better weather the next day – but without access to updated forecast information, who knew how many days that might go on for, or how far south we would drift?

Two: Keep beating to windward, indefinitely, until the weather eased. Not very different from option one, except that we would not lose anything to drift. This was not an instantly attractive idea though; it would be very hard, and everyone was tired and cold. It was impossible to operate the gas stove while beating in those conditions the way the boat was slamming over the waves, and we were reduced to eating cold, limp sandwiches on soggy, salty bread.

Three: Reach west across the wind to Tramandai – about which we could tell nothing from the chart except that it exists in name. There was just no detail of an entrance or a harbour – no depth markings, no yacht club, in fact no facilities at all – and once in, it would be impossible to get back out in these onshore conditions. I was not at all keen on this option; it was a lot safer to remain offshore, at sea, where there was nothing to hit.

Four: Turn and run downwind for maybe thirty-six hours, all the way back to Rio Grande, and wait for a weather change. That could mean a week or more. It would also mean all the paperwork again with the *Capitania dos Portos* and the *Policia Federal*, who would no doubt be highly suspicious of our movements. And the girls would be in Florianopolis waiting for us. This would be massively inconvenient, but a safe final option if it came to it. However it had not yet reached that stage; we could endure this a bit longer so long as nothing (and nobody) broke.

Then a fifth option occurred to me. If we could somehow make thirty-five miles more to windward, we might be able to sneak into Laguna. Fabrizio – a bottle-blond Brazilian sailor we had met briefly in Piriapolis – hailed from Laguna, and had told us of his home yacht club in a sheltered lagoon that was home to no less than "sixty-three dolphins". Again, my pilot books were silent but the chart showed a sizeable lagoon with a navigable channel.

We opted to ride out another night beating then try to make Laguna the next day if the wind eased. Whether or not we could make it would be dependent on the severity of the wind and the waves, but we would lose nothing trying. Except rest; but we were not getting much of that anyway.

Beating to windward during the night turned out to be impossible with the wind over fifty knots again, and we spent a second night mostly hove to, drifting south at two knots. However when day broke the wind backed off a little and by midday the sea had settled somewhat with waves no more than eight feet high. With the wind at thirty-five knots we were able to beat northwards despite fighting against both wind and current. By mid-afternoon we were only twenty miles short of *Cabo de Santa Marta* but the wind was threatening to build again. I hoped there would be some respite from the wind closer to the cape, and figured twenty miles was close enough to use up some valuable diesel. We decided to press straight on into the wind for as long as we could under a combination of sail and motor. It made for very rough going, slamming the boat over the steep waves, but at engine revs that would normally give us six knots we were able to make about two against the current and rough sea. Like this we would get there – eventually. If we did not break the boat.

After an interminable evening of bashing head-on over the waves we drew east of *Cabo de Santa Marta* at ten o'clock. I reckoned on eleven miles more straight into the weather would see us north of *Punta do Tamborete* ("Drum Point") and able to double back into the breakwater of Laguna, but by now the wind was up in the high forties again, gusting over fifty, and the waves were like houses. The pounding was merciless and I had been vomiting for twenty-four hours. It was exhausting, shattering stuff, but apart from a locker door breaking off its hinges and a box of books emptying itself on the floor there was no damage to the boat, and with the motor we were still able to progress about a mile and a half each hour.

We endured another six hours of this purgatory. Edu latched onto the helm for a marathon five hour shift so Rupert and I could rest. In this screaming wind, these roaring waves, everything drenched above and below, no sleep, Edu came into his own and was a soldier. I could not have prized him away from the wheel with a crowbar, and was immensely grateful that he had chosen to join us for the trip.

With a mile yet to go to the Laguna breakwater, it was all hands on deck to prepare for what was shaping to be a nail-biting entrance. All we had to go on was an incomplete electronic chart, which had a very basic outline of the coast and the lagoon entrance, and what Fabrizio had sketched for me with a pencil six months before.

"The breakwater faces north east", I struggled to make myself heard above the din. "So we will have to get past first, then turn and come back downwind to get in."

I watched their faces, and Rupert was first to voice what I could see them both thinking.

"Shite! That means the wind will be blowing straight in the entrance. It'll be unprotected…."

"*Si,*" Edu cut in, "And the waves also!"

"Exactly. So we'll have to plan this very carefully. We'll take our time when we are close enough to see everything, and keep working north until we are sure we have gone well past. That should be easy enough to tell, I expect a clear view of both entrance lights."

Edu and Rupert nodded without speaking.

"We want to be at least half a mile upwind before we turn. Turning is going to be an exciting manoeuvre in this weather." I stole a glance at the anemometer to see the needle vibrating well above the fifty knot mark. "We want to have enough sea room, and enough time, to cope with any unexpected complications. Once we get going downwind in this, there will be no second chances."

I paused to let them reflect.

"FUCK, FUCK, LOOK OUT!" and Edu was a whirr of action, leaping about behind the wheel, eyes wide. He was still shouting at the top of his lungs as he heaved the boat over to starboard off the wind. "LOOK OUT! EEN THE WATER! ROCKS!"

The savage wind slammed into the side of the tightened mainsail and the boat heeled over, plunging the starboard deck under the water and sending Rupert sprawling down the leeward rail in a welter of flying ropes and boots. I was thankful he was wearing his lifeline.

Almost in slow motion I hauled myself up the windward side, hanging onto the radar arch, to see the danger. My mind was racing. Rocks, *here*? If so I had really messed up the navigation. Any rocks should be at least half a mile to port.

Sodden gloves clamped around the guard rail I peered over the side through the salt and spray as someone released the mainsheet. *Josephine* leapt forward and crashed over another wave. My stomach dropped in anticipation of the juddering, shattering impact of fibreglass on rock, and my mind was running over the "abandon ship" procedures that all skippers are happy to know but a lot happier never to need.

With saltwater gushing off my hood and over my nose I blinked down at two huge black shapes awash with foam between the waves as we scudded by no more than three feet off.

"Whales!" I yelled as they disappeared astern. "Shit, that was really close."

The immediate danger was over.

Rupert had gathered himself and was sitting in the cockpit rubbing a barked shin, as Edu wrestled the wheel back under control.

"Well," I said ruefully, "at least they weren't rocks and we still know where we are!"

We bashed on for a further hour, until the dark bulk of *Punta do Tamborete* – appropriately named in these conditions, the echoes of the pounding surf booming through the night – reared against the sky to our left and we could make out the green winking of the port entrance light. That was our first fix on the end of the south eastern breakwater. The red light marking the other side was still obscured by the headland, so we kept pounding, pummelled by the merciless waves, for half an hour more until I reckoned we were far enough past to be able to turn back and get the right angle.

The wind was far too strong to risk a gybe, especially with these mountainous waves, and I waited for a gap in the sea to put in a 270 degree tack instead – a "chicken gybe". A surreal calm* descended on the boat as we were lifted by a wave and rampaged off downwind at thirteen knots, the entrance lights beckoning through the gloom.

There was a very real danger of a crash-gybe, as the approach and entrance were dead downwind. I engaged the motor with engine full ahead. Not because it would make any difference whatsoever to the boat speed – the wind and waves would have us going much faster than the motor ever could – but because the propeller and the rudder could be used together as a stern thruster, to swivel the back of the boat on the wave as we surfed and allow better control of our alignment with the wind. This way, in theory, we were less likely to be turned sideways and rolled under a wave, or smashed against the sea-wall.

We were carried away downwind on galloping white steeds, their manes shredding in the wind like ocean spray. With three reefs in the main, the boom out sideways and just enough headsail to balance the boat, we could surf under some semblance of control rather than being overpowered by the waves, tipped over and spun out onto the rocks. Now speed was our friend.

---

* Anyone who sails is familiar with the relative calm of sailing downwind. If you go into a 20kt wind at 5kts, the combined effect is 25kts in your face. This is what you feel. By the same token, going downwind in a 20kt wind, with the boat moving at 7kts, provides for an overall sensation of only 13kts – about half. Thus the experiences of the same wind, heading in opposite directions, are vastly different.

The entrance between the lights would have to be followed by an immediate ninety degree turn to starboard to stay in the channel and avoid running straight across into the opposite cliff where we would be pounded to oblivion by the waves. It was all going to be very quick, very noisy and very rough, and there would be no time for hesitation or mistakes. We talked through the drill as we thundered on, then fell silent.

For the last hundred yards the waves heaped up ever bigger, the decreasing depth combining with the action of the out-flowing current causing them to rear up high and steep before crashing over with a roar. We were riding the breaking water now, and could barely hear each other over the tumult.

Ahead of us the giant waves were piling unchecked through the narrow entrance and exploding against the opposite cliff like bombs. Rocks in the water close to the port light were sending geysers of spray high into the night. We would have to stay close to the starboard light to avoid those rocks, but here the waves were if anything bigger, smashing relentlessly against the concrete. We would have to aim well. Fifty knots of wind from behind was not going to allow us any last second adjustments.

Just as we were lining up for the final approach we saw a second, smaller green light in the middle of the channel, mounted on a nasty rock, and realised we had only half the width we originally thought. We were by now fully committed, flying down the face of a wave, while angling sideways ever closer to the wall. The wave curled and tumbled beneath us, hurling us headlong at the gap on a bellowing white monster. We would have to stay as close as possible to the breakwater on our right. Surging towards the red light, the spray of the smashing waves cannoning off the rocks and drenching us, we swept past the end of the wall. Fizzing with adrenalin we collapsed the sails and made the sharp right turn to avoid the upcoming cliff face, sliding across a wave and spilling onto the calm black water of the lagoon. The wind was still screaming in the rigging and the waves erupting against the outside of the wall, but the water was calm behind the resolute concrete and with the sails down, the motor gave us control at last.

That had been an exciting few minutes. Sailing downwind in fifty knots, surfing fifteen foot breaking waves, is not an approach I would recommend into an unfamiliar entrance at three o'clock on a dark night.

"No depth."

"What's that?"

"No depth," repeated Rupert somewhat nonchalantly, drawing my attention to the fact that in all the pounding we had lost the use of the depth sounder. The little screen was blank. Not great. The prospect of groping five miles along an unlit channel of dubious depth with no readings was not, after what we had already been through, an appealing one. We brought the navplotter up into the cockpit and motored carefully up the channel, eyes glued to the screen, keeping the boat where the deeper water *should* be – at least according to the GPS.

A little way in we encountered a large, unlit buoy of indistinct shape, by which we passed as close as possible as we could not tell by either its colour or its shape which side we should be. In the process we almost hit another whale lazing in the channel. Fortunately it blew at the last second and the double-barrelled spray of a Southern Right lit up orange against the lights of the approaching town.

After another hour feeling our way up the channel in the murk, we found Fabrizio's *Iate Clube Laguna* off to our right. We could see only one small sailing yacht with a short mast, and without a depth sounder decided to anchor in the channel and wait for daylight. But the wind even here was blowing thirty knots, and there was a two knot stream running. Our anchor promptly dragged, finding the soft, sludgy bottom no match against the combined effects of wind and current.

"No bloody freebies on this trip!" muttered Rupert darkly as he set about getting the anchor back up. He heaved it on board to find a muddy pair of men's Y-fronts wrapped around the shank.

For a minute we motored in circles debating what to do, until Edu noticed a night watchman over on the club quay gesticulating with a torch. We sidled the boat over towards him, working the current and wind, but the keel found the mud before we were close enough to be able to tie up. We aborted the manoeuvre and went back out, then came alongside a moored motor yacht in deeper water and made fast to that.

After we clambered across the motor yacht and onto the concrete dock, the kind guard took us to his little office and poured strong coffees with a very welcome shot of whisky. In spite of our exhaustion, we were pumped with adrenalin so there was no point trying to sleep straight away. We were still hyped up but with nothing left to worry about; it was disappointingly anticlimactic.

A nattily dressed young man in his mid-twenties then appeared out of nowhere and after acknowledging us with a curt nod of the head, as if it were commonplace to find three dishevelled gringos having coffee with the guard at four o'clock in the morning, mumbled some instructions and left. The guard told us the young man was the son of the club commodore, and that his friend had rolled his car. We trooped out after him into the car park, where we came across a flatbed truck carrying a little van with its engine still running. Covered in grass and dust, the van had newly battered sides, no mirrors and a shattered windscreen. An overweight youngster with greasy black hair sat smoking a cigarette in the driver's seat. Apparently he had "fallen asleep" at the wheel, but when he staggered down clumsily to hang all over us and embrace us like dear friends it was perfectly obvious what had happened.

We eventually got to bed after six o'clock and slept till ten, then awoke to luxuriate in the club's fantastic hot showers. It had been a difficult few days, but I could not have wished for a more determined, cheerful crew. We were all bruised from being tossed around like rag dolls inside the boat and fortunate not to have picked up any serious injuries. Rupert, still only nineteen years old, sleep deprived, hungry, wet, cold, sore, and undoubtedly scared at times – like all of us – had complained only once; that he would like to *shave* of all things. And Edu had pulled that heroic five hour shift on the wheel after *Cabo Santa Marta* to ensure Rupert and I, being more familiar with the boat, would be rested for the entrance into Laguna. It showed once again that the most important attribute for this type of adventure is the right attitude.

"Let your boat of life be light,
packed with only what you need
– a homely home and simple pleasures,
one or two friends worth the name,
someone to love and someone to love you,
a cat, a dog, and a pipe or two,
enough to eat and enough to wear,
and a little more than enough to drink
– for thirst is a dangerous thing."

– Jerome K. Jerome

21

The peasants of Brazil's southern state of *Rio Grande do Sul* rose up against their Portuguese rulers in 1835, protesting over economic mismanagement, in what has become known as the "*Guerra dos Farrapos*" – referred to in English as the "War of the Tatters" (the Portuguese name "*Farrapos*" meaning literally "Ragamuffins", as the rebels were poor and dressed in rags). Following the successful expulsion of Portuguese troops from their own state, the Ragamuffins were emboldened and launched more ambitious attacks into the neighbouring state of *Santa Catarina*, conquering the town of Laguna (founded in 1676 by the local farming community as an agricultural trading hub) and declaring it the capital of their new *Republica Juliana.* (The rebel army numbered among its leaders one Guiseppe Garibaldi of Nice, who later, following the collapse of the Napoleonic Empire, put the military experience he gained in South America to use in unifying Italy.) This status quo lasted all of six months – from July to November 1839 – until the Portuguese regrouped and counterattacked, crushing the rebellion. The Juliana Republic was no more, and Laguna, its erstwhile capital, has remained a rural town ever since.

Nestled a little way inside the mouth of a twenty-five mile long chain of three lagoons threaded like giant baubles onto the *Rio D'Una*, the town has recently come to the attention of the world's media for the special working relationship that appears to exist between the resident pod of tucuxi dolphins (*Sotalia fluviatilis*, a sub-species found in freshwater) and local fishermen. The fishermen line the beach inside the breakwater and wait with their throwing nets while the dolphins herd shoals of fish inshore. The dolphins then signal to the fishermen by rolling over, at which point the nets are cast. The catches are bounteous, and the dolphins make easy pickings of the fish struggling in the nets. Everyone wins (except the fish). This is said to have been going on for generations, and documentary footage of the phenomenon has been shown on the BBC's "Wildlife Frontiers".

Now that *Josephine* was securely moored at the *Yate Clube Laguna*, it was time for Edu to get back to work in Uruguay, so we sought out a taxi driver to take us to Florianopolis while Rupert stayed with the boat to clean and dry just about everything.

We found a short, spindly man poking out from under an oversized beret. He gawked at us with bulging eyes, his scrawny arms looking like they would reach the ground if he straightened his elbows. He moved in sharp, nervous twitches that lent him the uncanny appearance of a Capuchin monkey. Florianopolis was a little off his regular beat, but Edu assured him not only did he know his way around the city, but could in fact direct the fellow to Alistair's very house where the girls were waiting for us. A hundred dollars settled the deal and we piled into a shabby white Fiat.

The horrors of the storm at sea paled in comparison with that hundred mile taxi ride around the lakes. Our simian driver was obviously taken with us, the novelty of carrying foreigners almost too much for him, and he spent much of the trip jabbering into his mobile phone at the top of his voice, telling everyone he could reach he was going all the way to Florianopolis. He sounded like a first time international traveller. Seemingly oblivious of the road, he wandering onto the grass verge three or four times, nearly smashing into the back of a stationary truck and narrowly missing a jogger who escaped certain death by diving headlong into a bush. Then on reaching the city of Florianopolis our little Laguna Capuchin appeared to have his first ever encounter with lanes, meandering from one to another and back again, creating havoc with the normally efficient city traffic. I found it particularly nerve-wracking having not driven city streets for almost a year.

After criss-crossing the entire breadth of the island, I began to doubt Edu's grasp of its geography; and when we stopped for directions at an intersection we recognised from twenty minutes before, it was obvious we were in for a long afternoon. We drove around with no apparent sense of purpose for over an hour, asking directions from probably ten different people in the process, Edu and the Monkey screeching at each other with ever-rising pitch the longer it went on. Eventually we settled on being dropped off at a shopping centre and calling Abi's cousin to pick us up.

***

With Edu packed onto a plane home to Montevideo two days later, I was on a bus back to Laguna to find Rupert and sail the remaining sixty miles to Florianopolis. The weather outlook was good, with a gentle southerly breeze forecast. Back on the boat I found it had been raining heavily, and everything Rupert had washed and dried was now wet again, but as he cheerfully pointed out, at least it was now *clean* and wet.

After filling two diesel drums at a local garage, we lifted the floorboards to look at the depth transducer (which had given out on us as we surfed between the breakwaters into Laguna). Finding nothing amiss, we removed the instrument in the cockpit to discover one of the data cables had worked loose in the storm. It was a relief to be able to reconnect it and get readings again.

We left Laguna in sparkling weather. Two of the legendary dolphins escorted us out of the lagoon and we dodged yet another whale lazing just beyond the seawall. It was a superb day; bright sun, a gentle following breeze and no swell to speak of. We motor-sailed up the coast past the rocky *Ilha das Araras* to the port of Imbituba, where a lifetime before we had been saved by that fishing net from being blown against the breakwater in a midnight storm. After the bare cliffs of Garopaba and the steep sided *Ilha da Coral* with its circling frigate birds, we reached the entrance to the south bay of *Ilha Santa Catarina* at the rocky *Punta dos Naufragos*. It was getting dark, and rather than pick our way the last fifteen miles in water that ranges from ten feet down to two, we anchored close to the island and fired up the barbecue. The evening was spent lounging in the cockpit drinking first beer, then rum, then whisky, listening to music wafting over the bay from a fisherman's house hidden somewhere in the depths of the forest where a party was in full swing.

We knew it was morning when the black of night turned to a miserable damp grey. Fog lay thick and after a fried breakfast we sat about until ten o'clock waiting for it to lift. When it at last thinned, we broke out the spinnaker in the clammy breeze and ghosted up the bay towards the city. By early afternoon we arrived at the Santa Catarina Yacht Club, and after getting stuck twice in the shallows, finally forced our keel through the soft mud to the walk-on moorings inside the southern wall.

It was nice to have access to all the mod-cons that go with an up-to-date yacht club – bathrooms, restaurant, a chandler – but the southern wall was not really a wall; it was really little more than a concrete walkway on piles, so when the south wind blew the waves swept straight underneath causing the first row of boats – which included *Josephine* – to rear and pitch like the giant keys of some demented piano. It would have been far too dangerous trying to get on and off over the leaping pulpit with a baby and we were grateful to have Alistair's house to go to. (We had not considered putting the boat here the previous year because the little harbour at the club was new and did not appear on any of our charts. At the time of writing there is still no pilot book available that includes information about this marina – not even a Brazilian one.)

***

Undoubtedly one of Brazil's most spectacular attractions is *Foz do Iguacu*, and it was too close to Florianopolis for us to ignore, so we hired a car and headed inland.

Depending on the season, anything from five hundred to eight thousand tons of water thunders over the three hundred foot drop in two hundred and seventy-five separate cascades, creating the phenomenon that is Iguazu Falls – higher than Niagara and, with its two miles of cataracts, wider than Victoria. The falls (the Tupi-Guarani name "*Iguacu*" meaning "Great Waters") were declared a UNESCO heritage site in 1986, the same year Jeremy Irons was nailed to a cross and sent plunging over the watery abyss in that epic film "The Mission." In 2008 *Foz do Iguacu* had the dubious distinction of being the world's most popular suicide spot.

The falls, below which the Iguacu River is squeezed into a hundred metre wide gorge, are shared by Brazil and Argentina. While the greater portion is on the Argentine side of the gorge, it is the Brazilian side that offers the more panoramic view; but the Argentine side provides a more dramatic close-up experience, and it would be a waste to not take the time to explore both.

After filming the awe-inspiring vista from the Brazilian side, and getting drenched on the viewing platform, we retired to the restaurant perched above the lip of the main drop. Sitting outside on a wooden deck, the roar of Devil's Throat – the main cataract – all but drowning out conversation as thousands of tons of water rushed directly under our feet before flying out into space thirty feet on, we enjoyed a few "Antarctica" beers (yes, it is a Brazilian beer, and even has two penguins on the logo) and a delightfully decadent buffet lunch. Between taking orders and bringing plates, our waiter's time was spent shooing the opportunistic coatis that were snuffling about under the tables back out into the forest.

No visit would have been complete without stopping in at the nearby *Parque das Aves*. At eight dollars a head, the bird park was excellent value, and Lucy particularly enjoyed stroking the friendly toucans, walking through a blue and crimson cloud of flapping macaws, and kissing a boa constrictor.

For our trip to the Argentine side the next day, we found it easier to go with a "tour" organised from our hotel. A minibus arrived to pick us up, and we met our guide. Michel was a shrivelled, grey, bewhiskered old man with yellow teeth and carried with him a flashing silver coloured parasol. After struggling some hours to keep up with us in the heat, he pointed out a marshy bit of land and announced with great authority "*This is a svemp!*" following which he retired under a tree with his parasol and slept. We did not see "Svempy" again until home time.

***

By early October we had spent five weeks ashore in Florianopolis, house-sitting for Alistair's neighbours and using the opportunity to capture six months' worth of video tape to a hard drive, and now it was time to return to life afloat. Water and diesel tanks were filled at the club fuel jetty and we ploughed our way out of the shallow marina under a dense blue sky, the keel cleaving a furrow through the soft mud.

Our first excitement came almost immediately after leaving the yacht basin. To go north up the coast from the city of Florianopolis, we had a choice: either take the long way round the island by beating back south into the wind and nasty chop for half a day, sailing round the southern tip then back up the outside for a total trip of maybe a hundred miles which would see us to Jurere on the north of the island – a prospect that appealed to nobody; or go straight up the bay from the club and slip under the road bridge, staying in calm waters, and reach Jurere in a mere four hours. Hardly surprisingly there was a unanimous vote for option two – but there was a catch.

The height of the multi-lane road bridge joining the island of Santa Catarina to the mainland is variously estimated at between sixteen and seventeen metres. *Josephine*'s mast is just over fourteen metres long; add to that perhaps a metre and a half for the boat itself, and the masthead should be some sixteen metres above the water – so, in theory, we should have no problem getting under the bridge. However with the real height of the bridge somewhat vague, and considering that water levels would affect the clearance (higher water = less space) we approached the bridge with some trepidation.

The closer we came to the bridge, the lower it seemed to be; until, looking up from the deck, it seemed we would be lucky to clear the second spreader. Of course looking at it from this angle was misleading; we would have been better off with someone watching from shore with a cell phone. I considered sending Rupert up the mast, but had visions of leaving him hanging from the bridge by his fingertips as the rig crashed down around our ears if we got it wrong. We motored slowly closer until the bow of the boat was under the bridge and the mast was about to hit the road, and aborted. It looked like a definite no-go from down on deck. We pulled back from the bridge and debated what to do. In theory we *should* make it, but it looked impossible from our angle, and if the mast touched the bridge it was almost certain to snap, sending a ton of steel rigging crashing onto the boat, quite possibly inflicting serious injury. Yet the idea of going south around the island and losing a whole day was dispiriting, not to mention the near certainty that Abi would be seasick beating into the wind.

A hundred yards away to our left was a little wooden dinghy carrying two fishermen with a net. They had been watching us quietly, and when we pulled back from the bridge to have a second look they rowed over, smiling broadly. They had a clearer view than we did, being off to the side, and said we had a good metre to spare above the mast.

"*Facil, facil!*" they encouraged us. "*Nenhum problema senhor!*"

They had no reason to lie, so trusting in the centuries-old Brotherhood of the Sea we came around for another try. I was still going to be very cautious and go slowly enough that if the mast touched we at least stood a chance of reversing out before it came crashing down. Just as we were shaping our approach, Jo joked ominously about them not really being fishermen at all; she suggested instead that they hang about under the bridge waiting for *gringos*, encourage them to sail under and destroy their yachts, then claim salvage. Very funny.

In the event we were clear under as the fishermen had predicted, but by how much I do not know. It looked like two inches, though it could as well have been five feet. It was just impossible to tell from below. After waving a cheery farewell to our fishermen, the rest of the trip up the bay was unremarkable, until we arrived off the beach at Jurere on the northern end of the island and dropped anchor for the night. When it was well set I pressed the engine kill switch and… nothing. The engine kept running as smoothly as you like. I pressed it again, harder. Still the engine purred along. I gave the switch an annoyed stab with my thumb and bent my nail back, but the engine did not skip a beat.

"Oh come on, this we don't need!" I lamented. "All that money spent in Uruguay fixing the engine when it wouldn't start, and now it won't stop!"

I was at a complete loss. How do you stop a diesel engine that simply won't turn off? I stood there dumbly with the ignition key in my hand as the sun set over the island, the engine rumbling away beneath my feet, wasting diesel. Although I am not much of a mechanic, I can come up with a few reasons an engine might not start; but not *stop*? This was a new one. All I could think of, other than waiting two and a half days for it to run out of diesel, was to dismantle the kill switch and check for a loose wire. I took off the instrument panel in the cockpit and with a screwdriver poked at the wires by the light of a head torch.

The procedure yielded some spectacular sparks but nothing else. The engine remained oblivious to my endeavours.

"Cool shot!" exclaimed Rupert, with the video camera glued to his face. He had enjoyed the orange flashes.

"Hey Andrew, tell us what you are doing," prompted Abi, as Rupert fanned the camera in my face. I was irritable, and that camera was not helping. My crew were taking the idea of reality television too far and I lost my sense of humour.

"For shit's sake put that thing away! Nobody will be interested in this. It's boring! Let's just worry about getting it fixed, shall we?!" I snapped petulantly.

I then sat for a long moment, head in hands, my mind a complete blank. I pretended I could not hear the stifled giggles.

"I don't know what to do. I don't bloody know what to do. I have no idea."

Morose and grumpy, I went below to make a pot of tea while the engine rumbled happily on. A pocket-sized booklet on marine electrics lying on the chart table caught my eye. It was part of a set called "*Little Companion*". I scrabbled around in the half light until I found "*The Little Diesel Companion*" and started to read:

"Diesel engines are stopped by cutting off the fuel supply at the injection pump..."

'So what, and where, is that?' I wondered out loud.

"Prepare for the day it fails by familiarising yourself with how it works..."

Yes, thank you very much...

"Get someone to operate the stop control. Look at the engine in the region of the fuel injection pump to see what moves."

Now *there* was something we could try I supposed – not that I knew where this "injection pump" thing was, but if I saw anything move… I wedged myself next to the engine with a torch while Rupert repeatedly pressed the cut-off switch, and I heard a dull clicking sound before my eye caught a narrow rod sliding backwards and forwards. Its end was not attached to anything; it had obviously come loose. I followed its direction until I found a little lever. I pulled the lever, and hey presto, the engine stopped. Smug as you like I wriggled out of the engine space to a round of applause and all grumpiness was forgotten.

That night the wind blew up a gale from the south, pushing us back from the beach and dragging the anchor, which we re-set with 140 feet of chain even though the depth was no more then twelve. We were getting sick and tired of all this anchor dragging every time the wind blew, and congratulated ourselves again on finally heading northwards in search of more benign climes.

By the light of the following morning we reattached the rod on the engine cut-out thingy with plastic cable ties. As good as new. This is the way with cruising – you learn as you go by applying common sense to good old trial and error (though in my case, mostly error it must be admitted).

***

The sail up the coast started with the overnight southerly gale having reduced itself to a fresh breeze. We were reaching beautifully, and agreed it would be a splendid idea to break out the spinnaker, and before long were bowling along at a merry ten knots. But the wind started to build again, and an hour later *Josephine* was rolling drunkenly on the verge of losing control. The spinnaker was as tight as a drum, bulging out ahead of us like a great parachute and dragging us over the waves. In these conditions the cockpit was no place for a one-year-old, but below, in the saloon, Lucy had turned a greenish-grey and Abi was on the verge of throwing up.

Rupert and I set about hauling the big sail down again to calm matters, so it would be safer for Lucy out on deck where she and Abi should feel less sick. Unfortunately we had left it a little late and the wind was by now blowing thirty five knots. *Josephine* has a particularly large masthead spinnaker and it was like trying to wrestle an inflated hot air balloon. Rupert was on the foredeck as I manoeuvred the boat to keep the wind out of the spinnaker as much as possible, but the rough sea was making it tricky. Half the sail was bundled into its bag before we were spun by another swell, the boat twisting into the wind which tore across the deck and snatched the spinnaker, tearing it out of Rupert's hands and ripping it from its bag, sending it high in the air above us to fly like a giant purple and yellow kite at the end of its lines.

We had to start again. The wind gusted viciously, making it hard work on the foredeck for one man; but in time the errant spinnaker was forced into its bag. When Rupert picked his way across the swaying deck and back to the cockpit – barefoot – he was hobbling with a very nasty rope burn, having lost the skin off the inside arch of his left foot when one of the spinnaker sheets ran fast across it. I cringed at the sight of his wound, pinkish-grey and weeping lymph, and as Jo dressed it I marvelled at Rupert's stoicism. No sissy. I would have squealed like a piglet if that were my foot, and refused to walk on it for a week at least.

Eighty-four miles saw us to a muddy overnight anchorage in a river mouth in the lee of *Ilha da Sao Fransisco*, and forty seven more the next day brought us opposite the entrance to the vast lagoon-like Bay of Paranagua. The city of Paranagua boasts Brazil's second busiest port (as opposed to Rio Grande which has the second *biggest*) which serves the state's landlocked capital of Curitiba, Brazil's third biggest city. The third edition of the Great Soviet Encyclopaedia reassures us that Paranagua "also has building materials and woodworking enterprises", which may well be, but the city is better known to tourists as the lower terminal of the famous three hour train ride down the spectacular escarpment from Curitiba, through no fewer than thirteen tunnels and over some sixty-seven bridges. Paranagua's other big attraction is *Ilha do Mel,* or "Honey Island", which sits bang in the middle of the entrance to the bay. The shipping lane runs past the south side, the channel to the north of the island being shallower, rocky and poorly marked. *Ilha do Mel* is uninhabited except for a handful of traditional fishermen and a few locals with government permits operating restaurants near the popular surfing beaches on the southern tip. There are no cars, and no roads.

To us the north side, with its deserted beaches and the promise of overnight shelter from the south wind, was more attractive and we picked our way between the rocks and in through *Canal do Norte* in the late afternoon. After dropping anchor close to the beach at *Praia do Cassual* we fired up the barbecue. With the sun suspended like a fiery lantern over the western horizon Rupert and I stood side by side in the cockpit prodding sizzling steaks with a fork, beers in hand, when, as if on cue, a dolphin jumped clear of the water not twenty yards from us. It hung for an eternal second in the air, perfectly silhouetted in the centre of the pulsating orange disc of the hovering sun before it dropped back beneath the orange ripples. If it were not real it would have been corny.

With sun-up we went ashore to explore, but that part of the island being an ecological reserve there are no paths through the dense bush and apart from a quarter mile long strip of beach littered with floral detritus there was nothing to see – though we did manage to dig up an old television set after Rupert stubbed his toe on something poking out of the sand. After exhausting all possibilities of entertainment on the overgrown beach, we set off on the thirteen mile sail through the mangrove channels and mudflats to the town of Paranagua. It is a tricky pilotage, and on the way we passed a big ketch with a Dutch flag stranded in the shallows waiting for the tide to float her off.

The narrow river opposite the waterfront of the old town presented the perfect anchorage, and we paddled ashore in the rubber dinghy to a promising-looking restaurant perched atop the stone wall overlooking the water and a raft of brightly painted wooden fishing canoes pulled up on the sloping bank, gleaming lapis blue and crimson in the sun. While the waitress jotted down our requests for steak rolls and beers with one hand, with her other she was tweaking on a nylon line that ran over the wall into the river. I had never before had a waitress actively fishing while she took my dinner order.

The leafy old town of Paranagua, tucked up the creek from the concrete industrial sprawl that has erupted around the commercial harbour, was timeless and enchanting with smooth cobbles glistening in the afternoon sun. We spent two nights riding gently at anchor on the languid river. By day we explored the streets of ancient stone that meander between restored colonial buildings, their facades freshly painted in pastel blues and butter yellows, and ate our fill of the local "*feijao*" (hot black beans) with freshly caught fish.

The vast bay, with the city to the south and mangrove forest to the north, is relatively undeveloped, and we found the idea of crossing to the far side in search of a quiet anchorage, away from everything for our last night before heading back to sea, irresistible. The pilot book was once again mute. We determined to sail across the bay and explore the north-western section during the day, knowing we could return to town in the evening if we did not find a suitable spot.

We sailed off downwind at a sedate four knots. The chart showed a few rocks and some islands, but with no buoys marking any hazards outside the shipping lane, we had to be careful. Jo was on the helm while I popped in and out of the hatch like a gopher checking our progress on the electronic plotter. I had an uneasy feeling that I could not put my finger on. Everything looked fine, but it did not feel right. The plotter showed us getting ever closer to a small island dead ahead, but up on deck the island was well over to our left. I went below and checked again. Yes, it was dead ahead according to the GPS.

"Jo," I called up. "Can you see that island?"

"Yes," she replied. "It's about half a mile away, thirty degrees to port."

"Well the GPS says we are sailing right onto it. I don't get this…"

I went back on deck and had another look. An island, well off to our left; ahead of us, nothing but open water. It made no sense. There was absolutely nothing there. I was inclined to trust my own eyes rather than this electronic gizmo.

Then I recalled that GPS units all come with a warning that they are not infallible; that the satellites are not always perfectly accurate; and that the American Military reserves the right at any time to render them even less so. That had to be it; the GPS was a little out. Anyway, as long as we could see the island, we were not about to hit it.

"Alright, maintain your course then," I affirmed and ducked back inside. No sooner was I down the hatch, than I heard the shouting.

"What are they doing?" came Rupert's voice. "Are they trying to tell us something?"

Now Abi. "Those fishermen are waving at us. Something must be wrong…"

She did not finish.

There was an almighty BANG as *Josephine* slammed to a violent halt and lurched over sideways, sending me sprawling over the saloon table. I felt sick to my stomach. Up on deck I looked over the side to see only rocks, covered by maybe an inch of water. We had sailed right onto them and were firmly aground. We furled the genoa – fortunately we had not been sailing with the mainsail – and I went below again to lift the floorboards and check for water, while listening carefully for the sound of any leaking. Nothing, thank goodness. I could scarcely believe it; we had hit the rocks at a good four knots.

Outside a strong current was running, pinning us hard, and try as we might we could not work *Josephine* off with the motor. The fishermen Rupert had noticed whistling and waving at us arrived alongside in their aluminium skiff, shouting indecipherable instructions at us in Portuguese. With a lot of signalling I managed to get them to understand what we wanted (as if it weren't pretty obvious) and threw them a line which they hitched to their boat. Then with their powerful outboard motor they tried valiantly to drag us off against the current. That their motor kept cutting out did not help, but pulling eight tons of stranded yacht off the rocks against a two knot tidal flow was never really on. We would have to be patient and wait for the incoming tide to float us off.

After about an hour, with a little more water and gunning the engine full astern, *Josephine* twisted free of the rocks sending a collective sigh of relief through the crew. The next thing was to check for damage, so we found a quiet tree-lined bay and dropped anchor while I donned a mask to dive underneath and check the hull and keel. Apart from some severe scratches there was no obvious damage. The keel was straight and the seam between the keel and hull sound. It appeared we had got away with it yet again. I clambered back on board reflecting ruefully on the Dutch ship we had seen aground the previous day and answering my own question as to why this is not a popular cruising ground. There is just nothing easy about sailing these waters; if the wind does not get you, the unmarked rocks will.

Reflecting later on the day's excitement, the problem had been the chart showed the hazard as an *island* rather than a submerged rock;

so I had my mind set on spotting an island and was not thinking of anything else. When I saw no island, I reckoned we were clear. But when the chart says there is something there, there is probably something there. This was an error similar to the one I had made off Uruguay when I confused a local hazard for a distant lighthouse; being a slave to a preconception. Either of those mistakes could have cost us the boat, or more.

Abandoning the idea of crossing to the other side, we anchored in the lee of *Ilha Cobras* in the middle of the bay. It is a small, high island shaped like a croissant with a tiny inlet and pretty beach, complete with feral rabbits hopping about on the sand. The hill offered good protection from the south wind which was now blowing yet another gale and pushing a procession of whitecaps past either side of the island. All was calm in our little haven though and we relaxed for the first time that day as the descending sun lingered a final minute over the distant mainland.

Most of that night passed uneventfully. Until three o'clock in the morning, when we were awoken by the screaming of the anchor drag alarm. Outside there was chaos. The wind had veered to the west and was howling across the face of our bay at forty five knots, dragging us with it, anchor and all. Heavy rain was lashing down. It was difficult to see through the deluge as I stood shivering in my underpants at the wheel powering the boat against the elements with the engine to keep us in position, water gushing off my forehead. There was nothing else to be done.

Half an hour went by, then the wind died away to nothing and the squall was over. We put *Josephine* back in position and reset the anchor before I wriggled into some dry clothes and swallowed three cups of hot tea. It was a quarter to four by the time I burrowed back into my sleeping bag. I had barely stopped trembling from the cold when the anchor alarm squealed again – like a banshee I thought – and the wind was once more ripping across the deck. Outside the island had completely disappeared – until I realised the wind had swung a full 180 degrees and we were now facing the opposite direction. This time we were dragging straight towards the rocks that formed the western tip of the crescent bay. We were in a maelstrom of wind and rain, the squall this time even stronger, gusting to sixty knots. A mere four knots short of hurricane strength.

Another half hour of motoring on the spot to arrest the anchor drag followed, then the wind abated to a manageable twenty knots and the rain stopped. A third change of clothes and more tea brought us to five o'clock, by which time Rupert and I had decided to stay up until sunrise. We huddled together beneath the spray dodger and were entertained for the last hours of night by the most magnificent display of nature's fireworks either of us had ever seen. Bolts of distant lightning fizzed and cracked, tearing open the sky and illuminating the cockpit in vivid colour.

***

Our next planned stop was Cananeia, recognised as the site of Brazil's oldest European settlement, dating back to 1531. A brief search of the internet revealed that "Cananeia" actually means "Canaanite"; that it has been the site of extensive studies into the feeding territoriality of the Little Blue Heron; and the city was founded in the same year as Turtle Creek, Pennsylvania (1892 if you want to know). A more auspicious claim to fame is that it marks the site where the first European landed and stayed, though it appears from historical records that the so-called "Bachelor of Cananeia" was probably a convict, who was either marooned there, or escaped ship, in 1501. Either way, legend has it he ruled amongst the indigenous people like a king. He was feared along the length of Brazil's south coast for decades, building himself an army of Indian warriors and profiting massively from the slave trade.

A twenty mile sail from Paranagua Bay brought us opposite the entrance to the lagoon at Cananeia. Or at any rate, it brought us to where the lagoon should have been, but not one of the six channel buoys shown on the chart seemed to exist. The coast is low beach backed by mangrove forests, and we could see no gap in the uniform green shore that looked anything like the entrance to a lagoon. Yet it had to be there. Somewhere, behind those mangroves, was a fifty mile long lagoon and a town of some thirteen thousand people. We were determined to find it.

To complicate matters, the water is very shallow for two miles out, and while the depth of the (now unmarked) channel ranges between fifteen and thirty feet, there is less than four feet everywhere else. We could hear the roar of the surf where the South Atlantic swells rolled and tumbled in the shallow water, but from behind it was impossible to make out the breaks.

The only way in was to be guided by the GPS, and the plotter was brought up into the cockpit. The deep water of the channel was clearly marked on the electronic chart. Using that, in conjunction with the depth sounder that gave us a real, live reading of the water below the hull, we inched ever closer to shore. To complicate matters, a strong rip was pulling us sideways towards the banks, and we had to constantly adjust our heading to counter it. Closer to shore, with still no sign of an opening in the trees to guide us, the swells started to pile up higher and staying in twenty feet of water was more difficult as the boat was thrown off course by the cross-currents. As in our previous approach to Laguna, speed would be our friend in the waves and I gunned the motor. There could be no chickening out now. Eyes glued to the depth sounder, we surfed *Josephine* through the shore break, at one point surging at ten knots in water down to a mere eight feet. A few tense moments passed, and then, as if by magic, an opening manifested itself in the trees and we coasted into a quiet, deep river mouth, surrounded by dolphins.

A mile in, following a sharp turn to the right, the town of Cananeia unfolded before our eyes. A row of brightly painted buildings reflected yellow and green off the still water to our left, and at the far end of town we made out the mast of another yacht. A public jetty on heavy wooden piles provided the ideal place to tie up before walking into town to buy diesel, then we were back out in the river dropping the anchor for the night. The anchor had not been down long before there was a dull thump-thump-thump against the hull.

"Now what?" I grunted. "Always something!"

The thumping was persistent. Then came a voice.

"Hey there, *Josephine*! Come and say hello!"

It was definitely English, with an unmistakable Irish lilt. Alongside was a dinghy, and in it a man and two small children. A broad, jolly individual who almost never stopped talking, Brian was a whirlwind. He was cruising with his Brazilian wife and their two children, aged six and eight. They had been in their boat eight years, and had recently arrived from cruising some of the inland waterways of the United States. It was their yacht we had seen on our way in.

"What're yer doin' here?" he enquired.

"Oh, just cruising, you know. Exploring Bras..."

"No, I mean here?" he interrupted me.

"Cananeia? It sounded interest…"

"No, no!" he cut me short again, pointing down with his finger. "*Here!*"

I was nonplussed.

"Where?"

"*Here*, in th'river. You don't need t'anchor here. Yer man says yer can use his jetty fer the night!"

"My man? What ma…?"

"Yer man! Over at the club!" He looked at me as if *I* were the raving lunatic.

"I'm sorry, I have no man, and I know nothing about a clu…"

"Follow me then, I'll show yer. Come on!" and he roared off at top speed.

Brian's yacht was tied to a buoy next to a small floating jetty with a diesel pump, backed by a restaurant and bar, with a "Cananeia Yacht Club" sign above the door. It was not really a club at all, but in the absence of such, the owner of the place – "my man", Franco – who had done some sailing in his time, painted the sign to make the occasional cruising yacht feel welcome. And feel welcome we did. That evening, with *Josephine* securely tied to Franco's jetty, we shared a few pizzas and several beers with Brian and his delightful family.

"How long're yer stayin'?" asked Brian.

"Just a few days, we …"

"Why? It's a lovely place, yer should stay awhile!"

"Well, um, we need to get to Ilhabela to…."

"What on earth for?"

"…to pick up Rupert's mum, who …"

"Tell her to come here for heavens sake!"

"….who is flying in for a two week holiday." I managed to finish my sentence. "Anyway, we don't have much time left in Brazil, and…"

"Now what're yer talkin' about? Yer can stay in Brazil as long as yer like yer know!"

"…and we want to go north, and …"

"That tree month tourist visa is a lot a' tosh. Just apply for a residence permit. Then yer can stay as long as it takes for them ter turn yer down. It takes ages. Up ter tree years! And even then yer can appeal it."

Brian stopped just long enough for his mind to catch up, then "North?" he asked, looking amazed. "It's much nicer down here! Yer haven't finished yer beer. Do yer need anyting from town?"

I sensed a subject change.

"Actually, cooking gas. But the fittings on our bottles are different from the Brazilian ones, so...."

"Oh that's fine, yer man'll sort it out fer yer!"

"Who, Franco?"

"No, not him!" and he made a clucking sound. He seemed to think he was dealing with someone a bit dim. "No, yer man at the gas shop."

It seemed I had another man.

"I had the same problem," he went on. "Yer man sells an adaptor, we'll get yer one in t'mornin'."

"My man at the gas shop?"

"No, yer man doesn't sell adaptors!" he clarified for stupid me. "We'll get that from yer man at the hardware, then yer man at the gas shop will sort out yer gas!" He threw his arms wide in triumph and topped up my beer.

For three nights we stayed in the river at Cananeia as my various men sold us an adaptor, topped up our gas bottles, delivered the groceries, moved us to a buoy and filled us with beer. Every night we lay in our bunks on that tranquil river listening to the pops and rattles and squeaks of the estuary dolphins rooting about in the silt in their quest for shrimps. Brian was right; it would have been wonderful to have stayed longer.

But Rupert's mum was due in Ilhabela in a few days, and we had to leave our new friends too early. They could not have been kinder, and seemed as sorry as we were when we left.

***

Getting out of Cananeia the way we came in was easier in the sense that from this side we could clearly see the breaking waves, which told us where the shallow water was. But it was rougher, as we were meeting the waves head on, instead of riding with them. It took nearly half an hour of bashing through breakers and over swells to get beyond the channel into the deep water, but once we were out there the sea was shimmering in the still heat and we motored all day. At night we ghosted through the big ships' anchorage outside the busy port of Santos, and counted no fewer than fifty-four freighters and tankers anchored up, deck lights ablaze, waiting to go in. Rupert remarked in the dark it was like approaching the star fleet in a science fiction film. It took almost two hours to pass through this enormous parking lot, then we were back in clear water and as we pulled away from the floating city of lights, the sea glowed with electric green phosphorescence. Some time in the early hours of the morning a pod of dolphins joined us. They chased each other around and under the boat, rolling and diving like fighter planes in a dogfight, laying down twisting contrails of glittering stardust much like Tinkerbell as she flits across the screen in the Disney films.

Sunrise revealed the tree-clad island of Ilhabela ahead of us, high peaks jutting out of the mist that shrouded its lower slopes. We bimbled up the channel past the Sao Sebastiao oil terminal and dodged the ferries traversing between the island and the mainland laden with excited tourists. The tropical sun lifted the curtain of mist to reveal the familiar thick green jungle alive with parrots and toucans. The turquoise sea was dead calm. Passing Ludi's little sailing club and the tourist jetty in the town, we rounded the point into the next bay and moored at the swanky *Yate Clube Ilhabela* for the second time on our travels.

YCI is a very upmarket affair. It boasts walk-on moorings for over two hundred yachts, complete with drinking water and electricity. The club has a restaurant, two bars, a supervised playground for small children, a gym, an internet centre and a lovely swimming pool (where we had started Lucy swimming on our previous visit to the island at age seven months) overlooking a private beach. In the street to one side is a very good – though expensive – chandlery, and to the other the equally good – and only marginally cheaper – fresh fish market. The Yacht Club offers a courtesy mooring for four days to foreign boats and we took grateful advantage of this hospitality, revelling in the luxury of hot showers and good coffee.

Rupert's mum, Meg, arrived the next day amid great excitement. She was our first visitor from home in a year, and came bearing wonderful gifts. Her reaction to the exotic tropical environs – the sultry air, aquamarine water, coconuts and bananas in the streets – and the novelty of yacht life made us aware, once again, how fortunate we were to be living this dream.

Unfortunately the idyll was not to last long. On her very first evening Meg went on deck after dark and fell heavily in the cockpit, landing awkwardly on her shoulder. The next morning she was severely bruised and in great discomfort. X-rays revealed a fracture of the humerus, and her arm was put in a sling where it stayed for the full two weeks of her visit. Not that a broken arm was going to stop her enjoying her holiday. Far from it. We visited the nearby islands of Anchieta with its capybaras and marmosets, and Couves with its excellent snorkelling and pretty fishing boats. We took Meg to Paraty Mirim and she convinced us to lower her, broken arm and all, into the water with the boatswain's chair so she could swim amongst the giant starfish. Never once did she complain. We admired her greatly for getting on with it and making the most of her holiday.

***

It was early morning in Paraty Mirim, and Abi and I were on deck to greet the dawn with steaming mugs of coffee. As the forest was stirring with the early hoots, whistles and shrieks of waking birds and monkeys we marvelled at how we had come to regard this as our "backyard". We saw our lives again though Meg's eyes and appreciated how what had become "normal" for us was the ultimate fantasy for so many people; indeed as it had once been for us, slaving away at our corporate jobs in the city.

Now we were about to embark on an even more magical adventure. We had spent the best part of a year south of here, where the water is cold, the seas rough and the winds strong. It had been exciting, but not easy. We had lost track of the number of times we ran aground or dragged anchor in a storm, but now we were in the tropics, and heading north. We had warm seas and beautiful sunny beaches littered with coconuts to look forward to. We would spend more time barefoot, eating fresh fruit and catching our own fish. We would be able to sleep late, but want to get up early. All the way to the Caribbean.

"Better is knowledge than mechanical practice.
Better than knowledge is meditation.
But better still is surrender of attachment to results,
because there follows immediate peace."

– Bhagavad Gita

22

It turned out to be a beautiful day. Little wind to speak of – maybe a knot or two, no more; warm, scented air wafting out of the hills from the direction of Rio. A good night's sleep followed by a refreshing farewell swim with the giant starfish of Paraty Mirim, then a freshwater *ducha* under a tap we found on a private jetty near the beach. We scraped fresh oysters off the rocks and gulped them down as we showered.

Now here we were, around noon, coasting past the last tree-clad headland on our approach to the historic little town of Paraty, nestled in a crescent of verdant forest. Abi and Lucy were sunning themselves on the foredeck as The Crew-Cuts serenaded from the CD player.

"*Hey Nonny ding dong, a-lang a-lang a-lang...*"

The water was an iridescent jade as only in Brazil. A dreamy turtle poked its snout up and fixed us with a somnolent gaze as we ghosted by.

"*... Boom ba-doh, ba-doo ba-doo ba-doo...*"

To our left, a series of pristine little beaches tucked under the coconut palms, and coming up on our right the wooded cliffs of the uninhabited *Ilha da Bexiga.*

"*... Sh-boom sh-boom, ya-da-da-da-da-da-da...*"

Ahead I was just starting to make out a thicket of masts against the deep green of the hills. The sun was warm on my face and I was having one of those moments where you know you love your life.

" *... If I could take you up to paradise up above...*"

Our plan was to top up the diesel at one of the marinas, then come back out and choose a quiet beach off which to anchor for another swim and spend the night. A beach braai would be a good idea. Yes, I agreed with the Crew-Cuts as they concluded "*life could be a dream, Sweetheart!*"

Then it struck me that the music seemed louder. I could hear the sound of the water against the hull too. Why had I just noticed that? I listened, and slowly it dawned on me – nothing was really louder; it was just that there was no engine noise. And we were slowing down, definitely.

"Oh no! A mile to go, one little miserable mile; after travelling five hundred!"

"What's the matter?" came Abi's voice from the foredeck.

"Diesel!"

This couldn't be happening – running out, *one mile* short of the fuel jetty? You could not make this up. I could see the *Petrobras* signs against the backdrop of the trees, and here we were drifting to a standstill. And, of course, there was no wind.

Jo gave a resigned chuckle.

"At least we're consistent. There always seems to be *some* sort of drama when we arrive in a new place!"

The spell had been broken and I shut the Crew Cuts off with a grump. Inane noise.

We were floating about in the middle of a fairly busy channel. No ships, but lots of tourist schooners and power boats. I checked the anemometer. A knot of wind. The air was barely moving. Great. You'd struggle to blow a leaf over a puddle with that, never mind push an eight ton yacht.

There was nothing else for it but to roll out the headsail, keep a sharp lookout, and wait for wind. It occurred to me that I could have used the dinghy with its five horse power outboard motor to push us slowly along, but for the fact the motor had refused to start the day before because it was overdue for a service. My fault.

After about an hour spinning lazy circles on the flaccid water, I felt the air move over my cheek. It was almost imperceptible, but when I stood up on the radar arch and looked north I could see the dark line on the water that showed the approaching breeze.

"Alright folks, here it comes!" I announced to weary cheers.

The wind built to about five or six knots, enough to get us sailing again. We took half an hour to run down to the fuel dock on a broad reach, gybing between the moored boats outside *Marina Engenho* for the last hundred yards before furling the sail and gliding side-on to the quay. Except that we never quite got there.

The tide was on the ebb, and there was not enough water at the dock. Our keel fouled the mud and we lurched to a halt a tantalising two metres short. I shot a look at Jo next to me and this time she thought better of it and said nothing. Lines were thrown, jerry cans tossed across, and diesel swung aboard.

Now the real problem presented itself. Anyone who knows anything about diesel knows it is a very bad idea to let your engine run dry. Unlike petrol engines, there is no carburettor, and you cannot just crank the starter and wait for the fuel to pump its way back into the system after you have filled the tank. No, you need to bleed the engine, to remove all the air bubbles that block up the myriad little tubes, jets and ducts that make up a diesel line. It is a fiddly little job, involving spanners and some considerable mess, though I understand it is not a complicated procedure – if only you know how.

I, unfortunately, had never done it before; so now, for want of a little practice at something so elementary, we were likely to be stuck here for some time. In fact, as was pointed out to me by the fuel attendant, we might be here a lot longer than we bargained, because not only was the water low, it was getting lower. This meant every minute I dithered about with the engine, the keel was embedding itself deeper and deeper in the mud making it all the less likely that we would be able to escape at all before the next tide. And that would be midnight. The thought of spending the night stuck in mud alongside a fuel quay was not an appealing one – not with all those quiet, pretty beaches so close by – so I jumped ashore and set off in search of a mechanic who might, for a few *Reais*, show me how to bleed an engine. Little did any of us foresee the malign chain of events this was about to trigger.

I loped off behind the fuel station and found myself at the entrance to the rather rundown commercial marina "Pier46". To one side of the car park was a metal garage door, rolled up to reveal a workshop where two smudged men hunched over an outboard motor.

"*Bom Dia!*" I called, as friendly as you like.

They stood up, and the older one nodded.

"*Disculpe,*" I went on in awful Portuguese, "but I was wondering if it would be possible for you kind fellows to give me a hand?"

They blinked through their grime, impassive. I went on to explain my dilemma as best I could with my limited Portuguese while they stood staring at me, and eventually I saw a light come on.

"*Ah, sangrar*!" said the older one, standing a little straighter.

"*Sim, sangrar*!" I enthused, pouncing on the word that sounded like the Latin root for blood. "*Sangra meu motor por favor*!"

I lead them back to the boat. The older one, the boss, Jorge, around fifty, jocular, well built with thinning hair, and his silent teenage assistant with a shrivelled leg and a bad limp.

Jorge and The Mute were received aboard with due ceremony, and shown below. I whipped off the floor of the cockpit and squatted over the engine, watching Jorge from above. He fiddled and poked around in the depths, whistling between his teeth and shaking his head all the while. Eventually he signalled me to start the engine.

Chug chug chug chug it went but would not fire. Jorge fiddled some more with the same result. Then he rubbed his cheek and shook his head mournfully. Evidently this was not going to be so simple. Hauling himself up, he pointed out that if we stayed there any longer we would be well and truly stuck in the mud, and offered to tow us around to the marina. We all agreed a marina – even a paying one – would be a far better option for the night that the fuel quay, so we let Jorge drag us out of the mud and tow us with his fishing boat and deposit us on the jetty next door with a promise to return in the morning and sort out our engine.

The new day dawned hot and steamy as it does in Paraty. It was not so much a sunrise, as someone opening a door to a giant sauna in the sky. There was not a breath of wind on the marina and we were sweating by eight o'clock.

Jorge arrived with his sidekick and was soon at it again – fiddling and fussing below and tut-tutting under his breath, throwing the odd

"*No Andres, no!*" in my direction for good measure. I had no idea what he was doing down there but I was getting an uneasy feeling. After a time he surfaced, wiping his greasy hands on a rag and shaking his head. An expression of infinite sorrow clouded his face and he gave me a long pitying look.

"There is something very wrong with this motor," he whispered with great sympathy. "The diesel is not the problem. It is something infinitely worse."

Not what I wanted to hear. What could it be? We had just had the ruddy thing completely overhauled in Uruguay. I told him so.

"Uruguay?!" He looked aghast. "No, not Uruguay, please! Oh, no wonder! You've been ripped off my friend. This motor is a mess! A disaster!"

"So what's wrong with it?"

"I can't tell you now, but it's something very bad. It will have to come out."

It was my turn to look aghast.

"Out? That's crazy! It's just been out for two months! It's like a new motor, it was running perfectly yesterday!"

"Well," he shrugged, "it's not running so perfectly now, is it?"

I did not know what to say. I tried to stay calm. I looked from Jorge to the engine; to the pile of injectors, pipes, cogs and bolts he had accumulated on the deck, then back to Jorge. I felt trapped.

"Alright, what do you suggest?" I asked, trying to sound like the one in control.

"I must strip this engine down properly in my workshop to see what the problem is. But first we need to remove it from the boat. That I can do tomorrow, no problem, by the fuel jetty, at high tide. We can use the boom to lift it out."

I was horrified. Who knew what he might find, or how long it could all take? In Piriapolis we had already been without the engine for months.

"And the cost?" I ventured, as if it were purely an academic question. He sucked his teeth and whistled softly, staring over the distant hills for inspiration.

"Three thousand dollars. That's for the labour. Plus parts, depending on what I find."

I felt sick. We had spent so much money on this cursed engine. If I'd known we were going to be in this situation again, I'd have cut my losses early and bought a new one. I needed time to digest it all.

"I need to think it over. In the meantime, please put the engine back together, then tomorrow we can talk again."

"Oh, don't worry about that, I'll put all the parts in a box in my workshop, they won't go missing".

I sensed we were wrestling for jurisdiction.

"No, I want the engine in one piece while I think."

"But why, what's the difference? It will take more time, and I will have to charge you more."

"Because that's what I want, okay? I'm not sitting here with my engine scattered all over Paraty. Put it back together now." Then, to encourage him, I added "Tomorrow we can talk about taking it out."

The truth is I did not yet have any idea what I was going to do tomorrow. Grudgingly he went below and after an hour everything was tidied up. Before he left he leaned close to me and spoke most earnestly, as to a dear brother.

"*Andres,*" he said, almost in a whisper, his hand on my shoulder. "*Andres, por favor. Nao arranca,* okay? Do not start the engine, whatever you do."

"Well, I wasn't planning to, but why ever not?"

"Because I don't know what is wrong with it yet. If you try you could damage it really badly. Promise me you won't try. Please. *Por favor.*"

He had my attention. I was terrified. "Alright then, I understand. *Eu nao arranco o motor.*"

He gave me a supportive pat on the back and I watched him walk off up the jetty, his crippled teenager limping along behind with the toolbox.

This was a pretty pickle. I had no idea what to do. Gerald, my one-time mentor – who introduced me to sailing – had said to me "*If you are in a hole and don't know how you are going to get out, at least stop digging.*" Sage advice. I had no intention of digging, and I certainly was not going to let Jorge take the engine out willy-nilly. Not tomorrow at any rate.

As the sun set over the hills behind us and picked out the white boats bobbing on their yellow mooring buoys in the bay, Abi and I sat on the end of our wooden jetty with our feet in the warm water sharing a beer. A flock of vultures dialled black and high above the green peaks, and to our left the day's last schooners were returning to the town pier to disgorge their sunburnt but happy day-trippers. We could see the horses and traps lined up next to the old church, ready to take the tourists back to their hotels, and the coconut sellers on the lawns. We agreed there could be worse places to have to spend two months if it came to that.

Our reverie was broken by the sound of feet rattling the planks behind us. A friendly voice said "Hello, Yeah!" and we turned to see a stout, jolly man with a ponytail and bushy grey beard beaming down at us. The creases around his soft grey eyes made him instantly likeable. "I am Marcio. Welcome to Pier46, yeah!"

I stood and shook his hand.

"This is my boat, where I live," said Marcio, jabbing a fleshy thumb over his shoulder at a particularly unkempt looking thirty-two footer with a fringe of barnacles crusting her waterline. We were neighbours. "I believe Jorge is working in your boat?"

"Yes in fact he is – I think…"

"Ah. I saw him now, and he telled me – *told* me – to tell to you, '*don't start the engine*'. Yeah. A message for you!"

"Yes, he told me that himself, thanks."

"Ah, yeah! He look very worried that you will try it. I don't know why."

We invited Marcio on board for a beer, and I gave him a rundown of our day. He listened quietly, the smile never leaving his face. When I had finished, he chuckled.

"Okay. The first, you don't to take out the engine. Is not necessary. I am sure. Yeah." He flicked his ponytail over his shoulder. "The second, don't take Jorge for the mechanic. You must take another mechanic. Yeah. A better one. A *good* one!"

I would have believed my mum if she had told me at that moment it was not necessary to remove the engine, so badly did I want to avoid doing so.

Marcio was still talking. "Reinaldo know a good mechanic, yeah, we speak with Reinaldo tomorrow. This Reinaldo's boat," pointing to the ketch moored opposite us. "He in the restaurant tonight, he play music. But tomorrow, yeah, we speak with him. For sure."

Things were looking up. At least we felt like we had a friend. After a few more beers Marcio leaned towards me and disclosed in a low voice, "Jorge is not mechanic. Jorge knows only outboards motors. He don't know your engine. He will take out and then you will pay, just more and more, and nothing else. Yeah."

"You think so?"

"Yeah, I am sure, for sure. Why to not start the motor? I think because probably he put the points out so it does not work, and if you try, you break it. I don't think there was something wrong. Just diesel, yeah! Only this."

This sounded grim and I tossed and turned that night. Everything had been going so well, and now it was spinning away from us again. We were once more losing control of our destiny. '*Why does a sailboat need a ruddy engine anyway?*' I asked myself. '*A hundred years ago, Joshua Slocum sailed around the world with no engine. But then he didn't have power for his GPS, or his laptop, or his i-pod, or his fridge, or the fan in the saloon…*' until eventually I fell asleep.

The sun always rises again though, and true enough the next morning it did exactly that. I poked my head out of the hatch to clear my blurred mind, and there on the jetty beheld the smiling Marcio. With him was an older man with smartly cropped silver hair and twinkling blue eyes who, if anything, sported an infectious grin even broader than Marcio's filled to capacity with perfect, square white teeth. I decided I liked Reinaldo straight away too.

"You are lu-cky, you find-ed the best ma-ri-na in Pa-ra-ty!" He enunciated every syllable with great care. "Here wee leeve een our boats, so wee are neigh-bours. Wee help each oth-er. So to start you don't need to wo-rry a-bout no-theeng, o-kay?"

"Sounds good to me!" I said as we shook hands.

"Marcio tell-ed me you had Jorg-e on your boat," followed by an unrepeatable curse. "Now you come weeth me and I take you to Meester Feesh. Feesh ees ve-ry good, hee works on all the feesh-ing boats. He work-ed al-so on my boat, he ees not *ess-pen-sseef.*"

"That's good for me, I don't think much of expensive. Let me put a shirt on…"

"Ha ha, don' to wo-rry weeth shirt, Mee-ster Feesh ees not *so-phis-ti-cat-ed!*"

With that I was bundled into Reinaldo's van in my shorts and driven to town.

Mister Fish's workshop almost defied description. Never have I seen a bigger mess. It consisted of a corrugated tin roof stretched over two walls and boarded off on the street with a little creaky door for access. The far end was open to the elements and looked out over the bay. The floor was slimy clay, black with old oil and littered with springs, loops of wire, old engine blocks, grimy cardboard and assorted gearbox skeletons. At one end was a steel table sagging under a pile of greasy engine parts. Plastic drinks bottles had been glued into holes in the roof to make surprisingly effective skylights. Outside the back, amongst the tangled wet bushes and muddy puddles, were more rusting engine blocks, loose pistons and a heap of shafts. Mr Fish was quite obviously not *so-phis-ti-cat-ed*. Neither was he in. Reinaldo seemed unperturbed, and left a message with the neighbour; a stooped old man repairing starter motors and alternators in a gloomy shed next door.

Back at the marina Reinaldo told everyone our problems had been solved. This sounded over-optimistic to me, especially as I had not even met the mechanic, but optimism was good and I liked Reinaldo. Later that morning we met the rest of Reinaldo's "crew". Abi and Jo struck up an immediate rapport with his wife Bernadette, while Lucy and their dachshund puppy Billy fell in love with each other. It felt like catching up with old friends we had just never met before.

In the event I never did meet Mr Fish. It seemed *Senhor Pesce* was very busy on a tourist schooner, but he sent along one of his better mechanics, who was known to Reinaldo. "Lerdo" (Portuguese for "Slow") was a sight. His heavy, squat body was supported on impossibly short, stumpy legs and he appeared to have no neck. He puffed and wheezed around the boat with the slow deliberate movements of an overweight sloth, as if at any moment he might either fall asleep, or suffer some sort of attack. I was afraid to make sudden movements near him. I will never be able to figure out quite how Lerdo contrived his bulk into the little space under the steps which provides the only access to the front end of the engine, and once in there I seriously doubted he was ever going to come out again. He brought to mind those awful scrunched up fat-faced dolls you used to buy in jars, or Winnie the Pooh stuck fast in Rabbit's hole. No more honey for Lerdo.

Lerdo confirmed what Marcio had suspected; Jorge had indeed replaced everything with all the points set wrong to ensure the engine would never start. The problem was that Lerdo did not have the "specs" for our engine, so could not correct the problem. He would have to come back the following day.

Nothing is ever simple in Brazil, however. The next day Reinaldo came to tell us that Lerdo had suffered "prob-lems" the previous night and was now in hospital. We were relieved to be assured he was okay, but he had stripped the engine and now we were stepping over and around all the bits in the saloon. I certainly had absolutely no idea how to put it all back together, and there was no point asking Jorge who we no longer trusted. We had little option but to await the recovery of Lerdo.

It was three long weeks before Lerdo was back, still breathing like a kettle but evidently none the worse for wear. He admitted however that he could not put the engine back together correctly (even though I had downloaded the specs from the internet and had them bound and ready) as the job was too technical for him. This was a blow, but I was thankful for his honesty – a lot of mechanics would have "had a go" and possibly inflicted mortal damage.

And so as we moved into our second month at Pier46, we moved on to our third mechanic. Reinaldo knew another one, even better than Meester Feesh, but more *ess-pen-seef* (which was why he had not introduced me to Ricardo the first time around.)

Ricardo owned a company called "*So-Diesel*" and employed a thoroughly competent team of mechanics. They descended on the boat *en masse*, and while they got stuck in Riccardo insisted on leaving them to it as he took us off in his car – all of us – to meet his wife for a pizza. It turned out Ricardo and I had a lot in common, having both started out as school teachers, then both moved into banking, before I quit to pursue the sailing dream and he quit to run his own business. We became instant friends, and by the time we returned to the marina, awash with *cerveja,* his men had performed their magic and *Josephine*'s engine was running perfectly. Marcio and Reinaldo were looking on and nodding their approval in unison, their broad sunny smiles lighting up our world.

"You see!" beamed Marcio, "I tell you is no problem! Just diesel! Now you go! Yeah!"

Of course we had been there six weeks; but then, what is a mere six weeks to a jolly Brazilian?

"Not everything about fishing
is noble and reasonable and sane."

– Harry Middleton

23

I do not know what possessed me to buy a spear gun. I suppose I associated it with some concept of being a hunter; liberated, living off the sea, heroically providing for my family. Whatever the reason, I bought one from the little boat shop in Paraty, down by the tourist schooner dock, and propped it proudly in the saloon, in full view. It looked good there. It told everyone what type of man I was. Free, tough, resourceful, brave. Abi thought it was ridiculous.

My only prior experience with spear guns was up the east coast of South Africa, near the border with Mozambique. I drove there with three friends, all very accomplished spear fishermen, who had talked me into coming along to learn the ropes.

Driving to Cape Vidal is like driving into an up-country game park; it does not have the feel of the beach at all. For several miles you drive with caution along a dusty track hemmed in by dense bush, keeping an eye out for giant kudu that tend to burst unexpectedly from the thorny undergrowth and throw themselves in front of your car.

Cape Vidal itself, once you reach it, is little more than a hamlet with a very busy bar and a muddy campsite nestled under tall trees. But it is something of a fishing Mecca: there are very few cars coming and going that do not have a boat in tow.

We drove into the campsite and Dan saw some friends rinsing off under the outdoor showers in the car park. They were surrounded by the paraphernalia of spear fishing; spear guns, floats and bits of rope lay in a tangle on the gravel and wetsuits dripped in the trees. Nearby was an open truck and I could see the heads of a number of fish poking over the tailgate. Those heads were bigger than my torso, with teeth like my thumbs.

"How is it?" asked Dan through the car window.

"Not bad!" came the reply. "The viz is excellent, but the tax man is around. We didn't see him, but a number of other people saw him patrolling yesterday."

"How big?"

"Not too big. Sounds like about ten feet."

Dan grunted and wound up the window. The rest of the guys were quiet.

'*The tax man?*' I wondered to myself. Being the new guy I didn't want to give the impression of being nervous so thought it best to keep quiet and not ask too many questions. It was just as well I did not ask, as I would not have liked the answer and probably would not have got in the water.

First light found us on the deserted beach. We had driven several miles along the sand in the frigid air of pre-dawn, and were now kitting up. Wetsuit, fins, mask, snorkel, gun, float, stringer, flashers, knife… It was all very new and strange to me, but the others were in their element. Mark talked me through the gun, showing me how to load it and warning me about the obvious dangers of getting entangled in the line. I tried to load the gun myself but could not pull the rubbers back far enough to hook them round the back of the spear.

"Don't worry, its easier in the water."

Spear fishermen are an odd lot. Well my friends are at any rate. There is an almost indecent haste about the way they kit up and race each other into the water. Everybody wants to be in first in case, God forbid, somebody else sees a fish before they do. Or worse, actually shoots one. So by the time I was ready, I found myself alone on the beach struggling across the sand dragging a mangle of gear behind me.

The spear gun itself, once loaded, is about five feet long and has a very sharp end which one is advised to avoid. You swim with this gun in your hand, the spiky bit pointing ahead. Behind you your feet extend at least another two feet in their fins, so the overall effect is that you are twelve feet long. This horribly confuses your spatial awareness, causing untold problems of manoeuvrability.

The back of the spear is attached to the gun by a thirty foot long cord that should play out freely off a reel after you fire. That way you can get the spear back after you miss; or, if you know what you are doing, keeps you attached to the fish you have shot so it cannot escape before you wrestle it into submission and stab it in the brain with the knife strapped to your leg. In addition you have a thirty metre nylon rope, one end of which is attached to the handle of your gun, and the other to a float – really a small buoy – that bobs along on the water behind you. The float serves two purposes: Firstly, if you shoot a very big, powerful fish and need to breathe again before fighting it, you can apparently let go the gun and swim to the surface, holding either the rope or the buoy, and be towed about by an enraged ten foot man-eating marlin as you scream for your friends to save you. Secondly, there is a sharp metal hook (called a *stringer*) hanging beneath the buoy, to which you attach your slaughtered fish by the head as you go off in search of your next victim.

As if this is not enough, you need to deal with "flashers" too – a collection of mirrors and shiny bits of metal hanging on strings from your waist, which tangle around your legs and are meant to attract predatory fish like barracuda and tuna with big teeth, and then the idea is for you to try to kill them before they eat you.

It was thus laden that I attempted my first beach entry. No easy introduction for me, being lowered over the side of a boat – no, a beach entry, through a considerable shore break.

It was pitiful. I fell flat on my face twice as the ankle deep water rushed over my fins and trapped me, before I discovered it is easier to walk in backwards, only to be knocked over by the first wave and lose my mask, being forced to retrieve it from the beach and start again. Once I got deep enough to actually swim, I could not get through the breaking waves as the buoy, floating behind me on its rope, was all the time trying to surf back to the beach with me in tow. So it all had to be gathered together in my arms, which made swimming exceedingly difficult. By the time I did manage to get beyond the breakers I was exhausted. My calves were cramping and I could not see a thing through my misted up mask, my legs were entwined by the flashers, and I was nauseous.

"Well done, you made it!" It was Mark. "Now let the rope play out, you don't want to be too close to your buoy. Let it float away from you, like that. It's especially important once you have fish on your stringer."

"Huh?"

"Tax man."

That again.

"Mark, just a minute," I spluttered as I trod water. "Who is this tax man?"

"Great White!" he grinned and was gone.

Oh fantastic. Was he serious? Of course – all those struggling, bleeding fish – we would be chumming the very water we were swimming in. Why oh why, I wondered, does anybody do this, and why on earth am *I* doing this? I reached down my thigh and fingered my pathetic little knife. Cold comfort.

I peered down into the murky depths but could see nothing. Just flitting shadows in the green that gave me the creeps. I gripped the gun tightly and resolved not to fire it for fear of not being able to reload. I was not going to be unarmed when I was attacked by the tax man. And I certainly had no desire to fill the sea around me with fish blood. That was plain silly.

I saw Dan swim down and watched him merge with the darkness. I looked at my watch, and waited. A minute passed, then another, and another. It was well into the fourth minute before I saw him again, rising slowly upwards. It looked like a scene out of "Big Blue", only he carried a gun. He popped up alongside me.

"Fun, hey?!" he exclaimed, but did not wait for me to answer. He could not afford time on the surface; not when his mates were down there and might get some action that he would miss out on. He had just held his breath for four minutes, but was up for less than sixty seconds before he went back down. Where was he going, what was he doing? What was down there? I decided I did not want to know.

By now I was sea sick. Bobbing about on the surface, face down with nothing to focus on in the marble green, was no good. I threw up into my snorkel and nearly choked. I wondered miserably whether the Tax Man would be attracted to human vomit and swam away from the spreading stain in a panic, clutching my gun tightly.

A shadow appeared suddenly below me, and I almost stood up and ran over the water with the adrenalin. Then I saw a school of eight to ten large fish, each some six feet long, swimming in a straight line about thirty feet down. They were too far away for a shot. My heart thumping with excitement, I sucked a breath and tried to dive but my foot was tangled in the buoy rope and as I thrashed the surface with my trapped fin the fish vanished.

Alone again and regaining my senses I realised what I had almost tried to do.

'Are you nuts? What did you think you were going to do with one of those? It probably would've beaten you up. And anyway, I thought you weren't going to fire your gun. Now don't try anything like that again, you arse!'

I need not have worried: I did not see another fish all day. I lolled in the water feeling miserable, sweating in the rubber suit and vomiting into my mask, not wanting to show weakness and be the first out of the water. My friends were hardcore and I would have to endure.

I suffered for over four hours. For four hours those clowns dived, dived and dived again as I drifted around imagining the Tax Man stalking me from every direction. It was close to midday when the decision was taken to call timeout and I turned towards the beach.

But where was the van? Had it been stolen? I was too weary to care, and only too happy to be getting out. Once in the white water I let the waves roll me around and carry me, except that this time the infernal buoy was stuck *behind* the waves, and pulling me backwards so I could not surf in. I was tumbled in the breakers several times before I could get all the gear under control and eventually collapsed, thoroughly spent, face down on the wet sand.

Mark came next, then Brian.

"Where is the van?" I gasped into the little puddle formed by the salt water running out of my nose.

"Where we left it this morning. We've been drifting on the current. It's about a four mile walk back."

I was horrified. "What, with all this gear?"

But Mark was not listening. He was looking out to sea.

"Typical!" he spat. "Dan always has to be last out of the water. He seems to think the fish all want to be shot by him, and him alone!"

My Boys, competitive to the last. We sat on the sand and watched as Dan entered the break. He missed the first curling wave as it collapsed around him, and as he bobbed about in the white foam behind the wave he appeared to be struggling to gather his gear. Then there was a violent jerk and Dan vanished under the water. He was gone for no more than a few seconds, but when he popped up he had moved twenty metres down the breakline.

"How did he do that?" I asked.

Mark was silent, staring at the sea. Dan was gesticulating wildly, thrashing at the water.

"Something's wrong," Mark said, standing now, tense.

Dan was swimming hard. I could see his buoy trailing behind at the full extent of its rope and he did not appear to be holding a gun. He swam, surfed the breaks up onto the beach, stumbled in the shallows and sprinted out of the water. Then he turned screaming at the sea.

"Fuck you!" he bellowed. "You sneaky fucker! Come out here and I'll cut your fucking head off! For fucks sake, you son of a bitch!"

He was apoplectic with rage, but Mark and Brian were now giggling like school girls. Dan eventually regained control and stomped up the beach towards us, a look of dark fury on his face.

"I've been taxed!" he snapped. "Fucker took all my fish, and my gun. Fuck!"

He held up his buoy. Impaled on the steel hook were two fish heads, each the size of a basketball. They looked as if their bodies had been sliced away with a power saw. The White Shark had probably been shadowing us for some time, waiting for an opportunity, and just as Dan was distracted by the breaking waves, the rest of us out of the way, the shark struck.

"I just saw this grey hulk rushing at me in a cloud of bubbles, and then everything went pink in front of me. I shoved my arms up in front of my face and then I was jerked so violently my mask was ripped off and I was being dragged so fast I couldn't make out what was happening. Then I realised my gun was in the shark's mouth. I tried to hang on, thinking he would spit it out, but he was swimming too fast and I lost my hold. Bastard! Took my fish, and snatched the gun right out of my hands. That was a brand new gun!"

Dan was inconsolable. He was a lot more upset about the loss of the precious new gun than concerned about the fact that he had almost been bitten in half. The others found it all rather amusing. I seemed to be the only one shaken by this incident.

That afternoon, unbelievably, they were back at it. I swallowed my pride and stayed on the beach. And the Tax Man?

"I don't think he's hungry now!" quipped Dan as he grabbed his old gun and raced his mates down the beach to be first into the surf.

"We live in an age where unnecessary things are our only necessities."

– Oscar Wilde

24

It does not take much to trigger a *festa* in Brazil. The successful conclusion to our engine woes was met with much celebration by the closely-knit community of Pier46, and an impromptu "jetty party" was thrown. An assortment of folding chairs, camping stools and diesel drums were arranged around a long wooden table down the centre of our floating pier, and the braai fired up on one of the boats. Reinaldo staggered up with the biggest ice box I had ever seen, filled with beers, and we found someone competent to play my guitar. From town could be heard the sounds of drumming as the local samba schools rehearsed for the upcoming *Carnival*, now only a couple of months away.

Marcio was there, nodding his head vigorously, "Yeah!" Bernadette was ladling out *Moheca* (local fish stewed in fresh pineapple and coconut milk) as an *hors d'oevre* and Reinaldo was entertaining the crowd with hilarious stories from their tourist charters.

"A reech man from Sao Paulo wan-ted to char-ter the boat for four days, for hees son's eigh-teenth birth-day. There should be just the son, and hees five friends. Seex boys. We were too tir-ed, we deed not want eet, so we feex-ed a price very high, but they ac-cept-ed eet. So we must make the char-ter. Hooo! Ber-na-dette was cross, ho-ho-ho…"

His eyes twinkled in the candle light.

"When they arriv-ed, I ask-ed '*O-kay, we have four days, where do you want to go?*' and they said '*take us to Praia de Pie-da-de, on Il-ha Gi-poia*' and I ask-ed them '*where af-ter that?*' and they said '*no, just Praia de Pie-da-de.*' I ask-ed them '*for four days?*' and they said, '*yes, four days!*' And thees was fun-ny be-cause there are so ma-ny is-lands and beach-es, but they just pay me and they can go where they want. When we arriv-ed at *Praia de Pie-da-de* I thought '*hoooo, what ees thees?*' There was a lot of peo-ple, a lot of boats, a stage on the beach, loud mu-sic PUM PUM PUM and the beach eet was clos-ed with a beeg rope and float-ing theengs and you could not go there. We put down the an-chor and een the night the boys ask-ed me to take them een the deen-ghy. The teeck-et for thees par-ty should be ev-ery day one hun-dred doll-ars, so we go qui-e-tly een the dark un-der the rope and hide from the lights and I leav-ed them on the beach for the par-ty, no tick-ets. In the mor-ning they were all sleep-ing. I don't know when they came back, but they sleep-ed all day. Then een the night eet was the same a-gain. And ev-ery day was like thees. It was a ve-ry eas-y char-ter for us, no work-ing, on-ly the mu-sic was terr-ib-le PUM PUM PUM all night."

Reinaldo roared with laughter and slugged on his beer.

"On the last night Ber-na-dette and I de-cid-ed to go and look the par-ty so we went slow-ly swimm-ing with the pool noo-dles un-der the rope een-to the beach al-ways look-ing to the se-cu-ri-ty guards. Hoooo, where are they? Where are they?"

He made little swimming motions with his hands and peered over his shoulder for the guards.

"Walk-ing then on the beach, with seex-ty five years I am the old-est peo-ple een the is-land, with thees pool nood-les and I am weeth the speed-o on-ly, no shirt, noth-ing, and the peo-ple are with par-ty clothes, ve-ry *so-phis-ti-cat-ed*. I tell-ed to Ber-na-dette we should go we have not the cor-rect u-ni-form, and then we hear "*Hi*!!!..."

Reinaldo struck a teapot pose to demonstrate as he spoke.

"...and we turn and there we see two young mens een speed-os, ve-ry prett-y mens, beau-ti-ful, hold-ing hands, and they are wav-ing to me and Ber-na-dette tell-ed to me '*No Reinaldo, you* do *have a uniform!*'"

At which point, tears shining in his eyes, Reinaldo threw his head back and guffawed until the jetty shook.

Reinaldo and Bernadette made a decent living from running charters in the bay of Ilha Grande. They knew the islands well, having plied them for fifteen years, and had their favourite places. From time to time, however, they would have clients who knew better and came with a shortlist of islands printed off some internet site. It always seemed to be the same list, and for the most part they were relatively uninteresting islands with inaccessible beaches and private homes tucked away behind trees, but the clients always seemed happy to see them and would jabber excitedly and point at them and high five each other and tick them off the list.

Then one day Reinaldo discovered the secret behind the list: they were islands with the homes of famous football players or *telenovella* (soap opera) stars. After this discovery, Reinaldo would tell such clients the list was out of date, but that he could show them the *real* homes of these demigods, and he was then free to go to his own favourite anchorages and beaches, pointing out along the way any house that looked even slightly grand, and making up things like "*Thees was Ayrton Sen-na's house be-fore he died*" and "*O-ver there be-hind those trees ees a house be-long-ing to Ma-donn-a.*" His clients always went home *hap-py*.

In addition to charters, our friends supplemented their income playing music in a local restaurant. Reinaldo played the piano and Bernadette sang. Bernadette told us how in their breaks Reinaldo would mysteriously disappear, and eventually she discovered he was sneaking over the road to the old age home to sit with his geriatric friends and watch the local *telenovella* in their TV room. She joked that he was doing this to ingratiate himself with an eye to his future.

Although they owned a house in the town, they rented it out as they preferred living on the boat. They had the ideal life. Every couple of years they would up anchor and sail north to Bahia for a change of scenery, where they would spend several months at anchor among the islands of *Baia de Todos os Santos* near Salvador, and play music in a friend's restaurant.

Also on the jetty the night of the party was Wilson. Wilson lived in a rather scruffy boat called *Go For It,* a little way down from Reinaldo and Bernadette. An engaging fellow who could not speak English, he was always trying to help us. A retired veterinary surgeon, he too offered charters, only his were a little more "budget" than Reinaldo's. We later saw his website, which Marcio had built for him, and it made *Go For It* look rather more grand and smart than she actually was. In reality she was something of a mess. Mornings invariably found Wilson sawing or banging away at his beloved boat with great industry, his favourite beer at his elbow, but by midday he seemed incapable of managing anything much more than the next beer. Marcio told us an amusing story of how a couple once arrived on the pier for a charter, but after taking one look inside Wilson's boat the woman stormed off back to their car and made her husband drive her home to Sao Paulo. Wilson was delighted as they had paid upfront and it was non-refundable. The perfect charter!

In the time that we were there, we saw with our own eyes a family arrive for a charter with Wilson and immediately change the arrangement so they could stay in a local hotel and just use the boat for day trips. That way they could spend their days on deck, in the clean air, and avoid the dank, mouldy cabins at night. Wilson was thrilled, as he made his money but no longer needed to provide meals. In the evenings he could be seen sitting alone in his cockpit, trusty beer in hand, grinning at the passing world. The man had not a care.

Marcello was another interesting character at Pier46. Now about forty, he had left work, cashed in his pension, sold his house, and bought a thirty-three foot sloop that he was preparing for a round-the-world voyage. The remainder of his funds had been sunk into a tract of land somewhere in the surrounding hills which he had then planted with several thousand seedlings of some or other indigenous hardwood tree.

"Now I go sailing for fifteen years, and when I come back I cut down the trees and sell the wood and I am a rich man!" he explained.

***

Being stuck a while in Paraty meant we had come to know it well. A pretty old town, it was established by the Portuguese in 1667 to serve as a port for shipping gold from the mines at Minas Gerais to Rio and on to Europe. A curiosity unique to Paraty is the way the Portuguese engineered flood holes in the sea wall that separates the old town from the bay, such that at high tide the water floods the streets to a depth of about ten inches, to drain away again a few hours later leaving the cobbles washed clean. The phenomenon of horses towing traps through knee-deep water reflecting the colourful shop fronts is very popular subject matter for photographic-minded tourists.

We had become part of a happy, close-knit community at Pier46, and it was the perfect base from which to launch forays to the outlying beaches and explore the nearby islands. We spent several happy days anchored off the beaches of *Praia de Bom Jardinho* or *Jurumirim,* swimming with Lucy and romping on the sand, snorkelling beneath the wooden deck of the restaurant on *Ilha do Catimbau* and exploring the wooded cliffs of Mamangua. I even dived with my new spear gun (though the biggest fish I saw was not much bigger than my hand – couldn't shoot that – shot it anyway and felt guilty immediately). Everywhere the aquamarine water was warm and the coconuts, bananas and breadfruit were dropping off the trees. This area must be the cruising world's best kept secret.

Some time after our arrival, a catamaran appeared at Pier46, skippered by its Swiss owner Pierre Louis accompanied by his best friend Gabriel, from Barcelona. Pilou and Gabi had mutual business interests in Europe, in top-end yacht hire for corporate hospitality at events like the America's Cup. Two jollier fellows could not be imagined, and they were to be seen every evening in their spacious cockpit sipping on freshly made *caipirinhas* and playing dice. It was not long before I joined them and many happy hours were thus idled away.

One evening Gabi was talking about the nearby town of Angra dos Reis (old Portuguese for "Anchorage of the Kings") and Marcio asked if we were familiar with *Piratas Mall.* I had no idea what he was talking about. My pilot book, though it seems to be the only English language one in existence, was, as I may have mentioned, hopelessly inadequate. (It talks, for example, of the opportunities for anchoring off Paraty, but makes no mention of the seven commercial marinas now in existence, crammed with yachts. The same for Angra dos Reis; there is no reference at all to the marina development of *Piratas Mall.)*

"Oh, Abi, you and your mother should like it *Piratas Mall*, yeah!" exclaimed Marcio, bobbing his head so his ponytail jumped. "You stop the boat in the jetty direct in front the supermarket, then you walk inside and you buy what you want, and you deliver again direct on the boat. Is beautiful, yeah! You should like very much this. I am sure!"

I too was sure they should like it very much this *Piratas Mall* for shopping with its own jetty, but wondered what the point would be of a hundred mile roundtrip just to visit a supermarket.

Pilou was up for an adventure however.

"Ah, per'aps we go togesser!" he suggested in his French Swiss accent, "and sen we vissit Angra and some new islands on se osser side of se bay. We go a few days, why not?"

I was going to lose this one fast. I had to admit it would be fun to spend a few days sailing together discovering new places, and it would be a good test of our *rehabilitated* engine; we would be coming back here, so if anything went wrong I could just call Riccardo and his mechanics from *So-Diesel* back to Pier46.

We reached Angra dos Reis after one overnight stop anchored off *Ilha Scandri*, the white dome of Brazil's *Alvaro Alberto* nuclear power plant obtrusive in the background, and found *Piratas Mall* with no difficulty. Marcio was absolutely right of course; the girls sacked the supermarket and soon had five trolleys laden with loot lined up on the jetty. As Rupert and I were heaving it all aboard, I was approached by a tourist who offered me a hundred dollars to take him and his girlfriend to the islands for the afternoon. I realised how easy it could be to subsidise our travel habit that way.

From Angra we sailed two hours on a perfect breeze, beam reaching between eight and nine knots, across the bay to the island of *Ilha Grande* itself where we anchored in a cosy, protected cove just off *Praia de Freguesia*. The secluded yellow beach was fringed with coconut palms and backed by steep jungle-clad hills. At sunset the forest came alive with the hoots of night birds, the occasional shriek of a monkey, the chirruping of tree frogs and the rustling of the tropical breeze through the canopy. We roped our boats together and sat on deck late into the night, ice tinkling in fresh glasses of *caipirinha*, enchanted by the magic lantern show of fireflies dancing above the beach.

***

One thing I have learnt about cruising is that whatever your plans, something else will happen. In the long run, not necessarily for the worst; but it can be most frustrating when you set your heart on a course, and fate deals you unexpected cards that change everything. I suppose that is how life is generally, not just if you are living on a boat; its just that on a boat you do seem to need to "plan" every day, whereas back home your "plans" are longer term, so dealing with day to day contingencies is the norm.

Morning brought with it a steady downpour of rain which made lying on the beach unappealing, so we resolved to spend the rainy hours travelling to our next spot, in the hope that by midday the rain would have let up and we could do some snorkelling.

I turned the key and the diesel engine roared into life. It was such a welcome sound after the drama with Jorge and his "*don't start the engine*". But when I shifted it into gear, nothing happened. I could rev it up no problem, but the boat would not go. I tried reverse. Same result. My heart sank. I lifted the floor and had a look at the gear cable. It was fine. Rupert fiddled the throttle and I watched the little lever on the gearbox flick up and down, engaging alternately forward and reverse. Nothing wrong there. No, the problem was *inside* the gearbox. The mysterious, inscrutable gearbox. The one thing I knew even less about than the engine.

"Unbelievy," muttered Rupert doing his best imitation of Alex from Piriapolis.

And so, hearts heavy, we sailed the fifty miles back to Paraty, arriving at Pier46 after dark. We had been gone less than forty-eight hours with our happy engine and were now back with a decidedly *un*happy gearbox and in need of another mechanic. I called Riccardo to be told that his mechanics did not do gearboxes.

As luck would have it, the very next morning there was a mechanic coming out to look at the gearbox on one of the other boats, so when he arrived we co-opted him. Alberto was his name. He was in his sixties, short and bony, with wire rimmed spectacles that lent him a schoolmasterly air. Almost before I knew what was happening, he had whipped the gearbox out and whisked it away in his rusty little van, promising to have a look at it in his workshop. He assured us he would hurry back the next day with a prognosis.

We did not see or hear from Alberto again for over a week, during which time we got to choose between roasting beneath the open furnace of the tropical sun, or squelching around in pools of our own sweat under a steamy plastic tarpaulin. The hills around Paraty do a fine job of stifling the breeze, and not even the regular afternoon downpours cooled us down; they merely increased the humidity. When Alberto did eventually show up he was not the bearer of good news. He arrived on the jetty waving a nine-inch long metal shaft in his hand. It was the output shaft from our gearbox, and he showed me where the teeth had been stripped away. Apparently this explained why the gearbox would not work; there was nothing there for the gears to hold onto and turn the propeller.

"Can this be fixed?" I asked him.

"*Au, nao senhor, impossivel!*"

It seemed I would need a new one.

"And a new one would cost me how much?" I asked cynically. I was not going to be had twice.

"*Eu nao se senhor*!" He did not know. What he did know was I would not find one of these in Brazil. This was an old gearbox, and this make had never been popular in Brazil. I would need to import one. Import one! That could take three months, and I knew the taxes would be at least as much again as the cost of the shaft.

"I don't have the time to sit here and wait for an imported shaft. My visa will run out!"

Senhor Alberto came into his own.

"Nenhum problema senhor!" Today I had *"muito sorte!"*

Hmmm. Lucky me.

"I have in my workshop a used gearbox from another boat. There is nothing wrong with that gearbox. It is the same make as yours, just one size up, but the attachments are the same and it will fit your engine."

That sounded too convenient, and I was suspicious.

"How much?" I asked.

Alberto closed his eyes to do some complicated arithmetic in his head, then opened them and said brightly "*mil quinhentos dollar.*"

I was floored. Fifteen hundred dollars!? When was the pillaging of our finances going to end?

Alberto continued that he had the spare gearbox right here in town, that luckily for me I was his friend, that putting it in would take a mere half a day, and then we could be happily on our way. Life was indeed rosy.

That certainly sounded attractive, but fifteen hundred dollars? I thought again of Gerald's sage advice about not digging your hole deeper, and decided not to commit to anything just yet.

"I need to think about this, give me a few days. I will talk to you next week." I was stalling for time because, once again, I did not know what to do.

For a week I agonised. I discussed it with Marcio, with Reinaldo, with everyone I trusted, but nobody had an easy solution. There was consensus that the shaft could not be reconstructed; the damage was complete, and the shorn off spline very fine, with a very precise curve to it. Neither could a replacement shaft be bought "off the shelf" in Brazil, that was certain. In the end it appeared there was little option. We were running up a formidable bill at the marina; every day of indecision was costing another twenty five dollars. We were also eating into our visa time and there was a good three thousand miles of Brazilian coast still to be explored before we reached the Caribbean.

A few days before Christmas I managed to get a message to Alberto, and he arrived in the Pier46 car park in his clapped out van. Edu had flown in from Uruguay to join us for a two week holiday, and I felt very guilty about him having to spend his time sweating in the humidity under a tarpaulin on a boat stuck in a marina, so was doubly relieved to be biting the financial bullet and getting the job over and done with. As Edu and I were escorting Alberto to the jetty, lugging the replacement gearbox between us, I enquired in my best Portuguese about the whereabouts of my old gearbox. Alberto waved his bony hand in dismissal. That gearbox was useless, totally useless. I could never use it.

"Well, that may be so, but I should like to have it please."

"*Para que?*" he asked, frowning over his glasses.

"Well, I don't know – for parts I guess…"

"Oh, it is no use for that, it is destroyed," he said with authority. And anyway, he no longer had it. It was in the rubbish. *Lixo.* He had thrown it away.

"Oh." I could think of nothing else to say.

"But, not to worry," he said, brightening. "You'll see, this one is perfect!"

And so to the boat. We made a harness with some rope and I carefully lowered the gearbox down into the engine compartment where Alberto was lying with his arms through a side hatch waiting to bolt it in place.

He tinkered and fiddled away for a short while, then heaved and hammered and banged for a while longer, but no amount of cajoling, gentle or otherwise, was going to get the new box in place. The gearbox was indeed compatible with this engine, in the sense that it could easily have been bolted on in a workshop; but fitting it *en situ* was another matter altogether. The gearbox was patently not compatible with the *boat*; it was simply too big and would not fit in the tight space of the engine compartment. Alberto took longer than anyone else to reconcile himself to this fact (it being worth *mil quinhentos dolar* to him to make it fit) and I left him sweating several minutes more, until he finally surrendered and lay still.

"Okay Alberto, now what?" I had no patience for more nonsense.

"*Nenhum problema,*" came the muffled reply from the depths of the hull. He would just hack away at the inside of the boat to make more room.

I could not believe what I was hearing. I hauled the skinny rogue by his collar out onto the jetty where he could not cut anything and was just giving him the third degree when he suggested, without batting an eyelid, that a better course might be to have the damaged shaft repaired. I was speechless. Had he, or had he not, already told me that was *impossivel*?

"*Au nao senhor, es possivel, certo!*" And, what is more, it would be cheaper. Only *mil dolar.*

I could feel my blood rising.

"That's all well and good, except that you've thrown my old gearbox away, haven't you, you stupid dick! It's in the bloody *lixo*!"

But not at all, he assured me without a falter; in fact he had it right here, in his van. It must be my lucky day.

I was almost beside myself. If Edu had not been there to restrain me I fear I would have committed a most violent act and got myself into a lot of trouble with the police. Once I had calmed down sufficiently to not be a threat to public order, we retrieved my old gearbox from Alberto's van and sent him packing. At least he had not been paid anything, but I was back to square one, forlorn on the jetty with a broken gearbox.

"Don' worry my friend," said the ever dependable Edu. "Thees ees no problem. Come to Uruguay, we repair everything easy. I go weeth you."

Uruguay? What was he talking about? Back fifteen hundred miles the way we had come? After all we had been through; the storm off Laguna, running onto the rocks at Paranagua, surfing the shore break in to Cananeia… dragging anchors, seasickness, drug searches… what a notion!

That evening we sat down and discussed our options. If we stayed in Paraty much longer we would have a problem even if we *did* eventually resolve the gearbox, as our visas would expire and we would have to leave Brazil. We had already extended them once, and there is no second extension. In fact even if the gearbox *had* been repaired today, we would have been faced with rushing north and getting out of the country within two months; not nearly enough time to do justice to the three thousand miles of tropical coastline we had been so looking forward to exploring.

"This is like a bad dream," I lamented. "We've been away a year, and at least half of that time has been spent marooned somewhere or other with mechanical problems, and now, just as we get to the nice warm tropical parts, this!"

We were despondent, but the more we discussed it, the more obvious it was to us that Edu was right. Quite apart from resolving the mechanical drama, it made more sense – given the time we had already lost – to go south again, and leave the rest of Brazil, and the Caribbean, for next year. So, by the end of that eventful day, our life's course had changed again, and we were planning our return to Uruguay.

A few days later was New Year. We combined it with a farewell party on Pilou's catamaran, and the *caipirinhas* flowed well into the night. The warm tropical rain came streaming down unnoticed. Then, as the clocks struck midnight, wondering where Pilou had disappeared to, I popped up on deck to find him standing by the mast, squinting through the rain at the damp fireworks above the town. He was silent, and when I looked at him closely I could not tell at first whether it was rain or tears rolling down his cheeks.

"You okay?"

Pilou looked at me but could not speak. He had spent the previous New Year here too, on his boat, but had just been diagnosed with cancer and was preparing to fly back to Switzerland for treatment. Back then he had stood in the same spot, watching the same fireworks, believing it to be the last New Year he would ever see. When he said goodbye to his boat he thought he would never see her again. Back now on his beloved *Tavae* watching the fireworks herald another year in his life was to him a miracle. I slung an arm over his wide shoulders and without saying a word we stood there, together, in the downpour. And to think how stressed I was about our stupid gearbox.

"There Leviathan, hugest of living creatures,
in the deep stretched like a promontory sleeps...
and at his breath spouts out a sea."

– Milton, Paradise Lost

25

The return trip south, involving some thirteen hundred miles of sailing down a busy coast in potentially rough weather, would need to be planned carefully. I did not want Lucy on board, and that meant Abi would have to fly to Uruguay, or take a bus. Edu had to fly back to Montevideo for work after his holiday with us in Paraty, but promised to meet up with the boat in Florianopolis, thereby helping with the second leg of the journey. With Rupert now back home at university, Jo and I were in for a sail of around five hundred miles before meeting up with Edu. No gearbox meant complete reliance on the wind, and we knew with the capricious weather around Rio, five hundred miles could easily take as long as five days; quite a long time for two people on a boat with no autopilot. And we had no radar either, so not only would there have to be someone physically steering at all hours, we would have to keep a sharp lookout for ships too – in all weather. If we were going to eat, we needed a third crew member.

As luck would have it, we were put in touch with Oliver Yeates. A tall, blonde, twenty-six-year-old from Devon, Oli was a surfer who had spent several years working on, and in, boats around the world. He also had a RYA Yachtmaster qualification. Now he was freewheeling in Brazil with his surfboard and guitar.

Oli came to meet us at Pier46. We lashed the dinghy alongside and, with its outboard motor fired up, coaxed *Josephine* four miles across the bay to the little beach at Jurumirim. There we spent the day swimming and snorkelling, and getting to know Oli. He was very good with Lucy and shared my taste for Radiohead. We all liked him.

That evening, as we were nudging *Josephine* home, a sudden squall whipped up and before we could get to our mooring the rain was pelting down and the wind was gusting to forty knots. In this gale there was no way of shunting an eight ton yacht onto a crowded jetty with a 4hp outboard motor, so we were obliged to drop anchor in the bay and ride it out. It was messy – all the drama that goes with howling wind, driving rain and dragging anchor in a congested anchorage, but it was over quickly enough and half an hour of that was all I needed to know that Oli would be a good fit. He was practical, bright and had a quirky sense of humour.

***

Abi took Lucy by bus to Florianopolis to wait at Alistair's, while the three of us – Jo, Oli and I – made ready to sail from Paraty. There was considerable algal growth on *Josephine*'s underside, as well as a generous encrustation of barnacles. This could cost as a knot and a half of boat speed, which over a thousand miles could translate to a loss of as much as two days. And so when we finally left Pier46, which had been our home for three months, under a kind tow from Reinaldo and Bernadette on their ketch *Leoa Louca,* we made straight for our favourite local beach, *Bom Jardin,* where we anchored for a couple of hours so Oli and I could swim under the boat and scrub her clean. It was fun under the hull with a cloud of yellow striped fish snapping up the barnacles as we scraped them away. Above, while we worked, Bernadette cooked up a "*mukeka*" with baked bananas and we were treated to a royal farewell lunch by our generous friends.

Over lunch Reinaldo and Bernadette debated whether their next adventure should take them north once again to Bahia, and then on to the Caribbean; or whether they should try something new and follow us south.

"That ees why I love a seem-ple life!" remarked the ever smiling Reinaldo. "Thees boat ees my home for ma-ny years now, and I have here ev-ree-theeng what I need. With Ber-na-dette, I can go a-ny place, and eef we don't like eet, we go to an-oth-er place, no prob-lem. May-be we see you een U-ru-guay. Heh heh heh!"

I was sure we would be seeing them again – somewhere, sometime – but we said our farewells with heavy hearts nonetheless. Time to go. A perfect warm breeze lifted us away from the beach and out into the bay at six knots. Cleaning the hull had indeed been two hours well spent; it was all *Leoa Louca* could do under motor to keep pace with us, and after ten minutes we drew away with full sails and full stomachs. It was to be the last time any of us would ever see Reinaldo.

Getting out of *Baia da Ilha Grande* with no engine was never going to be easy. The bay is notorious for its wind – or lack thereof – and it did not disappoint. Within half an hour of waving our final goodbyes to *Leoa Louca,* our kindly breeze exhausted itself some twelve miles from the open ocean. Even out there it was probably still: we might have to go some thirty to fifty miles offshore to pick up more reliable wind and hook into the south-flowing Brazil current.

The dinghy was once again lashed alongside and we burned precious fuel using the little outboard motor to coax *Josephine* across the bay. We calculated this could take around four hours, and we might just make it to the open ocean by nightfall.

Then as we dropped the mainsail we let one of the lazy jacks escape, and the end ran up to the top of the mast. The only way to get it back was for someone to be sent aloft to retrieve it, and Jo being the lightest meant she would be the one. Standing on the deck of my yacht bellowing instructions to my mother-in-law as she dangled from the end of a rope some forty feet up in the air was something people might pay good money to do.

Once the sail was packed away and the outboard motor running in the dinghy, we made progress, albeit slowly. There was no need for a big dinner (Bernadette's "*mukeka*" having filled us up) so we picked at some sandwiches as we watched for the last time the sun slip behind the steep green hills of Paraty.

The Bay of *Ilha Grande* is not simple with its numerous coves, headlands and islands, and the local weather conditions can be extreme. About an hour after deploying the dinghy the wind rose, without any warning, to thirty knots. The little inflatable reared and bucked alongside like a truculent pony, the propeller cavitating wildly as it leapt out of the water with each wave. We had a desperate job retrieving the engine before letting the dinghy out on a tow line, but in time we brought everything under control and were once again sailing. We surged out to sea with two reefs in the main.

Once out of the bay our aim was to work our way south as much as possible during the night, and the wind blowing thirty knots from the west was perfect. We forged south at seven or eight knots, but gradually the wind backed, forcing us south-east. As Florianopolis lay to the south-west this was not helpful, but at least we were heading offshore. Shortly afterwards the wind strengthened and we were forced to reef again, until it was blowing fifty knots, tearing white sheets off the foaming sea and pushing us due east. *Josephine* was rampant, surging along at nine knots parallel to the coast. I was thankful for the sea room we had garnered earlier in the evening but we were still no more than twenty miles out to sea and could see the lights of the little fishing villages on the southern edge of Ilha Grande over to our left. Sailing along a lee shore in a storm, without a motor, can be very dangerous indeed.

All through the night the wind blew and we were pushed further and further east, towards Rio – the wrong way. The distance to Florianopolis was increasing, but there was nothing we could do about it. We would just have to keep sailing and stay away from the shore for as long as this wind lasted.

Dawn revealed pink and red ruffles of cloud strung across the eastern sky. The wind of the previous night was no more, and the sheets hung slack as the boom flopped from side to side on the slow swell. Sixty miles had been racked up since the previous evening, but the distance to go had actually *increased.* Now we were becalmed. There was nothing we could do, and we spent several anxious hours watching massive container ships ploughing in and out of Rio before the west wind came through again in mid-morning and we were able to head south, further out to sea. Soon after lunch we locked into the offshore current and made a consistent six knots the rest of the day as we settled into a comfortable routine of two-hour watches.

The next two days passed peacefully, punctuated by one sudden squall on the second afternoon that caught us with the headsail poled out and caused some chaos on deck. I had watched the sky darkening ominously ahead of us, but we were flying along at ten knots and although I knew better, I waited to reduce sail. The maxim about reefing should have applied here: "*When you think about reefing, reef.*" I contemplated taking the pole down ahead of the threatening weather, but hesitated; we were sailing so well; then the storm hit us with a sudden violence I did not expect, the fifty-five knot wind laying *Josephine* over on her side as we struggled with the sails. The genoa, still attached to the end of the spinnaker pole, flogged badly, tangling the sheets and tearing its foot before Oli was able to wrestle it under control.

Our third and last day was serene. Flying fish were springing from the bow wave, skittering over the shining crests like silver dragonflies, and we welcomed the return of the albatrosses and petrels as we forged south into cooler waters. Most of the day we reached at eight knots, and in the early afternoon, about thirty miles short of Florianopolis, we caught a beautiful Dorado which Jo buttered and baked in the oven with thinly sliced potato and onion. (Sometimes referred to by its Hawaiian name *Mahi Mahi*, or the English name "Dolphin Fish" – though it is not remotely related to the dolphin, being a fish – the Dorado is renowned for its beautiful flashing gold, blue and green colours, and its soft, delicate white meat.) It was delicious and we approached the yacht club at Jurere in high spirits.

The engine on a sailing boat is a bit like a parachute; you can do just fine without it, until you reach the end of your trip. We arrived in Jurere just after dark, and I was thankful this was the third time I had been there. Local knowledge gives one a lot more confidence, especially in the dark. A thirty knot wind was blowing straight onto the beach from the north and there was a nasty chop running. Anchoring would have been dubious without the engine; if the anchor dragged we would have few options and probably end up on the beach. Then, out of the gloom, there appeared a lone man in an inflatable – a "*marinheiro*" from the club – and we stalled the sails and threw him a line which he attached to one of the club's mooring buoys. We were safe. It was a rough night however, *Josephine* leaping about on a choppy swell, and at some point I felt compelled to swim through the waves to the buoy in the dark and attach a second rope as insurance.

***

We had a good rest in Florianopolis. The morning after we moored in Jurere, Abi arrived at the club in Alistair's car and took us back to his house on the east side of the island, near the popular surfing beach of Campeche. Edu flew in four days later, and Laurence – our Irish friend in Piriapolis – put us in touch with an American woman with some sailing experience who was in town and up for a sail to Uruguay. The biggest plus for me was that Betsy was a chef, and seeing as Jo was going the rest of the way to Uruguay by bus with Abi and Lucy, a talented cook was a godsend.

Betsy, Oli, Edu and I left Jurere in a stiff northerly, beating briskly away from the beach before working around the cliffs of *Punta do Rapa* into open water. We then turned southwards and let out the sails. *Josephine* responded eagerly, running with the light swell at seven knots. The first twenty-four hours yielded a hundred and sixty eight miles; at this rate we might cover the eight hundred miles to Piriapolis in less than five days.

***

By 5pm on the fourth day the wind fell away, and although we had covered some six hundred miles were reduced to sailing at a mere two knots. We had reached the latitude of the Brazil-Uruguay border, but Piriapolis was still two hundred miles away. The pressure had dropped steadily from 1010mb to 996mb and an ominous band of dark cloud lay low in the sky to the south. The air was sultry as the wind held its breath, and we slopped around on an indifferent, restless grey sea.

We eyed a growing bank of cloud with apprehension, knowing that while it was early in the season, it was not unheard of for the first *Pampero* to strike the River Plate in February. We were a hundred miles offshore; surely there could be no *Pampero* out here?

I had experienced one the previous year, in Piriapolis, though not at sea. That time *Josephine* had been moored to the quay in what is the best sheltered harbour in all of Uruguay, yet when that tell tale black tube of twisting cloud screwed itself across the horizon and the wind backed in something less than a minute from a twenty-five knot northerly to a hurricane force southerly, hell was unleashed. The water piled up so high in the harbour that *Josephine's* fenders floated over the top of the dock and the gel coat ground off the side of her hull against the concrete. If it were not for the additional lines I had earlier rigged to mooring buoys to hold her off she would have been severely damaged. As it was no fewer than eight yachts were destroyed in neighbouring Punte del Este when they were torn from their moorings by eighty-five knot winds, hurled upon the rocky shore and battered to splinters in the main road. I remember watching with Laurence the approach of that big rolling tube of cloud, and remarking that if I ever saw that out at sea I would be frightened.

Now here we were, a hundred miles offshore, looking at exactly that. Small consolation was that we were out on the ocean; there would be no danger of being washed onto a lee shore, and these storms, though violent, seldom last much more than an hour or so. And we were thankful there had not been enough time for the wind to build a dangerous sea. No, the danger was all in the wind itself, and I knew if we prepared the boat properly she would weather well. After all, *Josephine* had sailed in hurricane force winds off Cape Town and proved her seaworthiness.

We bunched in the cockpit watching the cloud build, aware of what was coming but sipping tea and discussing it as if it were an academic exercise. Edu was the most excited, being the "local". He had seen terrible damage inflicted by these malicious storms. Betsy and Oli were more bemused that anything, having never even heard of the *Pampero*, much less seen one.

And so we prepared for the worst. The headsail was furled to the size of a storm jib. The main was fully reefed. Everything that could be brought below deck was bundled into the locked forepeak, and everything that could not was lashed down double. The grab-bag, with radio, flares, water, food, fishing tackle, passports, sun cream and seasickness tablets was kept to hand, and the life-raft checked. Life jackets were stacked within easy reach. Then we had another cup of tea.

Daylight faded as a dark roof was pulled over the world behind the rolling black funnel that stretched across the sky with all the appearance of a horizontal tornado. Or, as Oli wrily noted, a steamroller.

The first breaths of wind from the north sent nervous shivers across the water. This was the beginning of the pre-wind; the air ahead of the storm being sucked back into the system and up into the vortex that was now looming large above. The wind rose to twenty knots, held there for some minutes, then stopped as abruptly as it had started. We braced for the *Pampero* proper.

The water ahead of us was being whipped up into whitecaps but we were still becalmed. Waiting like that, silently, in the still air, was surreal. I felt my heart trying to thump its way out of my chest. Then the wind burst upon us. In an instant it was blowing thirty knots and *Josephine* leapt forward like a racehorse. We would try to break through the wall of pressure and get behind the cloud, to lessen the time we were in the high winds directly beneath the giant roller. This meant a close reach, which increases the apparent wind and makes it all the more difficult on deck. The wind rose to forty knots. *Josephine* heeled over on her gunwale but sailed strongly under full reef at nine knots. It was thrilling. If only it could stay like this; this was perfect!

We waited for the wind to rise to a crescendo – and waited. And all the while we waited, we were tearing along across a sea blown flat by the squall. Then we seemed to be escaping behind the front; the wind settled back to thirty-five knots. It didn't seem right, but we took it. This was nothing more than a gale. Where was the real windstorm?

Still making eight knots, we bore off a little and put *Josephine* onto a beam reach to try and stay with this wind; if this was going to be its maximum strength, then we did not want to run through the back of the system and lose the wind altogether. This was too good to waste. Now we were chasing the storm, riding its wind, and it was exhilarating. A more benign *Pampero* we could not have imagined.

The wind fell away gradually as the storm front forged north away from us. We tried to sail perpendicular to it as long as possible, making way west towards the continent, trending slightly northwards to get as much use as we could from its remains. For perhaps an hour we made good progress, reaching under the cloud at seven knots, but eventually it outran us and we slowed down. We were still managing four or five knots, when Edu, now on the helm, called my attention to a disturbance in the water about half a mile to the north.

"Hey, Man, what ees thees?" he asked, pointing. "Ees whales?"

He was right. I saw the spray of a whale blow over the wave tops – then another, and another – then more. It had to be a lot of whales, no lone whale breathes that fast. It certainly was not spray off rocks – the depth was over a mile straight down.

"Go downwind a little, let's have a closer look," I said, then almost as I spoke I saw it. My first glimpse of that unmistakable high black dorsal fin. At first it did not register. Then I saw it again. No, two of them. Orcas!

Adrenalin surged under my skin like liquid metal.

"Killer Whales!" I yelled down the hatch for Oli and Betsy, grabbing the video camera from under the spray dodger.

As the boat turned downwind we saw more whales blowing, but no fins. Had I been mistaken? The blowing continued; it was frenetic. Man, that had to be a lot of whales! What was going on?

Suddenly we were upon them; big, rectangular hulks lying black in the water, side by side. Sperm Whales. The first I had ever seen. And the closer we got the more there were. We counted fifteen, just lying there, side by side like a fleet of tightly parked busses.

"There, over there! Orcas!" This time it was Oli, and sure enough, coming up behind us were the unmistakable hooked dorsal fins of two female Killer Whales. Then Edu shouted: "Another one, over here!" pointing beyond the pod of whales.

As we watched, spellbound, two of the orcas charged at the wallowing behemoths and there was a great thrashing in the water around one of the smaller whales. They closed ranks and the orcas moved out again, but continued to circle. We counted four orcas. The big bull had a very high, straight dorsal fin, the tip torn and ragged. He had obviously seen his share of battle.

Tacking to go about we made another pass as the pattern continued. The whales rafted up tight for protection, the orcas dashed in, two at a time, trying to separate the smallest whale from the pod. It was like watching lions work a herd of wildebeest. The bull, with his tattered fin, held back while the females tormented the pod. The whales were so close together it looked like you could walk across them.

After three passes to get good video, the bull orca decided he had had enough of us. Swimming a deliberate arc around the boat at a distance of about fifty yards, he seemed to be sizing us up; until he was dead ahead. He then turned to face us, held his massive head high out of the water for a few seconds – and charged. I was on the foredeck with the video camera, and he was coming head on. A confusion of half thoughts fell over each other in my scrambling brain. "*Orcinus*", Roman god of the underworld; root of the English "ogre". A big orca can weigh twenty tons; *Josephine* weighs eight, almost half of which is in the keel – a chunk of lead hanging underneath, held in place by eleven steel bolts. The fibreglass hull would offer little resistance to the mass and power of an enraged killer whale.

There was no point trying to take evasive action. We did not have the boat speed to manoeuvre, and in any event the orca was so agile we could never have avoided him if he really wanted to hit us, even if we had a motor. We would have to call his bluff. I shouted at Edu to hold his course as I tried to operate the video camera with shaking hands. The bull loomed ahead, a great bow wave standing up around his rushing bulk. We were about to be rammed by a submarine. I stopped breathing.

At the last possible moment, he sounded and swept beneath us, his dark mass ominous under *Josephine*'s hull. He was wider than the boat. There were shouts and whoops from the cockpit as he surfaced in our wake, but already he was coming around for another charge. Perhaps he had just been setting his sights?

This time the cameras were ready as he lifted himself high in the water and charged again. Never have I experienced such a feeling of awe. I had been this close to much bigger whales; I had been soaked by a Humpback breaching a few yards from the boat off Cape Town, and been close enough to smell the fishy breath of a Southern Right, but this was different; this was an apex predator at the very peak of the food chain, and he was coming for us.

The water piled up over his glistening back, then broke into a wave as he accelerated straight towards *Josephine*. I clung as tightly as I could to the forestay with my free hand, the other trying vainly to keep the camera steady as the orca's image swelled to fill the viewfinder. But just as impact seemed inevitable, he dived and rushed beneath us as before.

Now we had sailed a little way beyond the pod of whales and were presumably no longer seen as an immediate threat to the orcas' lunch, and the bull broke off his attack. He made his feelings clear by displaying with his tail high in the air then slapping it down hard on the surface with a crack that echoed off the sail. He followed up with several more smacks then vanished.

In the confusion the whales must have sounded for they were nowhere to be seen. Sperm whales are known to dive to depths of up to three miles as they hunt for giant squid, and can employ that diving ability as a defence strategy. Presumably the orcas had caught them on the surface as they were recovering from a dive and they had not been able to go back down straight away.

It was all over, and we were breathless. Nobody spoke. It had been one of those experiences that none of us expects to have again, and that very few people on this earth will ever have. We felt enormously grateful and privileged, and nobody wanted to break the spell.

Eventually Edu burst the bubble of awed silence.

"Maaan! What a day!" he shouted. "Pampero, Whales, Orcas…!" counting on his fingers, "…now let's go to Uruguay and make an *asado*!"

***

The euphoria we felt at that moment did not stay with us. As the last signs of our *Pampero* disappeared into the north the stillness returned, and we spent that night drifting rudderless over the flat sea in great lazy loops. There was not a breath of wind, and to make it worse the GPS showed the Falkland current was carrying us a mile back north with each passing hour. Maddening. Watches were spent keeping an eye out for ships with not much else to do should we see one other than make sure all our lights were on, try to call them over the hand-held radio and warn them of our position, or ultimately send up a flare to grab their attention. In the end there was no need for any of this; we were totally alone in our watery limbo.

Sunrise brought wind, but from the south-west. Exactly the direction we wanted to be sailing. This was not going to be easy. We were close hauled heading west-north-west at six knots, closing on the coast. It was frustrating to be northering but a lot better than just bobbing around. Before midday we landed our second dorado. We cleaned it in the cockpit, and Betsy baked it in the oven with lemon.

Not wanting to get too close to the coast, we tacked again late in the afternoon and aimed back out to sea for the night, heading south-east. The north-flowing Falkland Current was against us, and the wind picked up in the night to thirty knots, so with northwards drift we were really going east. It was infuriating. There seemed to be no options. At every turn, at every change in tactics, the wind seemed to shift and hold us in the north, hundreds of miles from Uruguay. That first day out of Florianopolis, sailing due south at seven knots, seemed a long time ago.

Early the next morning we tacked again onto a north-westerly heading, and were lucky enough to land a fifteen pound skipjack tuna that took care of lunch. The wind did not co-operate though, and soon after midday it had risen to forty knots. It was once again blowing straight up at us from the direction in which we needed to go.

The next two days were a grind, beating into the relentless gale. We were covering miles over the water, but not in the right direction, and not getting any closer to our destination. Two fish in the afternoon of day five broke the monotony and made another welcome meal, but there were no more whales to amuse us. In fact nothing at all to lift the gloom that was settling over the boat.

By the night of the seventh day, as we tacked once more inshore, we saw the lights of La Paloma, conjuring images of hot showers and a good night's rest; but it has a small, rocky harbour with a tight entrance, and to have attempted it in the dark, in forty knots of wind, without an engine, would have been suicidal. Reluctantly we went about and headed back offshore, banging over the waves as we took the running sea head-on.

With the morning sun we sighted the gleaming white tower of the Punte del Este lighthouse away to the north west. But overnight the wind had veered and was now a westerly; just when we rounded the bulge of Uruguay and needed to head west into the River Plate. You could not make this up.

The lighthouse in its two hundred foot tower marks *Isla de Lobos*, a rocky islet about three miles off the popular eastern beaches of Punte del Este (*Isla de Lobos* – or "Island of Wolves" – was a confusing name to us until we understood that the Spanish name for a sealion is "sea-wolf"). Seeing the tower glistening bright in the morning sun filled us with hope that today would be the day. We were ten miles south of it, and Piriapolis was another forty miles to the west. We would beat northwest towards Punte del Este, then back past the lighthouse by midday. With a succession of tacks from there we should be able to work our way west along the coast to Piriapolis. That was the idea at any rate.

By 11am we were close to land, about four miles east of the light, but the wind had strengthened again and was blowing a full gale from the west. It was like a bad dream. Wearily we turned south again and beat back out to sea. For four hours we fought the wind and the waves until we thought we must have made sufficient way westwards to allow us to tack back up and get past the light. We went about just after 3pm and fought our way north, but by 5pm could see that we had not managed to get far enough across. As the sun set for the evening, we were once again close to the beaches, and still to the east of *Isla de Lobos*. I checked our position – three and a half miles from the light. In eight hours of incessant beating we had made good a mere half mile to the west. It was soul destroying, being so close…

We endured a third consecutive night of relentless beating, every thumping wave shaking *Josephine* to her spine. In truth we were just marking time, waiting for the wind to change. There was an unusually strong current running out of the River Plate on account of heavy rains in Paraguay that was pushing us back out to sea, so until the wind played along there was really not much we could hope for. Picking my way between the waves and stealing inches here and there was my way of dealing with the frustration. Lashing the wheel and sitting back with a *mate* was Edu's way of coping.

Our eighth morning saw us still south-east of *Isla de Lobos*, but the wind had moderated somewhat in the night and, best of all, veered northerly. This enabled us to fall onto a starboard tack and approach Punte del Este close hauled. It was an offshore wind, which blew the sea flat, and once the sun warmed us up it was sailing heaven.

We slipped between *Isla de Lobos* and the beaches before midday, then round the rocky point of *Punta das Salinas* with its ostentatious holiday homes. As Maldonado Bay came into view to the north, we saw a mass of white yachts clustered around the tree-clad little island of *Goriti* and an enormous cruise liner somehow crammed between the island and the hotels of Punte.

All afternoon we sailed west on the warm breeze, lazing about on the deck taking pictures while Edu and Oli swapped turns putting me to shame with my guitar. The sun was warm on my face as I listened to the bow wave burbling along to Edu's flamenco, and the firm pressure in the sails trembled through the rigging into *Josephine*'s deck beneath my back where I lay dozing.

There remained, of course, one last challenge for us: We still needed to get into the harbour at Piriapolis – with no engine. The northerly breeze stiffened as we got nearer and was up to thirty knots when we arrived south of the entrance beacons. And, for good measure, it was dark.

Fortunately this would be the third time I had visited Piriapolis. I was familiar with the port and its approaches, and confident we could manage. I knew the layout of the harbour, and had a clear picture in my mind of exactly where I wanted to moor *Josephine*. I did a rough sketch of the harbour and explained to the crew where I wanted to dock. Edu and Betsy had both been there before and understood. It should not be too difficult.

After sailing past the town and beyond the entrance to get upwind, we dropped the main and flaked it away. Under headsail alone we then turned with the wind and bore down on the harbour mouth. Running between the lights, past the breakwater to our left, then round it, we tightened the sail to keep the pressure and reached up past the line of boats moored stern-to along the seawall, past the travel lift wall on our right, then… horror of horrors, there was another boat tied up exactly where we wanted to go. The wind was blowing, we could not stop, and we certainly could not turn round.

There was a space against the wall directly ahead of us, but it would involve an unlikely stunt of parallel parking. My heart beat fast as the adrenalin rose.

"Too fast!" Edu was shouting from the bow.

"Hold it… hold it… okay, now!" I shouted and Oli hauled on the furling line hand over hand. Edu and Betsy stood amidships with bow and stern lines, awaiting the command to jump.

Earlier I had stressed "Don't throw the ropes to anyone ashore, whatever you do. Take them yourself, or don't go; but never throw them to a stranger who doesn't know what we are planning."

Now I was glad because a night guard appeared on the quay, signalling for a rope. He was in completely the wrong place and would have tied us onto the wrong bollard, causing *Josephine* to blow backwards in the wind against an adjacent boat.

As the headsail rolled away and we shed speed, it seemed the bow would touch the wall before I spun the wheel to bring the boat up into wind. The well-meaning guard nearly fell in trying to grab the pulpit as it swept by him, but luckily for everyone he missed. Still nobody threw him a line. *Josephine* stalled perfectly and slid sideways onto the quay.

"Now, go, go!" I shouted above the wind, and Edu and Betsy leapt ashore and had us secure before the wind could push us off again. It was a neat manoeuvre, and an emotional cocktail of happiness and tiredness welled up inside me, together with admiration for the crew and the way each of them handled what had turned into a difficult trip. So much had happened in a week; it felt like we had been at sea a month. With all the beating and gybing over the last three days we had managed to turn a 600 mile doddle down the coast into a 1000 mile meandering odyssey. It was one o'clock in the morning when we trudged up the hill to Laurence's house to find my girls and help ourselves to his beer.

"Sometimes, if you stand on the rail of a bridge
and lean over to watch the river
slipping slowly away beneath you,
you will suddenly know all there is to be known."

– Winnie the Pooh

26

Prices in the port of Piriapolis had trebled since the previous year and we felt no inclination to dally there. It was in Montevideo, after all, that we were expecting to solve our gearbox problem, so after six days catching up with Laurence and Alex we were keen to be on our way again. We paid the ridiculous port bill, cleared the paperwork with the *Prefectura*, and sailed out at eleven o'clock at night, aiming for a daytime arrival at Edu's yacht club in Montevideo's little harbour of Buceo.

The night was a downwind romp on heavy swell in winds gusting over fifty knots with consistent boat speeds of eight to nine knots, and we arrived so early we were forced to heave to and wait outside

Buceo for first light before we could see to sail in. We charged into the harbour on rolling waves in yet another gale, dropped the sails and tossed out the anchor with all its chain, only for it to trail ineffectively through the soft mud as the strong wind blew us backwards across the basin, ever closer to the shore. Several frantic minutes were spent fending off other boats as we dragged with the waves between the buoys until we were able to raise Edu on the radio (he had arranged to meet us on arrival and was having coffee in the club) and the *lancha* came out and took us in tow. With the strong south easterly wind, enough water had been pushed into the harbour to make it deep enough to reach the jetty – the jetty we had been unable to reach the previous year, on account of the depth. '*Thees ees normal!*' Edu rejoiced.

Following a welcome breakfast in the club restaurant after a hard night's sailing, I was off with Edu, gearbox shaft in hand, in search of his mechanic friend. But it was eleven o'clock and the workshop was shut for lunch. A little way down the road was another workshop, outside which an overweight, grimy mechanic leaned against a flaking green wall in the shade of the plane trees sipping on his mate.

"We stop here just to ask. I don' know thees guy, but we see what he say," suggested Edu, bringing the car to a halt under a tree.

After an exchange of greetings, Edu proffered the shaft, and did the good mechanic know of a place where we might find a replacement for this shaft, or where we might get this one fixed?

The mechanic, surveying it solemnly and turning it over in his grubby hands, asked after a considered pause, "What is this from?"

"It's from a gearbox. On a boat."

The big man rolled it in his hands some more and squinted at it.

"What did you say you need?"

"We either need to replace it, or get it fixed."

Another wait while he studied it again. He looked up.

"Why?"

"Well, because this one is damaged, it doesn't work."

A longer pause while he perused it yet again.

"Where is it damaged?" he asked with a shrug.

Edu indicated the spline on the end, where it seemed pretty obvious the teeth had been cut away. I was having my doubts about this bloke. '*Here we go again,*' I thought.

The mechanic stared at the shaft, as if now seeing it for the first time, then gave a little grunt and held it out to Edu. There was nothing wrong with this shaft. It was made like that. Those teeth had been cut away on a machine. It was supposed to look like this.

I was incredulous. "*Made* like that...?!"

"This is a very clean cut. There is no twisting of the remaining spline. It has been machined off. And it is not a new cut either; you can see by the uniform discolouration and the oxidation that this shaft has been like this for a long time. There is nothing wrong with this shaft."

We were speechless. Not in our wildest imaginings had we expected to hear this. After lunch I finally met Edu's friend Dante. An enormous man, built like a giant bullfrog, eyes pressed into his pasty face like currents in a bun, two upper canines the only teeth evident in his large head. He looked a bit like Jabba the Hutt. Dante worked on gearboxes behind his house, the yard stacked high with the rusting skeletons of those who could not be saved, and the grimy wooden shelves under the corrugated tin roof of a home-built lean-to sagged under the weight of hundreds of rusty shafts, bearings and cogs. In the middle of all this was a steel bench with a high stool, where Dante fiddled all day cajoling the myriad moving parts of all manner of mysterious transmission boxes and transfer cases, ancient and modern, into magical synchronicity.

Dante confirmed there was nothing wrong with our shaft; the gearbox just needed new bearings and some cleaning up. It transpired the problem had been caused when the threads of the screw-in oil-filler cap had been stripped, so the cap no longer seated firmly and the measuring stick attached to its underside had been waving about inside the gearbox knocking against the moving parts. This had worn the aluminium dipstick down and the metal filings had jammed up and destroyed the bearings. Within two days, Dante had the gearbox working, and we had a new clutch plate made up (to replace the one our shyster mechanic Alberto had kept as "surety" in Paraty pending a rather optimistically anticipated $150 payment for all the effort of his work-not-done). In all it had taken no more than three days and cost less than two hundred dollars to get everything working like new again. We were indebted to friend Edu and the honest mechanics of Uruguay.

***

With a fully functional boat again at long last, it was decision time once more. A return to Brazil was not feasible for at least six months if we wanted to be able to start there again with fresh six-month visas, and being early February, the most we could expect here on the River Plate was three more months of warm weather. Another consideration was that we now had some fifty hours of video footage to be edited, a job that would require a more reliable power supply as well as adequate space in which to spread the two computers, external hard drive, two cameras and heap of books I would need to get the job done. We were keen to explore a little more of Uruguay, as the previous year we had been confined, by our lack of engine, to Piriapolis and its surrounds, and agreed it would make sense to spend the rest of this summer working our way up the *Rio Uruguay* and exploring the towns there, then move off the boat and rent a small house somewhere – perhaps in Piriapolis – for the winter.

So with Edu on board keen for more adventure, we left Buceo after dark on a warm, gentle offshore breeze. Reaching along the coast through the night would have been an idyllic sail but for a plague of mosquitoes. It was impossible to use a torch in the cockpit without being attacked by squadrons of the whining little bloodsuckers, and in the dark we were tormented by invisible clouds of them. They swarmed in our ears and up our noses, and when we dared to speak we took in mouthfuls.

After sun-up we edged closer to shore looking for the entrance to *Rio Rosario*, a river that by all accounts was navigable and where we expected to be able to anchor for a couple of days of peace and tranquillity after the bustle of Montevideo.

The approach to the mouth ("*Boca del Rosario*") was marked with buoys but we hit the sand three times nonetheless, the outflow of the river having shifted the channel around since the buoys were laid. With care and perseverance we scraped the keel through the sediment in six foot deep water until we made it past the beach and found ourselves on the still, willow-lined river, motoring slowly past a ruined quarry works and the rusting hulk of a dredger overgrown with vines that had spilled down the bank and reached out to envelop the dead ship.

Less than a mile upriver we came to a split; the right fork being the river proper, the left a creek leading to a *cul-de-sac* about five hundred yards in.

"Must be ees the place," announced Edu, "Everyone talk of thees. Ees a farm, very quiet place for put the anchor and make an *asado*."

A braai sounded a like a great idea, but after trying twice to enter the creek and running into mud both times, we tethered *Josephine* to the rusting dredger on the main river and Edu and I took the dinghy to see if we could find '*thees farm*'.

Both banks of the creek were a tangle of impenetrable bush, but near the far end the jungle on the left gave way to a sweeping lawn under majestic willow trees exploding with shimmering green Monk Parakeets. Beneath the trees several cows and a piebald pony grazed between the lichen-encrusted remains of a wooden fishing boat and an old clinker dinghy.

We dragged our inflatable onto the grass in the dappled shade and strode up the lawn to a low orange house behind white window frames. An old man with flowing silver hair came out to us, his lively eyes a sparkling royal blue. He introduced himself as Angelito. Bustling out behind him was his wife Primavera. '*Little Angel*' and '*Spring*' were good names for them; a kinder, friendlier couple we could not have hoped to meet. Angelito assured us the creek was deep enough for our boat, and that we only needed to force our way over a narrow mud bar at the entrance. I was not so sure, having visions of us stuck inside unable to get out again, but when their daughter Maria appeared in the doorway Edu took up the cause with religious zeal.

"Of course ees fine, okay, we try! Yes, yes, we come inside here! Ees deep!" he proclaimed, as if he knew from personal experience, never taking his eyes off Maria.

Angelito was right; in the event it proved easy enough to barge our way through what was indeed only a narrow strip of mud, encouraged by Edu who was now on a quest: *"Yes, yes! Again! More power! Okay!"*

With *Josephine's* anchor securely buried in the mud opposite the farmhouse, we trooped back up the lawn to where Primavera was waiting for us with a pot of tea and a large plate of homemade pastries. We stepped through the front door into a spacious living room with red painted pine chairs and tables, a brick bar at one end, and a green fishing net hanging from the ceiling. They were obviously set up for entertaining visitors; it turned out we had just missed the busy summer cruising season when there were up to twenty yachts anchored in the creek, all Argentinian.

Behind the bar a single wooden shelf held a ship in a bottle, a framed black and white family photo, two identical Christmas cards and a six-inch high porcelain friar. On the opposite wall hung a green board advertising "FORDSON super major diesel tractors," that presumably used to grace the outside of a garage but now had nails in it upon which were hooked an old .22 short rifle, a pump-action air-rifle, two swords, a very old double-barrelled revolver, a set of silver riding spurs and a collection of sinister looking implements like branding irons and Burdizzo castrating tools (for disabling the testicles of young bulls by crushing their blood vessels). Just outside the door, over a sooty *parilla*, was a very weathered piece of old planking with green copper nails in it. Angelito proudly announced it to be a piece of wreckage from the British ship the "Lord Clive", that in 1763 was bombarding the nearby Colonia del Sacramento when it became disorientated in fog and ran aground, to be broken up by the vengeful besieged. The officers were hanged in the town plaza and bits of the ship carted off as souvenirs.

Primavera hustled Lucy over to a big wooden toy-box in the far corner, filled with an assortment of teddy bears, hand puppets, plastic balls, a set of wooden castanets, model boats and a red and yellow checked bowler hat with a tangle of blue nylon clown-hair glued into the inside of its rim.

Several carefree days were spent on the farm, helping Primavera harvest figs using a bamboo stick with a wire hook on the end to reach the higher branches, playing with Juanita the pig, or lying in the cockpit on the tranquil river immersed in the cool liquid cooing of doves and contemplating the feathery cirrus brushed against a limpid blue sky, looking like swirls of cream before you stir it into your morning coffee. We escaped the heat of midday by swimming in the creek, where we were delicately nipped by inquisitive little fish that had set up home under the boat (from where they voraciously attacked any leftovers that were scraped overboard after meals).

The little fish put me in mind to demonstrate my higher angling skills and I attached my one and only homemade fly – a hideous, furry little beast with big silver bauble pop-eyes and a day-glo green tail – to a stick with two yards of gut. Choosing to maintain the moral high ground and ignore the disrespectful jibes of my family and erstwhile friends, I set to the task and surprised even myself by swinging a small catfish aboard (Heaven knows what it thought it was about to eat when it attacked that garish fly) which disconcerted Lucy with its long whiskers and toad-like croaking. This strange noise is produced by grating the bones of the pelvic girdle when they erect the spines of their caudal fins as a defence mechanism – much like crickets produce noise by rubbing their hind legs against their hard outer wings – which is amplified in the body cavity. We would lie in our bunks at night listening to the sounds of the catfish "burping" through the hull as they shovelled about in the mud of the riverbed in their never ending quest for crabs.

Being on the farm presented us with a welcome opportunity to get a bit of running in and explore some new countryside, so Abi and I set off down the sandy track that lead out of the front gate through the meadows past a copse of tall eucalyptus trees, heavy with the giant communal nests of a whirring swarm of parakeets. An arboreal petshop. A mile down the track we came upon the heavy wooden gate of another farm, above which a Uruguayan flag hung limply in the still air from a high pole, and a hand painted sign proclaimed the property to be the home of "*el Monarca del Oeste*". An engaging billy goat allowed Abi to scratch the top of his head through the gate, and as we trotted off down the road to resume our run the goat appeared behind us, trailing ten yards of frayed white rope in the dust. We dragged the fugitive creature back to the gate and handed custody over to a thin, wizened old man with a toothless grin. We wondered whether he was the Monarch of the West.

"*Ah si!*" exclaimed Angelito when we arrived home. "*Monarca del Oeste. El dueno esta un ex-presidente de Uruguay!*"

So the owner of the farm was a real monarch then.

We had just walked into an animated conversation between Edu and Angelito. It turned out that Angelito and Edu's late grandfather had been lifelong friends, and Edu had now been accepted into the home as a long-lost nephew. He was holding forth about our adventures with the orcas on our sail back from Brazil, all the while stealing surreptitious glances over at Maria quietly helping her mum lay the table for lunch. It was quite obvious who he was really trying to impress with his tales, and the pretty Maria, while feigning indifference, was studying him carefully through doe eyes hidden behind fluttering lashes.

***

About a week into our stay a local family arrived at the farm towing a wooden motorboat behind a van. The boat was backed down a ramp into the river, and Carlos introduced himself to me and asked me to help him tie a loop in the end of a rope. I showed him how to tie a bowline and in spite of my patchy Spanish we hit it off straight away. Carlos, in his early forties, wore a somewhat bemused expression on his face, but his perpetual grin made you feel like he'd been missing you for years. He turned out to be a farmer based in the rural town of Valdense, about a fifteen mile drive inland, who had bought a boat with which to entertain his children on weekends. Over lunch we met his family, where Abi and his wife – who spoke excellent English – forged the beginning of what was to become a meaningful friendship. The effervescent Marina (yes, another one) was ten years younger than her husband, with tumbling brown hair and a ready, hearty laugh. Absolutely nothing at all seemed to be any trouble for her, and by the end of the meal we had been invited to their farm and they had volunteered to help us find a suitable house for the winter. Up until then we had assumed we would rent a house in Piriapolis, as we knew the town and had friends there; but we had made no commitment and graciously accepted the Gardiols' offer to look around for something suitable in their home town of Valdense. If it worked out it would be fun to get to know another part of Uruguay, and we liked our new friends. Was life about to take another unexpected turn?

"Funny how the New Things
are the Old Things."

– Rudyard Kipling

27

"Okay, bye! See you! Yes, don' worry man! She take me home to Montevideo, no problem!"

Leaving Edu behind in the safe hands of Maria, we edged out of *Boca de Rosario* in chilly weather so we could take advantage of the extra water pushed into the shallow river mouth by a fresh southerly wind, and arrived off Colonia del Sacramento, twenty miles to the west, in cold rain that stung our faces with its icy needles. The only colours on nature's palette were the turgid brown of the water, the smudged black of the tree-line, and battleship grey of the heavy sky.

Founded by the Portuguese in 1680, overrun by the Spanish the same year and subsequently fought over and reconquered no fewer than ten times before Uruguay achieved independence in 1828, Colonia is Uruguay's oldest town. The historic quarter, with its original cobbled streets and old city walls, is a UNESCO World Heritage Site and popular tourist magnet, and regular ferries ply the river from Buenos Aires laden with *Argentinos* and their pesos.

The so-called "sport" harbour – as opposed to the commercial harbour, which caters for the enormous *Buquebus* ferries – is tucked around the western end of the point on which the original old town was built. The north side of the harbour is bounded by a rickety-looking wooden "town jetty", while the south side, behind a sea wall, offers moorings against a concrete quay with running water and electricity. There looked to be room for up to thirty boats along the wall, but we were spoilt for choice as we arrived to find only five there. Settling for a spot with lots of space on either side, we tried to moor stern-to but the rudder struck rock just short of the dock, forcing us to turn the boat around and moor bow-to. It made things just that little more complicated getting Lucy on and off the boat, as she had to be passed over the pulpit.

Within an hour, sailing in on the now increasing wind, came first one, then two, then an armada of Argentine-flagged yachts. By four o'clock in the afternoon the marina was full. We had docked just ahead of a race fleet from Buenos Aires; a couple of hours later and we would have had to pick up a buoy in the bay, which would have meant no fresh water and no electricity, not to mention the inconvenience of launching the dinghy and rigging the outboard motor in the rain to get ashore.

The old town of Colonia starts just outside the harbour. In spite of the obvious reliance on tourism (all prices in the shops are labelled in Argentine pesos and U.S. dollars) or perhaps because of it, the old town has managed to maintain its charm; stone streets are swept clean and avenues of Plane trees lined with rustic restaurants. The ubiquitous gift shops sell leather *mate* gourds made in Uruguay and T-shirts made in China with "STARBABY SWEAT HONEY" and "MAKE A HAPPY DAY" printed on them. The roads are all cobbled – the original, rougher ones by the Portuguese (with a drainage channel down the middle) and the more recent, cambered ones by the Spanish. There are several shady *plazas* in the old town, and vintage motor cars are scattered about like props in a Chicago gangster movie. One car has a tree growing out through its roof. Another, parked outside "El Drugstore" – which is actually a restaurant – has a small table where the front seats used to be, and two people can sit on the back seat to enjoy a romantic, private dinner. Well, maybe not so private, as the car is something of a tourist attraction in its own right and anyone having a meal in it is bound to have their picture taken by every second tourist who passes by.

The biggest attractions are the original city gate – a carefully preserved wooden drawbridge under a crumbling stone archway – and the lighthouse in its high white tower, from the top of which one is afforded a spectacular view of the town and across the River Plate to the skyscrapers of Buenos Aires as they rear up out of the water like distant fangs. A helpful sign next to the lighthouse tells us "*1740-1760,1890-1910 (Lighthouse) Religious building made of thick walls of 1.2m. The lighthouse which was constructed later is a referent not only for its function but also for its dimensions.*"

The skies cleared after lunch and in the gentle light of afternoon the pretty cobbled streets were burnished copper. We found an outdoor table in the dappled shade of the plane trees, and worked our way through a menu offering such mouth-watering enticements as a "Mixture of egg and sugar that is beaten stiff and browned in the oven, and topped with a gravy of eggs and wine", "Fish Miniatures with smashed potatoes, small portion (square shaped) at your choice" and "French Fries Scrambled with Egg and Pollack to the Garrison".

On the menu for the not so hungry was a "Croissant" (described as "a salty or sweet biscuit") or a "Stuffed Biscuit" (described as "a ham and cheese croissant"). It was hard to resist the "Cold Crafty Cakes" with the "spherical fries and milk-jam"; and how better to round off the meal than with "coffee or tea with milk accompanied by exquisite proposals to his election"?

The stiff southerly winds did not let up during the night, and by the following day the water was so high the bollards and taps on the quay were under a foot of water and the depth sounder showed over ten feet under the boat. But the next night the wind switched, and by morning the water was so low the hull under the bow was grinding on rock and we had to winch *Josephine* away from the wall with stern lines attached to mooring buoys behind us. The depth near the quay had dropped to a mere four feet. It brought home to us again the extent to which the water levels in the River Plate are dependent on the prevailing winds rather than any tidal rhythm.

The only way to get ashore once the boat had been pulled back from the wall was to lie prone along one of the bow lines and pull oneself commando-style across the gap to the quay. This provided much entertainment for passing pedestrians, and made for rather amusing video, but what proved the most exciting distraction to those fortunate enough to have witnessed proceedings from the public jetty was an ill-advised attempt to get Abi back on board by swinging her across the gap suspended from a halyard. Trusting my judgement (naturally), she launched herself from the quay, but my calculations were a little out and my hapless wife flew straight down the side of the boat clinging to the end of the rope until she hit the hull with a wallop and fell in the water. In spite of rousing applause from the public gallery I was not popular on board, and that technique was abandoned.

***

With all the difficulties getting on and off the boat in Colonia, not to mention the exorbitant mooring fees levied by the *Hydrografia* (it is the most expensive harbour in Uruguay) Colonia's attractions soon exhausted their appeal and it was time to move on. Roughly thirty-five miles upstream, where the river narrows to a mere five miles across, is the sleepy town of Carmelo, which officially marks the upper limit of the River Plate and the "mouth" of the *Rio Uruguay* (though the smaller town of Nueva Palmira, a further ten miles up where the river is only a mile wide, stakes a convincing claim to the title.)

Hoping to reach Carmelo in time for lunch the next day, we left Colonia at night, the orange glow from the megalopolis of Buenos Aires reflected off the low cloud twenty-five miles off our port bow creating an illusion of sailing towards a perpetual sunset. An icy wind sweeping north up the continent from Antarctica made it unseasonably cold, and we shivered in the cockpit as we huddled over a steaming pot of spaghetti Bolognese, later snapping shards of frozen chocolate with heavy leather mittens after the whisky-spiked coffee in the stainless steel flask had gone cold.

Making barely two knots under motor and wondering if we were dragging something, I stopped the boat and backed up to clear whatever might be caught round the keel, but there was nothing there. We could still only manage two knots on the GPS.

"Oh please don't let it be the transmission again!" I lamented. "We could do without more gearbox problems."

At this speed we would not reach Carmelo until the following evening. That was a complication we could do without, as the chart showed a lot of rocks, unlit buoys, islands and mud banks close to our destination and I really did not want to have to deal with all that in the dark.

"Everything seems to be working fine; the revs are good, we just have no power."

Then a thought struck me. The River Plate is such a wide body of water, one tends to forget it is in fact a river. I turned the boat around, and almost immediately we were sweeping along at nine knots. We had been working against a three and a half knot current. Because the impellor on the speed log was jammed up with barnacles and in need of a clean, we were unable to measure our "speed through the water" and had been using only the GPS – which measures "speed over the ground" and cannot take account of current. Our true boat speed through the water was six knots – quite normal.

The realisation there was nothing wrong with the engine or gearbox came as a welcome relief, and we were happy to accept that we would get there "*when we get there.*" By daybreak, however, our speed was up to five knots, and after breakfast six and a half, a brisk south-easterly wind pursuing us up the river and pushing the water back upstream, stalling the current. We had plenty of time to reach Carmelo in daylight after all. (Current, like depth, appears to depend to a large extent on the wind that blows across the river as well as over the Atlantic Ocean beyond Punte del Este. When strong winds blow from the east, it is not uncommon for the flow of the river to stop altogether, or occasionally even to reverse back upstream.)

Working our way upriver between the buoys of the shipping channel we noticed several flat barges lying very low in the water loaded with – well, Uruguay. They were Argentine vessels transporting tons of rock from quarries on the Uruguay side of the river to the delta near Buenos Aires to be used as landfill. I remembered Edu lamenting this phenomenon: "*They buy land een Uruguay, on the reever, then they take away the land een these sheeps, and when the land ees feeneesh they abandon. Ees stealing Uruguay thees Argentinos!*"

A few hours upstream from Colonia the channel splits in two. The main shipping channel, dredged to a depth of thirty feet, veers westwards and crosses several miles to the Argentine side of the river where it describes a circuitous loop through deeper water before heading north again, while the smaller *Canal del Infierno* hugs the Uruguayan bank. We kept to this quiet route up the eastern side, as it would make the trip to Carmelo at least eight miles shorter.

Some two thirds of the way to Carmelo, just after "San Juan" (where a quiet river mouth with a sandy swimming beach had been a popular anchorage until being declared out of bounds after a weekend retreat was built there for the President of Uruguay) the eastern channel dissipates in the mud flats and it is necessary to cross about a mile of shallow water to intersect the commercial shipping channel. We did not foresee a problem with this, as the chart indicated buoys in the river marking the way across.

After all our previous experiences of these things in South America, why then were we surprised, some hours later, to run out of channel but find no buoys? We had two options: to turn back the way we had come and join the shipping channel closer to Colonia, which would cost us six or seven hours; or try to find a way across here using the depth sounder, hoping to not get stuck.

"Going back will cost us about seven hours. There would be no way of reaching Carmelo before nightfall," I explained to the family. "It's a tricky approach to the town which we don't want to negotiate in the dark, so we'd have to stay out in the river all night waiting for daylight."

A universally unpopular proposition.

"And if we cut across here?" asked Abi.

We could see the main channel buoys a mile to our left where a freighter steamed its way down the river from Paraguay, bound no doubt for Buenos Aires.

"If we can find a way across, we should reach the channel in half an hour, even going slowly. The risk though is that we don't reach it at all."

"What does that mean?"

"It means if we run into the mud and can't get out again. We could be stuck out here for days waiting for the water to rise and float us off."

There was silence on the boat as everyone contemplated the implications of that. In the end though the temptation was too great, and we could not help ourselves. We had to try.

Looking at the chart and estimating the narrowest part of he mud flats, we edged our way westwards. The depth dropped sharply from twelve to five feet, and we could feel the keel ploughing through the upper layers of sediment. It was very soft mud, and with extra power we were able to keep the boat moving.

The first couple of hundred yards was fine, then *Josephine* started to labour as the depth dropped again. We were now in four and a half feet of water, the propeller throwing a turbid brown cloud out behind us, and unable to go faster than about a knot and a half on almost full power. It was touch and go.

"We have to turn back!" I yelled over the noise of the engine. "If it gets any shallower and the keel goes in any deeper, it'll stick fast and we won't be able to turn around."

But it was already too late. Turning the wheel scrubbed off enough speed for the mud to grab the keel and *Josephine* swayed drunkenly to a halt. We were now stuck in the mud a good mile from the nearest land.

Backing out, of course, was impossible, due to the propwalk; the spinning propeller just rotated *Josephine*'s stern over to the left. But this gave me an idea. I alternated reverse under full power, which swivelled the stern to the left a little way, then forward under power with the wheel hard over in the other direction, throwing the stern out even harder. Like this I was able to twist *Josephine* on the spot, grinding out a hole in the mud with the keel in the process. Once we had her facing back the way we had come, I engaged forward gear and under maximum power we ploughed slowly back through the mud, picking up speed as the depth increased again to six feet.

Emboldened by our escape, we tried again, picking a new path slightly to the south. This time we kept the revs and the speed up, and charged through the mud, slowing to less than a knot at one point, with the depth below five feet, but never stopping; and after fifteen minutes the depth began to increase again until eventually we reached the far side and the deep water of the shipping channel. There were cheers all round as we set off exultant for our last ten miles to Carmelo.

Carmelo is a small, drowsy town about a mile up the tributary "*Arroyo de las Vacas*", or Cow Creek. It was founded in 1816 by Uruguay's national hero Jose Artigas, who lead a successful revolt against the Spanish in 1811 and declared Uruguay independent. He was subsequently defeated by the Portuguese in 1821 and fled to Paraguay, from where his followers launched a counter-attack two years later which lead to the final liberation of Uruguay under a treaty brokered by the English in 1828. The local economy is agricultural, and it is said the town owes its name to the area's superior caramel.

It was mid-afternoon when *Josephine* motored into the languid Cow Creek and tied up at the concrete quay that stretches along its south bank. The adjacent area has been developed into something of a tourist facility for boaters, with cement picnic tables and brick built *parillas* under shady trees. The only other boat there was a locked-up yacht with a South African flag we were told had been abandoned the previous year.

I remarked to the attendant in the office they seemed to have a very large facility for so out-of-the-way a town.

"*Ah senor*," he replied with a knowing look. "*La semana que viene esta la semana del turismo. Esperamos muchos barcos!*"

"Tourism Week?" asked Abi when I repeated this news to her. "Is that some kind of marketing stunt? Where will all the tourists come from do you think?"

"No idea. Anyway, he says they expect lots of boats next week, and that we were lucky to arrive when we did as there wouldn't have been room."

We both laughed at this fanciful idea. The quay stretched for hundreds of metres along the river bank. In no port in Uruguay had we ever seen close to enough boats to fill a place this big.

Towards evening we were woken from our siesta by the sounds of a motor and shouting voices. I stuck my head out of the hatch to see a lovely old wooden motor-sailor, about forty feet long, her hull painted a gleaming white, deck varnished to an immaculate shine and polished brass fittings glinting in the sun. At the wheel was a very short, stocky man topped off with a thick shock of white hair, who was trying to manoeuvre his boat alongside ours while shouting contradictory instructions to his son, in the stern with a rope ready to throw, and the *marinero* on the bank who was waiting to receive it.

More in the interests of protecting *Josephine* from collision than anything else, I scurried ashore to assist. I wondered why, with all the room in the world, our new neighbour thought it necessary to park up hard alongside us.

"*Hola!*" the silver haired skipper greeted me once he was securely moored. "*Gracias, gracias. De donde son?*"

I told him where we were from.

"*Ah, muy bien! Hablan espanol?*"

I told him we were trying.

"I no good English," he announced with a proud grin. "*Soy Argentino*. Ha ha! Now is tourist week!"

"Yes, I believe so…"

"And we very luck, first to this place. Near to the *banos*. Ha ha!"

So that was it. He had nestled up against us as we were directly opposite the bathrooms.

"Tonight my wife arrive with ferry. Not like to sail. Ha ha! Then we make *asado* with pizza and you come, *esta bien*?"

What a lovely family Nestor, his much taller tango-teaching wife Alicia, and grown-up children turned out to be. Son Ariel – who had arrived on the boat with his father – was recently returned from several years studying flamenco guitar in Barcelona and had started playing with a music group in Buenos Aires. Their daughter Isis was a pretty, slim girl in her mid-twenties. "Poe-kee-toe!" she replied in a mock English accent, and giggled, when I asked her whether she *hablas ingles*.

We spent a fun evening over beers and hand-made pizzas on the grill, Nestor practicing his English by telling his women to be more '*organizated*' and to remember to '*make the salsation to the pizza*' before committing it to the flames. He and I stayed up late into the night round the fire drinking whisky after the beer ran out, becoming progressively more '*emotionated*' until by around three o'clock in the morning we had agreed I would run for President of Argentina.

Early the following day, long before the effects of the previous night's imbibing had worked their way through my alcohol-soaked system, the Gates to the Hell of Tourism Week were flung open. In fact they were not so much flung open, as smashed down. The arrival of the Flotilla was presaged by the BOOM-BOOM-BOOM of a distorted sound system thumping out unimaginative dance beats from a hundred foot long motor yacht bedecked by painted clowns and dancing girls as it careened up the river, its hull emblazoned in the livery of a well-known Argentine ice cream chain.

"*La lancha* 'Freggo'!" trumpeted Nestor, who was already up and about. It would appear Argentina's Freggo ice-cream tycoon made a habit of coming here for Tourism Week and the holiday would not be the same without the incessant noise he was expected to contribute.

By lunchtime the hitherto tranquil Cow Creek was packed solid with power launches and luxury yachts, some seventy-odd jammed together stern-to along the quay. It seemed by arriving early and mooring opposite the *banos* we had upset the accepted pecking order whereby the bigger, flashier *lanchas* get pride of place. Yet that did not stop them from barging in alongside, without fenders, and shoving us over to make room. I wondered that they did not come with mechanical elbows. The boats were so tightly packed we could have released all our mooring lines and run not the slightest risk of drifting off anywhere.

The restful, shady park was transformed into a *latino* mini-Glastonbury for the rest of the week, with permanent queues for bathrooms and people sharing *parillas* and cooking in relays on the same fires. It was certainly not the week we had anticipated, but very festive and a fun change to the sedate lifestyle to which we had become so accustomed. The only sensible strategy was to throw ourselves headlong into the spirit of it.

***

Sometime in the blur of Tourism Week I stumbled upon two bewildered Germans cowering in their little green tent under the trees between the inflatable jumping castle and the pony hire. Sixty years old and impossibly skinny, the husband and wife pair of Alexandre and Sabina were coming to the end of a three month bicycle trip around Argentina and Uruguay, and had heard about the peaceful little oasis that is Carmelo. It seemed they were the other two people who had never heard of Tourism Week. They looked in a state of shock, and when we invited them aboard for dinner they were grateful for the temporary escape from the hysteria of the campground.

Their cycling stories were fascinating, but we were most entertained by the tale of their departure from Berlin. They lived in a flat in the city, and had called a taxi to take them to the airport. As it was snowing and very cold, they watched through a first floor window until they saw the taxi pull up outside, then bundled all their luggage onto the pavement with their bicycles, locked the door and tossed the key through the letterbox (having arranged with a relative – who had a spare key – to collect them from the airport three months later.) It was only then they realised the taxi that had pulled up was not theirs. They hung about in the snow, stamping their feet to stay warm, for a taxi that never arrived. There they stood, surrounded by luggage, beginning to run late for their flight, with no taxi, no phone and no house key.

"So what did you do?" Abi asked.

"Vell, ve didn't know vot to do, but zen our neighbour asked us '*vot are you doink in ze snow like ziss?*' and ven ve told him, he said '*ach, but I take you!*'"

"That was lucky!"

"Ja, but first he haf to find ze car. It vos snowink a lot, and he don't remember vere he parked ze car! So now Sabina vos votching ze luggage, and I vos helping ze neighbour to locate ze car. Ve haf to dig each time to find a car and see if it is his or no, and zen ven ve find ze correct one ve haf to deliver ze car from ze snow wiss ze hands. Ach, it voss so cold!"

***

The social highlight for us in Carmelo was Lucy's second birthday. An impromptu little party was thrown under the trees with cake and beers to which we invited Nestor and Alicia (their children Ariel and Isis had gone home), our German cycling friends, and Jose and Viviana, a fun couple off one of the motor yachts from Buenos Aires. The very tall Jose was an ex-professional volleyball player who was fond of his beer, and lamented while caressing his round tummy that he could no longer play because he had 'swallowed the ball'.

The biggest treat of Lucy's party was the unexpected arrival of Edu, who had driven up from Montevideo with his new *amore*. He and the lovely Maria were now very much an item (though they confessed that her parents Angelito and Primavera were as yet none the wiser) and looked very happy together.

"Ah," sighed Edu when we were alone. "I don' want any more problems. I am tired. She is very nice, very nice… and you see the farm, wonderful people. Yes, I like a lot!"

"So when are you planning to tell Angelito?"

"Ah, I dunno. We wait, ha ha, ees not easy thees!" then, looking around, "Thees ees a very nice place, I like! Ees the first time I come here. Always weeth my gringo friends I see new theengs, haha! Even I find a good girl! So, where you go after?"

"Not sure Edu," I confessed. "The summer is coming to an end, we need to find somewhere to settle for the winter. I have a lot of work to do, editing a year's worth of video footage, and we could all use a break from the boat."

"You gonna stay een Piriapolis, yes?"

"It's a possibility, but furnished houses are expensive there. It's a popular tourist spot, so houses are typically rented by the day. Carlos and Marina have offered to look for a suitable house in Valdense."

"Ah, I remember them. Carlos ees farmer een Valdense, no?"

"Yes, that's right."

Just then Abi came over with the cell phone in her hand.

"It's Marina. She says they found us a house."

"To the bird a nest, to the spider a web;
To a man, friendship."

– William Blake

28

The streetlamps lining the promenade upstream from Buenos Aires flashed on under a fading purple sky as I squinted again at the GPS screen. According to the co-ordinates given to us by Carlos, his friend's club was dead ahead. The flashing red and green lights marking the main shipping channel we had just left were receding behind us, and with the depth now down to seven feet we had packed the sails away and were motoring slowly across the shallows, keeping a close eye on the depth sounder. There was no more than ten or twelve inches of clearance under the keel, and Puerto Olivos was still two miles away.

"How much longer do you think?" asked Abi.

"Not long," I replied. "Half an hour maybe, so long as it's deep enough all the way. Then we should just have enough light to get in."

Not that it should be too traumatic in the dark – there was a lot of ambient light from the city; but it is never fun going into a new harbour and tying up on an unfamiliar marina without full light. We had been assured that someone would be on duty to welcome us, but had anticipated arriving a little earlier; the current had unexpectedly failed for our trip down the river from Carmelo, setting us back several hours. The radio battery had died too, so we were unable to call ahead.

"I just hope the *marinero* hasn't knocked off and gone home by the time we get in."

***

To be honest we could have done without this side trip to Buenos Aires. We were keen to get to Juan Lacaze, the nearest port to Valdense, and meet up with Carlos to go and look at the house. His cousin had bought a farm and moved out of his house in the town, leaving it unoccupied but fully furnished. If we liked the house, there was every chance we would rent it; but first we needed to renew our visas for Uruguay, and the cheapest way to do that was to leave the country then go back. So here we were, picking our way across the shallow water between the city of Buenos Aires and the Parana Delta, so we could have our passports stamped in Argentina.

Carlos had arranged a mooring for us at the "*Club Graduados del Liceo Naval Militar*" – the club affiliated to Argentina's Naval Academy – where he had a friend who owned a boat. He had given us the co-ordinates of latitude and longitude, and mentioned that the club was to be found in Puerto Olivos. We had never been to Puerto Olivos, but I had heard of it and knew it was somewhere along this stretch of the river. Our chart had no detail, but when I entered the co-ordinates the GPS showed a basin or little bay in the otherwise featureless shoreline. I assumed that must be Puerto Olivos, and now we were aiming straight for it in the fading light.

"Over there!" cried Jo. "Is that a buoy?"

"Ah, yes," I confirmed, peering into the gloom. "Red and white stripes; that's a fairway marker. If we head for that, we should be fine. Then we'll be inside in ten minutes."

Presently we passed the buoy, from where we could clearly see the entrance to the little basin marked out with tall white poles. It had been a long day and we were looking forward to a hot meal in the club restaurant.

Another, smaller yacht, with five or six crew on board, had fallen in behind us in our approach, and they returned our greetings with cheerful waves and smiles, giving us once again that warm fuzzy feeling we had developed for Argentina the previous year. I throttled back as *Josephine* glided between the first pair of poles marking the start of the short entrance channel, and on the port side breakwater we saw a welcome sign that made me do a double take. "BIENVENIDO A PUERTO NUNES" it trumpeted in big letters.

"Oh crap!" I exclaimed. "Where the hell are we? This isn't Puerto Olivos… what is this? Puerto *Nunes*? What the…?"

"Oh my God," lamented Abi. "Please no, let's not be lost again. No phone, no radio, and its getting dark!"

I shouted across to the crew on the other boat, "*No es Puerto Olivos?*"

"*No!*" came the reply. "*Es Puerto Nunes. Puerto Olivos es cinco millas mas!*" he confirmed, pointing westwards.

"Five miles! How did we get it *that* wrong?" asked Jo.

I turned *Josephine* around and headed back out onto the river which was by now quite dark. A check on the GPS confirmed that we had navigated correctly according to the co-ordinates we had been given – which was some small comfort to my ego at least, but did not take away the fact that we were evidently in the wrong harbour. Puerto Olivos was five miles further up the coast; it would take another hour to reach it.

"Well at least now we know where we're going," said Jo stoically as we set off.

After an hour we made out the shape of another safe water buoy in the gloom, which told us we must be close to the next harbour – Puerto Olivos. As we were scouring the shore lights for the red and green that should show the port entrance in the dark, another boat loomed out of the night just ahead of us.

"*Hola!*" I shouted across. "*Perdon, una pregunta por favour!*"

The helmsman pulled the tiller over and let out his main sheet, slowing his boat and coming close alongside.

"*Estamos buscando Puerto Olivos. Es aqui?*" I asked, pointing to the shore.

"*Si, es Puerto Olivos!*" came the confirmation, and we cheered.

"*Muy bien!*" I shouted with relief. "*Y el Club Graduados del Liceo Naval Militar – esta dentro, no?*"

"*Club Graduados? Ah no, no es en Puerto Olivos.*"

My heart sank. The club was not in this port?

"*Donde es?*" I asked, already trying to figure out what we were going to do for the night. Buenos Aires has a lot of clubs, but no public marinas; not like Uruguay. You need to make arrangements ahead of time if you want to come in with a boat.

"*Club Graduados es en Puerto Nunes!*" came the reply.

In Puerto Nunes. Brilliant.

"Unbelievy!" exclaimed Jo.

By the time we got back to Puerto Nunes, woke the night watchman and made fast to the marina, the restaurant was shut, so Jo rustled up some omelettes before we sank into a welcome sleep that not even the jumbo jets roaring two hundred feet above us on their approach to the nearby airport could disrupt.

***

First thing in the morning we were up and ready to take on Argentine bureaucracy. I figured we knew the routine from last year, so it should be a cinch.

How wrong one can be.

For starters there was no *Prefectura* in Puerto Nunes so the club secretary called a taxi to take us the five miles up the road to Puerto Olivos (yes, *that* Puerto Olivos). But the *Prefectura* in Puerto Olivos declined to attend to us and for some unfathomable reason referred us to San Isidro. Another six miles by taxi took us to San Isidro, where we were again refused. The officer behind the big desk was of the opinion that we first needed to clear Immigration in Tigre – which was another ten miles away. I remembered from the previous year that the Tigre *Prefectura* knew the ropes and were likely to send us back to the city to clear Immigration. The only person enjoying this was Juan the taxi driver, who was charging by the minute.

In Tigre we avoided the *Prefectura* and marched into the little immigration office at the ferry terminal where we had blustered a young girl into stamping our passports the previous year, to find her on duty again. I held my breath while she cleared us into the country and was almost giddy with relief when she handed the passports back. I asked her where the customs office was. Just outside, first door on the left.

I found behind the tiny desk in the cramped customs office a large, amorphous, wheezing mass of man around forty years old, great rolls of flesh enveloping the chair on which he squatted. His bald head was divided by a wide mouth with too many little yellow teeth, and he brushed hamburger crumbs from his jowls as I presented myself and proffered my papers.

"*Donde esta su barco*?" he grunted, scooping a gob of tomato sauce from his jumper with a finger like a sausage.

"*Puerto Nunes,*" I replied, then for added effect "*Club Centro Graduados del Liceo Naval Militar*", imagining that the mention of this august club would enhance my image as a man of great standing.

It did not.

"*Donde?*"

I told him again. "*Puerto Nunes…* "

"*Donde es Puerto Nunes*?" he rasped, staring balefully at me over his sagging chin.

That caught me. It seemed I was not the only person never to have heard of *Puerto Nunes.*

"Umm… it's uh… just down the river here," waving at the window, "towards the city… beyond *Puerto Olivos.*"

"*Aja!*" with a flicker of recognition. "*Su barco esta en Puerto Olivos*?"

"Um, well not exactly…it's in *Puerto Nunes.*"

"*Pero donde es Puerto Nunes*?"

"Where?" I repeated. "It's right next to *Puerto Olivos. Al lado de Puerto Olivos.*"

"So your boat is in *Puerto Olivos?*"

"Well, close enough, if you would prefer…" I tailed off.

Now the mound of customs person was getting restless. "*Senor,*" he gasped breathlessly at me. "*Su barco esta en Puerto Olivos, o no*?"

I could not see what difference it would make if my boat was actually parked up the road outside the local pub. All I wanted was to declare that it was in Argentina, and once I was stamped in I would be free to move it around the country at whim anyway.

Yes, Okay, I told him, it was in *Puerto Olivos*, then followed up with a throw-away "*mas o menos*" which I regretted immediately.

Now I was exasperating him. What did I mean, *more or less*? It was either in Puerto Olivos or it was not?

I admitted that, well, no, it was not actually *in* Puerto Olivos…

"*Entonces, donde esta?*" he growled again.

I paused, uncertain how to play this. He clearly had no knowledge of Puerto Nunes. Was I missing something?

"*Esta en Puerto Nunes.*" I noted firmly, as if for the first time, with as confident a face as I could contrive.

And where exactly, he asked, rocking his little chair back, was this *Puerto Nunes* of mine?

This was going nowhere. I was inclined to grab him by the collar and shake the hamburger out of him and yell into his face that I was the tourist and shouldn't be expected to give him a local geography lesson. I wondered how I could explain where Puerto Nunes was without reference to the better-known Puerto Olivos that was next door.

Perhaps, I suggested, we could get someone else in here to clear this up, as my Spanish was not too good and I had become a little confused?

He contemplated me like a hungry bullfrog for a few seconds, and I had visions of him flicking out a gooey tongue and gobbling me up. Then he turned and yelled through the door.

"*Pilar!*"

Pilar appeared and they launched into a dialogue that was too fast for me to follow, so I said nothing and waited. Eventually Pilar left, and the obese man turned to me again.

"*Donde esta su carta?*"

"I'm sorry, my what? My *letter*?" I asked, puzzled.

A letter to who, for what? I didn't have any letter. He exhaled noisily. He needed to see a letter from the club. On their letter-head. I was beginning to wonder if I was being had. I asked him what exactly this letter was to say. He needed to see a letter certifying that my boat was actually there. At least he had stopped asking me where Puerto Nunes was, I assumed Pilar must have enlightened him; but now it appeared there was nothing else for it but to return by taxi to Puerto Nunes and get the club secretary to bang out a quick note on their stationery.

Two hours later I was back in Tigre, letter in hand, but the feeling of triumph as I entered my fat friend's office was short lived.

"*Aha, su carta, muy bien!*" he rejoiced. *"Y donde 'sta su barco?"*

He really was asking me again.

"My boat," I replied, deliberately enunciating every syllable and tapping the letter he held in his fleshy fingers, "is at this club, in Puerto Nunes."

He folded his arms, rocked his chair back, and beheld me with reptilian eyes.

"Well then, you've come to the wrong place *senor*. Puerto Nunes is not in my jurisdiction. Puerto Nunes falls under *el Capital*, you will have to go to the city to clear customs."

I was gobsmacked. He was not serious? Indeed he was. He was not going to stamp me in after all this? No, he was not.

He started to make a show of shuffling papers around on his crowded little desk, and I knew our relationship had come to an end. There would be nothing for it but to trek into the city the next day.

As luck would have it the next day was Friday, and after spending a good couple of hours walking around the seedy area below the flyovers of Buenos Aires, wheeling Lucy in her pram past the cardboard shelters of the city's homeless drug addicts, we found the cement block that is the customs office tucked away behind a bridge. It had closed for the weekend. That was the final straw.

"Okay, that's it!" I exclaimed in exasperation. "Now I've lost interest. *Mi importa un rabano.*"

Coming back here Monday to register the boat was a ridiculous notion, given that we wanted to leave the country by the end of the weekend, and I had no intention whatsoever of extending our stay an additional few days for the ridiculous purpose of declaring the boat only to clear it out again in the same breath. Our passports were stamped, and the girl at immigration had been kind enough to stamp the boat's papers too; I was sure that would be more than enough to satisfy the authorities back in Uruguay that we had been out of their country. Customs in Argentina could take a rain check.

***

The next three days in one of our favourite cities turned into something of a social whirl. Nestor and Alicia took us tango dancing, where two-year-old Lucy amazed us all by taking to the floor for an impromptu solo after having stared fixated at the dancers for several minutes. Alicia – a tango teacher – told us they have trouble teaching kids of six some of the moves Lucy picked up for herself that evening. We watched in awe as our toddler cavorted around the floor to generous and genuine applause.

Fabian, our friend from the yacht club in Puerto Madero the year before, hosted an *asado* at his home; Jose and Viviana (Jose the volleyball eater) took us out to dinner; and our dear friends Marcelo and Lili (Marcelo whose fortieth birthday party we had attended the previous year) took us to the zoo for a day out with their family. In addition I found time to catch up with Dado and Marco, two close friends from Italy who were in town. It all made the "admin stopover" well worth the while, but we were impatient to get back to Uruguay and looking forward to seeing the house in Valdense.

The start of the new week saw us once more out on the river, headed to a new port in Uruguay; this time Juan Lacaze, the nearest harbour to Valdense. We had decided on a night crossing from Argentina in order to ensure a daylight arrival. The glow from the lights of Colonia, which marks the half-way point to Juan Lacaze, was obvious in the moonless sky, providing us with a useful directional reference. I knew that closer to Colonia, when we could expect to make out individual features on shore, we would be guided by the light on the outcrop of rock a mile before *Isla San Gabriel* as well as the green and red lights marking the ferry channel, but until then, we need merely head in the general direction of the loom in the sky to the north-east.

We just needed to keep our eyes open for the double flashing white lights of the "dangerous water" buoys marking the multitude of wrecks that litter this area of the River. I knew these buoys had been placed in pairs, marking the bow and stern of each sunken ship, so the obvious requirement would be to not sail between them. It should all be fairly straight forward. Or so I thought.

The biggest problems with lights at sea come when it is too dark to actually see anything other than the light, and is nigh impossible to judge its distance. And so it was that night. As we left Buenos Aires behind and struck off northeast for Colonia, all we could see ahead of us was blackness punctuated by a sprinkle of twinkling white lights. Apart from the alien glow in the clouds caused by the reflection of the Colonia town lights, there was nothing else. No horizon, nothing; just these flickering lights that seemed to be everywhere, suspended in a black ether. I thought they looked like fireflies, the way they flitted about with the rolling and yawing of the boat under its press of sail.

The problem, of course, was that we needed to avoid them all, but had no idea where they were – which ones were closer, which were further away. Any one light could have been fifty yards or two miles away.

It occurred to me that seeing as each wreck was marked with two lights, it should be elementary enough to identify the pairs, and just avoid going *between* them. For a while that was fine; until, that is, around ten o'clock, when I was on the wheel, confronted by what seemed like rather a lot of these infernal twinkly lights. I was trying to identify the pairs, but somehow it wasn't so simple. I could see at least three pairs quite clearly, but then there was a bright, single light off the starboard bow, and another, almost as bright, some way off the port bow. Neither of them seemed to have a partner, which struck me as a little strange, but then maybe they were just marking smaller underwater obstructions – like single points of rock – which did not need two lights. Anyway, as we were well clear of both of them, I redirected my attention to the other, fainter lights up ahead that I knew I would have to reckon with shortly.

Almost too late, with the two lone lights about to pass either side of us, I realised with horror they *were* a pair. In the dark they had seemed a long way off, but were in fact so close I had failed to identify them as being together. Now I was sailing *Josephine* at a full six knots directly between them; we were about to run straight onto a wreck.

"Hold on!" I yelled to anyone who might be awake below, and spun the wheel, heart in my mouth, hauling the boat round and losing all power as the wind spilled out of the sails. Fortunately we hit nothing, but it was a chastening experience and I slowed down and took extra care the rest of the way. After that near mishap the trip was uneventful, and dawn broke a muted shell-pink on the eastern horizon shortly after we passed the lighthouse off Colonia. Ahead the smoke from the paper factory at Juan Lacaze rose straight up into the still sky as we motored the last ten miles, being careful not to venture too near *Punta Artillero* with its submerged rocks.

We were excited at the prospect of finding a house, not least because Abi was pregnant again and we liked the idea of having neighbours and friends. It presaged a temporary end to a fantastic adventure and a freewheeling lifestyle afloat. Aside from getting some writing and video work done, we had no real plans. What new adventures lay in store for us? When would we next take to the sea? I was excited but at the same time a little melancholy, and savoured the pretty sunrise alone in the cockpit with *Josephine* aware that it may be our last together.

***

Juan Lacaze is a small town twenty miles east of Colonia, very near *Boca de Rosario* and Angelito's farm where we had abandoned our friend Edu to the tender mercies of Maria a month before. The town originally sprang up around the paper factory that still dominates the skyline, chimneys spewing foul-smelling smoke twenty-four hours a day and sprinkling the harbour with an evil peppery coating of fine grey acidic ash whenever the wind blows from the east. Now the harbour was in the process of being spruced up by the authorities to attract "tourists", but for all the secure mooring facilities with fresh running water and electric plugs we could not see what there was in Juan Lacaze to attract tourists in the first place. Perhaps the life-sized statue of a heavily pregnant woman in the centre of the main roundabout, or the sailing club swimming pool with its garish pink changing rooms. The extensive concrete quay, with its paved walkways, had all the feel of a white elephant about it, but was very convenient for us, and when we tied up ours was the only boat on the dock. We boarded a bus and twenty minutes later arrived in Valdense to be met by Carlos and Marina who whisked us off in their car to see the house.

It was perfect: three bedrooms, two bathrooms, an open-plan sitting and dining room with a wood-burning *parilla* outside the back for summer barbecues. The ample garden was enclosed by hedges and sturdy wooden gates could be closed to keep Lucy off the road. The price was right and we committed to a year.

Back on the boat that afternoon it all seemed surreal. We had left our jobs, sold our home and set sail into the unknown eighteen months ago, but never had we imagined we would be moving off the boat into a house in Uruguay. In fact I am not sure we knew back then where Uruguay was. For a year and a half we sailed the south coast of Brazil and the River Plate, coping with vicious squalls and intense cold, running onto rocks and being washed onto a beach, enduring countless mechanical dramas and even being charged by a killer whale. Yet we had never seen Rio. The fantasies of tropical islands and trade winds had never quite materialised. The Caribbean was almost as far away now as it had been when we left home. Now instead of diving into a warm sea to snorkel over a coral reef, we were squatting on a concrete quay in the shadow of a stinky paper factory loading our belongings into cardboard boxes we had extorted from the staff of Juan Lacaze's supermarket. *What the hell are we doing? I don't want to live in a house.* A feeling of *déjà vu* came over me, similar to the sense I had when I walked out of the bank two years back; the feeling you get after you have made a momentous decision and realise you have wrested back control of your life but the consequences of that decision assume a force of their own, and the only thing to do is hang on tight and hold your nerve.

That evening the owners of the supermarket came to the port and invited us to dinner. The brothers Yuri and Igal could not have been more welcoming and we were delighted to be making new friends so soon. "*Casa del Nino*" – Home of the Child – struck me as a strange name for a supermarket. Apparently a defunct kindergarten had been demolished to make room for the store. Not only had the brothers named the supermarket after the kindergarten; they had saved the playground toys and had them re-erected in the car park to keep children amused while their parents shop. Uruguay is such a safe country, nobody found it odd that there could be six or seven children, all under the age of ten, playing unsupervised on the swings and slides while their parents were off buying groceries. I noticed it was a very classy supermarket too, in what came across as a somewhat lowbrow town.

"Yes, it look like a poor town," Yuri explained. "The people don't care to paint their houses or something, but there are two thousand people here from when the original factory was shut down, and they have very good pensions. The high in all Uruguay. So for this they like to buy everything in the supermarket. Of course they will die, and it will stop. But now it is good."

A couple of beers later he owned to the fact that although he has a nice house and earns good money, he gets no satisfaction from '*selling things to people that they don't need*' and would sooner live on a beach in Brazil, own a few windsurfers and '*cook nice food for people*'. I thought he sounded like us a few years ago. What he needed was a Plan.

Half way through dinner we were startled by the sound of fireworks.

"*Cebolla!*" said Yuri.

"What was that?" I asked. "Did you just say *Onion*?"

"Yes, onion. *Cebolla.* He is a football player. He made big success in Europe. He play now in Spain and earn something like two hundred thousand Euro every month. When he come home to Juan Lacaze for visit, he always make this firework from his house so the whole town know he is back. This is invitation to party, and everybody of his friends go to his mother house. Tonight it should be crazy in Juan Lacaze."

"I feel sorry for his mother!"

"Oh no, she very happy. For some years she was look after his money, but then after a time he get a financial advisor and they discover she buy thirty houses in Juan Lacaze with his money. He had to tell her to stop doing this. He had to tell her '*this is a no good investment!*'"

Later that night, bloated with good food and awash with red wine, we were poured out of Yuri's car at the port basking in self-satisfaction at our decision to call a timeout in Uruguay and finding such kind and friendly people to live amongst. I was so infused with love for my fellow man that I did not even care when I clambered aboard *Josephine* and noticed the water level had dropped so far that she was tilting over away from the quay with her keel obviously resting on the sand. That would be a problem for tomorrow. Tonight I was looking forward to a long and deep sleep.

"How paramount the future…
when one is surrounded by children."

– Charles Darwin

29

We woke with the bow resting on bare sand, and walked beside the boat, under the jetty, without getting our feet wet. *Josephine* was tilted over away from the quay and only the mooring ropes, taut as steel cables, prevented her from rolling all the way over onto her side. A warm northerly wind had blown the waters of the River Plate to Argentina.

Carlos and Marina arrived mid-morning with two vans that were quickly filled to overflowing with our belongings. Carlos wore an incredulous grin.

"*Navegan con todos estas cosas?*"

"Uh... this is nothing Carlos," replied Abi. "We'll have to come back for the rest!"

It is always amazing how much you can squeeze into a boat. The vans were loaded with bags of clothes, cameras, prams and computers, three bicycles, thirty bottles of Argentine wine and a new washing machine that had been smuggled across from Buenos Aires under the radar. We would have to come back another day for the numerous boxes of books, tripods, tents and sleeping bags, cooking utensils, toolboxes and yet more baby toys. We might need a separate trailer just for Lucy's LEGO. Carlos stared in awe, shaking his head and questioning how the boat had stayed afloat.

The last thing to be done before we could bid *Josephine* farewell was to get her off the sand away from the jetty and moored to one of the steel buoys in the little harbour. This was easier said than done. With the front half of the boat lying firmly on the hard sand, it proved impossible to get her away with the motor. The diesel engine roared and the propeller spun until the spectators on the dock were enveloped in exhaust smoke but *Josephine* would not budge.

"We're no longer living on the boat, and we're *still* having drama with her!" chuckled Jo, shaking her head.

A kind soul from the local sailing club, who had been watching us struggle, came over to offer a tow which was gratefully accepted. We looped the end of a rope around the top third of the mast and tied the other end to the stern of a little tug. The tug was then positioned off to the side, and powering up was able to roll *Josephine* far enough over on her side that the keel was raised and we were able to slide her sideways into deeper water to a round of applause from a band of workmen who had downed tools on the quay to watch the process unfold. We tethered *Josephine* to a buoy, dogged down all the hatches, and piled into the loaded vans for the drive to our new home.

Our route took us away from the port along the shore where indolent fishermen dozed on the rocks as their horses waded in the shallows with packs of wagging dogs splashing around them, bounding after stranded catfish. The road was lined with old Dodge pick-ups from the fifties, their chrome bumpers gleaming in the morning sun. Through the town of Juan Lacaze we meandered, giving way to the knife sharpener – a swarthy, moustachioed *gaucho* on a bicycle, tinkling his bell to announce his arrival as the butchers, bakers and candlestick makers of Juan Lacaze came out of their *carnicerias, panaderias* and *ferreterias* to line up on the pavement with their hatchets, cleavers and World War Two bayonets. Then it was out of town on gravel roads through rolling green fields, the last of the morning mist lingering in the shade of the Eucalyptus groves. A horse was being lead in slow plodding circles by a man in wellington boots, both up to their hocks in wet mud, treading it in preparation for firing into bricks. Two gauchos in leather trousers were erecting a fence, one of them drilling holes in a freshly hewn wooden post with a two foot long hand drill. The greens gave way to the dark rust of ripening sorghum and the gold of wilting soya, leaves yellowing ahead of the bean harvest. The gentle curves of the landscape were interrupted by lone poplar trees, standing like pins in a map. A pasture in the foreground held nine or ten calves, each tied to a stake with its own trough of feed, their stark black and white contrasting with the soft autumnal colours of the fields, where rolled hay bales squatted like giant snails. In the gentle light of the changing seasons, Uruguay had been painted in watercolour.

Twenty minutes later we drove into our new hometown behind an old Ford truck with a wooden tailgate, a lone pig eyeing us suspiciously through a gap in the planking. Carlos drew to a halt outside a low building painted the signature bubble-gum blue that is the colour of choice for all Uruguayan police stations, '*just to make introduction*'.

I was propelled up a short footpath of whitewashed rocks with an orange blaze of marigolds lapping the edges, to be presented like "Exhibit A" to Andino, the local police *jefe*, under the watchful eye of The Father of the Nation, Sr. Artigas, who gazed imperiously over the room from his gold frame mounted over the door.

The rural town of Valdense, home to some four thousand people, was established in 1856 by Italian settlers from the Valley of Pellice near Turin, who called themselves "*Los Valdenses*", or 'The Valley People', and named their settlement "*Colonia Valdense*". One of the founding fathers was Pastor Daniel Armand Ugon, who in 1888 founded Uruguay's second high school in Valdense, and has given his name not only to the school, but to the town's main avenue. Both Carlos and his cousin Marcelo, from whom we were to rent the house, were great-grandchildren of Armand Ugon, and thus highly esteemed figures in the community. Staying in an Armand Ugon family house, on *Avenida Armand Ugon* to boot, conferred certain status on us straight away and it was never difficult getting groceries, firewood or mineral water delivered to the house. "*Ah si, casa de Marcelo Armand Ugon!*" Everyone knew it.

Most of the inhabitants of Valdense are either farmers, or live indirectly from farming by providing services to the farmers. Half the floor space in the local supermarket is taken up with agricultural tools, leather *guacho* apparel, wire fencing, irrigation systems and bottles of armadillo repellent. The townsfolk entertain themselves with a monthly rodeo in a field next to the motorway, and even the local rock band is called *Hereford,* after the popular breed of cow. A clutch of teenage boys drove by in a car with low profile tyres and dark tinted windows, the heavy thump-thump-thump of the latest dance music turned up to distortion volume, and a MASSEY FERGUSON sticker on the rear window. Marina said that evening the country would be celebrating the annual "Night of Nostalgia".

"What's that?" Abi asked.

"Ah, it is a Uruguayan tradition! A lot of dancing, to old music. Every place in Uruguay! It is fantastic."

Abi and I glanced at each other. We were both a little tired.

"Traditional music?" I asked.

"Yes," Marina went on, "Music from long ago."

"What, *gaucho* music?"

"No, not *gaucho* music – *traditional* music."

"What is that?"

"You know – like Pink Floyd."

***

In the tranquil Valdense people leave their keys in their cars and we soon lost the habit of locking our bicycles when we were out and about, or shutting the front door. How nice it was to fall asleep in the evenings to the chorus of frogs and be woken in the mornings by the clip-clop of passing horses. The girls were delighted with the additional space afforded by the house, but as much as I enjoyed the serenity of Valdense I was a little disorientated. The boat had been the focus of my life for several years, and to now be back on land with no travel plans was anti-climactic. It was not as if I had nothing to do; there were hours of video to download, and I wanted to write, but what after that? I was not used to not having a "plan". My mountain bike was my escape.

The bicycle is one of mankind's greatest inventions. It is a quite remarkable machine, the basic design of which has scarcely changed in a century; yet still, in our modern world of unmanned aircraft, camera-operated spinal surgery, i-pods and atom splitting, something close to half a billion bicycles will be ridden somewhere in the world the day you read this.

As bicycles were relatively cheap in Argentina we had decided to treat ourselves before we crossed back to Uruguay. In the outskirts of Buenos Aires I had found a corner shop called "ROBERT'S BIKES" (owned and run by a "Diego" – a smiling, hefty man with black oily fingers and a grimy apron around his waist). At the back of the shop was a workshop with a red cross above the door, and he introduced himself to me as *el medico das bicicletas* – "the doctor of bicycles". On the shop floor were a gold painted three-man tandem bicycle (tran-dem?), a bright red three-wheeler with a large cage on the back for luggage, and several rows of second hand bicycles in various stages of decomposition. The only one my size was a red and silver affair with torn rubber grips on the handlebars.

"*Ah senor, no te preocupes, yo las cambio,*" Diego assured me, pulling open a drawer full of spare handlebar rubbers. *"Mira!"* and he pointed at the carpet, strewn with a liberal scattering of chewed up rubber fragments.

"*Era el pajaro de mierda*!" he spat, extending a damning finger at said shit bird up on its perch in the loft overlooking the shop floor. "Whenever I turn my back, he flies down here and attacks the handle bars. Look, here, and here," flicking his fingers across the torn grips of yet more bikes. "He eats all of them!"

"*Hola!!*" screeched the parrot with disdain, sweeping the shop floor with a beady eye lest he should have missed any.

The red and silver bike was just what I needed, and after Diego replaced the rubbers I was more than happy to part with a hundred dollars. Two more bikes – bright purple and metallic sparkly blue – were procured for Abi and Jo. They were to prove useful additions to the already crowded boat, for nipping off to the bakery or just getting to see the countryside. For me, it would be more than that – a new toy.

In Valdense I took off for two or three hours at a time exploring the countryside, and soon fell in with other cyclists and made new friends.

After being in Valdense a couple of weeks, I came home from an afternoon ride to find both Abi and Jo looking shocked and in tears.

"Oh God, what's happened?"

Abi looked at me with red eyes.

"There is an e-mail in your inbox. From Bernadette. It's Reinaldo. He died of a heart attack yesterday."

"What?" I asked, sitting down next to her. "Reinaldo, from Paraty?"

Abi nodded.

"They were doing a charter, everything was fine, then in the middle of making lunch he just collapsed. One of their clients was a doctor but couldn't save him."

I was empty. Reinaldo had been so lively, so positive, so full of… of *life*. I could see his sunny smile, and him telling me "*we are fam-i-ly on this ma-ri-na, we solve your gear-box prob-lem, do not wo-rry, heh heh!*" The last time we spoke he and Bernadette were thinking of sailing south to meet us here. Life is so fragile.

***

I didn't know whether to mourn Reinaldo, or celebrate the new baby. The irony of grieving and rejoicing at the same time was making me nauseous. In turmoil I called my best friend in Uruguay.

"Edu?"

"Ah, ees my friend, how are you?"

"I'm fine, but I have some news…"

"Okay, me too." He interrupted me. "I have news for you!"

"Oh?"

"Yes! Can you believe, oh man, I am so happy…"

"That's nice…"

"Of course! Yes, you know, I am going to be a father!"

Too much to process.

"Wha-aat?"

"Yes! Maria, she ees pregnant! Ees wonderful, oh man! Yes, ees true, I want to change my life, thees ees what I want, I tell you. You remember Reinaldo, in Paraty?"

"Um… ye-es…"

"I remember he said to me, '*I like a simple life, because you never know when ees feeneesh.*' Okay, now I am to be quiet for a simple life, like Reinaldo. He ees wonderful man, I am lucky to go to Paraty and meet heem!"

We rejoiced together. I did not have the heart to tell him about Reinaldo. Not at that moment.

***

From the time we wriggle into this world and gasp our first lungful of air, it is a certainty that we will not live forever; and from time to time, before we die, we will have to endure the loss of people we have come to love as they die before we do. But these tragic interludes can be offset against the joy of new life when a child is born. This is the cycle of life, and nothing new. Whatever our dreams, whatever our goals, our birth and subsequent death are the two things we cannot write into the plans. Instead of being sad to have lost Reinaldo, we are happy to have had him. And he is not gone: our lives are the better for having known him, and we live on carrying something of him inside us. Soon I will meet our second daughter and I hope she will one day think as much of me as I do of Reinaldo.

We don't know what will happen to us next year. We have no plans, and that is how I like it. For now I am content to sit on the garden swing in Valdense with our happy two-year-old gazing up at the wide sky, tracing horses and dragons in the clouds with our fingers. And it is all that matters. My purpose in life is to sit there with my child, in the sun, eating sticky pastries and Dreaming the Sky.

"All men dream, but not equally.
Those who dream by night in the dusty recesses of their minds
wake in the day to find that it was vanity.
But the dreamers of the day are dangerous men,
for they may act out their dreams with open eyes,
to make them possible."

– T S Eliot

Josephine in Piriapolis

Sunrise over the River Plate, heading east out of Buenos Aires

Lucy gives Edu some helming tips

Fishermen's homes in Laguna, Brazil

Iguazu Falls

The author approaching IlhaBela from the south

on our return to Brazil, late 2009

Josephine at anchor in IlhaBela

Jo on Josephine in Pier 46, Parati 2010

A quiet street in Parati

The pampero approaches, South Atlantic

The bull orca displays afer mock-charging our boat

Josephine aground in Boca de Rosario, where water levels are dependent on wind direction over the River Plate

Primavera and her daughter Maria, who went on to marry Edu, in the kitchen at Boca de Rosario

Lucy meets Petisa, our neighbour in Valdense

Visiting Wilson in our neighbourhood shop, Colonia Valdense

GLOSSARY OF BIG SAILING WORDS

Anchor Light – a small white light up the mast, used when anchored in the dark, to flatten the batteries before morning.

Anchor – a heavy, spiky metal thing kept in the bow, for throwing into the sea to find fishing nets and underwater electric cables. They are often to be seen rusting in flowerbeds outside seafood restaurants.

Bait – stuff used to feed live fish.

Beating – the art of sailing upwind and smashing the boat and crew to bits over the waves.

Bilge – drain area under the floorboards for storing spilt diesel, saltwater and lost biscuits.

Bow – the sharp end of the boat. Under normal circumstances, that is the front.

Chart – a type of map that tells you exactly where you have run aground, and shows you where you should have been.

Cockpit – the open area in the back of the boat where it is your turn to stand and steer between midnight and three in the morning when it is very cold, it is raining, and waves are breaking over your head. It is also where you go to be hit in the face by flying fish in the dark.

Compass – a thing that tells you which way is north, but is no use at all if you don't know where you are in the first place. Can be made to point anywhere you like with something metal, like a beer can or a belt buckle.

Depression – low atmospheric pressure that brings bad weather and makes everyone sad.

Fishing Net – nylon webbing spread in the sea to catch propellers.

Fish – frozen stuff you buy on land.

Foulies – waterproof clothing that keeps you wet long after the storm has passed.

Furler – a jamming device on the forestay that prevents you from getting the headsail down in a storm. Other times it serves to prevent you from deploying the sail at all.

Gearbox – I do not know what this is. Probably a box of stuff.

Guardrail – a steel cable, supported by stancheons, running around the outside of the deck, for draping yourself over when you have been seasick for ten hours and can no longer support yourself.

Hatch – a square hole in the deck that allows waves into the saloon in a storm. Can also be useful for getting in and out of the boat. Has an ingenious wooden ladder for barking shins.

Heaving To – a manoeuvre that involves pulling the headsail around to the wrong side of the boat and stalling the wind flow, which stops the boat while keeping it balanced in the wind. The past tense is "hove to". "Hove to" also refers to the position of the boat after the manoeuvre, i.e. "the boat is now hove to". It has nothing to do with sea sickness.

Jibe (or Gybe) – a risky downwind manoeuvre involving turning the boat that usually leads to injury for which the skipper is blamed. Called a jibe because crew make inappropriate remarks about the competence of the skipper afterwards.

Keel – a heavy wedge-shaped fin bolted to the underside of the boat for testing the depth. It can be used to plough through the mud of the River Plate, and is also useful in rough weather for keeping the boat upright.

Knot – The unit of measurement of speed at sea, it is applied to boats, current and wind. One knot is one nautical mile per hour (so a knot is a little faster than one mile an hour, or almost two kilometres an hour). "Knots per hour" do not exist, in spite of what one sometimes hears in bad films.

Lazy Jacks – Lines that run from the top of the mast down either side of the boom to snag the head of the main sail when you try to hoist it. They are, however, useful for guiding the sail into the stack pack as it is dropped.

Locker – place for keeping foulies wet for as long as possible after you have taken them off.

Nautical Mile – The unit of measurement of distance at sea, it is slightly longer than a Statute Mile, at 1850 metres. It is actually the distance of one sixtieth of a degree of latitude (or one second of latitude).

Propeller – a spinning metal thing under the stern of the boat for finding loose ropes in the water.

Propwalk – a phenomenon that makes the boat go sideways instead of backwards when you reverse. Makes the skipper look like a complete idiot in tight places like marinas.

Pulpit – a frame of stainless steel tubing above the bow to prevent you from climbing onto the jetty when you are moored "bow to".

Reaching – sailing more or less parallel to the wind. The fastest, safest and most comfortable point of sailing, it is called "reaching" because it almost never happens.

Reef – the action of making the sails smaller to reduce power, usually after a storm when it is too late. Also something hard and sharp discovered by that depth device, the keel.

Rudder – another fin thing under the boat, this time at the back end. Good for testing the depth when you reverse. Can also be used for turning.

Sheet – a commonly heard expletive. Also a rope for adjusting a sail.

Shroud – steel cables running from the deck to the top of the mast, designed for maximum entanglement on deck when you go under a low bridge and the mast falls down. Ironically designed originally to keep the mast upright.

Spinnaker – a large sail flown from the front of the boat like a parachute, for going downwind. Frequently causes the boat to "*spinn out*" and turn over. Not a favourite with wives.

Spraydodger – a canvas cover over the hatchway for obscuring the view of the helmsman. Also catches food scraps that would otherwise have been thrown overboard. Can be useful for keeping the hatch dry on occasion.

Spreader – little arms that extend sideways from the mast about halfway up for seabirds to sit on, from where they take careful aim at your scrubbed deck. Also used to brace the shrouds and add strength to the mast.

Stack Pack – a big bag with a zip, attached to the boom, where all manner of birds – even geese – will lay eggs when you are away from the boat a few days. It is supposed to be a bag to protect the mainsail when it is down.

Stern – the blunt end of the boat. Under normal circumstances, that is the back.

Swell – a wave that is just great.

Tack – a hard biscuit before it has been soaked in the bilges. Also the art of turning the boat into the wind at an inopportune moment and soaking the crew, hence the word "tactless".

Winch – an Australian girl. Also a round thing for pulling on tight sheets.

23602990R00255

Printed in Great Britain
by Amazon